Structuring XML Documents

ISBN 0-13-642299-3

 # The Charles F. Goldfarb Series on Open Information Management

"Open Information Management" (OIM) means managing information so that it is open to processing by any program, not just the program that created it. That extends even to application programs not conceived of at the time the information was created.

OIM is based on the principle of data independence: data should be stored in computers in non-proprietary, genuinely standardized representations. And that applies even when the data is the content of a document. Its representation should distinguish the innate information from the proprietary codes of document processing programs and the artifacts of particular presentation styles.

Business data bases—which rigorously separate the real data from the input forms and output reports—achieved data independence decades ago. But documents, unlike business data, have historically been created in the context of a particular output presentation style. So for document data, independence was largely unachievable until recently.

That is doubly unfortunate. It is unfortunate because documents are a far more significant repository of humanity's information. And documents can contain significantly richer information structures than data bases.

It is also unfortunate because the need for OIM of documents is greater now than ever. The demands of "repurposing" require that information be deliverable in multiple formats: paper-based, online, multimedia, hypermedia. And information must now be delivered through multiple channels: traditional bookstores and libraries, the World Wide Web, corporate intranets and extranets. In the latter modes, what starts as data base data may become a document for browsing, but then may need to be reused by the reader as data.

Fortunately, in the past ten years a technology has emerged that extends to documents the data base's capacity for data independence.

And it does so without the data base's restrictions on structural freedom. That technology is the "Standard Generalized Markup Language" (SGML), an official International Standard (ISO 8879) that has been adopted by the world's largest producers of documents and by the World Wide Web.

With SGML, organizations in government, aerospace, airlines, automotive, electronics, computers, and publishing (to name a few) have freed their documents from hostage relationships to processing software. SGML coexists with graphics, multimedia and other data standards needed for OIM and acts as the framework that relates objects in the other formats to one another and to SGML documents.

The World Wide Web's HTML and XML are both based on SGML. HTML is a particular, though very general, application of SGML, like those for the above industries. There is a limited set of markup tags that can be used with HTML. XML, in contrast, is a simplified subset of SGML facilities that, like full SGML, can be used with any set of tags. You can literally create your own markup language with XML.

As the enabling standard for OIM of documents, the SGML family of standards necessarily plays a leading role in this series. We provide tutorials on SGML, XML, and other key standards and the techniques for applying them. Our books vary in technical intensity from programming techniques for software developers to the business justification of OIM for enterprise executives. We share the practical experience of organizations and individuals who have applied the techniques of OIM in environments ranging from immense industrial publishing projects to websites of all sizes.

Our authors are expert practitioners in their subject matter, not writers hired to cover a "hot" topic. They bring insight and understanding that can only come from real-world experience. Moreover, they practice what they preach about standardization. Their books share a common standards-based vocabulary. In this way, knowledge gained from one book in the series is directly applicable when reading another, or the standards themselves. This is just one of the ways in which we strive for the utmost technical accuracy and consistency with the OIM standards.

And we also strive for a sense of excitement and fun. After all, the challenge of OIM—preserving information from the ravages of technology while exploiting its benefits—is one of the great intellectual adventures of our age. I'm sure you'll find this series to be a knowledgable and reliable guide on that adventure.

About the Series Editor

Dr. Charles F. Goldfarb invented the SGML language in 1974 and later led the team that developed it into the International Standard on which both HTML and XML are based. He serves as editor of the Standard (ISO 8879) and as a consultant to developers of SGML and XML applications and products. He is based in Saratoga, CA.

About the Series Logo

The rebus is an ancient literary tradition, dating from 16th century Picardy, and is especially appropriate to a series involving fine distinctions between things and the words that describe them. For the logo, Andrew Goldfarb incorporated a rebus of the series name within a stylized SGML/XML comment declaration.

The Charles F. Goldfarb Series on Open Information Management

As XML is a subset of SGML, the Series List is categorized to show the degree to which a title applies to XML. "XML Titles" are those that discuss XML explicitly and may also cover full SGML. "SGML Titles" do not mention XML per se, but the principles covered may apply to XML.

XML Titles

Goldfarb, Pepper, and Ensign
▌ SGML Buyer's Guide™: Choosing the Right XML and SGML Products and Services

Megginson
▌ Structuring XML Documents

Leventhal, Lewis, and Fuchs *(Coming Soon)*
▌ Designing XML Internet Applications

Goldfarb and Prescod *(Coming Soon)*
▌ The XML Handbook

Jelliffe *(Coming Soon)*
▌ The XML and SGML Cookbook: Recipes for Structured Information

SGML Titles

Turner, Douglass, and Turner
▌ ReadMe.1st: SGML for Writers and Editors

Donovan
▌ Industrial-Strength SGML: An Introduction to Enterprise Publishing

Ensign
▌ $GML: The Billion Dollar Secret

Rubinsky and Maloney
▌ SGML on the Web: Small Steps Beyond HTML

McGrath
▌ ParseMe.1st: SGML for Software Developers

DuCharme
▌ SGML CD

Structuring XML Documents

David Megginson

 Prentice Hall PTR, Upper Saddle River, NJ   07458
http://www.phptr.com

Library of Congress Cataloging-in-Publication Data

```
Megginson, David
    Structuring XML Documents / David Megginson.
        p.    cm. -- (The Charles F. Goldfarb series on open information
    management)
    Includes index.
    ISBN 0-13-642299-3
    1. XML (Document markup language)  2. SGML (Document markup
language)  3. Database management.  I. Title.  II. Series.
    QA76.76.H94M44    1998
    005.7'2--dc21                                         98-2691
                                                          CIP
```

Editorial/Production Supervision: *Craig Little*
Acquisitions Editor: *Mark Taub*
Marketing Manager: *Dan Rush*
Manufacturing Manager: *Alexis R. Heydt*
Cover Design: *Anthony Gemmellaro*
Cover Design Direction: *Jerry Votta*
Series Design: *Gail Cocker-Bogusz*

© 1998 Prentice Hall PTR
Prentice-Hall, Inc.
A Simon & Schuster Company
Upper Saddle River, NJ 07458

Prentice Hall books are widely used by corporations and government agencies for training, marketing, and resale.

The publisher offers discounts on this book when ordered in bulk quantities. For more information, contact Corporate Sales Department, Phone: 800-382-3419; fax: 201-236-714; email: corpsales@prenhall.com or write Corporate Sales Department, Prentice Hall PTR, One Lake Street, Upper Saddle River, NJ 07458.

Printed in the United States of America

10 9 8 7 6 5 4 3 2 1

ISBN 0-13-642299-3

Prentice-Hall International (UK) Limited, *London*
Prentice-Hall of Australia Pty. Limited, *Sydney*
Prentice-Hall Canada Inc., *Toronto*
Prentice-Hall Hispanoamericana, S.A., *Mexico*
Prentice-Hall of India Private Limited, *New Delhi*
Prentice-Hall of Japan, Inc., *Tokyo*
Simon & Schuster Asia Pte. Ltd., *Singapore*
Editora Prentice-Hall do Brasil, Ltda., *Rio de Janeiro*

This book is dedicated, with love, to Bonnie, Emma, and Tess.

Contents

Introduction   xxx

XML and SGML   xxxiii

The Book's Structure   xxxiv

Notations and Conventions   xxxv

Presentation of Examples   xxxv

Typographical Conventions   xxxvi

Figures   xxxvi

ı Part One

Background   1

Chapter 1
Review of DTD Syntax   2

1.1   Document Type Declaration   4

1.2   Elements   5

1.2.1   Element Type   6

1.2.2   Content Specification   7

1.2.2.1   Content Model   7
1.2.2.2   The ANY Keyword   12
1.2.2.3   The EMPTY Keyword   12

1.2.3   SGML: Elements   13

1.2.3.1   Multiple Element Types   13
1.2.3.2   Omitted Tag Minimization   13
1.2.3.3   Exceptions   14
1.2.3.4   Declared Content   15
1.2.3.5   Mixed Content   16
1.2.3.6   Unordered Content   17

1.3   Attributes   17

1.3.1   Attribute Type   18

1.3.1.1   String Type   18
1.3.1.2   Tokenized Types   19
1.3.1.3   Enumerated Types   20

1.3.2   Default Value   21

1.3.2.1   Literal Values   22
1.3.2.2   Keywords   22

1.3.3   Multiple Declarations   23

1.3.4   SGML: Attributes   24

   1.3.4.1   Attribute Types   24
   1.3.4.2   Attribute Default Values   25
   1.3.4.3   Multiple Attribute Definition Lists   26
   1.3.4.4   Global Attributes   27

1.4   Entities   28

1.4.1   Location   30

1.4.2   Definitions   31

1.4.3   Boundaries   32

1.4.4   SGML: Entities   32

   1.4.4.1   Default Entity   33
   1.4.4.2   External Identifiers   33
   1.4.4.3   Data Text   34
   1.4.4.4   External Entity Types   35

1.5   Notations   36

1.5.1   Declarations   36

1.5.2   SGML: Notations   36

   1.5.2.1   Data Attributes   37

1.6   Conditional Sections   38

1.7   Processing Instructions   39

*1.7.1   Why Bother with Processing
         Instructions?*   39

1.7.2   SGML: Processing Instructions   40

   1.7.2.1   PI Entities   40

Chapter 2
Model DTDs   42

2.1 Reading About the Model
     DTDs   45

  2.1.1 Sample Documents   45

2.2 A Note About Using Industry-Standard
     DTDs   46

2.3 The Five Model DTDs   47

  2.3.1 ISO 12083   47

    2.3.1.1 Background   48
    2.3.1.2 Quick Tour   49
    2.3.1.3 Sample Document   52
    2.3.1.4 Availability   54

  2.3.2 DocBook   54

    2.3.2.1 Background   55
    2.3.2.2 Quick Tour   56
    2.3.2.3 Sample Document   60
    2.3.2.4 Availability   62

  2.3.3 Text-Encoding Initiative (TEI) 62

    2.3.3.1 Background   62
    2.3.3.2 Quick Tour   64
    2.3.3.3 Sample Document   67
    2.3.3.4 Availability   69

  2.3.4 MIL-STD-38784 (CALS)   70

    2.3.4.1 Background   70
    2.3.4.2 Quick Tour   71
    2.3.4.3 Sample Document   74
    2.3.4.4 Availability   77

2.3.5 *Hypertext Markup Language
(HTML 4.0)*   77

2.3.5.1   Background   77
2.3.5.2   Quick Tour   78
2.3.5.3   Sample Document   81
2.3.5.4   Availability   82

ı Part Two

Principles of DTD Analysis   84

Chapter 3
Ease of Learning   86

3.1 DTD Size   89

3.1.1 *Logical Units*   90
3.1.0.1   Examples from the Model DTDs   92

3.1.1 *Learning Requirements*   94
3.1.1.1   Examples from the Model DTDs   96

3.2 DTD Consistency   97

3.2.1 *Naming*   98
3.2.1.1   Examples from the Model DTDs   99

3.2.2 *Parallel Design*   100
3.2.2.1   Examples from the Model DTDs   103

3.2.3 *Element-Type Classes*   104
3.2.3.1   Examples from the Model DTDs   106

3.2.4   *Global Attributes*   107

3.2.4.1   Examples from the Model DTDs   108

3.3   DTD Intuitiveness   109

3.3.1   *Naming*   110

3.3.1.1   Examples from the Model DTDs   110

3.3.2   *Structure*   112

3.3.2.1   Examples from the Model DTDs   115

Chapter 4
Ease of Use   118

4.1   Physical Effort   120

4.1.1   *Content Models*   121

4.1.1.1   Examples from the Model DTDs   124

4.1.2   *Attribute Definitions*   126

4.1.2.1   Examples from the Model DTDs   127

4.2   Choice   131

4.2.1   *Limiting Choices*   131

4.2.1.1   Examples from the Model DTDs   134

4.3   Flexibility   135

4.3.1   *Descriptive and Prescriptive*
DTDs   136

4.3.1.1   Examples from the Model DTDs   137

4.3.2   *Inline Element Types*   138

4.3.2.1   Examples from the Model DTDs   139

4.3.3   *Role Attributes*   140

4.3.3.1   Examples from the Model DTDs   142

4.3.4 *Generic Element Types*   142

4.3.4.1   Examples from the Model DTDs   143

Chapter 5
Ease of Processing   144

5.1   Predictability   146

5.1.1 *Constraint*   147

5.1.1.1   Examples from the Model DTDs   149

5.1.2 *Recursion*   150

5.1.2.1   Examples from the Model DTDs   153

5.1.3 *Generic Element Types and Role
              Attributes*   155

5.1.3.1   Examples from the Model DTDs   157

5.1.4 *Authors' Modifications*   158

5.1.4.1   Examples from the Model DTDs   160

5.1.5 *SGML: Placement of Data and
              Subdocument Entities*   163

5.1.5.1   Examples from the Model DTDs   164

5.2   Context   165

5.2.1 *Containers*   165

5.2.1.1   Examples from the Model DTDs   168

5.2.2 *Implied Attribute Values*   170

5.2.2.1   Examples from the Model DTDs   172

5.3   DTD Analysis:
        Final Considerations   174

▪ Part Three
Advanced Issues in DTD Maintenance and Design   176

Chapter 6
DTD Compatibility   178

6.1   Structural Compatibility   180

6.1.1   Repetition   181

6.1.2   Omissibility   183

6.1.3   Alternation   186

6.1.4   Changes in Combination   188

6.1.4.1   Changes to the Same Content Particle   189
6.1.4.2   New Element Types   190

6.1.5   ANY and EMPTY   192

6.1.6   Attribute Compatibility   193

6.1.6.1   Repetition   194
6.1.6.2   Omissibility   195
6.1.6.3   Alternation   196
6.1.6.4   Typing   196

6.1.7   SGML: Structural Compatibility   198

6.1.7.1   Ordering   198
6.1.7.2   Repetition of Data   201
6.1.7.3   CDATA and RCDATA Declared Content   201
6.1.7.4   Inclusion and Exclusion Exceptions   202
6.1.7.5   Additional SGML Attribute Types   202

6.2   Lexical Compatibility   203

   6.2.1   *Entities*   203

   6.2.2   *Whitespace*   205

   6.2.3   *SGML:*
         Lexical Compatibility   207

      6.2.3.1   Markup Minimization   207
      6.2.3.2   Record Ends   210

Chapter 7
Exchanging Document Fragments 214

7.1   Editing Fragments as Stand-Alone
     Documents   218

   7.1.1   *Ancestors and Siblings*   220

   7.1.2   *Cross-References*   220

      7.1.2.1   Changing IDREFs   222
      7.1.2.2   Creating Placeholders   223

   7.1.3   *Entities*   224

   7.1.4   *Summary*   226

   7.1.5   *SGML:*
         Stand-Alone Fragments   226

      7.1.5.1   #CURRENT Attributes   227
      7.1.5.2   Inclusion and Exclusion Exceptions   228

7.2   Reparenting in a Dummy
     Document   230

   7.2.1   *Ancestors and Siblings*   231

   7.2.2   *Cross-References*   232

7.2.3   *Entities*   234

7.2.4   *Summary*   234

7.2.5   *SGML: Reparenting*   235

    7.2.5.1   Inclusion and Exclusion Exceptions   235

7.3   Using Subdocuments   235

7.3.1   *Ancestors and Siblings*   237

7.3.2   *Cross-References*   238

    7.3.2.1   Simple External Reference:
          HyTime Scheme   239

    7.3.2.2   Simple External Reference:
          XLL Scheme   240

7.3.3   *Entities*   241

7.3.4   *Summary*   242

7.3.5   *SGML: Subdocuments*   242

    7.3.5.1   SUBDOC Entities   242
    7.3.5.2   Inclusion and Exclusion Exceptions   243

Chapter 8
DTD Customization   244

8.1   Types of Customization   246

8.1.1   *Simplifying a DTD for
       Authoring*   247

    8.1.1.1   Eliminating Unnecessary Choice   247
    8.1.1.2   Avoiding Markup Errors   248

8.1.2   *Adding Element Types to a
       DTD*   249

8.1.3   *Restructuring a DTD's Components*   250

8.2   Extension Mechanisms in the Model DTDs   252

8.2.1   *Customizing the DocBook DTD*   254

8.2.2   *Customizing the TEI DTDs*   257

8.2.2.1   Base and Auxiliary Tagsets   259

8.2.3   *Customizing the HTML DTD*   260

8.2.4   *Customizing the MIL-STD-38784 DTD*   261

8.2.5   *Customizing the ISO 12083 DTDs*   262

ı Part Four

DTD Design with Architectural Forms

266

Chapter 9
Architectural Forms: Concepts

268

9.1   Meta-DTDs   272

9.2   Documents   273

9.2.1   Types of Architectural Forms   274

9.2.2   The Architectural Document   275

9.3   Practical Uses of Architectural
        Forms   276

9.3.1   DTD Extension   276

9.3.2   Software Reusability   278

9.3.2.1   A Common Book Architecture?   278

9.3.3   Multiuse Documents   280

9.3.4   Extended Validation   282

9.4   Summary of Terminology   282

Chapter 10
Basic Architectural Forms Syntax 286

10.1 Setup and Configuration   289

10.1.1 Architecture Use Declaration
        Attributes   290

10.1.2 SGML: Original Syntax   292

10.1.2.1   Architecture Base Declaration   294
10.1.2.2   Architecture Notation Declaration   295
10.1.2.3   Architecture Entity Declaration   296
10.1.2.4   Architecture Support Attributes   297

10.2 Basic Forms   299

10.2.1 Deriving Elements   299

10.2.1.1   Element Form Strategies   303

10.2.2 Deriving Attributes   306

10.2.3 Deriving Notations   307

10.2.4 SGML: Basic Forms   308

10.2.4.1 Notation Forms   308

Chapter 11
Advanced Architectural Forms Syntax   310

11.1 Automatic Derivation   312

11.1.1 SGML: Automatic Derivation 313

11.2 Suppressing Architectural
    Processing   313

11.2.1 Suppressing Elements   314

11.2.2 Suppressing Data   316

*11.2.3 SGML: Suppressing Architectural
    Processing*   317

11.3 Architectural Attribute
    Values   318

11.3.1 Attribute Defaulting   318

11.3.2 Tokens   319

*11.3.3 Deriving Content from Attribute
    Values*   320

*11.3.4 Deriving Attribute Values from
    Content*   322

*11.3.5 SGML:
    Architectural Attributes*   323

11.4 Default Architectural Information   323

11.4.1 Creating a Default Notation   324

11.4.2 Resolving IDREFs   325

11.4.3 SGML: Default Architectural Information   326

11.5 Meta-DTDs   327

11.5.1 Meta-DTD Configuration   327

11.5.1.1 SGML: Meta-DTD Configuration   328

11.5.2 SGML: Meta-DTDs   328

11.5.2.1 Meta-DTD Quantities   329
11.5.2.2 General NAMECASE Substitution   330

ı Part Five

Back Matter   332

Model DTDs: Index of Element Types and Attributes   334

General Index   412

About the CD-ROM

Foreword

For many years the World Wide Web community has looked both longingly and fearfully at SGML.

Longingly, because the Web's HTML is based on SGML, and website developers need more of SGML than HTML can give them.

Fearfully, because the enormous power and flexibility of full SGML can be daunting to learn and implement. Which is what you might expect of an enterprise information technology that manages mission-critical Web-size document collections for industries and governments throughout the world.

Well, the World Wide Web Consortium has a solution, created during several years of work by an invited group of scores of the world's leading SGML experts. It is called XML, the eXtensible Markup Language, and it can satisfy the longing for SGML without the fear.

XML is a simplified subset of SGML that has been optimized for use on the World Wide Web. That sounds a lot like what you may have heard said of HTML, but there is a very big difference:

- HTML simplifies SGML by limiting it to a specific vocabulary of tags, aimed at describing the *rendition* of your data.
- XML simplifies SGML by eliminating its syntactic options, but allowing you to describe the *abstract structure* of your data using your own vocabulary.

And abstract structure is the gateway to the Brave New Web of smart data and electronic commerce. It is a new way of looking at your information and making the best use of it, something that David Megginson has been doing for some half-dozen years, as user, designer, and software developer.

With *Structuring XML Documents*, you can confidently apply David's methods and techniques to building your own information structures. It will unlock the gateway to the Brave New Web.

Charles F. Goldfarb
Saratoga, CA
February, 1998

Introduction

I have written this book to help you use XML and SGML to solve your document-structuring problems. The book is a result of my experience with and opinions about document structure after seven years' work with SGML (and more recently, XML), first as an academic and later as a professional document-management consultant and systems architect.

While XML and SGML DTDs provide a convenient syntax for defining a document's structure, most of the principles of document design and analysis covered in this book are not specific to any syntax. Though the book necessarily deals with some of the idiosyncracies of XML and SGML DTDs and uses XML syntax in its examples, it deals with issues—such as learning, usability, and ease of processing—that *all* document designers and analysts must understand, whether or not they use XML or SGML and whether they use DTD syntax or other notations to define their structures.

By itself, this book is *not* a general introduction to XML, SGML, or DTD syntax: I am assuming that you already know how to create markup in a document and how to write basic DTDs (though there is a review of DTD syntax in Chapter 1 if you're a little rusty). If you are entirely new to XML, you should start with a beginner's guide or with online resources such as the ones listed on the SGML/XML Web Page `<http://www.sil.org/sgml/>`.

This book concentrates on **book-oriented DTDs,** for applications such as technical manuals, literary texts, newspapers, magazines, advertisements, correspondence, regulations, legislation, and other material meant to be read by people rather than (or as well as) by machines. Both XML and SGML DTDs are also capable of modelling many other types of information, including commercial transactions and other types of data exchange; many of the principles described in this book can apply to **database-oriented DTDs** as well, but the book does not discuss that type of DTD explicitly.

In this book, I am also assuming that you already know how to collect information about the business problems you need to solve. You have to know about how people will create and process documents using your DTDs and about the projects that they will be working on. For this book, I have divided the people you have to know about into two groups:

1. the **authors**, who create documents
2. the **information-processing specialists**, who design software to process the documents in various ways

This division is, of course, an oversimplification (there are also editors, proofreaders, fact-checkers, etc., not to mention the end users of the information), but it is a useful one for developing a methodology for DTD analysis. When I want to refer to both authors and information-processing specialists together, I simply use the term **DTD users**.

It is essential that you know your users' requirements, because there are few absolute rights and wrongs in document analysis design: your goal is not to come up with an abstract, ideal DTD, but rather to come up with the best practical fit for your users. In fact, as I explain in Part Two starting on page 84, often you will have to make sacrifices in one area to meet your users' needs in another. Learning how to collect this information is an important skill in itself, as is learning to document your work—if you are interested in reading about good SGML (and XML) business practices, you might want to take a look at *Developing SGML DTDs: From Text Model to Markup* (Prentice-Hall) or any of the many software-engineering textbooks currently available.

∎ XML and SGML

From the perspective of document analysis and design, there are very few differences between XML and full SGML. XML DTDs can describe almost any structure that full SGML DTDs can describe (though they will sometimes present information differently); the following are the only major types of SGML structure that XML DTDs are incapable of modeling:

1. XML DTDs cannot model *inclusion exceptions* or *exclusion exceptions*

2. XML DTDs cannot model *unordered content*

3. XML DTDs cannot model arbitrary *mixed content* (only an optional and repeatable OR group is allowed)

Even when you are writing DTDs in full SGML, however, you should use inclusion and exclusion exceptions sparingly, you should usually avoid unordered content, and you should *always* avoid dangerous types of *mixed content*.

▮ The Book's Structure

There are four parts to this book:

- in Part One, you can read about the five industry-standard DTDs that this book uses as models and refresh your knowledge of XML (and SGML) DTD syntax
- in Part Two, you can read about how to analyze DTDs to see if they match your specific needs—this part contains many examples from the five model DTDs
- in Part Three, you can read about advanced topics like document disassembly and reassembly, configurable documents, DTD compatibility, and DTD customization
- in Part Four, you can learn about the important new standard for *architectural forms*, and see how to use them to produce simple solutions to complicated DTD problems

▮ Notations and Conventions

SGML Note: *XML documents are SGML documents; however, in full SGML you can use some additional facilities that are not available in XML.*

   Throughout the book, I include text like this whenever I think that you need to know about a difference between full SGML and XML or whenever I want to give you some extra SGML information.

Presentation of Examples

For the sake of consistency and readability, I present examples in the book (both DTD and document excerpts) using XML syntax whenever possible, even when the examples come from an SGML original. I also normalize whitespace and presentation, but preserve the name case of the original declarations.

For example, the following element type declaration appears in TEI-Lite:

Original SGML declaration

```
<!ELEMENT BiblioMixed - O ((%bibliocomponent.mix; |
                            BiblioMSet | #PCDATA)+)
                          -(%ubiq.mix;)>
```

Unless I am discussing SGML-specific syntax, I remove both the omitted tag minimization and the exclusion exception from the example. In this case, I also rearrange the presentation of the content model to conform to the XML constraints on *mixed content*:

Normalized XML-compatible declaration

```
<!ELEMENT BiblioMixed (#PCDATA | %bibliocomponent.mix; |
                        BiblioMSet)*>
```

Except for the absence of the exclusion exception, this is an equivalent content model; since the declaration is expressed in the subset of SGML syntax allowed by XML, however, both XML- and SGML-experienced readers should be able to read and understand it.

Typographical Conventions

When you are reading this book, you will notice different typefaces for some types of information:

- **sample term**
  This is a specialized term at the point in the text where I define it.
- *logical unit*
  This is the first reference in a chapter or section to a specialized term.

■ symbol/`filename`/`code`
I use this typeface to refer to text in an example DTD or document instance (such as the SGML name of an element type, entity, attribute, notation, or document type) or to the name of a file.

Figures

For some examples, the book provides figures to illustrate DTD or document constructions. For an explanation of the symbols that appear in the figures, see Figure Intro-1.

(✽) (DTD) Zero or more instances.

(?) (DTD) Zero or one instance(s) allowed.

(+) (DTD) One or more instances allowed.

x ———— a   (DTD or document instance) x contains a.

x ⌐ a, b   (DTD or document instance) x contains a followed by b.

x < a, b   (DTD) x contains either a or b.

x - - - - - - · a   (Entity structure) x contains a.

Example:

<!ELEMENT x ((a | b)?, c)+>

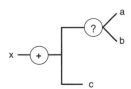

Figure Intro–1   Legend for Figures—The figures in the book provide
graphic representations of DTD and document instance structures.

Part One

In the first part of this book, you will find general background information to help you prepare for the advanced topics in the other three parts:

▌ a review of the DTD syntax you will need to understand the rest of the book, with a discussion of additional facilities available in full SGML (Chapter 1)

▌ an introduction to the five major industry-standard DTDs that this book uses as models (Chapter 2)

If you are already very experienced with XML or SGML, and with the major industry-standard SGML DTDs, feel free either to skip to the next part or to skim this one for a quick review.

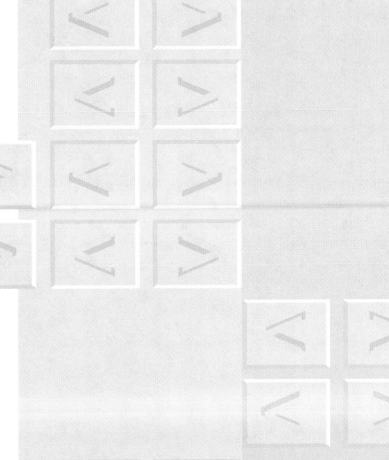

Background

Review of DTD Syntax

T his chapter reviews enough XML DTD syntax to allow you to read the examples in this book, including those relating to architectural forms, but it is not intended as a general introduction to DTD syntax and concepts. It also introduces additional SGML DTD facilities that are not available in XML.

The chapter deals with DTD markup declarations under seven major headings:

1. document type declaration (Section 1.1, page 4)
2. element types (Section 1.2, page 5)
3. attributes (Section 1.3, page 17)
4. entities (Section 1.4, page 28)
5. notations (Section 1.5, page 36)
6. conditional sections (Section 1.6, page 38)
7. processing instructions (Section 1.7, page 39)

At the end of each section, you will find a list of additional facilities available in full SGML.

There are a few general points to note. First, XML reserves all names (for elements, attributes, entities, notations, and processing instructions) starting with the letters "xml" (upper- or lowercase), so you may never declare an element type with a name like **xmli**.

Second, some of the examples in this chapter assume that your declarations appear in the *external DTD subset*. XML places syntax restrictions on the *internal DTD subset* that prevent you from using parameter entities within declarations. For example, consider the following markup declaration:

Markup declaration containing entity reference

```
<!ELEMENT para %para.model;>
```

XML somewhat confusingly allows this in the external DTD subset, but forbids it in the internal DTD subset.

SGML Note: In the notes on full SGML syntax, this chapter (like the book as a whole) deals only with the structural side of DTDs, entirely omitting short references and other optional features that relate only to typing such as DATATAG, OMITTAG, RANK, and SHORTAG. It also omits discussion of the optional CONCUR feature, which is rarely used or supported.

1.1 Document Type Declaration

XML documents with DTDs (and all SGML documents) include a **document type declaration**, like the following:

Sample document type declaration

```
<!DOCTYPE doc SYSTEM "document.dtd">
```

The external identifier after the document type name ("doc") is shorthand for a parameter entity reference to the external file containing most of the DTD. You could also write it like this:

Entity reference for external DTD subset

```
<!DOCTYPE doc [
  <!ENTITY % document-dtd SYSTEM "document.dtd">
  %document-dtd;
]>
```

What the external identifier (if any) points to is the **external DTD subset**. There is also an **internal DTD subset** that appears between "[" and "]>":

Document type declaration with internal subset

```
<!DOCTYPE doc SYSTEM "document.dtd" [
  <!ENTITY myname "David Megginson">
]>
```

Any entity or attribute list declarations in the internal subset take precedence over those declared in the external subset. Declaring the same element type or notation in both is an error.

Normally, you will put the bulk of your DTD in the external subset, so that it can be shared by many different documents. In the internal subset, you include local declarations (such as entities for the graphics used in a specific document) and parameter entities for configuration. When people use the term "DTD" informally, as I do in most of this book, they are referring mainly or exclusively to the (reusable) external subset.

1.2   Elements

Elements provide the basic logical structure for XML and SGML documents. Every document contains exactly one top-level element, and that element may contain others, together with character data. There is a mechanism for attaching meta-data to these elements using attributes (Section 1.3, page 17).

A basic XML *element type declaration* looks like this:

Element type declaration

```
<!ELEMENT list (item+)>
```

The declaration contains two important parts:

- the name of the element type that you are declaring ("list")
- the *content specification*—in this case, a *content model*— (item+), specifying what content can appear within that element

Instead of a content model, the content specification could also be one of the keywords ANY or EMPTY.

1.2.1   *Element Type*

In XML, the **element type** is always a single name:

Element type declaration

```
<!ELEMENT warning (para+)>
```

If you want to declare more than one element type with the same content specification, you have to use a separate declaration for each one:

Different element types with the same content specification

```
<!ELEMENT warning (para+)>
<!ELEMENT caution (para+)>
<!ELEMENT note (para+)>
```

As a convenience, however, you can define a shared content model as a parameter entity, so that you can make changes in a single place (with XML, this is allowed only in the *external DTD subset*):

Different element types with shared content specification

```
<!ENTITY % wcn.MODEL "(para+)">
<!ELEMENT warning %wcn.MODEL;>
<!ELEMENT caution %wcn.MODEL;>
<!ELEMENT note %wcn.MODEL;>
```

1.2.2   *Content Specification*

Your **content specification** must include one of the following:

- a *content model*
- the ANY keyword
- the EMPTY keyword

SGML Note: *Full SGML classifies these differently. In ISO 8879, the content model may be either a **model group** or the keyword* ANY, *while the keyword* EMPTY *designates a type of declared content.*

1.2.2.1   Content Model

The **content model** describes what you are allowed to put in an element (as well as how many and in what order). In the following example, the **section** element must contain a title, followed by an optional abstract, followed by one or more paragraphs:

Sample content model

```
<!ELEMENT section (title, abstract?, paragraph+)>
```

There are two types of content models in XML:

1. **mixed content**, containing character data, possibly mixed together with elements
2. **element content**, containing only elements

Mixed Content

If your content model allows only character data, you must declare it like this (you may optionally add "*" afterward):

Content model allowing character data only

```
<!ELEMENT para (#PCDATA)>
```

In the following case, nothing but character data may appear in a **para** element:

Character data only

```
<para>This is a paragraph, containing nothing but
character data.</para>
```

If your content model allows elements to appear mixed in with the character data, you must declare it like this:

Content model allowing character data and elements

```
<!ELEMENT para (#PCDATA | emphasis | link)*>
```

The "*" at the end shows that the whole content model is repeatable, and the "|" shows that either character data or an element can appear each time: in other words, a **para** may contain any amount of character data (including none), optionally interspersed with **emphasis** and **link** elements:

Mixed character data and elements

```
<para>This is a paragraph with an <emphasis>emphasized
phrase</emphasis> and then more text.</para>
```

Element Content

If it does not allow character data to appear directly, then your content model will consist of a series of **content particles** arranged either as a *choice* or as a *sequence*.

A **choice** requires content to appear in your document that satisfies exactly one of the content particles:

A choice of content particles

```
<!ELEMENT x (a | b)>
```

In this case, an **a** *or* **b** element must appear, but not both.

A **sequence** requires content to appear in your document that satisfies all of the content particles, in the order specified:

A sequence of content particles

```
<!ELEMENT x (a, b)>
```

In this case, **a** *and* **b** elements must appear, in that order.

Content Particles

In all of the examples so far, *content particles* have been simply element type names. In fact, most of the expressive power of DTDs comes from the fact that content particles can have *occurrence indicators* and that they can be groups of other content particles.

Element Content: Groups

A *content particle* can actually be a group of other content particles. For example, the following content model contains three content particles:

Simple content model

```
<!ELEMENT x (a, b, c)>
```

For the second content particle, you could include an entire group instead of a single element type name:

Simple content model

```
<!ELEMENT x (a, (b | d | e), c)>
```

There are still three top-level content particles in the content model, but now the second one is actually a group: an **a** element must appear, followed by a choice of a **b**, **d**, or **e** element, followed by a **c** element.

Note that the group can use a different type of connector than its parent: a group within a sequence can be a choice, and vice versa.

Occurrence Indicators

After each *content particle* (either a single element type name or a group), you may include one of three **occurrence indicators** or no occurrence indicator at all:

[NONE]

There must be content satisfying the content particle exactly once (*required* and *non-repeatable*).

?

Either there must be no content satisfying the content particle, or the content must appear once (*optional* and *non-repeatable*).

*

Either there must be no content satisfying the content particle, or the content may appear one or more times (*optional* and *repeatable*).

+

Content satisfying the content particle must appear one or more times (*required* and *repeatable*).

For example, according to the following content model, an **x** element must contain an optional **a** element, followed by a **b** element, followed by one or more **c** elements:

Example of occurrence indicators

```
<!ELEMENT x (a?, b, c+)>
```

You may also place an occurrence indicator after the entire content model:

Content model with occurrence indicator

```
<!ELEMENT x (a | b | c)*>
```

In this case, the content model allows a choice of an **a**, **b**, or **c** element to appear; however, since the entire content model is optional and repeatable, an **x** element can actually contain any number of **a**, **b**, or **c** elements.

In the following example, exactly one instance of an element of type a must appear before content satisfying the content particle (b, c) (a is *required* and *non-repeatable*):

No occurrence indicator

```
<!ELEMENT x (a, (b, c))>
```

In the next example, zero or one instance of an a element may appear before content satisfying the content particle (b, c) (it is *optional* and *non-repeatable*):

? occurrence indicator

```
<!ELEMENT x (a?, (b, c))>
```

In the next example, zero or more instances of an a element may appear before content satisfying the content particle (b, c) (it is *optional* and *non-repeatable*):

* occurrence indicator

```
<!ELEMENT x (a*, (b, c))>
```

In this example, one or more instances of an a element must appear before content satisfying the content particle (b, c) (it is *required* and *repeatable*):

+ occurrence indicator

```
<!ELEMENT x (a+, (b, c))>
```

1.2.2.2   The ANY Keyword

Instead of a *content model*, the *content specification* can simply use the keyword ANY to specify that any character data or declared elements are allowed to appear in any order:

ANY keyword

```
<!ELEMENT front ANY>
```

In this example, a **front** element may contain character data or any other element allowed anywhere in your DTD. ANY is always *mixed content.*

1.2.2.3   The EMPTY Keyword

Instead of a *content model*, the *content specification* can simply use the keyword EMPTY to specify that the element may never have any content:

EMPTY keyword

```
<!ELEMENT pointer EMPTY>
```

In this example, a **pointer** element may never contain character data or any other element. In your XML document, it will appear in one of the following two forms:

Single empty element tag

```
<pointer/>
```

Empty element with start and end tags

```
<pointer></pointer>
```

If you use the second form, you must not put anything between the start and end tags.

1.2.3 *SGML: Elements*

Most of the differences between XML DTDs and full SGML DTDs appear in element type declarations. This section covers the six most important additional facilities in full SGML:

1. multiple element types in a single declaration (Section 1.2.3.1)
2. omitted tag minimization (Section 1.2.3.2)
3. exceptions (Section 1.2.3.3, page 14)
4. declared content (Section 1.2.3.4, page 15)
5. unconstrained mixed content (Section 1.2.3.5, page 16)
6. unordered content (Section 1.2.3.6, page 17)

1.2.3.1 Multiple Element Types

In full SGML, you may apply a single declaration to more than one element type:

List of element type names
```
<!ELEMENT (warning|caution|note) - - (para+)>
```

The above example is exactly equivalent to the following three separate declarations:

Equivalent separate declarations
```
<!ELEMENT warning - - (para+)>
<!ELEMENT caution - - (para+)>
<!ELEMENT note - - (para+)>
```

1.2.3.2 Omitted Tag Minimization

Full SGML allows authors to omit start or end tags in the document instance. If your SGML declaration allows tag omission (and most do), then you *must* include **omitted tag minimization** immediately after the element type:

- -

Both the start and end tags are always required.

- o

The start tag is always required, but the end tag is optional.

o -

The start tag is optional, but the end tag is always required.

o o

Both the start and end tags are optional.

For element types declared EMPTY, some parsing software insists that you use "- o" or "o o" to show that an end tag is not present.

Nearly all SGML DTDs use omitted tag minimization, so a typical SGML element type declaration actually looks like this:

Typical SGML element type declaration

```
<!ELEMENT list - - (item+)>
```

In this book, however, examples that are not SGML-specific do not include omitted tag minimization so that they will work equally well in XML and in full SGML (assuming an appropriate SGML declaration).

1.2.3.3   Exceptions

In your full SGML content models, you may include two types of **exceptions—exclusion exceptions** and **inclusion exceptions**—to explicitly forbid or allow instances of the specified element types anywhere within an element or its children.

The following inclusion exception allows instances of **annotation** or **todo** anywhere within a **section** element and its children (except where explicitly forbidden by an exclusion exception), even though neither appears in the group `(title, para+)`:

Inclusion exception

```
<!ELEMENT section - - (title, para+) +(annotation|todo)>
```

The exclusion exception in the following example forbids instances of **footnote** within itself and its descendants, even though **footnote**'s content consists of **para** elements, which would normally allow **footnote** elements within them:

Exclusion exception

```
<!ELEMENT para - - (#PCDATA|list|footnote|emphasis)*>
<!ELEMENT footnote - - (para+) -(footnote)>
```

An exclusion exception consists of "–" followed by a group of element type names, and an inclusion exception consists of "+" followed by a group of element type names. Both must follow the main model group, and if you specify both, you must put the exclusion exception first.

Exclusion exceptions always take precedence over inclusion exceptions (once you have excluded an element type, there is no way to include it again).

1.2.3.4 Declared Content

In full SGML, you may include **declared content** for an element type (the EMPTY keyword is actually one type of declared content, but full SGML allows two others):

CDATA

Character data: no delimiters are recognized except "</" followed by a name start character.

RCDATA

Replaceable character data: no delimiters are recognized except "</" or "&" followed by a name start character.

For example, the following declaration would allow you to include a sample content model without escaping any special characters:

CDATA declared content

```
<!ELEMENT listing - - CDATA>
```

1.2.3.5   Mixed Content

While XML restricts mixed content to an optional and repeatable choice group, full SGML allows #PCDATA to appear anywhere you can put a content particle (or **content token** in SGML), though doing so can be dangerous.

In element content, a full SGML parser will ignore whitespace between elements; in mixed content, a full SGML parser will initially treat nondelimiters not caused by markup as character data, even if #PCDATA is not allowed at that point in the content model (it will later discard whitespace that is caused solely by markup, but at that point it may already have signaled a markup error).

As an example, consider the following declaration for a block quotation:

Dangerous mixed content

```
<!ELEMENT quotation - - (source?, #PCDATA)>
```

With this declaration, the following document fragment would *not* parse correctly:

Document excerpt

```
<quotation>
<source>Goldfarb 1990, 322</source>
The only reliable way to define mixed content is as a
repeatable "OR" group; in other words, the data can occur
anywhere within the content, intermixed with whatever
subelements are also permitted.
</quotation>
```

The problem is that, while reading mixed content, the parser will initially treat the record end after the **quotation** start-tag as #PCDATA, then will report an error because #PCDATA is not allowed at that point in the content model.

As a result, the only safe type of mixed content is the repeatable choice group that XML requires, as in the following example:

Safe mixed content

```
<!ELEMENT quotation - - (#PCDATA | source)*>
```

Since #PCDATA can now appear anywhere, record ends will not cause parsing errors (though they may still appear in unwanted locations).

1.2.3.6   Unordered Content

In addition to sequences and choices, full SGML also allows a different way to join content particles, using the "&" connector:

Unordered content

```
<!ELEMENT x - - (a & b & c)>
```

In this example, an **x** element must contain **a**, **b**, and **c** elements, but they may appear in any order.

In general, it is a good idea to avoid **unordered content**, since it makes it much more difficult for authors to create documents with most existing SGML authoring tools. Unordered content can be useful, however, for converting loosely-structured non-SGML documents to SGML.

1.3   Attributes

Attributes provide meta-data for elements, such as a security level, a revision status, or a unique identifier. You can declare attributes for an

XML element type using an **attribute list declaration**, as in the following example:

Attribute list declaration

```
<!ATTLIST sample
  id ID #IMPLIED
  n CDATA #REQUIRED
  status (draft|final) "final">
```

The declaration begins with "<!ATTLIST", followed by the name of the element type, and ends with ">".

In the main body of the declaration comes a list of **attribute definitions**, each of which has three parts:

1. the **attribute name** (i.e. "n")
2. the *attribute type* (i.e. "CDATA")
3. the *default value* (i.e. "#REQUIRED")

The first one is straightforward, but the other two require some explanation.

1.3.1   *Attribute Type*

In XML, the **attribute type** can be a *string type*, a *tokenized type*, or an *enumerated type*.

1.3.1.1   String Type

In a **string type**, the attribute's value will have most whitespace preserved (except that line ends will be replaced with spaces).

CDATA

The attribute value can contain arbitrary character data (except "<" in XML; full SGML does not have this restriction):

CDATA attribute type

```
<!ATTLIST interpretation
    type CDATA #IMPLIED>
```

Note that an attribute type applies to the value of the attribute, *after* the attribute string has been normalized—general entities will still be recognized as part of that normalization process.

1.3.1.2   Tokenized Types

In a **tokenized type**, the parser will normalize all whitespace to a single space character and will eliminate leading and trailing whitespace altogether. It will also validate the contents based on the declared type.

ENTITY OR ENTITIES

The attribute value can contain the name of a single general entity or a list of general entity names:

ENTITY attribute type

```
<!ATTLIST graphic
    source ENTITY #REQUIRED>
```

The parser will verify that you have declared any entity names used. In XML (but not in full SGML), the entity must be an NDATA entity.

ID

The attribute value is a unique identifier for the element instance:

ID attribute type

```
<!ATTLIST chapter
    id ID #IMPLIED>
```

You may include only one ID attribute for each element type.

IDREF O R **IDREFS**

The attribute value must be a reference to an ID or a list of references to IDs:

IDREF attribute type

```
<!ATTLIST xref
  target IDREF #REQUIRED>
```

A validating parser will verify that there are elements with the specified IDs somewhere in the document.

NMTOKEN O R **NMTOKENS**

The attribute value must be a name token or a list of name tokens:

NMTOKENS attribute type

```
<!ATTLIST procedure
  effectivity NMTOKENS #REQUIRED>
```

In XML, a *name token* contains only alphanumeric characters (and the characters ".", "-", "_", and ":"). However, the "alpha-" in *alphanumeric* includes characters from all of the world's major languages, and not just from the Western European alphabet.

1.3.1.3   Enumerated Types

An **enumerated type** requires the author to select values from a predefined list of names, as in the following example:

Name token group as attribute type

```
<!ATTLIST doc
  status (draft | proof | final) #REQUIRED>
```

In this case, the attribute `status` must take a value from among the three tokens "`draft`", "`proof`", or "`final`". Note that for interoperability with most existing SGML systems, it is best that each token be unique among *all* of the attributes for the element type. The following might cause a parsing error, because both the `status` and the `pos` attributes use the token "`final`":

Not Interoperable

```
<!ATTLIST doc
  status (draft | proof | final) #REQUIRED
  pos (initial | middle | final) #IMPLIED>
```

NOTATION Attributes

You may optionally precede the list of tokens with the keyword NOTATION; in this case, the allowed values are all names of notations that you have declared:

NOTATION attribute type

```
<!ATTLIST formula
  format NOTATION (tex|troff) #REQUIRED>
```

Only one attribute for each element can have a NOTATION and should not declare the element itself to be EMPTY. (Otherwise, why supply a notation?)

The typical use of a NOTATION attribute is to describe the contents of an element. In the following example, the contents are a TeX equation:

TeX equation with a notation attribute

```
<formula format="tex">
$\frac{\sqrt{x+y}}{\pi}$
</formula>
```

Note that using a NOTATION attribute does *not* prevent the XML parser from recognizing special markup characters like "&" or "<" in an element's content.

1.3.2   *Default Value*

There are two types of **default values** that you can provide:

1. a literal value (optionally preceded by the keyword
   #FIXED)
2. one of the keywords #IMPLIED or #REQUIRED

1.3.2.1   Literal Values

For an attribute's default value, you may provide a literal value just as
you would in a document instance:

Default value specified

```
<!ATTLIST report
  security (public|confidential|secret) "public">
```

In this example, the security attribute for the **report** element
defaults to the value public unless otherwise specified.

   If you precede the default value with the keyword #FIXED, then
authors will *never* be able to override your default value:

#FIXED default value

```
<!ATTLIST emphasis
  html CDATA #FIXED "em">
```

   In this example, an author will not be able to specify any value for
the html attribute other than em (in most cases, the author would not
specify the value at all). You may not use the keyword #FIXED for an
attribute with a attribute type of ID, because each element must have a
unique ID, if any.

   Note that the parser will not recognize parameter entity references
within a literal default value: it interprets it exactly as it would if the
default value appeared in the document instance.

1.3.2.2   Keywords

There are two keywords that you can use instead of providing a literal
default value for an attribute:

#REQUIRED

There is no default: document authors must always specify a value for this attribute, every time the element appears:

#REQUIRED default value

```
<!ATTLIST interpretation
  type CDATA #REQUIRED>
```

#IMPLIED

Document authors do not have to specify a value for the attribute, and when they do not, the processing software determines a default value in an application-dependent way:

#IMPLIED default value

```
<!ATTLIST interpretation
  type CDATA #IMPLIED>
```

This is by far the most common *default value* for attributes in typical book-oriented DTDs.

1.3.3   *Multiple Declarations*

More than one attribute list declaration may appear for the same element type. For example, the following is legal:

Multiple ATTLIST declarations

```
<!ATTLIST doc
  id ID #REQUIRED>

<!ATTLIST doc
  security CDATA #REQUIRED
  status (draft|final) #IMPLIED>
```

If you declare the same attribute twice, the first declaration will take precedence.

1.3.4   *SGML: Attributes*

For attributes, full SGML offers facilities not available in XML:

1. six additional types of tokenized attribute (NAME, NAMES, NUMBER, NUMBERS, NUTOKEN, and NUTOKENS)
2. two additional keywords for attribute default values (#CURRENT and #CONREF)
3. global attribute definition list declarations

The 1986 version of SGML also forbids multiple attribute definition lists for the same element type.

1.3.4.1   Attribute Types

Full SGML provides six additional tokenized attribute types (or **declared values**):

NAME O R **NAMES**
The attribute value must be a name or a name list:

NAME declared value

```
<!ATTLIST emphasis
  html NAME #FIXED "em">
```

By default, a name begins with an alphabetic character and contains only alphanumeric characters and the characters ".". and "-". In other words, although "1greenwich2" is a valid NMTOKEN, it is not a valid NAME.

NUMBER O R **NUMBERS**
The attribute value must contain only the digits "0" to "9":

NUMBER declared value

```
<!ATTLIST line
  n NUMBER #IMPLIED>
```

NUTOKEN OR **NUTOKENS**

The attribute value must begin with one of the digits "0" to "9", followed by alphanumeric characters or "." or "-":

NUTOKEN declared value

```
<!ATTLIST dossier
   fileno NUTOKEN #REQUIRED>
```

1.3.4.2   Attribute Default Values

In addition to the default values available in XML, full SGML offers the following:

#CURRENT

The default is the value specified on the most recent instance of the associated element type. Document authors must specify a value *at least* on the first instance of the element type in a document:

#CURRENT default value

```
<!ATTLIST interpretation
   type CDATA #CURRENT>
```

You may not use the keyword #CURRENT for an attribute with a declared value of ID, because two elements may not have the same ID.

#CONREF

The attribute is a substitute for the element's content—an element may have content *or* a value for this attribute, but not both (if the author specifies an attribute value, the parser will act as if the element were declared EMPTY):

#CONREF default value

```
<!ATTLIST interpretation
   type CDATA #CONREF>
```

An instance could look like this:

#CONREF attribute not specified

```
<interpretation>This is an interpretation</interpretation>
```

or like this:

#CONREF attribute specified

```
<interpretation type="this is an interpretation">
```

You may not use the keyword #CONREF for an attribute with a declared value of ID, and you may not specify it for an element type that is already declared EMPTY.

1.3.4.3   Multiple Attribute Definition Lists

Unlike XML, the 1986 SGML standard allows at most one attribute definition list declaration for each element type. If two element types share some attributes but not others, most SGML DTDs will use a parameter entity to hold the shared attributes, then will include a reference to the parameter entity in each attribute definition list declaration:

Shared attributes (standard SGML)

```
<!ENTITY % attr.xref "
  target IDREF #REQUIRED
  label CDATA #IMPLIED
">

<!ELEMENT table-ref - - (#PCDATA)>
<!ATTLIST table-ref
  n NUMBER #IMPLIED
  %attr.xref;>

<!ELEMENT ref - - (#PCDATA)>
<!ATTLIST ref
  %attr.xref;>
```

If your system supports the WebSGML adaptions to SGML (annex K), however, you can provide multiple attribute definition lists for the same element type (Section 1.3.3, page 23) just as you can in XML. In fact, since SGML allows multiple associated element types, you can actually declare shared attributes for many different element types in a single declaration:

Shared attributes (AFDR extensions)

```
<!AFDR "ISO/IEC 10744:1992">

<!ATTLIST (table-ref|ref)
  target IDREF #REQUIRED
  label CDATA #IMPLIED>

<!ELEMENT table-ref - - (#PCDATA)>
<!ATTLIST table-ref
  n NUMBER #IMPLIED>

<!ELEMENT ref - - (#PCDATA)>
```

Now **ref** will receive only the common attributes target and label, but **table-ref** will receive the attribute n as well.

1.3.4.4   Global Attributes

DTDs sometimes contain global attributes. Normally, they do so by declaring a parameter entity, then including a reference to it in each attribute definition list declaration (this method works for both XML and full SGML):

Global attributes (pre-WebSGML)

```
<!ENTITY % attr.global "
  id ID #IMPLIED
  class CDATA #IMPLIED
">

<!ELEMENT para - - (#PCDATA)>
<!ATTLIST para
  %attr.global;>

<!ELEMENT xref - - (#PCDATA)>
<!ATTLIST xref
```

```
target IDREF #REQUIRED
%attr.global;>
```

If your SGML system supports the WebSGML adaptions to
SGML (annex K), however, you have an additional choice: you can
use the associated element type #ALL to declare global attributes without declaring a parameter entity and including references:

Global attributes (WebSGML)

```
<!ATTLIST #ALL
  id ID #IMPLIED
  class CDATA #IMPLIED>

<!ELEMENT para - - (#PCDATA)>

<!ELEMENT xref - - (#PCDATA)>
<!ATTLIST xref
  target IDREF #REQUIRED>
```

Now both **para** and **xref** will receive the global attributes id and
class, but **xref** will receive the local attribute target as well.

1.4   Entities

Just as elements represent an SGML document's **logical structure**,
entities represent its **physical structure**—every XML document starts
with a single top-level entity, and the document's complete entity
structure provides a road map of how to put a logical document
together from objects defined internally or stored on the file system,
in a database, on the Internet, or anywhere else that is accessible.

There are two different types of entities, each with its own name
space:

1. **general entities** apply within the top-level element and
   in attribute values

2. **parameter entities** apply within the internal and external DTD subsets

The following *entity declaration* creates an internal **general entity** containing the text "Extensible Markup Language":

General entity declaration

```
<!ENTITY xml "Extensible Markup Language">
```

You can include a reference to the entity in attribute values or anywhere in *mixed content*:

Entity reference in document

```
<para>The &xml; is derived from ISO 8879,
an International Standard.
 <indexref label="&xml;"/></para>
```

This example is equivalent to the following:

Entity references expanded

```
<para>The Extensible Markup Language is derived from ISO
8879, an International Standard.
  <indexref label="Extensible Markup Language"/></para>
```

The following declaration creates an internal parameter entity containing the text "#PCDATA | emphasis | link":

Parameter entity declaration

```
<!ENTITY % inline "#PCDATA | emphasis | link">
```

In XML, you may include a reference to the entity in markup declarations in your external DTD subset (in the internal subset, it would have to match a complete declaration in XML; full SGML has no such restriction):

Parameter entity reference in DTD

```
<!ELEMENT para (%inline;)*>
```

This example is equivalent to the following:

Parameter entity reference expanded

```
<!ELEMENT para (#PCDATA | emphasis | link)*>
```

1.4.1   *Location*

You can declare entities that are either internal (the entity text is in the declaration itself) or external (the entity text is somewhere else). For an **internal entity**, you provide an entity value literal:

Internal entity declarations

```
<!ENTITY name "David Megginson">
<!ENTITY % inline "#PCDATA | emphasis | link | comment |
                   note">
```

In each case, the entity value (`"David Megginson"` or `"#PCDATA | emphasis | link | comment | note"`) provides the entity's replacement text internally—there is no need to look in other entities.

For an external entity, you must provide an **external definition** consisting of at least a **system identifier**, as in the following examples:

External entity declarations

```
<!ENTITY chapter1 PUBLIC "-//megginson//TEXT Chapter 1//EN"
                         "chap01.xml">
<!ENTITY pic SYSTEM "pic.tiff" NDATA tiff>
<!ENTITY % symbols SYSTEM "symbols.ent">
```

Each of these contains a system identifier that the parser will use to locate the entity text *outside* of the document entity (external entities normally reside in a different physical resource from the document entity, such as the file system, perhaps, in a database, or even over the Internet—in XML you may use any resource that can be represented by a URI). The first example also contains a **public identifier** that the parser can use to select a different (perhaps more convenient) place to look for the entity, and the second example contains an NDATA declaration.

If you provide both a public and system identifier, the public identifier should come first, and the system identifier should *not* be preceded by the word SYSTEM:

Public and system identifiers together

```
<!ENTITY preface PUBLIC "-//megginson//TEXT Preface//EN"
                         "preface.sgm">
```

1.4.2   *Definitions*

For internal entities (parameter entities or general entities) in XML, the definition is always a simple quoted literal:

Internal Entity

```
<!ENTITY % model "a | b | c">
```

For external entities, you use an external identifier (a system identifier, optionally preceded by a public identifier) to specify the value. If you include *only* the external identifier, the system will treat the entity as a **parsed entity** and attempt to parse the text at the point where the entity reference appears:

Declaring an external parsed entity

```
<!ENTITY % dtdmodule SYSTEM "dtdmodule.mod">
```

If you are declaring a *general entity* rather than a *parameter entity*, you can follow the external identifier with an NDATA declaration:

Declaring an external unparsed entity

```
<!ENTITY pic SYSTEM "scheme.gif" NDATA gif>
```

Note that the NDATA keyword is always followed by the name of a notation that you have declared somewhere else in your DTD. This declaration informs the parser that it should not parse the entity as part of the current document. In XML, you may use an unparsed entity only as the value of an ENTITY attribute (in full SGML, you may include references in the text as well).

1.4.3   *Boundaries*

Although the physical (entity) and logical (element) structures of an XML document do not have to correspond, they do have to be **properly nested**:

1. elements must begin and end in the same entity
2. comments, processing instructions, character references, and entity references must be contained entirely within the same entity

For example, consider the following entity:

Entity declaration

```
<!ENTITY overlap "</a><b>">
```

There is nothing wrong with the declaration in itself, but when you make a reference to it in your document, the elements and entities will no longer be properly nested, because the **a** element ends and the **b** element starts in the overlap entity:

Improperly nested structure

```
<a>text&overlap;text</b>
```

1.4.4   *SGML: Entities*

Full SGML offers the following additional facilities:

1. default entities
2. more flexibility with external identifiers
3. internal data text entities
4. three additional types of external entities

1.4.4.1   Default Entity

In full SGML, you can declare a **default general entity**, as in the following example:

Default entity declaration

```
<!ENTITY #DEFAULT "[undefined]">
```

If the entity `symbol` were not declared, then the two paragraphs in the following example would be equivalent:

Equivalent paragraphs

```
<para>Here is the entity reference: &something;</para>
<para>Here is the entity reference: [undefined]</para>
```

1.4.4.2   External Identifiers

In full SGML, you may provide the word SYSTEM without an explicit system identifier:

System identifier defaulted

```
<!ENTITY copyright SYSTEM>
```

You may also include a public identifier without an accompanying system identifier (in XML, you must always include the system identifier):

No system identifier

```
<!ENTITY disclaimer PUBLIC
    "-//megginson//TEXT Disclaimer//EN">
```

In this case, the parser must look up a system identifer itself.

1.4.4.3   Data Text

In full SGML, you can specify a special treatment for an internal entity value by declaring it as **data text** or as **bracketed text**. (This section does not deal with bracketed text, since it it is rarely used.)

For data text, you include the keyword CDATA, SDATA, or PI immediately before the entity value:

Data text

```
<!ENTITY auml SDATA '[auml  ]'>
```

The keywords have the following meaning:

CDATA

The entity text is treated as unparseable character data—markup characters have no special significance:

CDATA internal entity

```
<!ENTITY amp CDATA "&">
```

You may not use the CDATA keyword with parameter entities.

SDATA

The entity text is treated as **specific character data**, interpreted in a system-specific way. People often use SDATA text for character entities:

SDATA internal entity

```
<!ENTITY amp SDATA '[amp   ]'>
```

You may not use the SDATA keyword with parameter entities.

PI

The entity text is treated as a *processing instruction*, to be interpreted in a system-specific way:

PI internal entity

```
<!ENTITY authorize PI "authorize uid='105'
password='abcde'">
```

You may use the `PI` keyword for both general entities and parameter entities.

I.4.4.4   External Entity Types

In XML, external entities must either be text or NDATA. In full SGML, there are three other types available:

SUBDOC

The entity is a separate SGML document instance, with its own prolog. The declaration ends immediately after the keyword:

Declaring a subdocument entity

```
<!ENTITY wpaper PUBLIC "-//local//SUBDOC White Paper//EN"
                       SUBDOC>
```

CDATA

The entity is character-oriented data (such as a source-code listing) that should not be parsed. A notation name and an optional data attribute specification follow the keyword:

Declaring an external CDATA entity

```
<!ENTITY listing SYSTEM "main.pl" CDATA perl>
```

SDATA

The entity text is character data that has a system-specific meaning (such as system-specific processing code). A required notation name and an optional data attribute specification follow:

Declaring an external SDATA entity

```
<!ENTITY book SYSTEM "book.rtf" SDATA rtf>
```

1.5   Notations

You need to know about notations if you plan to include non-XML content—like graphics, sound, video, or source-code listings—in your XML documents. While the XML parser knows nothing about specific notations, it can pass them on to the processing software to let it know what kinds of data to handle.

1.5.1   *Declarations*

A *notation declaration* looks like this:

Declaring a notation

```
<!NOTATION TeX PUBLIC
   "+//ISBN 0-201-13448-9::Knuth//NOTATION The TeXbook//EN">
```

The body of the declaration contains the notation name ("TeX") and an external identifier ("PUBLIC "+//ISBN 0-201-13448-9::Knuth/ /NOTATION The TeXbook//EN""). Notation declarations are the only place in XML that you are allowed to supply a public identifier without an accompanying system identifier.

Notations have their own name space—you are free to choose the same name for a notation, an entity, and an element without causing an error.

You should declare a notation for every non-XML datatype in your document, including non-XML text such as source-code listings. You may also declare a notation for XML itself, if you wish.

1.5.2   *SGML: Notations*

In full SGML, you can declare and specify *data attributes* for notations.

1.5.2.1   Data Attributes

Like element types, notations in full SGML can have attributes associated with them. These data attributes provide extra information for the notation handler about a specific entity, such as the parameters that should be used for rendering a graphic.

In addition, both data attributes and notations are important for SGML Architectural Forms (Chapter 9), since they play a crucial part in the relationship between a DTD and the document's base architecture(s).

A data attribute declaration looks like this:

Declaring data attributes for a notation

```
<!ATTLIST #NOTATION tiff
   height NUMBER #IMPLIED
   width NUMBER #IMPLIED
   depth NUMBER 8>
```

Except for the keyword #NOTATION, and the use of a notation name instead of an element type name, it follows the same structure as the attribute definition list declaration for element attributes (see Section 1.3, page 17).

Data attributes allow you to specify parameters, such as the height and width of graphics or the default tabbing interval, for different external entities that share the same notation. You specify the attribute values in the *entity declaration* itself, as in the following example:

Specifying values for data attributes

```
<!ENTITY face PUBLIC "-//local//NONSGML Face Shot//EN"
   NDATA tiff
  [ height=16 width=32 ]>
```

1.6   Conditional Sections

In the external DTD subset and external parameter entities, XML allows **conditional sections** that the parser can include or ignore, depending on the value of the keyword at the start:

Ignored conditional section

```
<![IGNORE[
 <!ELEMENT para (#PCDATA)>
]]>
```

In this example, the declaration for the **para** element will be ignored.

Usually, you will use parameter entities for the keywords:

Parameter entities and conditional sections

```
<!ENTITY % include-para "IGNORE">
<![%include-para;[
  <!ELEMENT para (#PCDATA)>
]]>
```

Now, the declaration for **para** will be included if the include-para parameter entity has the value INCLUDE, and it will be ignored if include-para has the value IGNORE. In the example, include-para is set to IGNORE, but a declaration in the internal DTD subset would override it:

Overriding a parameter entity

```
<!DOCTYPE book SYSTEM "book.dtd" [
  <!ENTITY % include-para "INCLUDE">
]>
```

In this example, **para** will be included in the DTD because the declaration of include-para here will take precedence over the declaration in the external subset.

1.7   Processing Instructions

The final basic component of DTD design is the *processing instruction*. A processing instruction is a system-specific instruction that looks like this:

Processing instruction

```
<?IS10744:arch name="abc"?>
```

The actual instruction appears between the "<?" and "?>" delimiters. It consists of a name (in this case, "IS10744:arch") followed optionally by whitespace and character data (in this case, name="abc"). The first name may be the name of a notation that has been declared, but it is not required to be.

XML parsers will pass processing instructions on to your application, but it will be up to you to do something useful with them.

1.7.1   *Why Bother with Processing Instructions?*

The processing instruction was originally meant as a (somewhat awkward) work-around for some of the shortcomings in early SGML processing software. For example, authors could use a processing instruction to force a page break and avoid a widow (that is a different matter from declaring a **page-break** element type for document types such as medieval manuscripts, printed scientific papers, or some legal texts, where the location of page breaks is part of the document's structure rather than simply a formatting question).

Processing instructions have become important, however, for an entirely different reason: They make it possible for users to introduce new facilities into SGML without modifying the basic syntax. XML, for example, uses processing instructions to convey different types of extra information to processing applications, and processing instructions are crucial for architectural forms (Chapter 9).

1.7.2   *SGML: Processing Instructions*

The original SGML standard (ISO 8879:1986) does not require processing instructions to begin with a name.

1.7.2.1   PI Entities

In full SGML, you may also include a processing instruction by declaring an internal general entity or parameter entity with the keyword PI, and then referencing the entity at the points where you want the processing instruction to apply:

Declaring a processing instruction as an entity

```
<!ENTITY % arcbase PI "IS10744 ARCBASE abc">
```

Referencing the processing instruction

```
%arcbase;
```

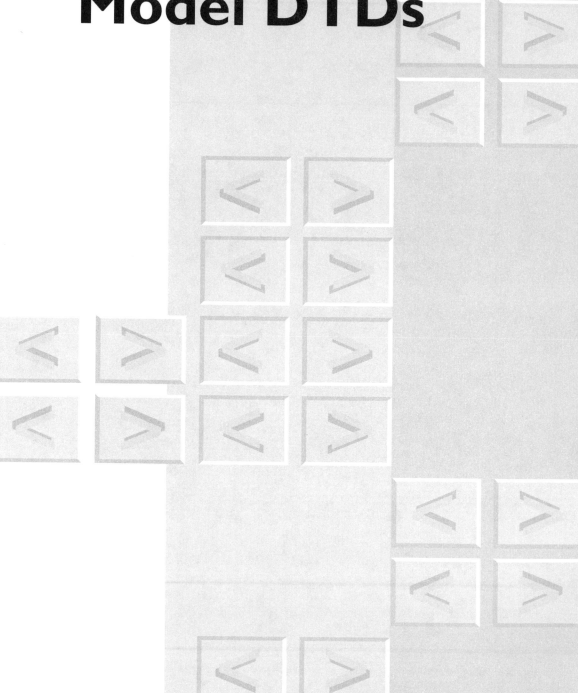

Model DTDs

Chapter 2

XML itself is new, but it has inherited a long history from its parent: SGML has been an International Standard since 1986 and was under development and discussion for more than a decade before that. The principles of document design apply equally well to both, so it makes sense to see what XML can learn from a generation of SGML experience.

For more than a decade, organizations have been working together to develop SGML **industry-standard DTDs** (or **exchange DTDs**). At the time of writing, most of these industry-standard DTDs still exist only for full SGML, but work is already under way to create stripped-down XML versions of some of them.

Whether or not you decide to use an industry-standard DTD yourself, you can learn much about DTD analysis and design by studying them. From the many available, I have chosen to use five as model DTDs for this book (for detailed descriptions, see Section 2.3, page 47):

1. ISO 12083, the publishing-industry DTD for books, serials, and articles (Section 2.3.1, page 47)
2. DocBook, the computer-industry DTD for technical documentation (Section 2.3.2, page 54)
3. the Text Encoding Initiative (TEI-Lite) DTD, derived from the family of academic DTDs used for literary and other research material (Section 2.3.3, page 62)
4. MIL-STD-38784, a U.S.-military DTD from the CALS initiative, designed for technical manuals (Section 2.3.4, page 70; for definitions of the acronym "CALS" see Section 2.3.4.1, page 70)
5. the Hypertext Markup Language (HTML), a DTD used for publication over the World Wide Web and on corporate intranets (Section 2.3.5, page 77)

These DTDs are designed for different purposes, but I have chosen them because they have several important features in common:

- They are all **book-oriented DTDs** rather than **database-oriented DTDs**—documents that use them tend to contain continuous text organized into paragraphs, sections, chapters, and so on
- They are all **publication-oriented DTDs** rather than **information-content-oriented DTDs**—they tend to emphasize general publishing element types, such as lists, sections, and paragraphs, over specific analytical element types such as introductions, tutorials, or explanations
- They are all designed for the exchange of information within a wide industry or discipline, so they are not closely modeled on any one user's needs or on any single class of documents (with the partial exception of MIL-STD-38784).

This chapter introduces the model DTDs, but more detailed analysis appears elsewhere in the book; in particular, see Part Two for specific, detailed examples from the DTDs. Near the end of the book, there is also a combined index of element type names and attribute names: you can use this to look up specific element type names or attribute names, or to compare naming conventions among the different DTDs.

2.1   Reading About the Model DTDs

This chapter contains one section for each DTD. In each section you will find the following information:

- history and background information
- a quick tour of the DTD's structure
- a short sample document using the DTD
- information on obtaining the DTD and its documentation

The "Quick Tour" in each section provides a very high-level overview of the main structure of the DTD, concentrating on the top-level element types, the most important structuring element types (such as chapters or sections), and the main paragraph-level and inline element types (such as lists and emphasized phrases).

2.1.1   Sample Documents

The sample documents are as similar as possible, so that you can compare the way that different DTDs structure information. I have put the following into each sample:

- a title and author's name
- two chapters, each with a title and an initial paragraph

- an ordered list of three items
- a cross-reference from the second chapter to the first
- an illustration in TIFF format, from the file `pic.tif`

2.2   A Note About Using Industry-Standard DTDs

If you need to exchange documents that conform to an industry-standard DTD, you have traditionally had two choices:

1. write the documents using the industry-standard DTD directly
2. write the documents using a simpler DTD customized for your own needs, and design software to convert the documents to use the industry-standard DTD when you ship them out

A new standard, *architectural forms* allows for a third approach—for more information, see Part Four.

There are both advantages and disadvantages to using one of these industry-standard DTDs directly instead of writing your own, simplified DTD.

Advantages of Customized DTDs
Because industry-standard DTDs are usually the result of collaboration and negotiation among many people, they include something for everyone and may end up being large, unwieldy, and loosely structured. If you start from scratch, you can write a customized DTD that is small, tightly structured, and easy to learn and use.

Advantages of Industry-Standard DTDs
Industry-standard DTDs are already designed, implemented, tested, and documented, and are well supported by existing software. If you write an entirely new DTD, you will have to do all of this additional work yourself. Furthermore, your customers, contractors, and collaborators may already be set up to work with one of the industry-standard DTDs, and your writers might already be trained to use one.

In fact, because the industry-standard DTDs are so well tested, documented, and supported, people often choose to use them even when they do *not* need to exchange documents. For example, I chose to write this book in SGML using the DocBook DTD unmodified, even though I do not require all of the facilities of the DocBook document type.

2.3   The Five Model DTDs

2.3.1   *ISO 12083*

ISO 12083 defines a set of four DTDs designed for general electronic publishing. Unlike the other book-oriented DTDs introduced in this chapter, the ISO 12083 DTDs are not customized for a specific industry or subject matter—they truly are general-purpose DTDs, designed for three different types of publications:

1. books (`ISO 12083:1993//DTD Book//EN`)
2. serial publications, such as journals and magazines (`ISO 12083:1993//DTD Serial//EN`)
3. individual articles (`ISO 12083:1993//DTD Article//EN`)

The Serial DTD includes the Article DTD, and all include the Math DTD (`ISO 12083:1993//DTD Mathematics//EN`).

The Book and Article DTDs are very similar. They contain 148 element types in common (out of a total of 169 element types for the Book DTD and 159 element types for the Article DTD), 35 of which are defined in the Math DTD and 113 of which are defined separately in each DTD. Some of the definitions differ slightly between the two—by allowing, for example, additional attributes or children that are appropriate only for books or articles—but they are generally very similar.

Of the remaining DTDs in ISO 12083, you cannot use the Math DTD by itself, because it requires that six parameter entities be defined externally. The Serial DTD simply includes the Article DTD and adds 27 additional element types for high-level structure. This book will refer mainly to the Book DTD, but many of the observations and examples apply equally well to the Serial and Article DTDs.

2.3.1.1   Background

The ISO 12083 DTDs are unique among the five model DTDs because they are defined by an International Standard; they also have a remarkably acronym-ridden history. The Association of American Publishers (AAP) developed the original version of these DTDs, which were released as an American National Standard by the American National Standards Institute (ANSI) in 1988.

With some modifications, the DTDs became an International Standard through the International Organization for Standardization (ISO) in 1993 and are now maintained for ISO by the Electronic Publishing Special Interest Group (EPSIG), which includes the AAP and the Graphic Communications Association Research Institute (GCARI), together with other members.

Within the ISO standard, the Book, Article, and Serial DTDs are final—that means that they will not be changed (barring error corrections) more frequently than every five years. (The Mathematics DTD is still under development, but this book does not deal specifically with scientific publishing.) None of the other DTDs introduced in this chapter has this level of guaranteed stability, though most try to make their changes backward-compatible. The HTML DTD, in particular, changes frequently (and sometimes reverses itself and discards previous changes), and DocBook comes out with frequent updates.

Keeping documents and software synchronized with constantly-changing DTDs can become very expensive; as a result, the stability of the ISO 12083 DTDs makes them especially attractive to SGML implementors and software developers. The problem with the stability, however, is that these DTDs cannot change quickly to meet new demands.

2.3.1.2   Quick Tour

What's on Top?

The ISO 12083 Book DTD starts with the document element type **book**, which permits the classic division of front matter, body, and back matter, with the addition of a separate division for appendices. Instances of the following top-level element types can appear within **book** (see Figure 2–1):

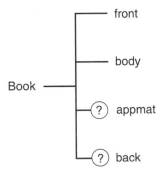

Figure 2–1   ISO 12083 Book DTD: Top Level—The ISO 12083 Book DTD has a simple, clearly-structured top level.

front

The book's front matter (required), containing, at a minimum, structured information about the author and title. Elements of this type may also contain information on the date of publication; various types of publication-related material, such as the copyright edition, location, and paper type; any number of special front-matter divisions such as forewords, introductions, and prefaces; and a table of contents.

body

The main body of the book (required), containing either one or more parts or one or more chapters.

appmat

One or more appendices (optional).

back

The book's back matter, other than appendices (optional). Elements of this type can contain three major types of divisions: afterwords, notes, and vitaes; glossaries and indexes; and bibliographies.

What's in the Middle?

As I mentioned earlier, the main body of an ISO 12083 document consists of one or more chapters or one or more parts. All of the major sectioning element types in this DTD are **nonrecursive element types**—that is, there is a different element type for each level, and the sectioning depth is limited by the DTD.

In addition to parts and chapters, there are element types for sections and six different levels of subsections in the main body of the text. Each sectioning element type begins with an optional number, followed by an optional title, followed by paragraph-level content, followed optionally by sectioning elements from the next level down (if any). Altogether, the following principle element types are available for sectioning in the main body of the document (see Figure 2-2): **part**, **chapter**, **section**, **subsect1**, **subsect2**, **subsect3**, **subsect4**, **subsect5**, and **subsect6**. The **part** element type permits a title and

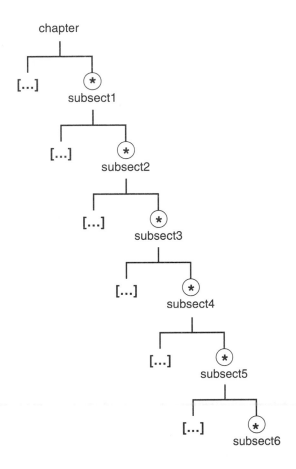

Figure 2-2   ISO 12083 Book DTD: Sectioning Hierarchy—ISO 12083 uses a straight-forward, non-recursive sectioning hierarchy.

various paragraph-level elements followed by one or more chapters, and all of the rest (except for the bottom-level **subsect6**) may contain zero or more instances of the next-lower element type.

There are also several sectioning element types that do not appear in the main hierarchy, such as **foreword**, **intro**, **preface**, **appendix**, **glossary**, and **index**.

What's on the Bottom?

The ISO 12083 Book DTD contains most of the usual paragraph-level element types, including paragraphs, lists, tables, block quotations, figures, graphics, and formulas. There are also some less common paragraph-level element types, such as **poem**. Most of these can also appear either between or within paragraphs.

Like HTML 4.0 and TEI, the ISO 12083 DTD does *not* use the CALS table model—instead, ISO 12083 develops its own, which is different enough that it could not easily be mapped onto a CALS table using Architectural Forms or a conversion utility.

For lists, there is a single, generic **list** element type, with an optional **head** before each **item**, and an optional attribute type to distinguish up to six list types (including both numbered and bulleted lists). List items contain paragraphs or other paragraph-level elements.

For figures and illustrations, there are empty element types **fig** and **artwork**, each with an optional attribute name specifying the entity containing relevant information.

The DTDs include the standard inline element types, including those for emphasis, direct quotations, various types of cross-references, notes, authors, literal text, keywords, cited titles, and dates.

2.3.1.3   Sample Document

This sample document contains the model document marked up according to the ISO 12083 Book DTD. As with all DTDs except HTML, this document includes the TIFF graphic as an entity: the external DTD subset already declares the tiff notation, so there is no need to redeclare it in the declaration subset. Especially note the single, generic **list** element type, the structure within the **author** element type, and the lack of other required front matter.

ISO 12083 sample document

```
<!DOCTYPE book PUBLIC "ISO 12083:1993//DTD Book//EN" [
  <!ENTITY pic SYSTEM "pic.tif" NDATA tiff>
]>
```

```
<book>

<front>
<titlegrp>
<title>Sample Text</title>
</titlegrp>
<authgrp>
<author>
<fname>David</fname>
<surname>Megginson</surname>
</author>
</authgrp>
</front>

<body>

<chapter id="first">
<title>First Chapter or Section</title>

<p>This is a sample chapter or section containing this
paragraph, an <emph>emphasised phrase</emph> and an ordered
list of three items:</p>

<list type="1">
<item>
<p>first item;</p>
</item>
<item>
<p>second item; and</p>
</item>
<item>
<p>third item.</p>
</item>
</list>

</chapter>


<chapter id="second">
<title>Second Chapter or Section</title>

<p>This is a second sample chapter or section, containing a
paragraph with a single <secref rid="first">cross-
reference</secref> to the first chapter or section. Here is
```

```
an illustration:</p>

<artwork name="pic">

</chapter>
</body>
</book>
```

2.3.1.4   Availability

As the ISO relies on selling standards to support its activities, the final versions of the ISO 12083 DTDs and their documentation are not freely available and have to be ordered from ISO or EPSIG.

The best source of information on EPSIG, the DTDs' maintainer, is the EPSIG home page `<http://www.gca.org/epsig/>` on the World Wide Web: it offers different levels of memberships, publishes a news-letter and holds regular meetings on ISO 12083 and other topics related to electronic publishing. EPSIG also sells *The Annotated ISO 12083*, an electronic book available from EPSIG for US$250 (at the time of writing), with discounts for EPSIG members. You can reach EPSIG by e-mail at `epsig@aol.com` or by regular mail, care of the GCARI, 100 Daingerfield Road, 4th floor, Alexandria, VA 22314-2888.

While the final, official versions of the DTDs are not available online, at the time of writing you can obtain the prerelease discussion versions at several sites on the World Wide Web, such as the Exeter SGML Archive `<ftp://info.ex.ac.uk/pub/SGML/ISO-12083/>`.

2.3.2   *DocBook*

The DocBook DTD is a book-oriented DTD like ISO 12083, but it contains additional element types that are particularly useful for software documentation. The designers built it to capture the existing structure of printed documents, from full software manuals to Unix man pages, and intended it chiefly for interchange—some projects, however, now use either the DTD itself or a stripped-down version of it for authoring original documents in SGML (including this book).

Unlike the ISO 12083 DTDs, which allow several different document types at the root, DocBook is designed to encompass many different structures inside a **Book**, or, alternatively, inside a **Set** of books. Like full TEI (Section 2.3.3, page 62) (but not TEI-Lite), DocBook includes hooks for user customization in restricted and well-specified ways, so that users can modify the DTD for their individual needs.

Earlier versions of DocBook used variations on the public identifier "`-//HaL and O'Reilly//DTD DocBook//EN`", but current versions use variations on "`-//Davenport//DTD DocBook//EN`" (the current DTD is "`-//Davenport//DTD DocBook V3.0//EN`").

2.3.2.1   Background

DocBook started as a joint project of HaL Computer Systems and O'Reilly & Associates, but it is now under the control of the Davenport Group, a broadly-based consortium whose sponsors include or have included software industry leaders like Microsoft, Novell, Fujitsu, Hewlett-Packard, Digital Equipment Corporation, The Santa Cruz Operation, Hitachi, Sunsoft, and Unisys.

Since it is a consortium standard, DocBook changes much more quickly than an International Standard like ISO 12083, so it can be more difficult to develop and maintain specialized tools for authoring and processing DocBook documents. To make things easier for software developers (and for other users), the Davenport Group has established a policy on changes:

1. there will be no backward-incompatible changes in minor revisions
2. backward-incompatible changes will be made in major revisions, which will appear no more than two times each year

3. the Davenport group will give at least six months'
   advance notice of any backward-incompatible changes

Although this policy means that documents themselves might need frequent update, and that tool developers will have to keep up with new, nonincompatible changes, it does at least ensure some predictability.

One of the major architects of the DocBook DTD, Eve Maler, is the coauthor of *Developing SGML DTDs: From Text Model to Markup* (Prentice-Hall). Although the book is not primarily about DocBook, it does present many of the design principles that Maler brought to the creation of the modular DocBook DTD (V2.3 and up).

2.3.2.2   Quick Tour

What's on Top?

The DocBook document instance usually starts with the document element **Book** (it may also start with **Set** for a set of books). Unlike the ISO 12083 Book DTD, the DocBook DTD does not require that the user include front matter, though typically a book will begin with a **BookInfo** element, containing bibliographical information such as the book's author and title.

Again, unlike the ISO 12083 Book DTD (and unlike the other DTDs introduced in this chapter), the DocBook DTD has no **body** element type per se; instead, it has four major sectioning element types, and every **Book** must contain an instance of at least one of them:

Chapter
  A regular book chapter.

Article
  An article in a collection.

Reference

A collection of structured technical reference entries (**RefEntry**), similar to Unix man pages.

Part

A collection of any or all of the above or of several other major section types.

Each of these has a compulsory title, and the **Article** element type also requires an explicit page range (**ArtPageNums**)—an unnecessary nuisance if the article is newly authored in SGML rather than converted from a printed original.

In addition to these, the **Book** element type can optionally contain tables of contents, lists of tables, indices, bibliographies, and appendices (see Figure 2–3).

What's in the Middle?

Like the ISO 12083 Book DTD, the DocBook DTD uses nonrecursive sectioning element types: there is a separate element type for each sectioning level, from **Sect1** (section) to **Sect5** (sub-sub-sub-subsection). The **Reference** element type has a slightly different structure, and has its own sectioning element types, from **RefSect1** to **RefSect5** (see Figure 2–4).

In addition to the generic sectioning element types, some specialized types are available, such as **Abstract**, **Sidebar**, and **Warning**. There is also a new **SimpleSect** element type that can appear at the end of any other sectioning elements but can contain no subsections.

What's on the Bottom?

The DocBook DTD contains many paragraph-level element types—even paragraphs themselves appear in three different forms:

SimPara

An untitled paragraph that cannot contain block-level elements, such as lists and tables. Inline element types like **Emphasis** can still appear.

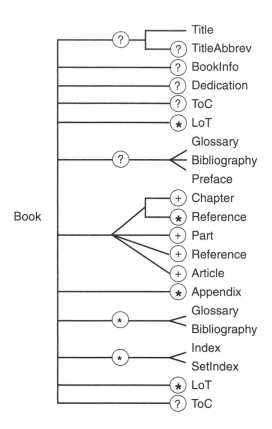

Figure 2–3 DocBook DTD: Top Level—DocBook has a complicated top level, without container elements to organise the element types into front matter, etc.

Para

An untitled paragraph that can contain both inline and block element types.

FormalPara

A titled paragraph structure, containing a title and a **Para** element. This element type is similar to **Para0** in the MIL-STD-38784 DTD (Section 2.3.4, page 70).

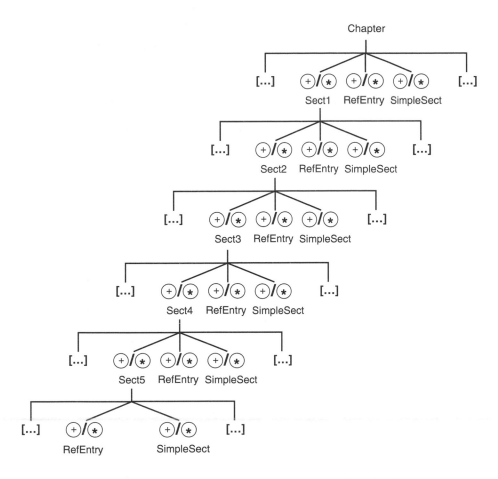

Figure 2–4 DocBook DTD: Sectioning Hierarchy—DocBook uses a standard, non-recursive sectioning hierarchy, but provides alternatives at each level.

This pattern appears a few times at the paragraph level in the Doc-Book DTD: there are also both formal and informal versions of lists, equations, examples, and tables, in addition to the **SimpleSect** element type mentioned in the previous subsection. In general, the informal (simple) versions allow the capture of less-structured information in legacy text, whereas the formal (structured) versions provide more guidance for the creation of new documentation in SGML.

DocBook provides six types of lists (**ItemizedList**, **OrderedList**, **VariableList**, **SegmentedList**, **SimpleList**, and **GlossList**), although the segmented list is more like a simple table. On the paragraph/block level, it also provides (among others) element types for change highlights, procedures, figures, and equations (including graphics), and many types of examples and listings. For tables, DocBook uses the CALS table model from MIL-STD-38784 (Section 2.3.4, page 70).

The DTD includes the standard inline element types, including those for emphasis, abbreviation, cited titles, inline quotations, indexing, cross-references, and so on. Since it is designed specifically for software documentation, however, its inline element types can make very fine distinctions among different types of technical information. The following list provides only a sampling: **Application**, **ClassName**, **Command**, **Database**, **Email**, **Filename**, **Function**, **Literal**, **Markup**, **MouseButton**, **ProductName**, **ProductNumber**, **ReturnValue**, **SGMLTag**, **Symbol**, **Trademark**, and **UserInput**.

2.3.2.3   Sample Document

Note the absence of a **body** element type—individual chapters appear directly as children of the root **book** element. For DocBook, the front matter (**BookInfo**) is optional—I've included it here for consistency with the other examples.

DocBook sample document

```
<!DOCTYPE Book PUBLIC "-//Davenport//DTD DocBook V3.0//EN">

<Book>

<BookInfo>
<BookBiblio>
<Title>Sample Text</Title>
<AuthorGroup>
<Author>
<FirstName>David</FirstName>
<Surname>Megginson</Surname>
</Author>
```

```
</AuthorGroup>
</BookBiblio>
</BookInfo>

<Chapter Id="first">
<Title>First Chapter or Section</Title>

<Para>This is a sample chapter or section containing this
paragraph, an <Emphasis>emphasized phrase</Emphasis> and an
ordered list of three items:</Para>

<OrderedList>

<ListItem>
<Para>first item;</Para>
</ListItem>
<ListItem>
<Para>second item; and</Para>
</ListItem>
<ListItem>
<Para>third item.</Para>
</ListItem>
</OrderedList>

</Chapter>


<Chapter Id="second">
<Title>Second Chapter or Section</Title>

<Para>This is a second sample chapter or section, containing
a paragraph with a single <Link Linkend="first">cross-
reference</Link> t

the first chapter or section.</Para>

</Chapter>
</Book>
```

2.3.2.4   Availability

All of the DocBook materials—both the DTD itself and the documentation—are available free of charge over the Internet, through the Davenport Group Home Page `<http://www.ora.com/davenport/>`.

There is also a mailing list, `<davenport@online.ora.com>`, open to anyone interested in the DocBook DTD: to subscribe, send a message to `<listproc@online.ora.com>` containing the line `subscribe davenport` in the main body. An archive of past discussions `<ftp://ftp.ora.com/pub/davenport/archive/>` is available through the Davenport site.

2.3.3   *Text-Encoding Initiative (TEI)*

Like the ISO 12083 DTDs (Section 2.3.1, page 47) and the DocBook DTD (Section 2.3.2, page 54), the full TEI DTD provides a general, book-oriented structure for SGML documents; however, just as DocBook contains additional features for software documentation, TEI contains many features especially designed for the encoding and study of research-oriented material, such as literary, historical, and lexicographical texts and linguistic corpora.

The current version (P3) of the full TEI DTD is complex, since it is designed to meet a wide range of technical requirements for advanced text-based research. To encourage use of TEI for simpler applications, the project has also released *TEI-Lite*, a fully-compatible subset of the full DTD for more routine text markup: because this DTD contains all of the core element types of the full TEI, it will be the basis for most of the examples in this book.

2.3.3.1   Background

The TEI project began in 1987 with the goal of creating a comprehensive and extensible standard for marking up texts in electronic form. SGML became the clear choice, since it was platform-independent and required no special software (many TEI researchers still create their SGML texts using plain ASCII editors).

The DTD is designed primarily for *researchers* rather than *publishers*—as a result, it emphasises element types and attributes that allow authors to make semantic distinctions and to attach interpretations and other critical information to the text, including information about the physical appearance of a printed or handwritten source. Many of these element types would not be necessary simply to create a printed book, but they are essential for scholars who want to perform computer-assisted analysis of a text.

Consider the following queries:

- What copying errors are typical of the second scribe of a medieval legal text?
- How often does a certain character in a play use foreign words or expressions?
- What stressed vowels are most characteristic of the New England dialects in American speech?
- What metrical variants tend to appear in a particular sonnet collection?

To allow a researcher to execute the queries, the TEI DTD provides element types that the researcher can use to mark up such information as scribal errors (and corrections), the use of foreign phrases, linguistic transcriptions, and metrical scansion (as well as many other types of interpretive information). Authors can usually ignore most of these element types, but they are available when needed.

Full TEI

Although this book concentrates on the TEI-Lite DTD, you might find a brief explanation of the full TEI DTD helpful, especially if you are considering beginning a TEI project. To mark up a full TEI text, you have to use parameter entities to enable what the TEI calls a *base tag set* (really, a base element type set), together with zero or more *additional tag sets*. The base tag set determines the type of document; currently, you can choose from any of the following:

1. TEI.prose for basic prose texts
2. TEI.verse for verse or mixed prose and verse texts
3. TEI.drama for dramatic texts
4. TEI.spoken for linguistic transcriptions of speech
5. TEI.dictionaries for lexicographical texts
6. TEI.terminology for terminological databases

Note that TEI-Lite does not use these parameter entities at all. To enable one of these base tag sets in full TEI, you simply declare the parameter entity with the value INCLUDE, as in the following example:

Including the base tag set for drama

```
<!ENTITY % TEI.drama "INCLUDE">
```

Full TEI will likely add additional base tag sets in the future.

In addition to the base tag sets, you will likely want to enable one or more additional tag sets, with special element types for marking up complex information about topics such as linking, analysis, probability, and textual criticism. (Again, TEI-Lite does not use these.)

TEI has become the standard both for interchange and for authoring within the humanities and social sciences. Scholars have marked up thousands of texts—such as manuscripts, novels, plays, historical documents, lexicons, and linguistic corpora—using the TEI standards and have made many of these freely available over the Internet.

2.3.3.2   Quick Tour

What's on Top?

A TEI document is actually two documents in one SGML document (see Figure 2–5):

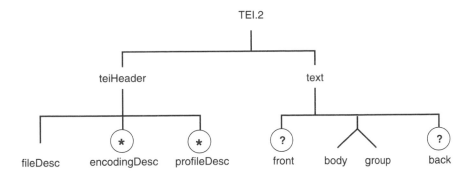

Figure 2–5 TEI-Lite DTD: Top Level—TEI-Lite adds an additional level at the top to contain both the text and its cataloging information.

1. a bibliographical record, **teiHeader**
2. the document proper, **text**

Both of these appear within the root element **TEI.2**. The **teiHeader** element type permits information about the electronic text and its printed original (if any), together with optional information about such subjects as the document's revision history, markup, and encoding practices.

The **text** element type itself permits the usual front and back matter for a printed document, and **teiHeader** permits additional information required by librarians and bibliographers. If the document is an anthology or some other sort of collection, it can contain a **group** instead of a **body**—a **group** element can contain a series of **text** or **group** elements, each with its own optional front and back matters.

What's in the Middle?

TEI sectioning can be either recursive (see Figure 2–6) or non-recursive (see Figure 2–7). The TEI-Lite DTD provides generic sectioning element types that are useful for general text (such as parts, chapters, sections, etc) and for verse (such as cantos and stanzas). For recursive sectioning, TEI uses **div** for general text and **lg** for verse; for nonrecursive sectioning, TEI-Lite uses **div0** to **div7** for general text (TEI-Lite has no nonrecursive equivalent for **lg**).

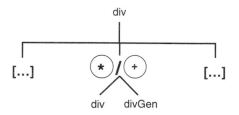

Figure 2–6   TEI-Lite DTD: Recursive Sectioning Hierarchy—One alternative for TEI-Lite sectioning is recursive element types, with no fixed limit on depth.

What's on the Bottom?

In addition to the usual paragraphs, lists, tables, figures, and formulas, TEI-Lite has a rich set of inline element types especially designed for textual research. For example, there are element types available for marking the following types of information:

- readings, changes, corrections, and gaps in a source text (such as a manuscript or typescript)
- stage directions
- numbers, times, dates, and proper nouns
- complex bibliographical references
- many different interpretations of emphasised text

Most of these would not be useful for writing software documentation or maintenance manuals (for example), but they are critical for academic researchers who wish to use a TEI-encoded poem or novel as a database. The full TEI application contains many more structures for marking up complex interpretations and analyses in an SGML document.

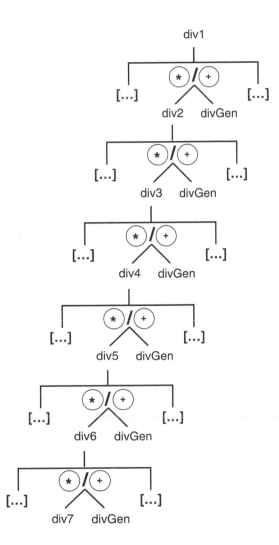

Figure 2–7   TEI-Lite DTD: Non-Recursive Sectioning Hierarchy—TEI-Lite also offers a standard, non-recursive sectioning hierarchy.

2.3.3.3   Sample Document

In the following document, note that the **text** element itself is similar to an entire document marked up according to ISO 12083 (Section 2.3.1, page 47) or DocBook (Section 2.3.2, page 54), with separate

front matter (optional) and a body. In addition to that, though, the
TEI document contains a **teiHeader** element, which contains cataloguing information for the text (like an electronic library card). The
TEI DTD makes provision for distributing the headers separately for
cataloguing purposes.

TEI-Lite sample document

```
<!DOCTYPE TEI.2 PUBLIC "-//TEI//DTD TEI Lite 1.0//EN">

<TEI.2>

<teiHeader>
<fileDesc>

<titleStmt>
<title>Sample Text</title>
<author>David Megginson</author>
</titleStmt>

<publicationStmt>
<p>Unpublished.</p>
</publicationStmt>

<sourceDesc>
<p>The electronic version is the original.</p>
</sourceDesc>

</fileDesc>
</teiHeader>

<text>

<front>
<titlePage>
<docTitle>
<titlepart>Sample Text</titlepart>
</docTitle>
<docAuthor>David Megginson</docAuthor>
</titlePage>
</front>

<body>
```

```
<div id="first" type="section">
<head>First Chapter or Section</head>

<p>This is a sample chapter or section containing this
paragraph, an <emph>emphasized phrase</emph> and an ordered
list of three items:</p>

<list type="1">
<item>first item;</item>
<item>second item; and</item>
<item>third item.</item>
</list>

</div>


<div id="second" type="section">
<head>Second Chapter or Section</head>

<p>This is a second sample chapter or section, containing a
paragraph with a single <ref target="first">cross-
reference</ref> to the first chapter or section.</p>

</div>
</body>
</text>
</TEI.2>
```

2.3.3.4   Availability

Both the full TEI DTD and the TEI-Lite DTD are available free of charge online—for general information, the full TEI DTDs, and electronic documentation in TEI format, see the TEI Home Page `<http://www.uic.edu/orgs/tei/>`. For the TEI-Lite DTD in particular, there is a separate TEI-Lite Page `<http://www.uic.edu/orgs/tei/lite/index.html>` with links to brief documentation and the TEI-Lite DTD.

If you do not wish to use the SGML documentation, you can purchase the (lengthy) printed documentation from the Text Encoding Initiative, or you can read a searchable, online version of the guidelines `<http://etext.virginia.edu/TEI.html>` at the Electronic Text Center `<http://etext.virginia.edu/>` at the University of Virginia.

2.3.4   *MIL-STD-38784 (CALS)*

What is now the MIL-STD-38784 DTD was one of the first important SGML DTDs. Like ISO 12083 (Section 2.3.1, page 47), DocBook (Section 2.3.2, page 54), and TEI (Section 2.3.3, page 62), MIL-STD-38784 is a book-oriented DTD. It is designed for technical documents, especially equipment maintenance manuals, and follows a much more restrictive structure than the other DTDs discussed in this book.

2.3.4.1   Background

For the sake of convenience, people sometimes refer to MIL-STD-38784 as "the CALS DTD"; in fact, there is no such thing as a single CALS DTD. The CALS initiative (CALS has stood for many things at different times, including "Computer-Aided Logistic Support," "Commerce At Light-Speed," and "Continuous Acquisition and Life-cycle Support") began as an attempt to limit the flow of paper documentation within the U.S. military. During more than a decade, it has evolved into an elaborate technical and business approach used by the military and commercial sectors in many countries, and different projects use DTDs appropriate to their sectors and subject matter.

Nevertheless, because of its early association with the initiative, what is now MIL-STD-38784 has become the best known of the CALS-related DTDs, both as a whole and through the table model embedded in it—in fact, the *CALS table model* has become a de facto standard for commercial SGML tools, and many other DTDs (such as DocBook and the ATA 2100 DTDs for aircraft documentation) include a variant of it.

During the early history of SGML, the U.S. military and associated defense contractors were the largest purchasers of SGML services in the North-American market, and as a result, many consultants and software designers became very familiar with earlier versions of 38784. When these specialists went on to help with the creation of more recent DTDs, they often kept 38784 in mind, whether as a model for what to include or as a model for what to avoid.

For its examples, this book uses the DTD with the public identifier `-//USA-DOD//DTD MIL-STD-38784 AMEND1//EN`, the most recent version of the DTD available at the time of writing (last modified October 9, 1996). Earlier versions include (among others) MIL-M-38784B, MIL-M-38784C, and unamended MIL-STD-38784.

2.3.4.2 Quick Tour

What's on Top?

The top-level element type is named simply **doc**. It has several specified attributes, indicating the military service (Navy, Air Force, etc) for which the document was written, the document's current revision status, and the document's security level. In fact, most of the major structural element types in the DTD contain attributes for specifying revision status and security level, so that different parts of a document can exist in different revision states or require different security clearances.

The top-level **doc** element type can contain either of the following (see Figure 2–8):

- **front** (front matter *and* a forward, preface, or introduction), **body**, and optional **rear** (end matter) elements
- two or more **volume** elements (essentially, documents within the document)

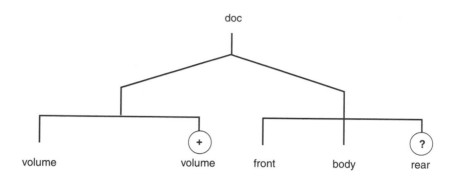

Figure 2–8   MIL-STD-38784 DTD: Top Level—MIL-STD-38784 allows either a series of volumes, or the typical containers for front matter, body, and back matter.

It also permits inclusion exceptions to allow arbitrary insertion of certain types of information, such as page- and line breaks and modification requests, anywhere in the document.

What's in the Middle?

The **body** element type permits at least two **chapter** elements. The **chapter** element type permits either two or more **section** elements, or one or more **para0** elements, and the **section** element type itself permits one or more **para0** elements (see Figure 2–9).

It is in the **para0** element type that MIL-STD-38784 differs the most from other book-oriented DTDs (though DocBook offers a similar, optional element type named **FormalPara**). Most book-oriented DTDs allow regular paragraphs to appear immediately within high-level sectioning elements such as chapters or sections—in MIL-STD-38784, regular **para** elements are always contained within another element type, such as **warning**, **step1**, or most important, **para0**, because in a maintenance manual for mission-critical systems, it is necessary that every paragraph have a title of some sort so that technicians can find information quickly.

A **para0**, or primary paragraph, consists of the following:

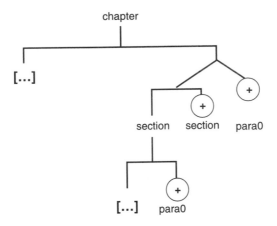

Figure 2–9 MIL-STD-38785 DTD: Sectioning Hierarchy—MIL-STD-38784 has a relatively flat sectioning hierarchy.

- a required title
- optional warnings, cautions, and notes (for safety reasons, these must *precede* the paragraph proper)
- a single optional **para** element
- an optional sequence of two or more **step1** elements
- zero or more **subpara1** elements

In other words, the **para0** element type is constrained to include at most one paragraph as a child—other paragraphs would have to appear within its children, such as **step1** or within subsequent **para0** elements. This structural principle holds throughout most of MIL-STD-38784: for the most part, only notes, warnings, and cautions allow more than one paragraph in a row; otherwise, each paragraph must appear as a separate step, substep, or other similar container element.

While this approach enforces highly-structured manuals, with frequent headings and relatively little consecutive (or block) text, it would work poorly for more narrative writing, like essays or works of fiction.

What's on the Bottom?

The MIL-STD-38784 DTD contains the three classic list types:

1. unordered (bulleted) lists (**randlist**)
2. ordered (numbered) lists (**seqlist**)
3. glossary lists (**deflist**)

It also contains an elaborate, publication-oriented table model and two types of figures (regular figures and fold-out figures).

In addition to the regular, titled paragraphs listed in the previous section, the DTD allows three levels of subparagraphs (**subpara1**, **subpara2**, and **subpara3**), again, each with its own title and (possibly) warnings, caution, and note. It also allows for different levels of steps and substeps, from **step1** to **step4**, each with a paragraph as its contents (together, again, with optional warnings, etc).

Within a paragraph, most of the usual inline element types can appear, including emphasized phrases, acronyms, internal and external references, and verbatim computer text—unlike the other DTDs, however, MIL-STD-38784 always implements cross-references as empty element types, so it is not possible to tag a sequence of text as a link. There are also element types for specialized requirements, such as change markup, applicability, footnote references, and external graphics.

2.3.4.3   Sample Document

Like the TEI-Lite DTD, MIL-STD-38784 requires a large amount of front matter for each document, though in this case the front matter is designed specifically for the military and for military contractors rather than for general bibliographical applications. In this example, the navsea value for the service attribute on the root element shows that the document is intended for Naval use, and the **tmidno** specifies the *technical manual identification number*. The front matter also requires a list of effective pages and a foreword, preface, or introduction.

Note also that each paragraph has a title of some sort.

MIL-STD-38784 sample document

```
<!DOCTYPE doc PUBLIC
    "-//USA-DOD//DTD MIL-STD-38784 AMEND1//EN">

<doc service="navsea">

<front>

<idinfo>
<tmidno>12345-67</tmidno>
<doctype>Example</doctype>
<prtitle>
<subject>SGML Sample Document</subject>
</prtitle>
<distrib>[distribution statement omitted]</distrib>
<authnot>Written by David Megginson</authnot>
<pubdate>1997</pubdate>
</idinfo>

<lep>
<lepcontents>
<lepentry>
<leppage>[list of effective pages omitted]</leppage>
<lepchg>[change pages omitted]</lepchg>
</lepentry>
</lepcontents>
</lep>

<contents>[table of contents omitted]</contents>

<intro>
<para0>
<title>Introduction</title>

<para>This introduction is necessary because MIL-38784
requires an introduction, preface, or foreword.</para>

</para0>
</intro>
```

```
</front>

<body>

<chapter id="first">
<title>First Chapter or Section</title>

<para0>
<title>Sample list and emphasis</title>

<para>This is a sample chapter or section containing this
paragraph, an <emphasis type="i">emphasized phrase</
emphasis> and an ordered list of three items:

<seqlist>
<item>first item;</item>
<item>second item; and</item>
<item>third item.</item>
</seqlist>
</para>
</para0>

</chapter>

<chapter>
<title>Second Chapter or Section</title>

<para0>
<title>Sample cross-reference</title>

<para>This is a second sample chapter or section, containing
a paragraph with a single cross-reference <xref
xrefid="first"> to the first chapter or section.</para>
</para0>

</chapter>
</body>
</doc>
```

2.3.4.4 Availability

The DTD for MIL-STD-38784 amendment 1 is available free of charge from various sites on the World Wide Web, including SGML University's DTD list `<http://www.sgmlu.com/dtds.htm>`. Brief descriptions of most of the element types in MIL-STD-38784 are available online from the U.S Navy in the Official Navy Baseline Tagset Library at:

`<http://navycals.dt.navy.mil/dtdfosi/tag_library.html>`.

2.3.5 *Hypertext Markup Language (HTML 4.0)*

 Note: This book uses the strict version of the HTML 4.0 DTD (1997-11-18) for all of its examples. There is also a transition version, with more presentation element types and attributes, and a frameset version.

At the time of writing, judged by the number of users and by general public awareness, HTML is by far the most successful application in the history of SGML. To a certain extent it has been a victim of that success—besides some problems stemming from the initial design, it shows deep scars from flawed software implementations and from marketing battles among major software producers—but as both a book-oriented DTD and the defining information format of the late 20th century, it certainly deserves a place beside the other four DTDs discussed in this book.

2.3.5.1 Background

The HTML 4.0 specification states that "HTML 4.0 is an SGML application conforming to International Standard ISO 8879— Standard Generalized Markup Language." When it was first introduced in 1990, HTML used SGML-like start- and end tags and then entity references, but it was by no means an SGML application (there was no DTD, for example). Even at the time of writing, most major HTML browsers ignore the DOCTYPE declaration (at best), cannot handle marked sections, and ignore all references to entities whose definitions are not built-in to the browser.

Nevertheless, the World Wide Web Consortium (the Web's standards body) now uses a DTD to provide a formal description of each new version of HTML, and it is possible to use these DTDs with standard SGML authoring tools to produce HTML pages that work with the major browsers.

The HTML DTDs show two strong influences. Their structure owes a fair bit to typesetting languages such as LaTeX—in particular, like LaTeX, the DTD models different levels of headings instead of different levels of sections, and the earlier HTML DTDs included only paragraph breaks rather than paragraph containers.

The HTML naming scheme, on the other hand, is largely based on the ISO 8879:1986 *General Document DTD*, an example included as Annex E to the SGML standard—in particular, HTML borrows element type names **H1** to **H4** (using them for section titles rather than sections), **DL** (definition list), **DT** (definition term), **DD** (definition description), **OL** (ordered list), **UL** (unordered list), and **LI** (list item). They also share some more common element-type names, like **TITLE** for the document title and **P** for a paragraph.

The HTML DTDs were designed to minimize typing, so that people can easily create their own documents in a simple character-text editor.

2.3.5.2   Quick Tour

What's on Top?

The root element type in an HTML 4.0 document (strict version) is always **HTML**, and it has two required children (see Figure 2-10):

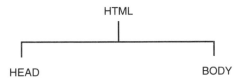

Figure 2-10   HTML DTD: Top Level—HTML has typical containers for front matter and the main body, but no provision for back matter (there are often better alternatives for online display).

1. **HEAD**, containing meta-information
2. **BODY**, containing the displayed information for the page

The **HEAD** element type must contain a formal title for the document, and optionally may also contain other elements for specifying such information as stylesheets, scripts, and generic meta-information.

The **BODY** element type is very loosely structured. Unlike most book-oriented DTDs, HTML does not contain element types for large structural elements, such as chapters and sections—instead, the body of an HTML document consists of a relatively flat stream of headings, paragraphs, tables, lists, etc.

What's in the Middle?

Traditionally, HTML documents contain no sectioning elements (see Figure 2–11); instead, there are six different levels of headings, from **H1** to **H6**. There is, in fact, a relatively new, recursive **DIV** container that you *could* use to delimit sections and subsections, but the DTD does not enforce its use.

Unlike the earlier HTML 3.2 DTD, the HTML 4.0 DTD makes a careful distinction between paragraph-level element types and inline element types: in HTML 3.2, the **BODY** element type allowed mixed content, including character data interspersed with inline elements (see below), paragraphs, tables, section headings, and most other

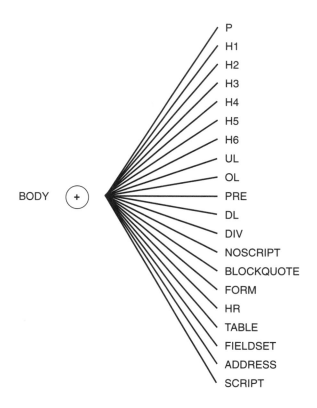

Figure 2–11   HTML DTD: Middle Level—HTML has no proper sectioning elements, so paragraph-level element types appear immediately inside the body.

HTML element types. In HTML 4.0, character data and inline element types are not allowed as children of **BODY**.

What's on the Bottom?

Like the other DTDs introduced in this chapter, the HTML DTD includes element types for various kinds of emphasized phrases (such as **EM** and **STRONG**, etc) verbatim text (such as **CODE** and **KBD**), symbols (**VAR**), and external graphics (**IMG**). Because the DTD is intended for online display, it also contains some element types especially designed for online publication.

The most important of these is the **A**, or anchor element type, which is the basis of an HTML browser's hypertext capability. Although HTML 4.0 does allow some elements to have ID attributes, HTML documents do not generally use the traditional SGML ID/ IDREF pairs for cross-references; instead, they use the CDATA attributes `name` for a target, or `href` for a cross-reference (either internal or external).

More recent additions to HTML include the **APPLET** element type, which launches an external program (such as a Java applet), the **OBJECT** element type, for generic embedded objects, and the **MAP** element type, which maps hyperlink anchors to regions in an image.

2.3.5.3   Sample Document

There are three points of particular interest in the following example:

1. the front matter (**HEAD**) permits no element type for the author's name, so it is necessary to use a generic **META** element
2. there are no container elements for sections—the section titles and the paragraphs are all siblings, immediately under the **BODY** element type (though it would have been possible to simulate containers with **DIV** elements, but that is not common HTML practice)
3. to allow cross-references to the different chapters (or at least to their titles), it is necessary to use additional **A** elements, since HTML browsers do not generally use IDs

HTML sample document

```
<!DOCTYPE html PUBLIC "-//W3C//DTD HTML 4.0//EN">

<html>

<head>
<title>Sample Text</title>
```

```
<meta name="author" content="David Megginson">
</head>

<body>
<h1>Sample Text</h1>

<h2><a name="first">First Chapter or Section</a></h2>

<p>This is a sample chapter or section containing this
paragraph, an <em>emphasized phrase</em> and an ordered list
of three items:</p>

<ol>
<li>first item;</li>
<li>second item; and</li>
<li>third item.</li>
</ol>


<h2><a name="second">Second Chapter or Section</a></
h2><p>This is a second sample chapter or section, containing
a paragraph with a single <a href="#first">cross-reference</
a> to the first chapter or section.</p>

</body>
</html>
```

2.3.5.4   Availability

The HTML 4.0 specification and DTDs are available through the
World Wide Web Consortium web site
    `<http://www.w3.org/MarkUp/>`.

Part Two

The second part of the book develops general principles for analyzing DTDs and illustrates the principles with many detailed examples from the book's five model DTDs (Chapter 2). You can read about DTD analysis from three different perspectives:

- how easily authors can learn the DTD (Chapter 3)
- how easily and effectively authors can use the DTD once they have learned it (Chapter 4)
- how easily and effectively information-processing specialists can work with the resulting documents (Chapter 5)

Principles of
DTD Analysis

Ease of Learning

This book uses the term **"authors"** to refer to anyone responsible for creating documents that conform to your DTD. The term actually includes three different groups of people:

1. writers creating new documents (with or without specialized XML software)
2. editors adding XML markup to existing non-XML documents (with or without specialized XML software)
3. engineers creating software that will generate XML documents automatically

Clearly, these groups will have some different needs: writers and editors are more likely to work with book-oriented DTDs, for example, while engineers are more likely to work with small, transaction-oriented DTDs. This chapter concentrates mainly on the first two groups, where humans (writers or editors) add markup to the documents directly; nevertheless, many of the comments apply to the third group as well.

When you are analyzing a DTD to see if it will be easy for your authors to work with, you really need to ask two different questions:

1. How easy will it be for authors to *learn* the DTD?
2. How easy will it be for authors to *use* the DTD effectively once they have learned it?

A DTD that is very easy to learn might cause serious problems after a few months, when authors find that the DTD is so simple that it cannot represent all of their information; a DTD that is very complex might cause serious problems right away, if authors cannot (or will not) learn it properly.

The next chapter (Chapter 4) will discuss ease of use; this one examines three areas that affect ease of learning:

1. **DTD size**, or the amount of information that authors must learn before they can create documents that conform to the DTD
2. **DTD consistency**, or the extent to which authors can predict some of the DTD's structures based on others
3. **DTD intuitiveness**, or the extent to which the DTD is consistent with authors' past experience

These areas imply goals that are not entirely consistent with one another. A larger DTD, for example, might be more intuitive, but a less intuitive DTD might be smaller. Even more importantly, intuitiveness is subjective: the DTD might be more intuitive for authors who are familiar with other XML or full SGML DTDs, or it might be more intuitive for authors who are familiar with the subject matter.

As you can see, it would be very misleading to grade DTDs (say, from 1 to 10) on ease of learning, because that grade would not show what choices and trade-offs the designers made. Like the chapters that follow, this chapter does not contain simple rules or rankings so much as a set of questions that you can ask when you are designing or analyzing a DTD.

3.1   DTD Size

When they have to determine how complex a DTD is, many people simply count the number of element types, just as many people count the number of lines of source code to determine how complex a computer program is. By this (misleading) criterion, the DocBook DTD should be nearly five times as difficult to learn as the HTML DTD:

- HTML 4.0: 77 element types
- TEI-Lite: 143 element types
- ISO 12083: 168 element types
- MIL-STD-38784: 181 element types
- DocBook: 362 element types

Even considering size alone, however, what really matters is not the number of element types, but the amount of general information that an author must learn to use the DTD. This section approaches *DTD size* from two different perspectives:

1. the total number of unique **logical units**—a combination of element types with significant attributes and contexts (Section 3.1.1, page 90)

2. the **learning requirements**—the amount of the DTD that authors will actually need to learn for specific projects (Section 3.1.1, page 94)

3.1.1   *Logical Units*

If you want to compare the sizes of two DTDs, you cannot do so simply by counting the number of element types. Most DTDs contain at least some element types that can fill different logical roles, depending (for example) on their context in the document or on the value of an attribute.

Each different role is a **logical unit** of the DTD's structure. This example shows a declaration for an element type that can represent two different logical units (see Figure 3–1):

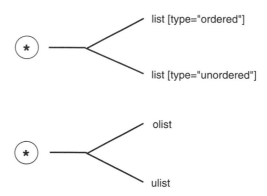

Figure 3–1   Multiple Logical Units from One Element Type—One element type can fill two or more roles: these two examples are structurally equivalent.

Two logical units in one element type

```
<!ELEMENT list (item+)>
<!ATTLIST list
  type (ordered | unordered) "unordered">
```

When the document contains a **list** element with the type attribute set to "ordered", the **list** element represents an ordered list; when the document contains a **list** element with the type attribute set to "unordered", the element represents an unordered list. I call an attribute that changes the meaning of an element type a **role attribute**.

It is easy to tell that there are really two logical units in the previous example, because you could declare two different element types to represent them (see Figure 3–1):

Two logical units in two element types

```
<!ELEMENT olist (item+)>
<!ELEMENT ulist (item+)>
```

The first example contains only a single declaration where the second contains two, but both contain the same number of logical units.

You can also create multiple logical units with context. Some element types, for example, may assume different identities, depending on their ancestors, children, siblings, or even data content:

- a **note** element might indicate a special paragraph if it appears inside a section but indicates a footnote or endnote if it appears inside a paragraph
- a **title** element might indicate a section heading if it appears at the beginning of a section but indicates a (cited) monograph title if it appears inside a paragraph
- an **item** element might indicate a definition if it follows a glossary term but indicates a simple list item otherwise, and so on

A DTD's true size is the total number of logical units that it contains, and that number is the sum of the products of each element and all of the attributes and contexts that can alter its identity. Usually, this number is impossible to calculate exactly, because many DTDs include unconstrained role attributes such as the following:

Element type with unconstrained role attribute

```
<!ELEMENT para (#PCDATA)>
<!ATTLIST para
  type CDATA #IMPLIED>
```

Since the attribute `type` may take any arbitrary value, the number of logical units is potentially infinite—one author might set `type` to "`caution`", another might set it to "`definition`", another might set it to "`key argument`", and so on.

3.1.0.1   Examples from the Model DTDs

Among the model DTDs, DocBook, HTML, and TEI-Lite (as well as full TEI) allow unconstrained role attributes with many or all of their element types.

In DocBook, for example, you can specify the role attribute `Role` for almost any element in your document:

Abuse of role attribute

```
<Para Role="main point">You can
<Emphasis Role="sarcasm">hope</Emphasis>
that the other party won't betray your trust <Emphasis
Role="accusation">again</Emphasis>, or you can
<EmphasisRole="reassurance">know</Emphasis> that our party
will work hard to deserve your trust day after day.</Para>
```

A campaign team could automatically analyze this document to determine which words are used sarcastically (etc); however, the `Role` attribute creates a whole new level of markup (one that cannot be validated using the DTD) and requires authors to learn many new logical units. It would make more sense to write a DTD that fits more closely with the campaign team's requirements.

HTML 4.0 uses the role attribute `class` for the same purpose, allowing it for 69 out of 77 element types. The `class` attribute is especially intended for use with stylesheets, to allow varied rendering of the standard HTML element types:

HTML `class` attribute

```
<H1 class="fancy-heading">This is a fancy heading</H1>
```

The TEI-Lite DTD uses the role attribute `type` in a similar way, but you are allowed to specify it for only 38 of the 143 element types defined in the DTD. However, the TEI-Lite DTD relies on the `type` attribute to identify several basic types of logical units that the other model DTDs usually distinguish with different element types. Here, for example, is typical markup for a chapter in TEI-Lite:

TEI-Lite chapter

```
<div type="chapter">
...
</div>
```

And here is typical markup for an ordered list:

TEI-Lite ordered list

```
<list type="ordered">
...
</list>
```

The values of the `type` attribute are entirely unconstrained by the DTD, so another author might use the values "chap" to mark a chapter and "num" to mark an ordered list.

When you are using the DocBook, HTML, and TEI-Lite DTDs then, the number of logical units may be much larger (potentially infinitely larger) than the number of element types. The other two model DTDs do not contain widespread, unconstrained role attributes like these, but they do occasionally use more constrained role attributes.

Like the TEI-Lite DTD, the ISO 12083 and MIL-STD-38784 DTDs use the role attribute `type` to create multiple logical units from a single element type; unlike the TEI-Lite DTD, however, both DTDs use the attribute sparingly and constrain its possible values to a group of tokens. ISO 12083 uses the `type` attribute for the **list**, **date**, and **emph** element types, whereas MIL-STD-38784 uses it for the **brk**, **dataiden** (unconstrained), **distrib**, and **emphasis** element types.

For example, the ISO 12083 book DTD would mark an ordered list as follows:

Ordered list in ISO 12083

```
<list type="1">
 <item>a list item</item>
 <item>another list item</item>
 <item>another list item</item>
</list>
```

The combination of the **list** element type with the `type` role attribute creates new logical units.

3.1.1   *Learning Requirements*

The previous section presented some of the difficulties involved in comparing the sizes of two different DTDs. Even if you can count the number of logical units in two DTDs, however, you still cannot be certain which of the two would be harder to learn.

With large, general-purpose DTDs—like the five model DTDs used in this book—some authors will never use or even be aware of many of the logical units available. Depending on the complexity and nature of each writing project, the logical units in a DTD fall into three learning categories:

1. logical units that authors must use to create a useful document
2. logical units that authors do not require, but that are visible to authors
3. logical units that authors do not require and that are not visible to authors

Authors need to learn the first group well, but they need only be aware enough of the members of the second group to avoid using them, and they do not need to be aware of the members of the third group at all.

These declarations show a case where an author might not need to learn about a logical unit in a DTD (see Figure 3–2):

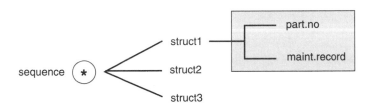

Figure 3–2   Limiting Learning Requirements—If authors never need to use **struct1**, then they never have to learn the part of the DTD beneath that element type.

Hidden logical units

```
<!ELEMENT sequence (struct1 | struct2 | struct3)+>

<!ELEMENT struct1 (part.no, maint.record)>
<!ATTLIST struct1
  class (service | purchase) #REQUIRED>
```

Inside a **sequence** element, an author may include any number of **struct1**, **struct2**, and **struct3** elements in any order. Assume, now, that an author works for a company that *never* uses **struct1** elements. That author would have to know not to include **struct1** elements, but that author would not have to know about **part.no** or **maint.record**, unless they could appear in other contexts. The author would not even have to know about the *role attribute* named class.

If there were ten logical units of various sorts that could appear only within a **struct1** element, they would make the DTD no more difficult to learn, since they would never be available as choices for the authors. In an XML or SGML document, it is possible to make simple decisions high up in the document tree without worrying—or in some cases, without even knowing about—the various branches and leaves underneath. Some of the model DTDs examined in this book are very large, containing hundreds of element types and, in some cases, a potentially infinite number of logical units; with most of them, though, authors can create useful documents after learning only 20 or 30 of the most important logical units.

3.1.1.1   Examples from the Model DTDs

As an example of learning requirements in the model DTDs, consider an author's choices at three points in a chapter of a typical book-oriented document:

1. within a chapter title
2. immediately following a chapter title
3. within a paragraph after the chapter title

At each point, the author will have to choose among a different set of elements to insert into the document. Within the chapter title, the author will usually be allowed to insert only restricted inline content (it would be awkward, for example, to include a list or table in a title); after the title, the author will be allowed to insert typical paragraph-level elements, such as paragraphs, tables, lists, and figures; and within a paragraph, the author will be allowed to insert inline elements and possibly also lists or tables.

To make the comparison, some adjustments are necessary for each DTD:

- for TEI-Lite, I have used a **div1** element to represent a chapter
- for MIL-STD-38784, I have used a **para** element within a **para0** element for the contents of a paragraph
- for HTML, which does not use sectioning elements, I have used an **H1** element for the chapter title and have

simply counted the number of element types that may follow it in a **BODY** element

The following table summarizes the results:

Table 3.1   Element Types Available

DTD	In Chapter Title	After Chapter Title	In Paragraph
ISO 12083	20	25	37
DocBook	78	52	110
TEI-Lite	54	30	54
MIL-STD-38784	21	12	27
HTML 4.0	33	22	33

Although the HTML DTD contains the smallest number of element types, it does not restrict the number of element types available at different points as effectively as the ISO 12083 and MIL-STD-38784 do: as a result, HTML authors may actually have to learn *more* different element types than they would to work with those other two (supposedly larger) DTDs.

3.2   DTD Consistency

Authors find it easier to learn a DTD if it names its elements and attributes consistently and structures its content consistently. Good

DTDs will often group element types into classes (implicitly or explicitly) and will use similar names, attributes, and content models for all of the element types in a class.

These first consistency criteria are internal to the DTD, and, as a result, they are relatively simple and objective; however, consistency is not always so easy to define. Authors find it easier to learn a DTD that is consistent not only within itself, but also with other DTDs and documents that they have used. In particular, they find it easier to learn a DTD that is consistent with the expectations that they bring from their professional, cultural, and social backgrounds.

Is it better, then, to create an internally-inconsistent DTD that is consistent with authors' outside experience or to create a internally-consistent DTD that is inconsistent with authors' initial expectations? The answer will, of course, vary from situation to situation, but the question itself shows some of the challenges you will face in designing or analyzing a DTD for consistency.

This section examines some of the most important consistency criteria under four broad headings:

1. naming (Section 3.2.1)
2. parallel design (Section 3.2.2, page 100)
3. element-type classes (Section 3.2.3, page 104)
4. global attributes (Section 3.2.4, page 107)

3.2.1   *Naming*

The easiest (and most obvious) place to look for consistency is in the DTD's naming scheme for element types and attributes. If a DTD uses the element type name **div1** for a major division, authors can reasonably expect to find **div2** and **div3** for subdivisions; if a DTD uses the element type name **list.ordered**, authors can reasonably expect to find **list.unordered**; and so on.

Designers of some of the earliest SGML DTDs wrote them to conform to an eight-character name-length limit—the minimum that all SGML parsers must support (XML has no limit)—and, as a result, they could not use informative names like **list.unordered**.

Some more recent DTDs continue this tradition by using relatively short, uninformative names like **em** for emphasized phrases, **ul** for an unordered list, and so on; for the sake of consistency, however, names like **phrase.emphasized**, **list.unordered**, or **paragraph.caution** are much more intuitive to the user. Authors learn the relationship between **paragraph.caution** and **paragraph.note**, for example, or **phrase.emphasized** and **phrase.foreign**, much more quickly than they learn the difference between **caution** and **note**, or **emph** and **foreign**.

Of course, this rule will not always apply. Some document authors have grown accustomed to short, cryptic names, either from experience with older SGML DTDs or from experience with non-SGML document-production systems such as TROFF and LaTeX (which, in turn, preserve some of the names from earlier typesetting codes)—if you try to introduce a more consistent naming scheme to authors who are already used to a cryptic one, they may end up confused or even openly hostile (DTD writing is not for the faint-of-heart). For further discussion, see Section 3.3, page 109.

3.2.1.1   Examples from the Model DTDs

The naming schemes for all of the model DTDs are (more-or-less) internally consistent, at least in the higher levels of the document structure. The TEI-Lite DTD, for example, allows you to use **div1** for a high-level section and **div2**, **div3** and so on for lower-level sections. The MIL-STD-38784 DTD allows only chapters and subsections, so such a structure would not apply to it. The ISO 12083 DTD, however, allows **subsect1**, **subsect2**, etc for different levels of subsections within a section; the DocBook DTD allows **Sect1**, **Sect2**, etc for different levels of sections within a chapter; the

MIL-STD-38784 DTD and the HTML DTD have a similar scheme for headings (**H1**, **H2**, etc.).

The differences are much greater when it comes to external consistency. The ISO 12083, MIL-STD-38784, and HTML DTDs, in particular, tend to use short, cryptic element type names such as **ded**, **ftnref**, and **H1**. The TEI-Lite DTD uses some longer names, but only the DocBook DTD consistently provides long, readable names like **Subtitle**, **BiblioEntry**, or **Sidebar**.

3.2.2 *Parallel Design*

The most important thing to look for in DTD consistency is **parallel design**: if two structures are similar, their SGML or XML representation should be similar as well. Take a look at these element type definitions for illustrations and tables:

Declarations demonstrating parallel design

```
<!ELEMENT illustration (heading, graphic.ptr, caption?)>
<!ATTLIST illustration
  id ID #IMPLIED
  placement (floating | fixed) "fixed"
  border (border | noborder) "noborder"
  height NMTOKEN #REQUIRED
  width NMTOKEN #REQUIRED>

<!ELEMENT table (heading, table.body, caption?)>
<!ATTLIST table
  id ID #IMPLIED
  placement (floating | fixed) "fixed"
  border (border | noborder) "border"
  rows NMTOKEN #REQUIRED
  cols NMTOKEN #REQUIRED>
```

In a traditional printed book, illustrations and tables have a great deal in common, and the SGML or XML element types and attribute definitions in this example reflect the similarities:

- both illustrations and tables have headings, bodies, and captions
- both may be floating or fixed on the page
- both may have borders
- both may be the target of cross-references
- both occupy two dimensions on the page

Whenever possible, the declarations presented above use identical or similarly-named components: the **heading** and **caption** element types appear in the same place in each content model, with the same degree of *repetition* and *omissibility*. The id, placement, and border attributes appear in both attribute definitions, with the same declared types.

This parallel design makes it much easier for authors to learn one element type after learning the other; however, a second (and less obvious) advantage is the fact that the parallels help to emphasize the *differences* between the two.

Because the element-type definitions and the attribute definitions are largely the same, the differences stand out:

- a table contains a **table.body**, whereas an illustration contains a **graphic.ptr**
- authors specify a table's dimensions in rows and columns, but they specify an illustration's height and width dimensions using some other unit (such as inches or points)

The only difference that is not obvious is the default value for the border attribute, though the attribute itself works the same way for both element types.

There are then, in fact, *two* rules of parallel design:

1. similar element types should be similar both in their content models and in their attribute definitions

2. similar element types should mark their differences as clearly as possible

If the example above used the `width` and `height` attributes for the **table** element type as well as the **illustration** element type, it would give the misleading impression that the attributes work identically on the two element types; the `row` and `column` attribute names for the **table** element warn authors to treat these attributes differently (using a row- or column-count instead of absolute measurements like points or inches).

There is no simple rule to determine whether element types should have similar or identical content. One DTD designer, for example, might choose the following element declarations for ordered and unordered lists:

Similar content for similar element types

```
<!ELEMENT ordered.list (ol.item+)>
<!ELEMENT ol.item (para+)>


<!ELEMENT unordered.list (ul.item+)>
<!ELEMENT ul.item (para+)>
```

Another might chose these declarations:

Identical content for similar element types

```
<!ELEMENT ordered.list (item+)>
<!ELEMENT unordered.list (item+)>
<!ELEMENT item (para+)>
```

In the first example, both the context and the element-type name distinguish the two types of list items, whereas in the second, only context distinguishes them. Both, however, contain the same number of logical units (see Section 3.1, page 89) and both demonstrate good parallel design—a list consists of one or more items of some sort, and an item consists of one or more paragraphs—so there should be little difference in the difficulty in learning one or the other.

3.2.2.1   Examples from the Model DTDs

The use of element-type classes is an important part of parallel design in two different ways:

1. all of the element types in a class can share the same (or similar) content models and attribute definitions
2. all of the element types in a class can appear in the same contexts

The DocBook DTD, for example, declares the parameter entity `list.class` as follows:

A class in DocBook

```
<!ENTITY % local.list.class "">
<!ENTITY % list.class
   "CalloutList | GlossList | ItemizedList | OrderedList |
   SegmentedList | SimpleList| VariableList
%local.list.class;">
```

(Note the `local.list.class` parameter entity for user-defined extensions.) Each of these list types has a slightly different purpose and content model, but all can appear in the same contexts. In fact, by using the `list.class` parameter entity in the content model declaration of various element types, the DTD ensures that any element type that allows one sort of list will allow all of them.

DTDs can use similar methods for applying attribute declarations to classes. For example, the ISO 12083 DTD declares the following parameter entity:

Class attributes in ISO 12083

```
<!ENTITY % a.sizes "sizex NUTOKEN #IMPLIED
                    sizey NUTOKEN #IMPLIED
                    unit CDATA #IMPLIED">
```

(Note the SGML-specific NUTOKEN where XML would have NMTOKEN). Both of the element types that can have size specifications include a reference to this parameter entity in their attribute definition list declarations:

Using class attributes in ISO 12083

```
<!ATTLIST artwork
  %a.id;
  %a.sizes;
  name ENTITY #IMPLIED
  %SDAFORM; "fig #attrib ID">

<!ATTLIST fig
  %a.id;
  %a.sizes;
  name ENTITY #IMPLIED
  scale NUMBER 100
  %SDAPREF; "<?SDATRANS>Figure: ">
```

Note the SGML-specific NUMBER attribute type (XML would use NMTOKEN), and the addition of the scale attribute for **fig** to mark the difference between the two similar element types.

3.2.3   *Element-Type Classes*

There are different degrees of similarity—sometimes, as in the cases of an appendix and a chapter, or an illustration and a table, element types are very similar and have many components in common. In other cases, element types may share only broader similarities.

XML makes no official provision for grouping element types by class, but most DTDs still contain groups of element types that can appear in similar contexts and/or convey similar semantic information. In a book-oriented DTD, classes might include the following (among many others):

- sectioning element types (chapters, sections, appendices, abstracts, prefaces)

- paragraph-level element types (paragraphs, notes, block quotations, displayed warnings)
- inline element types (emphasized phrases, inline quotations, cross references)
- block element types that can appear inline or as paragraphs (lists, tables, illustrations)

Many of these contain subclasses, such as emphasized phrases, lists, and cross-references, which in turn can contain still other element types or classes.

As mentioned in the previous section, DTD designers often use parameter entities to model the DTD's implicit class structure, as in the following fragment:

Class content models

```
<!ENTITY % phrases "emph | strong | sic">
<!ENTITY % xrefs "ref | ptr ">
<!ENTITY % inline "quot | %phrases; | %xrefs;">

<!ELEMENT para (%inline;)+>
```

Here, the `inline` parameter entity represents the most general, or highest-level class, whereas the `phrases` and `xrefs` parameter entities denote specific types of inline data (and, of course, the individual element types themselves are the most specific classes).

In object-oriented programming, classes inherit variables from their ancestors; in DTDs, attributes can fill something like the same role as variables for their associated element types, and attribute list declarations should reflect the DTD's implicit class structure as much as possible. It will often make sense to provide a set of common attributes for all element types in a class: all section-level element types, for example, might require a `security` attribute, whereas all cross-reference element types might require an attribute of type `IDREF` (named, for example, `target` or `ref`). If a DTD makes intelligent and consistent use of class-level as well as global attributes, it will be much easier to learn and use.

3.2.3.1   Examples from the Model DTDs

As explained in the previous section, all five of the model DTDs group element types into classes using parameter entities (the TEI-Lite DTD, which is derived from the full TEI DTD, preresolves all of the parameter entities that appear in the full DTD).

The ISO 12083 DTD, for example, uses the parameter entity `m.ph` to represent the content model for phrases (it contains several nested parameter entities for specific types of phrases). Eleven phrasal element types use this content model directly, and together they form an identifiable class. In the DocBook DTD, the corresponding parameter entity is named `para.char.mix`; in the full TEI DTD, it is named `paraContent` (the `phrase` parameter entity is rarely used directly); in the MIL-STD-38784, it is named `text`; and in HTML 4.0, it is named `inline`.

For example, the following declarations appear in the HTML DTD:

Class content models in HTML

```
<!ENTITY % fontstyle "TT | I | B | U | S | STRIKE | BIG |
                      SMALL">
<!ENTITY % phrase "EM | STRONG | DFN | CODE |
                   SAMP | KBD | VAR | CITE | ABBR | ACRONYM" >
<!ENTITY % special
   "A | IMG | APPLET | OBJECT | FONT | BASEFONT | BR | SCRIPT
    | MAP | Q | SUB | SUP | SPAN | BDO | IFRAME">
<!ENTITY % formctrl "INPUT | SELECT | TEXTAREA | LABEL |
                     BUTTON">
<!ENTITY % inline "#PCDATA | %fontstyle; | %phrase; |
                   %special; | %formctrl;">
```

In other words, the DTD creates four specific element-type classes—`fontstyle`, `phrase`, `special`, and `formctrl`—and then creates a larger class `inline` containing the other four.

3.2.4   *Global Attributes*

It is important, then, that the attribute definitions for an element type reflect the element type's class. In some document types, there will also be some attributes that apply to every element type:

- elements may have an ID
- elements may have a revision-status property (with values such as `draft` or `final`)
- elements may have a security property (with values such as `public` or `classified`)
- elements may have a property to specify additional information about their role
- elements may have a responsibility property (containing, for example, the author's initials)

The obvious way to model these properties is with attributes, and it is essential that the DTD containing the models adhere to three basic principles:

1. it should use the same names for the attributes wherever they appear
2. it should use the same declared types and (preferably) default values for the attributes wherever they appear
3. it should avoid using the same attribute names for unrelated properties on any other element types

From the point of view of consistency, it is a good idea to provide attributes like these for *all* and not just for *most* element types: users will become accustomed to global attributes quickly and will come to expect them everywhere; any inconsistency increases the time and effort that authors will need to learn the DTD.

3.2.4.1   Examples from the Model DTDs

Two of the model DTDs—the DocBook DTD and the TEI-Lite DTD—apply a set of global attributes to most (but in neither case, all) element types.

The DocBook DTD declares global attributes with the parameter entity `common.attrib`:

Global attributes in DocBook

```
<!ENTITY % local.common.attrib "">
<!ENTITY % common.attrib
 "%id.attrib;
  %lang.attrib;
  %remap.attrib;
  %xreflabel.attrib;
  %revisionflag.attrib;
  %effectivity.attrib;
  %local.common.attrib;">
```

Note the use of nested parameter entities for specific subclasses of attributes.

The TEI-Lite DTD has preresolved all of the parameter entities from the full TEI DTD. The original DTD, however, contains the following declaration for the parameter entity `a.global`:

Global attributes in TEI-Lite

```
<!ENTITY % a.global
 "%a.analysis;
  %a.linking;
  %a.terminology;
  id ID #IMPLIED
  n CDATA #IMPLIED
  lang IDREF %INHERITED;
  rend CDATA #IMPLIED">
```

3.3   DTD Intuitiveness

When you analyze a DTD's consistency (Section 3.2, page 97), you can use simple, objective criteria, since you are considering a closed system—the DTD itself. When you analyze a DTD's **intuitiveness**, however, you must use more subjective criteria, since you are considering how closely the structures and naming conventions in a DTD correspond with authors' experience in the world outside.

Differences such as language, nationality, education, profession, socioeconomic status, age, gender, professional specialization, and even employer might affect authors' expectations:

- a French author might expect a **phrase** element to contain an entire sentence, whereas an American author might expect it to contain only a small group of related words

- a lawyer might expect a **clause** element to contain a single legal statement, while a linguist might expect it to contain a subject and predicate, together with modifiers and function words

- an aircraft mechanic might expect rigidly-structured procedures, while a literary critic might expect a loosely-structured series of paragraphs and quotations

- a librarian might expect elaborate bibliographical headers, while a casual user expects no more than the title, author, and date of publication; and so on

This section examines intuitiveness from two different perspectives:

1. intuitiveness in naming
2. intuitiveness in structure

3.3.1   *Naming*

To speed up learning, a DTD's element types and attributes should use names that are familiar to the document authors. For example, if lexicographers at a dictionary normally begin an entry with a *lemma*, then it makes sense to name the corresponding element type **lemma** rather than **headword** (and vice versa).

Often, however, a DTD is intended for a group of authors who have significant cultural differences; perhaps they speak different languages, have different social backgrounds, work in different professions, work for different industries, or belong to different companies; in fact, sometimes the greatest disagreements will arise between different parts of the same company. For example, the consulting division of a company might use the term *status* to refer to the current revision number of a program (e.g., "version 1.1"), whereas the commercial-software division of the same company might use *status* to refer to a program's proximity to release (e.g., "alpha" or "beta").

In this case, if you choose the attribute name status for *either* the revision number or the proximity to release, the name could cause confusion among authors at one of the two divisions. It would be even worse if you used the same attribute name, on different element types, to describe *both* types of information—the result would be confusion on all sides.

Except in special situations you should compromise and select a third, neutral name in these circumstances.

3.3.1.1   Examples from the Model DTDs

In general, the shorter a DTD's element type names, the less intuitive they will be for the authors.

Assume, for example, that an author is using XML-aware editing software to create a document and wants to insert a numbered list between two paragraphs. With the HTML DTD, the author will have to choose from a list of the following element types:

**ADDRESS BLOCKQUOTE DEL DIV DL FIELDSET FORM
H1 H2 H3 H4 H5 H6 HR INS NOSCRIPT OL P PRE
SCRIPT TABLE UL**

For a new user, it can hardly be obvious that **OL** ("ordered list") is the correct element type to choose. In fact, the majority of the names—**DL**, **PRE**, **HR**, etc—would be difficult for a new author to guess or remember.

If the author were using the MIL-STD-38784 DTD, on the other hand, the following element types would be available (in this case, within rather than between paragraphs):

acronym applicabil brk change dataiden deflist emphasis esds extref figure foldout ftnote ftnref graphic hcp line location modreq nsp pgbrk randlist seqlist subjinfo table tabmat verbatim xref

Some of these are still cryptic and confusing, but many of the element-type names would be relatively easy to guess, even for a first-time author. For the numbered list, for example, the author could choose **seqlist** ("sequential list"). (If you already know some HTML, however, the element type name **OL** might at first seem more intuitive than **seqlist**—more on this point in a moment).

None of the other DTDs uses quite as many short, cryptic names as does the HTML DTD. ISO 12083 and TEI, for example, represent a numbered list using the **list** element with the role attribute type set to an appropriate value (though it would be difficult for an author to guess what that value might be), and DocBook represents it using the intuitively-named element type **OrderedList**.

At first glance, then, it would seem that HTML uses the least intuitive names of all the model DTDs, and that, as a result, it should be the most difficult to learn. Nevertheless, because of the popularity of the World Wide Web, HTML is the best-known SGML document type in the world (even if most people using it don't know what a DTD is), and millions (rather than dozens or hundreds) of authors use it daily.

This popularity leads to an interesting paradox. Once authors are familiar with HTML, they might actually find its element type names *more* intuitive than longer, more explicit ones, simply because they are familiar. As a result, many people design project-specific DTDs that use HTML element-type names whenever possible. Popular usage may dictate that **OL** is more intuitive than **orderedlist** after all.

3.3.2   *Structure*

Authors usually worry the most about a DTD's terminology, but they also bring conscious or unconscious structural expectations to their writing. They may expect, for example, that each item in a part list begins with a part number, that manual pages contain synopses, that a book contains chapters, and so on. The more closely a DTD meets these expectations, the easier authors will find it to use.

If the DTD is designed for a specific type of document for use among a small group of authors, the choice of structure is often straightforward. For example, authors in a single division of a single company might be used to writing maintenance-manual entries containing the following information:

- Assembly Name
- Assembly Number
- Overview
- Part List
- Regular Maintenance
- Troubleshooting

In this case, the DTD can model the structure exactly, as in the following content model:

Direct model of document structure

```
<!ELEMENT entry (assembly.name,
                 assembly.number,
                 sect.overview,
                 sect.partlist,
                 sect.maintenance,
                 sect.troubleshooting)>
```

For the sake of processing, it might make sense to add an extra structural level:

Direct model with container

```
<!ELEMENT entry (entry.head, entry.body)>
<!ELEMENT entry.head (assembly.name, assembly.number)>
<!ELEMENT entry.body (sect.overview,
                      sect.partlist,
                      sect.maintenance,
                      sect.troubleshooting)>
```

In either case, the structure is close to what the authors expect, and the similarity should help them to learn the DTD more quickly.

If, on the other hand, the DTD is meant for broader use, the problem of intuitive structure becomes much more difficult, since different authors may have very different expectations. Assume, for example, that one company uses this structure for its maintenance-manual entries:

- Assembly Name
- Assembly Number
- Overview
- Part List
- Regular Maintenance
- Troubleshooting

Another organization, however, might use the following structure:

- Task
- Required Tools

- Required Parts
- Safety Concerns
- Procedures

These two entries might hold the same information, but it will be scattered in different places: some of the information from Regular Maintenance from the first list will appear under Required Tools, some will appear under Safety Concerns, and some will appear under Procedures; likewise, whereas some of the information under Procedures in the second list will appear under Regular Maintenance in the first, other information will appear under Troubleshooting.

In this example, the problem is much more complicated than simply choosing names: authors at the two companies are accustomed to thinking about the *structure* of their information in very different ways, and a DTD that is well suited to one will work very poorly for another. If you are a DTD designer, there are four broad approaches that you might choose in this situation:

1. you can create a DTD that uses a new, neutral structure, different from either of the existing ones
2. you can impose one of the two structures arbitrarily
3. you can create a DTD that allows either of the two structures as alternatives
4. you can create a less-restrictive DTD that can be adapted to any appropriate structure

These approaches (in this order) provide increasing flexibility for authors, but at the cost of decreasing predictability for the processing software:

- creating a new structure (perhaps taking the best from both) requires authors at both companies to make some changes in their work habits, but it produces a predictable result

- imposing one company's structures is bound to aggravate authors at the other company
- allowing both structures essentially creates two separate DTDs, each of which needs to be processed differently
- creating a less-restrictive DTD allows a possibly infinite number of structures to appear for any entry

Most industry-standard DTDs use the fourth method more often than the others, because the DTDs need to be useful for a wide range of applications within a single industry; but, as a result, the DTDs provide a lower level of guidance for authors, validation for processing, and context-sensitivity for searching.

For an alternative approach to this problem, see Part Four.

3.3.2.1   Examples from the Model DTDs

All five of the model DTDs are meant for widespread use, for many different types of projects. As mentioned above, there are four different ways you can design a DTD to work with many different projects:

1. you can create a DTD that uses a new, neutral structure, different from either of the existing ones
2. you can impose one of the two structures arbitrarily
3. you can create a DTD that allows either of the two structures as alternatives
4. you can create a less-restrictive DTD that can be adapted to any appropriate structure

Industry-standard DTDs necessarily tend toward the fourth approach, with some nods toward the third.

A DocBook document, for example, might contain a chapter on maintenance, a tutorial chapter, and/or a chapter listing any required software. Instead of creating separate element types for each one, the

DTD simply provides the generic element type **Chapter**, and it allows users to specify the purpose using the **Title** element:

General element type in DocBook

```
<Chapter id="tutorial">
<Title>Tutorial</Title>
[...]
</Chapter>
```

Authors can adapt fairly quickly to this approach, but their work will be difficult to validate (the XML parser will not check that, for example, the tutorial and maintenance chapters are both present and in that order). It can also lead to inconsistencies, since one author might use the title "Tutorial", while another might use "Overview" and a third might use "Quick Start".

Such generic structures—which are present in all but the HTML DTD (though even there, **DIV** can serve as a substitute)—are intuitive to the extent that they match a minimum common denominator in most author's expectations (a structural division into generic chapters, sections, subsections, paragraphs, lists, tables, etc). They actually describe layout more than logical structure, but they describe layout at such a high level that they translate well to many different output targets.

Some of the DTDs also include some more specific structures. For example, the front matter for the MIL-STD-38784 and ISO 12083 DTDs allows specific elements for a preface, introduction, or foreword; DocBook provides only a preface; and TEI-Lite provides none. As a result, an author using TEI-Lite might mark up a preface as follows:

General element type in TEI-Lite

```
<div1 type="preface">
<head>Preface</head>
[...]
</div1>
```

An author using ISO 12083, on the other hand, could simply use the following:

Specific element type in ISO 12083

```
<preface>
[...]
</preface>
```

It is difficult to be certain which structure is more intuitive—the answer depends on whether authors prefer to think of a preface as simply a chapter with a special title or as a fundamentally different type of logical unit in a book. Certainly, the latter will be easier to validate.

Finally, some of the DTDs use specialized structures that are unique to their fields. The TEI-Lite DTD, for example, makes provision for complex, highly-structured bibliographies and for metrical and linguistic analysis, whereas the DocBook DTD makes provision for reference information following the model of Unix man pages. The MIL-STD-38784 uses the titled paragraphs (**para0**) standard in military maintenance documentation, whereas the HTML DTD allows for browser-specific features like applets and image maps.

Ease of Use

Chapter
4

The previous chapter described how you can analyze a DTD to see how easily authors can learn it; this chapter continues the discussion of usability by examining how to analyze a DTD to see how easily authors can use a DTD to mark up text after they have managed to learn the DTD's terminology, structure, and semantics.

There are three different categories that you can use to determine how easy it will be for a specific group of authors to use a DTD:

1. the amount of extra work—or physical effort—required to add the markup (Section 4.1, page 120)
2. the number and complexity of the choices the authors must make (Section 4.2, page 131)
3. the flexibility necessary to allow authors to mark up different and unexpected types of information (Section 4.3, page 135)

Again, the goals implied by these categories are not entirely consistent: a DTD that presents authors with more choices requires more mental (and often physical) effort from those authors; a DTD that presents authors with fewer choices may not be flexible enough to model their data.

In the end, you will have to pay special attention to your authors' writing conditions:

- if your authors will be entering or converting large volumes of data quickly, then physical and mental effort may be the most important criteria

- if your authors will be composing new documents at a more moderate pace, then flexibility may be the most important criterion

4.1   Physical Effort

Your authors—especially if they are new to structured documents—might think of markup not as part of writing but as something that they have to do in addition to writing. In other words, they might think of the time that they spend adding markup as overhead, and if so, they will want to reduce that time as much as possible.

The precise mechanics of creating an XML or SGML document vary by software package, but usually some or all of the following observations apply:

1. it requires more effort to enter tags and content than simply to enter content

2. it requires more effort to enter tags and attributes than simply to enter tags

3. it requires more effort to enter element types that allow choices in their content

 **SGML Note:**   *Full SGML does contain several optional facilities to help save on typing, such as* OMITTAG *and* SHORTREF, *but these work only in special circumstances and are not well supported by commercial SGML tools. They can be useful for data entry with an ordinary text editor under very controlled conditions, when your data is not mission-critical (in effect, since the parser can place the end tags itself, you miss one of the most important validity checks).*

In this section, you can read about the two aspects of DTD design that have the most to do with physical effort:

1. content models
2. attribute definitions

4.1.1 *Content Models*

If your only goal in DTD design were to minimize physical effort, then every DTD that you write would contain only a single document element:

Simplest DTD

```
<!ELEMENT doc (#PCDATA)>
```

Authors would simply type character data between the start and end tags, and the result would be a valid, if not very useful, XML document.

More practically, if your authors are using XML- or SGML-aware editing tools, the tools can do much of the work when the document's structure is straight-forward. Consider, for example, the following element type declaration:

Straight-forward content model

```
<!ELEMENT record (author, title, publisher, date)>
```

Once an author creates a **record** element, the editing software can determine that the element must contain **author**, **title**, **publisher**, and **date** elements, in that order, and the software can create that skeleton structure automatically without requiring any extra effort from authors:

Predictable content

```
<record>
 <author></author>
 <title></title>
 <publisher></publisher>
 <date></date>
</record>
```

For the effort of inserting a single element, the author ends up with five.

In the first example, the children of the **record** element were not all *required*—from the DTD alone, the editing software could determine that authors would have to insert each of the four children (in a specific order) to have a valid document. In the following example, on the other hand, two of the children are *optional* (see Figure 4–1):

Content model with omissible content particles

```
<!ELEMENT record (author, title, publisher?, date?)>
```

When an author creates a **record** element, the editing software can insert **author** and **title** elements because they are both *ordered* and *required*; because **publisher** and **date** are optional, however, the software cannot determine whether authors will decide to include them and cannot insert them into a skeleton structure without some

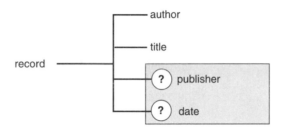

Figure 4–1   Predictability—Editing software cannot automatically insert optional elements for an author, so additional physical and mental effort is necessary.

additional input from the authors. Here's what the editing software could insert automatically:

Predictable content

```
<record>
 <author></author>
 <title></title>
</record>
```

In the end, the least flexible content models—those with *required* elements—usually require less physical effort than those with *optional* elements.

> ***SGML Note:***   *Unlike XML, full SGML allows unordered content, using the "&" connector instead of ",":*
>
> **Content model without explicit ordering**
>
> ```
> <!ELEMENT record - - (author & title & publisher &
>                       date)>
> ```
>
> *Although all four element types are required to appear, the DTD does not specify the order (****author***, for example, could appear in any of the four positions); as a result, the software can insert none of the children automatically.*
>
> *In general, it is best to avoid unordered content for DTDs that authors will be using directly; even experienced SGML authors will often have difficulty with it.*

4.1.1.1   Examples from the Model DTDs

Because they are designed to be flexible, the model DTDs tend to offer enough choice so that editing software can rarely predict what children an element type will have; custom-written DTDs, designed for a specific project or organization, can provide greater savings in physical effort.

Even highly-structured element types, like ordered lists, are not always predictable enough that editing software can insert extra markup. When an author inserts an ordered list into a document, for example, only the MIL-STD-38784 DTD would allow the editing software to insert the first item automatically. The MIL-STD-38784 DTD uses the following element-type declaration for ordered lists:

Predictable content model in MIL-STD-38784

```
<!ELEMENT seqlist (title?, item+)>
```

Since the content particles are required and repeatable, the editing software can determine that at least one item must appear and can insert it automatically when the author inserts the **seqlist** element:

Predictable content

```
<seqlist>
<item></item>
</seqlist>
```

None of the other model DTDs allows even this simple saving—in all of the others, either the list item is optional, or there is more than one option available. For example, the ISO 12083 DTD uses the following element-type definition for general lists:

List in ISO 12083

```
<!ELEMENT list (head?, item)*>
```

Because the group is optional and repeatable, XML or SGML-aware editing software cannot be certain that the first item *must* appear.

For sectioning elements and their titles, most of the model DTDs still provide few savings (HTML does not have sectioning elements per se), but both DocBook and MIL-STD-38784 use content models that allow editing software to insert titles automatically when the author inserts a sectioning element.

The DocBook DTD requires a **Title** element at the beginning of sectioning elements such as **part**, **chapter**, **appendix**, **sect1**, **sect2**, and so on. As a result, it is possible for editing software to insert the title automatically whenever the author inserts a new sectioning element.

For example, if an author inserts a **sect2** element into a DocBook document, the following markup could be generated automatically:

Subsection in DocBook

```
<Sect2>
<Title></Title>
</Sect2>
```

The author saves the physical effort of inserting the title, because the editing software knows that it must be there. The ISO 12083 and TEI DTDs—which make sectioning titles optional rather than mandatory—cannot offer the same savings in physical effort.

The MIL-STD-38784 DTD, however, has even more restrictive content models than DocBook. The **chapter** sectioning element works as it does in the DocBook DTD: it requires a title, and the simple insertion of a chapter can result in the following markup:

Chapter in MIL-STD-38784

```
<chapter>
<title></title>
</chapter>
```

The MIL-STD-38784 sectioning hierarchy is not deep, however, and extends only as far as sections (and formal paragraphs). When an author inserts a **section** element, the editing software can determine not only that the section must contain a title, but that the title must be followed by a **para0** (formal paragraph) element with its own title, because of the following element-type definition:

Section in MIL-STD-38784

```
<!ELEMENT section (title, para0+)>
```

Both the **title** and the **para0** elements are required (and **para0** also requires a title), so when an author inserts a **section** element into a MIL-STD-38784 document, editing software can insert *four* elements:

Predictable content

```
<section>
<title></title>

<para0>
<title></title>
</para0>
</section>
```

Again, a stricter (or less-flexible) content model often saves authors physical effort. This type of content model, however, is necessarily rare among the model DTDs.

4.1.2   *Attribute Definitions*

If your DTD allows attributes, then your authors must expend effort to insert both elements and attribute value specifications. The amount of extra effort will vary greatly depending on the XML or SGML editing software; generally, authors enter attribute values in pop-up dialog boxes or other similar input areas—to do so, they must interrupt the flow of their work and take their attention away from the main document.

As with elements, attributes that are *required* (using the "#REQUIRED" keyword) sometimes take a little less effort: The editing software can prompt for the values automatically whenever an author inserts an element. When an attribute is *optional*—if the DTD declares it as "#IMPLIED" or gives it a default value—then authors must take *two* steps to specify an attribute value:

1. they must inform the software that they wish to specify an attribute value
2. they must enter the new value

On the other hand, when an attribute is optional, authors can simply avoid specifying a value altogether when it is not needed. (Many attributes need specified values only occasionally.)

Depending on the editing software, attribute types that have a name token list as their attribute type may also simplify authors' work. Consider the following attribute definition:

Unpredictable attribute value

```
<!ATTLIST doc
  security CDATA #REQUIRED>
```

In this example, authors must type the name of the security level without any additional help from the editing software, because the software cannot guess at (or validate) the allowed values.

The following attribute definition uses a name token list:

Predictable attribute value

```
<!ATTLIST doc
  security (public | classified | secret) #REQUIRED>
```

With this definition, the editing software can either provide dynamic completion from the keyboard or (more likely) present authors with a menu of choices rather than a blank text-entry field.

4.1.2.1   Examples from the Model DTDs

Since they are so general, the model DTDs tend to define many special-purpose attributes that most authors can ignore most of the time. For example, in TEI-Lite, even a simple paragraph element can have up to nine attributes—ana, corresp, next, prev, id, n, lang, rend, and teiform—one of which (teiform) is defaulted, and eight of which are optional. In full TEI, depending on the modules enabled, this list can be much longer; for marking up routine prose, however, none (except possibly the already-defaulted teiform attribute) is necessary.

Since authors will rarely use most of these attributes, the model DTDs rightly declare them as #IMPLIED, as in TEI-Lite:

Paragraph attributes in TEI-Lite

```
<!ATTLIST p
  ana IDREFS #IMPLIED
  corresp IDREFS #IMPLIED
  next IDREF #IMPLIED
  prev IDREF #IMPLIED
  id ID #IMPLIED
  n CDATA #IMPLIED
  lang IDREF #IMPLIED
  rend CDATA #IMPLIED
  TEIform CDATA "p" >
```

It would make no sense to force an author to provide a number, a rendition string, or a link to an analysis (for example) with every paragraph. With most editing tools, the author can insert a **p** element without even seeing this list (unless the author specifically requests it).

It is not so obvious, however, that the id attribute should be #IMPLIED—if the author does not specify a value, then the paragraph cannot be the target of a cross-reference or hyperlink without using advanced linking mechanisms from the HyTime standard. An XML editing tool could easily generate a unique ID for every element that required one, but since some authors still create XML and SGML documents in character-data editors, the model DTDs (like most others) generally declare IDs as #IMPLIED, so that authors can include them only where necessary—authors are saved the burden of specifying an ID for every element that can have one, but they assume the different burden of adding IDs themselves whenever they need to make a cross-reference or link to another part of the document.

Cross-reference and linking elements do usually declare their IDREF attributes as #REQUIRED, as in this example from MIL-STD-38784:

Required #IDREF in MIL-STD-38784

```
<!ATTLIST xref
  xrefid IDREF #REQUIRED >
```

The difference between the IDs and IDREFs is one of semantics. Element types that may have IDs generally have another purpose, such as marking sections or phrases, whereas element types that have IDREFs are generally intended primarily for linking or cross-references. An emphasized phrase is still an emphasized phrase if the author does not specify a value for its ID attribute, but a cross-reference can hardly be a cross-reference without a value for its IDREF attribute.

Whenever an attribute value is essential to the meaning of an element, it should be declared as "#REQUIRED" (as in the case of **xref**, above) for two reasons:

1. so that authors will not forget to insert it
2. so that authors can insert it more easily (most editing tools can prompt for the value automatically when it is #REQUIRED)

For example, in HTML the empty **IMG** element type represents an inline graphic, using the src attribute to provide the actual graphic object's address. The **src** attribute is required, because without an actual graphic object, the element type is meaningless.

For an example of a poor implementation, consider the following element-type definition from the MIL-STD-38784 DTD (I have omitted an exclusion exception and most of the attributes):

Emphasis in MIL-STD-38784

```
<!ELEMENT emphasis (%text;)>
<!ATTLIST emphasis
  type (u|b|bu|i|bi|q|x|o|sup|sub|ui) #REQUIRED>
```

In this case, the **emphasis** element could make sense by itself, since the `type` attribute provides only rendition information—it is difficult to justify the annoyance (and extra effort) of forcing authors always to specify a value for this attribute.

> *SGML Note:*   A more unusual approach is to use the default value #CURRENT in an attribute definition (see Section 1.3.2, page 21)—this forces the author to specify an attribute value for the first instance of an element type but then silently allows all subsequent instances to inherit the same value.
>
>   TEI-Lite declares the attribute `type` as #CURRENT for the **lg**, **div**, and **div0 – div7** elements. These declarations can cause some confusion; consider, for example, the following fragment from a TEI-Lite document:
>
> **Sample sections in TEI-Lite**
>
> ```
> <div id="div01" type="chapter">
>  [...]
>   <div id="div02"> <!-- type="chapter"!!! -->
>    [...]
>   </div>
>   <div id="div03" type="section">
>    [...]
>   </div>
> </div>
> <div id="div04"> <!-- type="section"!!! -->
>  [...]
> </div>
> ```
>
> In this example, the parser will automatically assign the value "chapter" to the `type` attribute of the element with ID "div02", even though the element appears within a chapter, and it will assign the value "section" to the `type` attribute of the element with ID "div04", even though the element is a sibling of a chapter.

4.2   Choice

Whenever your authors have to choose whether to insert an element or choose whether to specify an attribute value, they expend mental effort on the document's structure instead of its data content. Although effort spent on structure is not necessarily a problem—information can lie as much in structure as in words—it is better to present authors with a few clear (and necessary) choices. Since XML (like full SGML) uses a DTD to control document structure, software can limit authors' choices based on where an author is in the document; how well the software can do so depends on whether your DTD was designed with choice in mind.

4.2.1   *Limiting Choices*

Even if a DTD contains hundreds of element types (and even more *logical units*), authors choose from among only a very small subset of these at most points in a document. Consider, for example, the following simple DTD (see Figure 4–2):

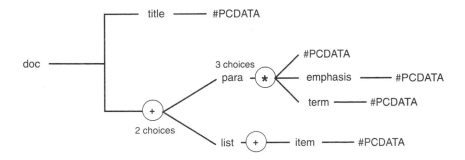

Figure 4–2   Limiting Choice—A DTD can limit choice to only a few elements at any point in a document. In this example, a user never has to choose from more than three options.

DTD with limited choices

```
<!ELEMENT doc (title, (para | list)+)>
<!ELEMENT title (#PCDATA)>
<!ELEMENT para (#PCDATA | emphasis | term)*>
<!ELEMENT list (item+)>
<!ELEMENT item (#PCDATA)>
<!ELEMENT emphasis (#PCDATA)>
<!ELEMENT term (#PCDATA)>
```

This DTD declares seven element types, but authors never have to choose from among all seven. The following list describes the different choices that authors will make after inserting the document element **doc**:

- in a **doc** element, authors must insert a **title** element, then they choose only between **para** and **list** elements
- in a **para** element, authors choose among data, **emphasis** elements, and **term** elements
- in a **list** element, authors may insert only **item** elements
- in all other elements, authors may insert only character data

In a DTD such as this, containing character data and seven different element types, authors never have to choose from among more than three options, including character data.

As a general principle, the more choices available to authors at any point in a document, the greater the mental effort required to create that part of the document. XML and SGML authoring tools deal with the insertion of elements in many different ways; but if there are, for example, 35 element types available at a certain point in a document, choosing from such a long list requires more mental (and possibly also more physical) work than choosing from a short one, whether the authors choose by scrolling down a list, selecting from a drop down menu, or simply typing the element-type name.

The structure of your DTD will determine how and how often authors must make three basic structural decisions:

1. whether to insert an optional element
2. how many times to insert a repeatable element
3. which element to insert from a list of alternatives

Consider, for example, the following element-type definition:

Predictable content

```
<!ELEMENT doc (a, b, c)>
```

The content is *required*, and *nonrepeatable*, with no alternatives—as a result, authors are not required to make any choices after creating the document element **doc**—the editing software may, in fact, insert the three child elements automatically.

With a slightly different content model, creating a document becomes more complicated:

Optional content

```
<!ELEMENT doc (a, b?, c)>
```

Now, authors must decide whether to insert the **b** element—the editing software can no longer do it automatically. A different change has a similar effect:

Repeatable content

```
<!ELEMENT doc (a, b, c+)>
```

Here, authors must decide how many times to insert the **c** element.

Finally, alternation also requires authors to expend mental effort on the document's structure, as in the following example:

Alternation in content

```
<!ELEMENT doc (a, b, (c | d))>
```

Here, authors would have to decide whether to insert a **c** or **d** element.

The worst case would be a combination of all of these facilities, as in the following example:

Facilities in combination

```
<!ELEMENT doc (a+, b*, (c | d))>
```

In this case, authors have to decide which elements, and how many, to include. It is usually necessary that DTDs provide authors with some degree of choice, but it is important to remember that each choice requires document authors to expend additional mental as well as physical effort.

SGML Note: *In full SGML, authors also have to decide how to order unordered elements:*

Unordered content

```
<!ELEMENT doc - - (a & b & c)>
```

*Here, authors would have to decide the order for the **a**, **b**, and **c** elements: they could insert any of the three elements in the first position, and either of the remaining two in the second.*

4.2.1.1   Examples from the Model DTDs

Generally, because of their flexible structure, the model DTDs require authors to choose from long lists of attributes and element types. The following list shows the number of element types within a standard paragraph for each DTD:

- the MIL-STD-38784 **para** element type allows a choice of character data and 17 element types in its content
- the HTML **P** element type allows a choice of character data and 33 element types in its content
- the ISO 12083 DTD **p** element type allows a choice of character data and 34 element types in its content
- the TEI-Lite **p** element allows a choice of character data and 48 element types in its content

- the DocBook **Para** element type allows a choice of character data and 112 element types in its content

As you can see, the amount of choice in a paragraph in the model DTDs varies greatly, and it is the MIL-STD-38784 DTD, not the (apparently) smaller HTML DTD, that limits choice most effectively.

It is also important to remember that role attributes can greatly increase the burden of choice by generating many logical units from the same element type. For example, the ISO 12083 DTD contains the **emph** element type, which uses an attribute to distinguish six types of emphasized phrases; the **q** element type, which uses an attribute to distinguish five different alphabets for citations; the **date** element type, which uses an attribute to distinguish five different date formats; and the **list** element, which uses an attribute to distinguish six different types of lists. If you interpret all of these as role attributes, then there are actually 52 *logical units* to choose from within an ISO 12083 paragraph, rather than simply 34 element types.

4.3 Flexibility

Limiting choice makes it easier for authors to write a conforming document, but it does not necessarily make it easier for them to write a good one. Often, the nature of the subject matter and of the intended audience requires the author to present information in ways that the DTD designers could not anticipate.

Of course, authors' choices are not necessarily always good ones, and house styles or writing methodologies often attempt to restrict them for the sake of consistency, especially when several authors are collaborating on a single document or on a set of related documents. A narrowly-targeted DTD (e.g., for a single, well-constrained documentation project) can enforce some of these restrictions, but a broadly-targeted one cannot, since it must be adaptable to different house styles if required.

This section will examine four aspects of DTD design that have a significant effect on flexibility:

1. descriptive and prescriptive DTDs (Section 4.3.1)
2. the placement of inline elements (Section 4.3.2, page 138)
3. the use of role attributes (Section 4.3.3, page 140)
4. the use of generic element types (Section 4.3.4, page 142)

4.3.1   *Descriptive and Prescriptive DTDs*

A DTD can deal with unpredictable requirements mainly by becoming more general (some specialists prefer the terms **descriptive DTD** or **enabling DTD**). For example, one company's software release notes might always consist of three sections:

1. New Features
2. Known Bugs
3. Corrigenda to the User Manual

In such cases, it is tempting to create something like the following DTD fragment:

DTD for a single company

```
<!ELEMENT release-notes (features, bugs, corrigenda)>
<!ELEMENT features (para+)>
<!ELEMENT bugs (para+)>
<!ELEMENT corrigenda (para+)>
```

If the DTD is meant only for that single company, it will work well. If it is meant for exchange, however, there will be difficulties if another company uses a different structure, like this one:

1. Interface Changes

2. Format Changes
3. Installation
4. Bugs and Corrigenda

A DTD intended to work for both companies would have to be more general: it would provide less guidance to authors—and less help in enforcing editorial standards—but it would be flexible enough to work in many different circumstances:

Exchange DTD for multiple companies

```
<!ELEMENT release-notes (section+)>
<!ELEMENT section (title, para+)>
```

Now, instead of creating a specific type of section, authors create a generalized **section** element and identify it with the appropriate title. The companies can share the cost of developing documentation and support software, but they will lose the stricter validation possible with a more prescriptive DTD.

4.3.1.1   Examples from the Model DTDs

All of the model DTDs are, for the most part, descriptive—each of the DTDs (with the partial exception of HTML) contains a hierarchy of generic sectioning elements, paragraphs, lists, tables, etc.

For example, the sectioning hierarchy in the DocBook DTD is **Part** (optional), **Chapter**, **Sect1**, **Sect2**, etc in the main body, or **Appendix**, **Sect1**, **Sect2**, etc, in the back matter. The DTD places no restrictions on the use of these sectioning elements: you can use the **Chapter** element type for any kind of chapter at all.

The sectioning hierarchy in the TEI-Lite DTD is even more flexible: it allows either an (indefinitely) recursive **div** element type (**lg** for verse), or the nonrecursive **div0** (optional), **div1**, **div2,** etc element types, without even restricting whether the divisions are parts, chapters, sections, cantos, books, clauses, acts, or scenes (you provide that information with the unrestricted role attribute type).

HTML has no regular sectioning element types—only different levels of headings—but the MIL-STD-38784 and ISO 12083 DTDs follow the same basic pattern as DocBook, with generic, nonrecursive sectioning element types.

Most of the model DTDs do provide some dedicated sectioning element types for common divisions such as introductions, prefaces, and abstracts, and some provide more specialized structures as options: TEI-Lite, for example, has a special list type for bibliographies, while DocBook has a special (highly-structured) section type for reference material. DocBook and MIL-STD-38784 both have element types for special paragraphs such as notes, cautions, and so on.

Finally, whereas MIL-STD-38784 uses relatively generic sectioning types, the structure itself is very restrictive: most notably, all **para** (paragraph) elements must appear within a **para0** container, together with a title.

4.3.2   *Inline Element Types*

A second, important type of flexibility is the placement of inline elements: the more places you are allowed to put a given element, the more likely it is that you will be able to deal with unexpected requirements. Take a look at the following element type definitions:

Inflexible inline content

```
<!ELEMENT section (heading, para+)>
<!ELEMENT heading (#PCDATA)>
<!ELEMENT para (#PCDATA | title | emphasis)*>
```

These definitions assume that authors may need to include a book title or emphasized text inside a paragraph, but only character data inside a section heading. As soon as an author needs to create a section whose heading refers to a book title—i.e., "Dream Imagery in *The Mabinogion*"—this design fails, because it is not possible to place a **title** element in the section heading.

A typical solution to this problem is to allow the same inline content everywhere:

More flexible inline content

```
<!ENTITY % inline "#PCDATA | title | emphasis">
<!ELEMENT section (heading, para+)>
<!ELEMENT heading (%inline;)*>
<!ELEMENT para (%inline;)*>
```

Because it provides so many choices at each point, this solution can lead to serious problems for ease of learning, ease of use, and ease of processing, but it does often provide the flexibility that authors require. The same basic principle applies to general attributes like id or security, which authors may wish to include for all elements (see Section 3.2.4, page 107).

4.3.2.1 Examples from the Model DTDs

In general, book-oriented DTDs, like this book's five model DTDs, allow two types of content to appear in paragraphs:

1. phrases, short equations, short quotations, cross-references, etc (**true inline content**)
2. lists, displayed equations, tables, long quotations, figures, etc (**block content**)

The second type—*block content*—contains element types that usually appear *between* paragraphs, but can also appear within them. Of course, whereas block content may be appropriate within a paragraph (e.g., a list or table), it is inappropriate within the inline content of a section title. Generally, only *true inline content* is allowed in titles, emphasized phrases, and other similar element types.

For example, the ISO 12083 DTD allows elements such as poems, bibliography lists, artwork, and tables to appear within a paragraph but not within a section title (or within a phrase, etc); DocBook and MIL-STD-38784 take a similar approach.

The TEI-Lite and HTML DTDs, however, provide exceptions to this rule. For the sake of (somewhat extreme) flexibility, TEI-Lite allows *block content* to appear inside paragraphs, section titles, and emphasized phrases, whereas HTML forbids block content to appear in any of the three (originally, since there was no DTD and most HTML documents omitted end tags, it was unclear whether block content appeared within or between paragraphs). As a result, it is not possible in HTML to include a list or table within a paragraph, but it is possible in TEI-Lite to include a list or table even within an emphasized phrase in a section title!

4.3.3   *Role Attributes*

There is also the problem that an author may discover the need for an element type that is simply absent from the DTD. There are two related approaches to this problem: the *role attribute*, described here, and the *generic element* (see Section 4.3.4, page 142).

In the first approach, most or all element types have a *role attribute*—an optional attribute named something such as `class` or `type`, that authors can use to derive a new, virtual element type from an existing one. For example, if there were a strong need to include special warning paragraphs, and the DTD did not declare a **warning** element type, the author might include something like this in the document:

Creating a new logical unit with a role attribute

```
<p type="warning">Do not mix these two chemicals together.
</p>
```

Here, the new virtual element type (or *logical unit*) is derived from the most similar existing element type: a warning is a more specialized type of paragraph, so authors begin with the **p** element and use the role attribute `type` to make it more specific.

Although they may be useful in very limited circumstances, role attributes have some very serious drawbacks. For example, they can greatly increase a DTD's effective size and thus can cause difficulties both for learning and for processing. Role attributes also require authors to expend more physical and mental effort—authors need both to insert the element and specify the attribute value—and weaken validation, since the XML parser cannot spot an incorrect usage.

In fact, taken to a ridiculous extreme, a DTD could contain only a single element type **element** with a required role attribute to specify its role:

Abuse of role attributes

```
<element type="section">
<element type="title">Required Study</element>

<element type="list">
 <element type="item">Read <element type="booktitle">Moby
 Dick</element> before next Tuesday.</element>
 <element type="item">Prepare a report on nineteenth-century
American
 novelists.</element>
</element>


</element>
```

When users need to derive many new structures from a common base DTD, it is a better choice to use architectural forms (see Part Four). In moderation, however, role attributes can perform two useful functions:

1. as a short-term escape mechanism for dealing with unexpected emergencies

2. as a tool for interim DTD development, to collect information on element types that should be added to the DTD in the next revision

4.3.3.1   Examples from the Model DTDs

The DocBook DTD assigns a role attribute `Role` to nearly all element types, so that you can create new ad hoc structures as you are writing a DocBook document:

Role attributes in DocBook

```
<Section Role="joke">
<Title>Chicken Joke</Title>
 <Para Role="setup">Why did the chicken cross the road?
 </Para>
 <Para Role="punchline">To get to the other side.</Para>
</Section>
```

Of course, it would be much better to extend the DocBook DTD or to create a new DTD with **Joke**, **Setup**, and **PunchLine** element types, but the `Role` attribute does provide a great deal of flexibility.

HTML 4.0 uses the `class` attribute in exactly the same way as DocBook uses the `Role` attribute. TEI-Lite uses a `type` attribute for some element types, but it is not global—paragraphs, for example, do not use it, but sectioning element types do.

ISO 12083 and MIL-STD-38784 do not use general role attributes at all.

4.3.4   *Generic Element Types*

An even more extreme measure for allowing flexibility is the creation of a new, **generic element type** that can contain itself (at least) and a required *role attribute*, as in the following DTD fragment:

Generic element type

```
<!ELEMENT extension (#PCDATA|extension)*>
```

```
<!ATTLIST extension
  class NMTOKEN #REQUIRED>
```

Authors can use such an element to create whole new structures. Book-oriented DTDs almost always include a list element type of some sort; if one did not, however, authors could use generic elements to construct one that looked like this:

List with generic element types

```
<extension class="list">
 <extension class="item">First Item</extension>
 <extension class="item">Second Item</extension>
 <extension class="item">Third Item</extension>
</extension>
```

An XML parser cannot validate this new structure, but it can report it to the program that is doing the processing. A DTD that allows generic elements to appear frequently provides authors with a great deal of flexibility, but at the cost of difficulty in learning, additional effort for both writers and editors, and much more complicated processing and validation (if, in fact, it is still possible to process the document at all).

Again, however, generic element types can be useful during the DTD design process, to collect information on the element types that authors require but that are not allowed by the current draft of the DTD. They should never be a long-term working tool (for that, you should use architectural forms [Part Four]).

4.3.4.1   Examples from the Model DTDs

None of the model DTDs uses a generic element type, although some provide fairly generic phrasal element types, like **hi** (highlighted phrase) or **seg** (segment) in TEI-Lite.

Ease of Processing

Chapter 5

You can process XML (or SGML) documents in many different ways: from the source documents you might create printed books, process a purchase order, execute context-sensitive searches, extract information for a database, display a table or chart, or even control a lawn-sprinkler system or satellite orbit. In nearly all cases, however, your **processing software** will have to meet these two requirements:

1. it must try to anticipate *all* of the different ways that authors might structure their documents
2. it must report errors or issue warnings when it finds something that it has not anticipated

Fortunately, a DTD makes this task much simpler: the processing software can assume that only constructions allowed by the DTD will appear in a document, and it can trust that the parser itself (a logically separate process) will report any structural errors. Because of these assumptions, XML (or SGML) processing software can be much simpler (and the software's source code, much shorter and clearer) than software that processes documents represented by other notations.

Of course, the DTD will simplify your processing only to the extent that it *does* constrain your authors' choices. A very flexible DTD (see Section 4.3, page 135) may constrain authors so little that the processing software cannot make reasonable guesses about what might appear.

This chapter introduces two major areas of DTD design that affect how easily—or even whether—you can create software to process conforming documents:

1. *predictability*
2. *context*

This chapter does not consider issues of cross-references or alignment: the XLL working draft <http://www.w3.org/TR/WD-xml-link> covers these issues for XML, and the HyTime standard, ISO/IEC 10744 <http://www.hytime/org/>, covers them for full SGML. This chapter also omits discussion of document-database issues, since these will vary greatly depending on the type of database (such as object-oriented or relational). In general, however, it is important to note that many database systems will do a poor job of modeling *mixed content* or unordered elements: DTDs designed to hold data for a database should usually assume relatively flat, simple structures, unless the database is itself XML-aware.

5.1   Predictability

All XML and SGML documents provide a certain degree of **predictability**: processing software never has to guess at the structural context of data, for example, because the tagging scheme marks the context unambiguously. No matter which DTD you use, all elements have explicit element-type names and (possibly empty) attribute specification lists, and all unparsed entities are associated with explicit notations.

None of this information, however, can guarantee the authors' intentions—if an author used an **emphasis** element instead of a **cite-title** element to mark a book title, and both were allowed in the same places, the parser would not detect an error. More importantly, the more flexibility allowed by the DTD, the less likely that software will be able to do a good job of processing its documents, because there will be more structural combinations available.

This section examines five aspects of DTD design, all of which can affect the predictability of the documents:

1. constraint
2. recursion
3. generic element types and role attributes
4. placement of data and subdocument entities
5. authors' modifications to the DTD

5.1.1 *Constraint*

Processing software written as part of an XML application does not have to deal with every possible combination of elements: if a document is valid, any given element can appear only in the contexts allowed by the DTD. For example, consider the following DTD fragment:

List element types

```
<!ELEMENT ordered.list (item+)>
<!ELEMENT unordered.list (item+)>
```

The XML or SGML parser itself will confirm that an **item** element appears only as the child of **ordered.list** or **unordered.list**, that it has no siblings of any other element type, and that at least one element will appear. Your software does not have to be prepared to deal with pathological cases such as items within titles, items between two table cells, or chapters within ordered lists.

Of course, not all DTDs constrain elements so tightly. A flexible (or **descriptive** or **enabling**) DTD may allow some element types to appear in dozens or even hundreds of different contexts: in such cases, the presence of the DTD is still an advantage—the processing software still deals with data in a finite and predictable number of possible contexts—but the advantage is relatively smaller that it would be with a more-constrained (or prescriptive) DTD.

Your software will likely also need to apply some constraints itself. A DTD can describe broad structural constraints—such as the number, location, and order where elements are allowed (or required)—but it cannot describe constraints that require an understanding of the data itself. Such constraints are a matter of **editorial policy** (or **business rules**, in the database world) rather than document structure: they clarify the kinds of data that processing software should be able to deal with, but they also place some of the burden of error-checking on your processing software itself rather than on the parser.

As an example of editorial policy, consider the following definitions:

Element types requiring editorial constraints

```
<!ELEMENT person (name, age, occupation)
<!ELEMENT name (#PCDATA)>
<!ELEMENT age (#PCDATA)>
<!ELEMENT occupation (#PCDATA)>
```

The designers of the processing software can safely assume that within **person** elements, the **name**, **age**, and **occupation** elements are always present and in the same order, and they can make optimizations based on that assumption. The XML or SGML parser will not, however, validate the *contents* of the three child elements: the parser will not report an error if an author leaves the contents of the **name** element blank, enters "5987" in the **age** element, or enters "rhubarb pie" for the occupation.

It is entirely reasonable for you to design processing software that works properly only with data that match additional constraints (e.g., ages between 0 and 150 or a list of occupations provided by a statistics agency), but if you do so, you have a responsibility to report an error when these constraints are violated.

5.1.1.1 Examples from the Model DTDs

As mentioned above (Section 5.1.1, page 147), the more a DTD constrains the placement of elements, the easier it will be to process the resulting documents. For example, the MIL-STD-38784 allows its **seqlist** (ordered list) element to appear in the content of only three parent element types:

1. **entry** (table entry)
2. **ftnote** (footnote)
3. **para** (paragraph)

A **para** element can appear in several different contexts (including steps), but in general, if you were designing processing software for a MIL-STD-38784 document, you would be required to handle lists only in these three contexts.

By comparison:

- the HTML DTD allows its **OL** (ordered list) element to appear in the content of 15 different element types
- the ISO 12083 DTD allows its **list** element to appear in the content of 30 different element types
- the TEI-Lite DTD allows its **list** element to appear in the content of 38 different element types

■ the DocBook DTD allows its **orderedlist** element to appear in the content of 43 different element types

As always, though, a simple count is deceiving. Depending on the type of processing, the number of element *classes* may be more important than the number of element *types*.

For example, in ISO 12083, the **list** element can appear in sectioning elements, paragraph-level elements, table entries, and list items; in DocBook, it can also appear in procedure steps (admittedly, a sort of list item); in HTML, the **OL** element cannot appear within most paragraph-level elements, but only between them.

If you were writing general formating software (rather than database or other types of software), you would be able to process an ordered-list element with roughly the same level of effort for each of those DTDs.

TEI-Lite, however, would cause much more difficulty, because that DTD allows its **list** element to appear within emphasized phrases and even sectioning titles. In other words, you would have to be prepared to format an ordered list within a chapter title, a foreign phrase, a line of poetry, or even a cross-reference or hyperlink(!!). This level of flexibility is useful for certain types of analytical markup, but it will make generalized processing very difficult.

5.1.2   *Recursion*

Sometimes, an element can contain instances of its own type; at other times, it can include other elements that can contain instances of its own type (and so on). This **recursion** can make for clean and elegant document models, but it can cause difficulties for the designers of processing software—recursion makes it impossible to predict the depth of a document's structure.

 SGML Note: *In full SGML, you can use exclusion exceptions to avoid some types of recursion.*

The following fragment contains a classic example of recursion:

Recursive content model

```
<!ELEMENT quote (#PCDATA | quote)*>
```

Quotations can contain data or other quotations, as in the the following excerpt:

Recursion in document

```
<para>
  <quote>I ran into him on the subway,</quote> she said,
  <quote>and he turned to me and said <quote>I'm sorry about
  last year</quote>.</quote>
</para>
```

In North American practice, the outside **quote** element would appear surrounded by double quotation marks, and the inside **quote** element would appear surrounded by single quotation marks:

"I ran into him on the subway," she said, "and he turned to me and said, 'I'm sorry about last year'."

In British practice, the two types of quotation marks would be reversed:

'I ran into him on the subway,' she said, 'and he turned to me and said "I'm sorry about last year".'

In either case, however, it would rarely make sense to nest quotations more than three levels deep (a person quoting a second person quoting a third person)—past that point, readers probably will not be able to keep track of who is saying what.

When you are designing processing software for a recursive DTD, however, your software will need to be able to deal with arbitrarily deep hierarchies, even when they do not make sense:

- the software must have the ability to determine the depth of the recursion

- the software must be able to treat the data differently depending on the depth

- the software may have to enforce an arbitrary limit for the depth and report an error if a document exceeds that limit

Just as the processing software may reject a valid XML document that does not meet non-XML editorial constraints, it may have to reject a valid document with deep recursion, if that recursion would affect the program's work: XML itself provides no general way to limit or validate the depth of recursion.

The recursion in the above example was fairly obvious, since the element-type definition included itself directly in its content model. The following example is more subtle (see Figure 5–1):

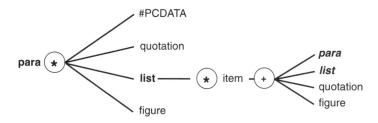

Figure 5–1   Hidden Recursion—An element type can contain instances of itself indirectly; if so, then the DTD imposes no limit on the depth of nesting, and the processing software will have to do its own error detection.

Hidden recursion

```
<!ELEMENT para (#PCDATA | quotation | list | figure)*>
<!ELEMENT list (item+)>
<!ELEMENT item (para | quotation | list | figure)+>
```

In fact, there are *two* examples of recursion here:

1. since a list consists of one or more items, and items can include lists, it is possible for lists to appear within other lists
2. since paragraphs can contain lists, lists contain items, and items can contain paragraphs, it is possible for paragraphs to appear within other paragraphs

In this case, software designers might not realize the problem until they begin to receive bug reports about incorrect output.

5.1.2.1 Examples from the Model DTDs

All of the model DTDs have recursive phrasal element types. For example, the HTML DTD contains the following declarations:

Recursive element types in HTML

```
<!ENTITY % fontstyle "TT | I | B | U | S | STRIKE | BIG |
                      SMALL">
<!ENTITY % phrase "EM | STRONG | DFN | CODE |
                   SAMP | KBD | VAR | CITE | ABBR | ACRONYM" >
<!ENTITY % special
   "A | IMG | APPLET | OBJECT | FONT | BASEFONT | BR | SCRIPT
    | MAP | Q | SUB | SUP | SPAN | BDO | IFRAME">
<!ENTITY % formctrl "INPUT | SELECT | TEXTAREA | LABEL |
                     BUTTON">
<!ENTITY % inline "#PCDATA | %fontstyle; | %phrase; |
                   %special; | %formctrl;">
<!ELEMENT CODE (%inline;)*>
<!ELEMENT EM (%inline;)*>
<!ELEMENT VAR (%inline;)*>
<!-- (etc.) -->
```

As a result, it is possible for a **CODE** element to contain another **CODE** element, either directly or through other phrasal element types. This arrangement leads to some simple and some fairly complex processing problems.

For example, it is fairly easy to decide how to create a printed rendition of an **EM** (emphasized phrase) element containing another **EM** element—simply toggle italics on or off, depending on their current state. It is trickier, though, to decide how to deal with a **CODE** (literal text) element within another **CODE** element. It is even less obvious how software extracting variable names should treat a **VAR** (variable) element within another **VAR** element.

Likewise, all of the model DTDs use recursive list and/or table models, where list and table element types can contain instances of themselves (or, in the case of MIL-STD-38784 and DocBook, of a **entrytbl** element that is recursive). As a result, none of the DTDs enforces an arbitrary limit on the depth of list or table nesting—a list could, in principle, be nested 100 levels deep or more.

For structural element types, the DTDs treat recursion differently. TEI-Lite allows recursive or nonrecursive sectioning elements. For example, a TEI-Lite document could model a chapter-section-subsection hierarchy in two ways. The first uses recursion:

Recursive sectioning elements in TEI-Lite

```
<div type="chapter">
  <div type="section">
    <div type="subsection">
      [...]
    </div>
  </div>
</div>
```

The second uses explicitly hierarchical elements:

Hierarchical sectioning elements in TEI-Lite

```
<div1 type="chapter">
  <div2 type="section">
    <div3 type="subsection">
      [...]
    </div3>
  </div2>
</div1>
```

Using the recursive **div** element from the first example, an author could create arbitrarily deep sections (sub-sub-sub-sub-sub-sub-sub-sub-subsections, for example), and processing software would have to be capable either of handling those sections or of reporting an error.

The ISO 12083, DocBook, and MIL-STD-38784 DTDs use only explicitly hierarchical element types for sections, whereas the HTML DTD does not contain sectioning elements at all (though it does use explicitly hierarchical section *titles*, such as **h1**, **h2**, etc.).

5.1.3   *Generic Element Types and Role Attributes*

Documents can become even less predictable if their DTD allows the use of *generic element types* and unconstrained *role attributes*. Consider, for example, the following three attribute definition list declarations:

Required role attribute

```
<!ATTLIST list
  type (ordered | unordered) #REQUIRED>
```

Optional role attribute

```
<!ATTLIST list
  type (ordered | unordered) #IMPLIED>
```

Defaulted role attribute

```
<!ATTLIST list
 type CDATA #IMPLIED>
```

The first definition is the simplest, because the processing software can trust the XML parser to ensure that the list type will always be specified as either ordered or unordered; the second is a little more difficult, because the processing application will have to assume a default if the attribute is not specified; but the third definition makes it difficult to write a comprehensive processing application at all, because the type attribute may assume any arbitrary value, and your software will have no easy way to determine how to handle arbitrary values: one author might set type to "ordered," for example, whereas another might set it to "numbered."

In other words, the more flexibility that the DTD provides for document authors, the harder it is to process the resulting documents.

Even in the third example, a information-processing specialist would at least know that the element type represented some sort of list and could fall back on a default format (like bullets) for any unrecognized type. DTDs that include *generic element types* rarely allow even that level of predictability. Consider the following definitions:

Generic element type

```
<!ENTITY % inline "#PCDATA | link | emph | extension">
<!ELEMENT para (%inline;)*>
<!ELEMENT extension (%inline;)*>
<!ATTLIST extension
 class CDATA #REQUIRED>
```

A *generic element type* such as **extension** is very convenient for document authors, because they can use it to create new structures. It complicates processing, however, in three ways:

1. every time an author supplies a previously unused value for the `class` attribute, you must rewrite the processing software
2. the XML or SGML parser can enforce no structural constraints, so your software must be designed to deal with arbitrary constructions (and to validate the structure itself in some less formal way)
3. there is no obvious default treatment for the generic elements (other than simply ignoring them)

 SGML Note: *Technically, the SGML standard actually prohibits generic element types, since an element type must describe the element; however, an SGML parser cannot enforce this requirement, because it cannot know the author's intention.*

5.1.3.1   Examples from the Model DTDs

The previous chapter has already discussed generic element types (Section 4.3.4, page 142) and role attributes (Section 4.3.3, page 140) from the perspective of usability and flexibility; this section discusses them from the perspective of processing.

When you are writing software to process a DocBook document, you will have to assume that the authors will not abuse role attributes in ways that will affect your software. For example, look again at this example from the last chapter:

Role attributes in DocBook

```
<Section Role="joke">
<Title>Chicken Joke</Title>

<Para Role="setup">Why did the chicken cross the road?
</Para>

<Para Role="punchline">To get to the other side.</Para>

</Section>
```

If you were writing formatting software, you might be able simply to ignore the `role` role attribute and treat the section and the paragraphs in the same way as all other sections and paragraphs; on the other hand, the authors might have expected you to format punch lines differently (say, by printing them upside-down at the bottom of the page). It is unlikely that the designer of general DocBook formatting software would have anticipated this particular use of the role attribute—instead, the software would have to report a warning or even an error here, to signal that it might be losing information.

The same problem can occur with TEI-Lite documents, though on a smaller scale.

5.1.4   *Authors' Modifications*

Some DTDs are designed so that authors can modify them by declaring parameter entities in the internal subset (where they will take priority over any declarations in the external subset). These parameter entities might alter content models, change element-type names, or trigger the inclusion or exclusion of marked sections in the external DTD.

Take a look at this simple example:

Extensible DTD fragment

```
<!ENTITY % ext.inline "">
<!ENTITY % inline "#PCDATA | emph | xref | list
%ext.inline;">

<!ELEMENT para (%inline;)*>
```

This fragment belongs to an **extensible DTD**—one that allows authors to make modifications for local requirements without editing the original DTD. In this case, if authors want to add the new element type, **date**, to the `inline` content model, they can do so by declaring the `ext.inline` parameter entity in the declaration subset (where it will take precedence over the definition in the DTD), and then by defining the new **date** element type itself:

Adding a new inline element type

```
<!DOCTYPE doc SYSTEM "doc.dtd" [
  <!ENTITY % ext.inline " | date">
  <!ELEMENT date (#PCDATA)>
]>
```

Now, after entity reference resolution, the content model for the **para** element type is

New content model

```
#PCDATA | emph | xref | list | date
```

instead of

Old content model

```
#PCDATA | emph | xref | list
```

In this situation, your processing software will have to deal with a new **date** element in all of the contexts where it might appear.

DTDs may also allow authors to use parameter entities for more general configuration, perhaps for including modules or selecting different versions of the same DTD. In the following example, the **list-item** element will have a different content model depending on whether the simpleLists or parameter entity is declared with the value "INCLUDE" or "IGNORE":

Ignorable section in DTD

```
<!ENTITY % simpleLists "INCLUDE">
<![%simpleLists;[
  <!ENTITY % listitem.content "(#PCDATA)">
]]>
<!ENTITY % listitem.content "(para | list | table |
                             figure)+">

<!ELEMENT list (listitem+)>
<!ELEMENT listitem %listitem.content;>
```

Since the first entity declaration is the one that counts, if `simpleLists` is declared with the value "INCLUDE" (as it is by default), the `listitem.content` entity will have the following value:

Default entity value

```
#PCDATA
```

However, the author might declare it in the declaration subset with the value "IGNORE":

Overriding default

```
<!DOCTYPE doc PUBLIC "-//local//DTD Generic Document//EN"
"doc.dtd" [
  <!ENTITY simpleLists "IGNORE">
]>
```

In this case, the `listitem.content` entity will have the following value:

Modified entity value

```
(para | list | table | figure)+
```

In such cases, your processing software has to deal with *all* possible combinations of parameter entities—in effect, with two or more related but distinct document types. Even with only five such parameter entities available for configuration, 32 different versions of the DTD are possible, and that number will double with each additional configuration parameter entity. (If you enjoy doubling games, then you probably already know that 16 configuration parameter entities would allow 65,536 possible document types, while 20 configuration parameter entities would allow 1,048,576 possible document types.)

5.1.4.1   Examples from the Model DTDs

As mentioned above, in both XML and SGML, the first entity declaration is the one that counts. As a result, authors can override the values of parameter entities in an external DTD by declaring the same entities in the document-type declaration subset.

For example, the ISO 12083 DTD declares the following parameter entity for floating elements:

ISO 12083 parameter entity

```
<!ENTITY % i.float  "figgrp|footnote|note">
```

An author could add a new element type **chgreq** (change request)—and include it wherever the other floating elements appear—simply by overriding the i.float parameter entity as follows:

Overriding ISO 12083 parameter entity

```
<!DOCTYPE book PUBLIC "ISO 12083:1993//DTD Book//EN"
"book.dtd" [
  <!ENTITY % i.float "figgrp|footnote|note|chgreq">
  <!ELEMENT chgreq (#PCDATA)>
]>
```

Because the parser reads the declaration subset first, this entity declaration takes precedence over the one in the DTD. The ISO 12083, DocBook, MIL-STD-38784, and HTML DTDs all use parameter entities for content models and attribute definition list declarations, so authors can modify them in unpredictable ways in the declaration subset. The full TEI DTD also uses parameter entities in this way, but the TEI-Lite DTD does not.

This kind of modification is awkward to make: the i.float parameter entity has to reproduce all of the content from its original declaration, and the element-type declaration for **chgreq** cannot use any of the parameter entities in its content that are declared in the DTD, since those parameter entities do not yet exist. (You could work around this second problem by referencing the DTD explicitly with an external parameter entity in the *middle* of the declaration subset, with the entity declarations before it and the element-type declarations after it.)

To deal with the first problem, the DocBook and full TEI DTDs (but again, not TEI-Lite) use two parameter entities rather than one for each class of content. For example, for paragraph-related element types, DocBook has the following declarations:

DocBook parameter entity

```
<!ENTITY % local.para.class "">
<!ENTITY % para.class
   "FormalPara|Para|SimPara %local.para.class;">
```

By default, `local.para.class` is empty, but authors could override it in the declaration subset to include their own paragraph-related elements without having to reproduce the entire definition of `para.class`:

Overriding DocBook parameter entity

```
<!DOCTYPE book PUBLIC "-//Davenport//DTD DocBook 3.0//EN"
"docbook.dtd"[
   <!ENTITY % local.para.class "|newpara">
   <!ELEMENT newpara (#PCDATA)>
]>
```

Full TEI and DocBook have other customization mechanisms as well, including parameter entities for including or ignoring entire sections of the DTD and (in the case of full TEI) parameter entities for renaming any arbitrary element types.

Clearly, even though they provide flexibility, these mechanisms can make DocBook and full TEI documents very difficult to process—if every author, or at least every project, uses what turns out to be a slightly (or substantially) different variant of the DTD, then you cannot write a single program to process or format arbitrary instances.

From this perspective, then, the choice to resolve all parameter entities in TEI-Lite was a very good one: unlike its parent, the TEI-Lite DTD is very difficult to modify in the declaration subset, and, as a result, TEI-Lite documents should be much more predictable (and thus easier to process).

5.1.5   *SGML: Placement of Data and Subdocument Entities*

Unlike XML, full SGML allows authors to place subdocument- and data-entity (*unparsed entity*) references anywhere they can place parsed-entity references. As a result, an author can insert a reference to a video clip (for example) at any arbitrary point in a document's content, and your processing software must attempt to deal with it at that point or must report an error.

All data entities have notations associated with them, and the processing application can use the notation to determine the type of data (and possibly some display parameters); however, since it cannot predict where these entities might appear, the processing requirements become more complicated.

It is possible, through editorial policy, to constrain the placement of entity and subdocument-entity references by using placeholders, as in the following example:

Placeholder for data entities

```
<!ELEMENT graphic - o EMPTY>
<!ATTLIST graphic
  ent ENTITY #REQUIRED>
```

The DTD can constrain and enforce the placement of the **graphic** element, and the processing software can simply report an error if a data entity reference appears elsewhere. Even here, however, SGML editors and parsers will not prevent authors from assigning an inappropriate type of entity (i.e., a subdocument entity) as the value of the `ent` attribute, nor will they prevent them from placing data entity references elsewhere if they wish: the processing software will be reponsible for detecting and reporting the error.

5.1.5.1   Examples from the Model DTDs

All of the model DTDs except HTML attempt to constrain the placement of external data entities by providing a (usually) empty element with an ENTITY attribute. For example, assume that you have declared an external data entity as follows:

External data entity declaration

```
<!NOTATION cgmbin PUBLIC "ISO 8632/3//NOTATION CGM Binary
text encoding//EN" >
<!ENTITY pic01 SYSTEM "pic01.cgm" NDATA cgmbin>
```

To include this graphic in an ISO 12083 document, you would use the following markup (note the SGML empty-element syntax):

Reference to data entity in ISO 12083

```
<artwork name="pic01">
```

To include it in TEI-Lite, you would use the following:

Reference to data entity in TEI-Lite

```
<figure entity="pic01"></figure>
```

Although there is no SGML mechanism to prevent authors from placing data-entity references wherever textual data is allowed, these element types allow at least some predictability—the DTDs can constrain the placement of graphics and other data entities to locations where they make sense.

Unlike the other model DTDs, HTML does not provide a container for data entities, chiefly because the major browsers do not support them. Instead, HTML uses an **IMG** (image) element with a CDATA attribute named src to specify an image's system identifier (A browser will guess at the notation based on the file extension.):

Reference to graphic URL in HTML

```
<IMG SRC="pic01.gif">
```

(Note that this example uses SGML empty-element syntax, instead of XML.)

5.2   Context

One of the greatest strengths—and strongest selling points—of XML and SGML is that the documents provide **context** for their data. In an XML document, you (or your software) can always know exactly where you are in the structural hierarchy and can trace your current element's ancestors right up to the root.

The context, however, will be only as good as your DTD allows. This section examines two of the most common situations where the context provided by the DTD design is essential for processing:

1. containers
2. implied attribute values

5.2.1   *Containers*

For many processing tasks, the context provided by the ancestors of an element is all you need. Here are some examples:

- your processing software can decide how to treat a heading element by checking to see if its immediate parent is a chapter, section, or subsection
- your processing software can decide how to treat a nested quotation by checking to see how many of its ancestors are also quotations
- your processing software can decide what sort of bullets to use for list items by checking how deeply the parent **list** element is nested

It is important, then, that the DTD provide this kind of context, by grouping related elements into **containers**—element types that can hold a group of related elements.

List items, for example, should all appear together in a single **list** container, the entire contents of a chapter (heading, paragraphs, sections, etc) should appear together in a single **chapter** container, and so on.

Consider, for example, the following definition for the root element of a simple book-oriented DTD (see Figure 5–2):

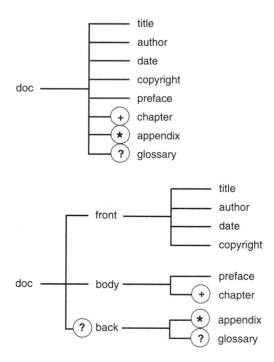

Figure 5–2 Using Containers—Containers can organize a document more clearly by collecting related information into easily-managed groups.

Flat element structure

```
<!ELEMENT doc (title, author, date, copyright,
          preface, chapter+, appendix*, glossary?)>
```

The **title**, **chapter**, and **glossary** elements all appear as siblings, even though they are not closely related. It would be difficult, for example, to grab all of the information for the title page and process it separately. In fact, there are three different types of information here:

1. front matter (title, author, date, and copyright)
2. the body of the book (preface and chapters)
3. back matter (appendices and glossary)

Your software will be able to process documents more easily if the DTD provides unambiguous containers for each type of information, as in the following example (see Figure 5–2):

Element structure with containers

```
<!ELEMENT doc (front, body, back?)>
<!ELEMENT front (title, author, date, copyright)>
<!ELEMENT body (preface, chapter+)>
<!ELEMENT back (appendix*, glossary?)>
```

With the containers, the program can easily gather all of the front matter (for example) and use it to create a title page or an external bibliographic record.

It can also be useful to collect repeated elements in a container. Consider, first, the following definition:

Flat structure

```
<!ELEMENT record (project, region*, contact)>
```

If the regions need to be collected and specially formatted (in a bulleted list, for example, or into a separate database record), it is much easier to process them if they appear inside an element of their own:

Container for repeated element type

```
<!ELEMENT record (project, region.group, contact)>
<!ELEMENT region.group (region+)>
```

Now you do not have to add extra code to your software to search forward and backward for the start and end of the sequence of **region** elements and to extract the elements from their siblings.

Finally, a container element is useful for specifying, in a single place, information that applies to all of its children: the container may have attributes whose values apply to all of the child elements, for example, or it may have top-level elements whose content applies to all of the children, as in the following example:

Container for grouping information

```
<!ELEMENT project.list (resp, project+)>
```

If the content of the **resp** element contains the name and contact information for the person (or people) responsible for the projects, then the same information does not have to be repeated within each **project** element—in this case, container elements simplify the work of both the authors and the information-processing specialists.

5.2.1.1   Examples from the Model DTDs

Four of the model DTDs use containers for grouping associated elements and for applying information to a group of elements, such as a chapter, list, street address, or block quotation. For example, MIL-STD-38784 uses the **figure** element type to hold a title together with one or more graphics, subfigure groups, or figure tables (note also the SGML exclusion exception to prevent recursion):

MIL-STD-38784 figure container

```
<!ELEMENT figure - - (title, ((subfig, subfig+) |
                             ((graphic, legend?) | figtable)+))
             -(figure | table | foldout)>
```

This scheme could be improved—it would make sense to group each **graphic** separately with its associated **legend**—but in general it puts all associated graphics or other figures together in the same container, and applies a single title to all of them.

The one DTD that does not use containers consistently is HTML, which provides no standard container element types for divisions. As a result, it is difficult to process or extract a section (for example) or a chapter from an HTML document.

An ISO 12083 document will mark chapters and sections with containers, as in the following example:

ISO 12083 chapter and section

```
<chapter>
 <title>Chapter Title</title>
 <p>[...]</p>
 <p>[...]</p>
 <section>
  <title>Section Title</title>
  <p>[...]</p>
  <p>[...]</p>
 </section>
</chapter>
```

If your processing software needs to extract a section from the document or to determine the context of a paragraph, it can do so easily. Now compare the same text in HTML:

HTML chapter and section

```
<h1>Chapter Title</h1>
<p>[...]</p>
<p>[...]</p>
<h2>Section Title</h2>
<p>[...]</p>
<p>[...]</p>
```

The paragraphs within the section are actually siblings of the chapter title.

5.2.2   *Implied Attribute Values*

DTDs often declare attributes with a default value of #IMPLIED: if authors leave the attribute value unspecified in the document, the processing software supplies its own default value.

When an unspecified attribute should always default to the same value, declaring it as #IMPLIED creates unnecessary extra work for the processing software—the software will have to supply the default value itself, rather than taking it directly from the document. Consider, for example, this definition:

No default value

```
<!ATTLIST section
  security.level NMTOKEN #IMPLIED>
```

If the security.level attribute were always 0 unless otherwise specified, it would be simpler (and less error-prone) to provide the default value in the DTD rather than hard-coding it in all of the processing software. The following modified definition provides the default value:

Simple default value

```
<!ATTLIST section
  security.level NMTOKEN "0">
```

Authors can now see more clearly what will happen when they leave the attribute value unspecified, and processing software can assume that a value will always be present for this attribute.

That said, sometimes the default value for an attribute is not fixed across all documents or is in some way dependent on its context in the document. Processing software might determine a default value from any of the following sources:

- the value of an attribute of an ancestor element (often the nearest one)

- the value of an attribute of a sibling element (often the closest left sibling)
- the attribute value or the content of a specific element in the document (possibly specified by an IDREF)
- system information (current time, date, host name, locale, user id, etc.)
- an external database query
- a hard-coded, project-specific default (that might differ among projects using the same DTD)

The first case is probably the most common: the processing software simply examines ancestors until if finds one that *does* have the attribute specified. Ideally, an element type higher up in the hierarchy should declare the attribute as #REQUIRED or provide a default value, so that the search will not fall off the top of the document tree. Consider, for example, the following very simple DTD:

Required value at top

```
<!ELEMENT doc (section+)>
<!ATTLIST doc
 security.level NMTOKEN #REQUIRED>

<!ELEMENT section (para+)>
<!ATTLIST section
 security.level NMTOKEN #IMPLIED>

<!ELEMENT para (#PCDATA)>
<!ATTLIST para
 security.level NMTOKEN #IMPLIED>
```

Since the security.level attribute is declared as #REQUIRED on the root element type, the processing software can trust that it will eventually find a default value in any element's ancestors.

Note that this technique assumes that the security level has the same meaning for different element types. XML neither requires nor enforces such an assumption, but as mentioned in Section 3.2, page 97, it is generally a good idea not to use the same attribute name for different purposes for different element types.

5.2.2.1   Examples from the Model DTDs

Because they are meant to be general, the model DTDs never specify an attribute as #REQUIRED (or provide a default value) near the top of the document hierarchy when the same attribute is #IMPLIED below (although TEI-Lite does use a full-SGML #CURRENT attribute for specifying the section type). As a result, when you are designing processing software, you cannot be certain that you will find a value for an element's unspecified #IMPLIED attribute specified for one of its ancestors.

The DTDs do occasionally provide default values for other attributes, however. For example, the DocBook DTD specifies the following attribute definition for the **step** element (other attributes omitted):

DocBook attribute

```
<!ATTLIST Step
  Performance (Optional|Required) "Required">
```

As a result, all steps will be required unless otherwise specified, and the processing software can assume that there will always be a value present for the performance attribute.

This approach has its risks, however. For example, the MIL-STD-38784 DTD declares the following parameter entity containing a single attribute definition:

Security attribute in MIL-STD-38784

```
<!ENTITY % secur "security (u | c | s) 'u'" >
```

For the security attribute, u stands for "unclassified," c stands for "confidential", and s stands for "secret."

When the DTD includes a reference to the secur parameter entity in its attribute definition list specification, it will have a security level that defaults to "unclassified" unless the author explicitly chooses a different level. The problem is that the DTD includes the attribute at many different levels, and that it will default to "unclassified" even if the element has an ancestor that is "confidential" or "secret."

Take a look, for example, at the following fragment:

Author's markup for MIL-STD-38784

```
<randlist security="s">
 <item>first item</item>
 <item>second item</item>
 <item>third item</item>
</randlist>
```

It would be a fair assumption that when an author specifies the value s ("secret") for the list, the list's items would be secret as well; however, because the attribute value defaults to u when unspecified, the processing software will actually see the list as follows:

Defaulted values for MIL-STD-38784

```
<randlist security="s">
 <item security="u">first item</item>
 <item security="u">second item</item>
 <item security="u">third item</item>
</randlist>
```

In other words, while the list as a whole is secret, all of its items are unclassified. If you were building processing software for MIL-STD-38784 documents, you would have to do additional work to ensure that you did not cause the military to release secret information because of an error in the DTD design; in this case, using an #IMPLIED value for the security attribute (with, perhaps, a #REQUIRED value on the document element) would have both saved work and protected national security.

5.3   DTD Analysis: Final Considerations

In the end, then, the three chapters in this part of the book have shown that document authors can learn a DTD more easily if the DTD meets the following criteria:

- it contains relatively few *logical units*
- it is internally consistent and similar to other structured documents that the authors have seen
- it uses names and structures that are relatively intuitive to the authors

On the other hand, after first learning the DTD, authors will be able to use it most effectively if it meets a different set of criteria:

- it demands relatively little physical effort to mark up a document
- it demands relatively little mental effort to choose among available *logical units* at different points in a document
- it is flexible enough to deal with a wide range of information structures

Some of these requirements are problematic or even inconsistent. Intuitiveness, for example, depends largely on the cultural, linguistic, social, and professional backgrounds of the authors—the larger the intended audience for the DTD, the less likely the DTD designers will be able to predict these backgrounds. Likewise, a more-constrained DTD may provide more guidance to authors, but it will do so at the cost of flexibility.

Even without considering processing requirements, then, DTD design or selection requires you to make a series of intelligent compromises. If your authors will be performing high-speed data entry, then avoiding physical and mental effort are your highest priorities, and you may choose to sacrifice flexibility, intuitiveness, and even internal consistency to achieve this goal; if, on the hand, your authors will be composing and revising their documents slowly and thoughtfully, then flexibility and intuitiveness are your highest priorities, and you may choose not to worry as much about overhead imposed by physical and mental effort.

Likewise, you may place greater emphasis on ease of learning and restriction of choice if your authors will have little time available for training, if they are volunteers, or if there is a high staff turnover; you may place a greater emphasis on ease of use and flexibility if your authors are highly-trained specialists who wish to create complex documents and will be working with the DTD over a long time.

The conflict between ease of learning and ease of use is actually greater, then, than the conflict between usability in general and ease of processing. You will be able to process a DTD's documents if it meets these criteria:

- it allows you to predict the structures that can and cannot appear in a document
- it provides for sufficient context to distinguish different logical units and to group related elements.

The first criterion makes the DTD harder to use—a more predictable DTD is generally a less flexible one—but it makes it easier to learn. The second criterion makes the DTD both harder to learn and harder to use—a DTD that provides more context contains more element types to learn and more context may require authors to enter more markup.

The next part of this book introduces several special, advanced topics in DTD design and analysis.

Part Three

The third part of this book examines several special, advanced issues in DTD design and maintenance:

- compatibility in different versions of the same DTD
- document disassembly and reassembly
- DTD customization

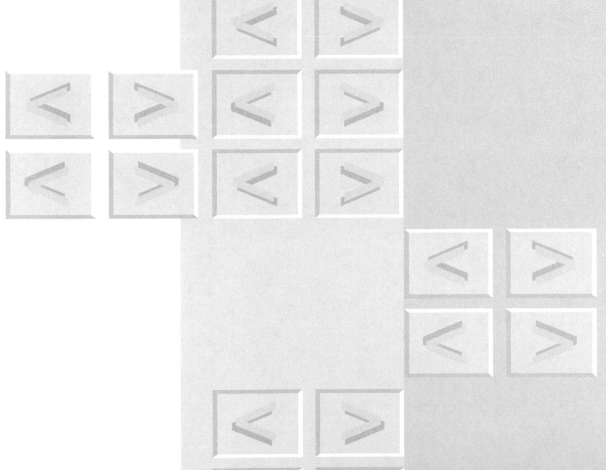

Advanced Issues in DTD Maintenance and Design

DTD Compatibility

Chapter 6

Like other types of software, XML and SGML DTDs evolve over time: they go through major and minor revisions, acquire new features, and lose old ones. All five of this book's model DTDs, for example, have been through several revisions since they first appeared.

XML or SGML document instances are closely tied to their DTDs, and even a simple change to the DTD can make existing documents invalid. To avoid this problem, some authors hard-wire their documents to a specific version of a DTD. An SGML DocBook document, for example, might begin like this (an XML document would also require a system identifier):

SGML version-specific document type declaration

```
<!DOCTYPE Book PUBLIC "-//Davenport//DTD DocBook 3.0//EN">
```

Even when new releases of DocBook come out, this document will always use version 3.0 of the DocBook DTD and thus will not run into parsing problems.

Freezing the DTD version used by a document does not always make business sense, however, for the following reasons:

- some documents need to be written and rewritten over years or even decades, and your Information Services department might not be interested in maintaining a different version of the DTD—together with all of the documentation and support files—for each document
- your suppliers, customers, or partners might require documentation that uses the newest version of the DTD
- future releases of a DTD may add new features that will allow your authors to do their work better or to adapt to a changing marketplace

If any of these conditions applies, then you will have to be ready to deal with the problem of DTD compatibility. This chapter cannot cover every detail of DTD compatibility—to do so would require a separate book—but it does introduce the most important aspects, organized into two groups:

1. structural compatibility (Section 6.1), covering the element structure described by the DTD (together with a note on attributes)
2. lexical compatibility (Section 6.2, page 203), covering the markup techniques used in individual documents

 SGML Note: *The chapter does not cover compatibility issues for some of full SGML's more obscure lexical features, such as* SHORTREF, RANK, DATATAG, *and* CONCUR.

6.1   Structural Compatibility

This section concentrates mainly on the element structure described by the DTD, while the next section—on lexical compatibility

(Section 6.2, page 203)—examines how individual XML or SGML documents can affect DTD compatibility through the use of common markup facilities like declarations in the document-type declaration subset. This section also contains subsections on attributes (Section 6.1.6, page 193) and SGML considerations (Section 6.1.7, page 198) as well as a discussion of the effects of changes in combination (Section 6.1.4, page 188).

The following three types of changes will make an element type's content model either more- or less-**restrictive**; in general, any change that makes the content model less restrictive can cause incompatibilities with previous versions of a DTD:

1. changes in repetition
2. changes in omissibility
3. changes in alternation

You can make changes like these to any element type's content model, and, for the most part, they can apply either to data or to element content (though XML's rules for the placement of character data are much stricter than the full-SGML rules).

SGML Note: *For SGML DTDs, you must also consider changes in ordering (Section 6.1.7.1, page 198). Specialists in regular expressions will know that you can express changes in ordering as changes in alternation; for the sake of simplicity, however, this book will keep the two separate.*

6.1.1   *Repetition*

There are two degrees of **repetition** allowed in a content model:

1. **non-repeatable**: at most, one instance of an element type or group may occur in an SGML or XML document

2. **repeatable**: more than one instance of an element type or group may occur in an SGML or XML document

To make a content particle repeatable, you use the occurrence indicators "*" or "+" immediately afterward. In the following example, the element type **name** is repeatable, so an **authors** element may contain more than one **name** element:

Repeatable content particle

```
<!ELEMENT authors (name+)>
```

To make a content particle non-repeatable, you use the occurrence indicator "?" or omit the occurrence indicator altogether. In the following example, the element type **name** is non-repeatable, so an **author** element may contain only one **name** element:

non-repeatable content particle

```
<!ELEMENT author (name)>
```

A repeatable item is always less **restrictive** than a non-repeatable item. As a result, the following hold true:

- if you change the repetition of a content particle from *non-repeatable* to *repeatable*, the change will be backward-compatible with existing documents
- if you change the repetition of a content particle from *repeatable* to *non-repeatable*, the change may not be backward-compatible with existing documents

For example, the MIL-STD-38784 DTD currently contains the following declaration:

Original MIL-STD-38784 declaration

```
<!ELEMENT figtable (tgroup+)>
```

In this content model, the element type **tgroup** is repeatable, so there may be one or more **tgroup** elements within a single **figtable**. If you were to remove the repetition, the content model would become *more* restrictive, because it would allow only one **tgroup**—any existing documents that already contained two or more **tgroup** elements in a **figtable** would be invalid:

Backward-incompatible change to MIL-STD-38784

```
<!ELEMENT figtable (tgroup)>
```

Elsewhere, the MIL-STD-38784 DTD contains the following declaration:

Original MIL-STD-38784 declaration

```
<!ELEMENT subfig ((graphic, legend?) | figtable)>
```

In this content model, the entire group "`((graphic, legend?) | figtable)`" is non-repeatable. If you were to add repetition, the content model would become *less* restrictive:

Backward compatible change to MIL-STD-38784

```
<!ELEMENT subfig ((graphic, legend?) | figtable)+>
```

Since existing documents could contain the group only once, and the new version of the DTD allows the group to appear one or more times, there is no construction valid with the original DTD that would not be valid with the new one.

6.1.2   *Omissibility*

There are three types of **omissibility** allowed in a content model:

1. **required**: the content particle must always be present
2. **optional**: the content particle may or may not be present
3. **forbidden**: the content particle may never be present

An optional content particle is always less restrictive than a required or a forbidden content particle. As a result, the following holds true:

- if you change the omissibility of a content particle from *required* or *forbidden* to *optional*, the change will be backward-compatible with existing documents
- if you change the omissibility of a content particle from *optional* or *forbidden* to *required*, the change may not be backward-compatible with existing documents
- if you change the omissibility of a content particle from *optional* or *required* to *forbidden*, the change may not be backward-compatible with existing documents

In other words, the only compatible omissibility change for a content particle in an existing content model is to *optional* from *required* or *forbidden*.

To make a content particle in a content model required, you can follow it either with no occurrence indicator (if it is non-repeatable) or with the "+" occurrence indicator (if it is repeatable). In the following example, the element type **name** is required (as well as repeatable), so at least one **name** element must appear in each **authors** element:

Required content particle

```
<!ELEMENT authors (name+)>
```

To make a content particle optional, you can follow it with the "?" occurrence indicator (if it is non-repeatable) or with the "*" occurrence indicator (if it is repeatable). In the following example, the element type **name** is optional (as well as repeatable), so it would be possible for zero **name** elements to appear in an **authors** element:

Optional content particle

```
<!ELEMENT authors (name*)>
```

To make a content particle forbidden, on the other hand, simply omit it from the content model.

For example, the HTML DTD currently contains the following declaration:

Original HTML declaration

```
<!ELEMENT TABLE (CAPTION?, (COL*|COLGROUP*), THEAD?, TFOOT?,
                TBODY+)>
```

In this content model, the **TBODY** element type is required, so at least one must appear. If you were to make the element type optional, the content model would become *less* restrictive, and the DTD would remain compatible with existing documents:

Backward-compatible change to HTML

```
<!ELEMENT TABLE (CAPTION?, (COL*|COLGROUP*), THEAD?, TFOOT?,
                TBODY*)>
```

Since existing documents will always have at least one **TBODY** (table body) element in a **TABLE**, and the new DTD allows zero or more, there is no construction valid with the original DTD that would not also be valid with the new one.

On the other hand, if you were to change the omissibility of **caption** so that it were required, the content model would become more restrictive, so it would not be backward-compatible:

Backward-incompatible change to HTML

```
<!ELEMENT TABLE (CAPTION, (COL*|COLGROUP*), THEAD?, TFOOT?,
                TBODY*)>
```

The original content model allowed the **CAPTION** element to be left out, so many existing HTML documents might not have it. If the new DTD requires it to appear, those documents will no longer be valid.

If you were to add a new optional element type **TITLE** to the content model, it would also be less restrictive:

Backward-compatible change to HTML

```
<!ELEMENT TABLE (TITLE?, CAPTION?, (COL*|COLGROUP*), THEAD?,
                 TFOOT?, TBODY*)>
```

Since the **TITLE** element did not appear in the original DTD, no valid existing documents will have it; since it is optional in the new DTD, its omission will not cause a parsing error.

If, however, you made the new element type required, the content model would become *more* restrictive, and the change would not be backward-compatible:

Backward-incompatible change to HTML

```
<!ELEMENT TABLE (TITLE, CAPTION?, (COL*|COLGROUP*), THEAD?,
                 TFOOT?, TBODY*)>
```

No document that is valid with the original DTD could have a **TITLE** element within a **table**, but every document that is valid with the new DTD *must* have a **TITLE** element within a table.

6.1.3   *Alternation*

Wherever a content model has a single content particle, it may include a list of alternative content particles instead (XML imposes restrictions if #PCDATA is involved); in fact, you can think of a single content particle as a list of one alternative, as in the case of **phone** in the following example:

A single alternative

```
<!ELEMENT contact-info (name, phone)>
```

If you needed to, you could introduce two other alternatives for the same position as **phone**:

Multiple alternatives

```
<!ELEMENT contact-info (name, (phone|email|fax))>
```

Now a **phone** element is still allowed after **name**, but authors of new documents may use **email** or **fax** instead.

There are, in fact, two types of changes that you can make to **alternation** in your content model (it is possible to make both at the same time):

1. add an alternative to a list
2. remove an alternative from a list

Adding an alternative makes a content model less **restrictive**, whereas removing an alternative makes a content model more restrictive. As a result, the following hold true:

- if you add an alternative, the change will be backward-compatible with existing documents
- if you remove an alternative, the change may not be backward-compatible with existing documents

Changing an alternative is the equivalent of removing one and adding another, so changing also makes the content model more restrictive (and thus backward-incompatible).

For example, consider the following DocBook declaration for a list of tables:

Original DocBook declaration

```
<!ELEMENT LoT ((%bookcomponent.title.content;)?, LoTentry*)>
```

In this example, no other alternatives are allowed for **LoTentry**. If you extended the alternatives to allow **LoTpart** instead, the content model would be less restrictive, and the change would be backward-compatible with existing documents:

Backward-compatible change to DocBook

```
<!ELEMENT Lot - o ((%bookcomponent.title.content;)?,
                  (LoTentry|Lotpart)*)>
```

Existing documents are allowed to have zero or more **LoTentry** elements at the end of an **LoT** element, and the new DTD also allows **LoTentry** in that position, so every document that is valid with the old DTD will also be valid with the new one.

The declaration for the **BookInfo** element type is a little more complicated (SGML exclusion exception removed):

Original DocBook declaration

```
<!ELEMENT BookInfo (Graphic | LegalNotice | ModeSpec |
            SubjectSet | KeywordSet | ITermSet |
                %bibliocomponent.mix; | BookBiblio)+>
```

This time, there is a list of alternatives that is required and repeatable. If you were to remove one of the alternatives from the list, the DTD would no longer be backward-compatible:

Backward-incompatible change to DocBook

```
<!ELEMENT BookInfo (Graphic | ModeSpec | SubjectSet |
  KeywordSet | ITermSet | %bibliocomponent.mix; |
  BookBiblio)+>
```

This declaration no longer allows the **LegalNotice** element to appear as an alternative in the content of **BookInfo**. Removing an alternative makes the content model *more* restrictive: as a result, any existing documents that use **LegalNotice** in that position will be invalid with the new DTD.

6.1.4   *Changes in Combination*

In summary, then, the following types of changes make a content model less restrictive, and are, as a result, backward-compatible:

■   changing the *repetition* of a content particle from non-repeatable to repeatable

- changing the *omissibility* of a content particle from required or forbidden (absent) to optional
- increasing the *alternation* of a content particle by adding an alternative

On the other hand, these changes make a content model *more* restrictive and are, as a result, backward-incompatible:

- changing the *repetition* of a content particle from repeatable to non-repeatable
- changing the *omissibility* of a content particle from required or optional to forbidden (absent)
- changing the *omissibility* of a content particle from forbidden (absent) or optional to required
- decreasing the *alternation* of a content particle by removing an alternative

6.1.4.1   Changes to the Same Content Particle

It is possible to apply more than one change to the same content particle. For example, consider the following declaration:

Original content model

```
<!ELEMENT a (b, (c, d)?, e)>
```

Currently, the content particle (**c, d**) is optional, non-repeatable, and has no alternatives. Now, look at this modified version:

Backward-incompatible change

```
<!ELEMENT a (b, (c, d)+, e)>
```

There are two changes to the content particle (**c, d**): the omissibility has changed from optional to required, and the repetition has changed from non-repeatable to repeatable; the first change makes the content model more restrictive, whereas the second makes it less.

Nevertheless, the two changes do not cancel each other out. Documents conforming to the first version are still allowed to contain *no* **c** or **d** elements within an **a** element, whereas documents conforming to the second version *must* contain **c** and **d** elements within an **a** element.

When you combine changes to a single content particle, then, any change that makes the content model more restrictive is backward-incompatible, even if there are also changes that make the content model less restrictive.

6.1.4.2 New Element Types

The changes described in this section apply only to existing content models. If you declare entirely new element types, their content models will not create backward incompatibilities.

Normally, however, you will need to attach the new element types to some point in your existing element structure, and that will require modifying the content model of at least one existing element type. For example, the previous version of your DTD might contain the following declaration for its front matter (see also Figure 6–1):

Original declaration

```
<!ELEMENT front (title, author, other)>
```

You might realize that you also need a date, so you declare some new element types:

New element types

```
<!ELEMENT date (year, month, day)>
<!ELEMENT year (#PCDATA)>
<!ELEMENT month (#PCDATA)>
<!ELEMENT day (#PCDATA)>
```

Since these element types did not appear at all in the previous DTD, no existing document can have used them, so nothing in their content models can affect backward compatibility; however, you do

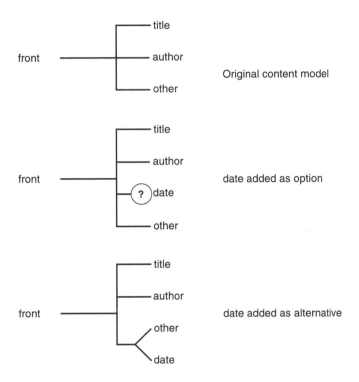

Figure 6–1   Adding a New Element Type—When you add a new element type to a content model, you can avoid backwards-incompatibilities by making the element optional or by allowing it to alternate with an existing content particle.

need to include them somehow in the existing content model for **front**:

Backward-incompatible change

```
<!ELEMENT front (title, author, date, other)>
```

In this first example, the omissibility for **date** has changed from *forbidden* (not in the content model) to *required*; that change makes the content model more restrictive, so it is backward-incompatible (no valid existing document can have an element that was not allowed by its DTD).

Backward-compatible change

```
<!ELEMENT front (title, author, date?, other)>
```

In this second example (see Figure 6–1), the omissibility for **date** has changed from *forbidden* (not in the content model) to *optional*; that change makes the content model less restrictive, so it is backward-compatible.

Alternative backward-compatible change

```
<!ELEMENT front (title, author, (other|date))>
```

The third example (see Figure 6–1) uses alternation rather than omissibility, adding **date** as an alternative to **other** in the final position of the content model. Adding an alternative makes the content model less restrictive, so this is also a backward-compatible change.

6.1.5   ANY *and* EMPTY

There are two further special cases for structural compatibility:

1. the content model ANY
2. the declared content EMPTY

In the content model ANY, every element type in the DTD (together with #PCDATA) is optional, is repeatable, and has every other element type as an alternative. As a result, it is the least restrictive of all content models, and almost any change you make will be backward-incompatible.

For example, the following two short DTDs are exactly equivalent:

DTD with ANY

```
<!ELEMENT doc (title, para+)>
<!ELEMENT title (#PCDATA)>
<!ELEMENT para ANY>
```

DTD with explicit content model

```
<!ELEMENT doc (title, para+)>
<!ELEMENT title (#PCDATA)>
<!ELEMENT para (#PCDATA|doc|title|para)*>
```

With the declared content EMPTY, every element type in the DTD (together with #PCDATA) is forbidden. At first glance, then, it might seem that adding optional content particles should be backward-compatible; consider, however, the following example:

Original declaration

```
<!ELEMENT break EMPTY>
```

The following declaration is backward-incompatible because of the way documents may represent empty elements:

Backward-incompatible change

```
<!ELEMENT break (desc?)>
```

EMPTY elements may have a special tag in XML and have no end tags in full SGML, but elements with content have end tags.

6.1.6 *Attribute Compatibility*

This section has concentrated on changes to the element structure of a document, but there are other areas that can cause backward incompatibility in a new revision of a DTD, such as the deletion of entity declarations, attribute definitions, notation declarations, short-reference maps, and link process definitions, among others. This subsection will concentrate on the most important of these, attribute definitions.

Like content models, attribute definitions can have the following properties:

1. repetition (Section 6.1.1, page 181)

2. omissibility (Section 6.1.6.2)

3. alternation (Section 6.1.6.3, page 196)

As a result, the rules in the previous subsections apply—with certain modifications—to attribute definitions as well as content models. Since attribute values are strongly typed, you will also need to consider changes in typing (Section 6.1.6.4, page 196).

6.1.6.1   Repetition

As explained earlier (Section 6.1.1, page 181), a repeatable content particle is less restrictive than a non-repeatable content particle, and, as a result, a change from non-repeatable to repeatable is backward-compatible.

Exactly the same observation applies to attribute definitions. In XML, there are three types of attribute types that imply repetition:

1. ENTITIES

2. IDREFS

3. NMTOKENS

Every one of these has a singular counterpart that does not allow repetition. For example, the following attribute definition has an attribute type of NMTOKENS, allowing more than one token to appear in its value:

Original declaration (with repetition)

```
<!ATTLIST bibref
   texts NMTOKENS #REQUIRED>
```

If you changed the definition from NMTOKENS to NMTOKEN, any existing documents that specified more than one token for the attribute's value would be invalid with your new version of the DTD:

Backward-incompatible change (without repetition)

```
<!ATTLIST bibref
  texts NMTOKEN #REQUIRED>
```

6.1.6.2   Omissibility

When you define an XML attribute with the default value #REQUIRED, then the author must specify a value for the attribute each time the corresponding element appears; if you provide any other default value, including #IMPLIED, then the attribute is optional, and the author does not have to specify a value; if the attribute has no definition, then it is, of course, forbidden.

As a result, any time you change the default value for an attribute of an element type that was in the previous version of the DTD, the change *must* make the attribute optional: you may change a #REQUIRED attribute to #IMPLIED (or provide another default value), or you may define a new attribute that is not #REQUIRED; any other change will create backward incompatibilities with existing documents.

Changes to Default Value

There is one other important point about default values. If you define an attribute and give it a literal value as its default value, any change to the literal value might create hidden incompatibilities; unfortunately, the older documents will still parse correctly, so the error may remain hidden until much later.

For example, consider the following declaration:

Original declaration

```
<!ATTLIST chapter
  security (public|classified|secret) "secret">
```

Any **chapter** element that does not specify a value for the attribute will receive the default value, "secret." In a different revision of the DTD, the attribute definition's default value might change:

Backward-incompatible change (different default value)

```
<!ATTLIST chapter
  security (public|classified|secret) "public">
```

Now, any **chapter** element that does not specify a value for the security attribute will receive the default value "public." This change would not cause a parsing error, but it would change the way that software interprets existing documents in possibly dangerous ways (in this case, it could cause a security breach).

6.1.6.3   Alternation

The attribute type in an attribute definition may be a list of tokens, as in the following example (the revision status of a chapter):

Attribute type with alternation

```
<!ATTLIST chapter
  revision (draft|final) "draft">
```

As with alternation in content models (Section 6.1.3, page 186), you may add tokens to the list, but you may not remove them without introducing backward incompatibility. For example, the following declaration would be backward-compatible with existing documents, since the list contains all of the previous tokens in addition to one new one:

Backward-compatible change (new alternative)

```
<!ATTLIST chapter
  revision (draft|approved|final) "draft">
```

6.1.6.4   Typing

Unlike content models, attribute definitions also have **typing** in their attribute types. This subsection has already dealt with repetition (Section 6.1.6.1, page 194), so plural forms such as IDREFS and ENTITYS will be ignored here.

The most restrictive types of attributes are those with the following attribute types:

- ENTITY
- IDREF
- ID
- NOTATION
- a token group

These are all mutually exclusive and (together with some plural counterparts) represent the strongest typing available for attributes in XML.

The attribute type NMTOKEN is less restrictive than any of these and can cover values allowed by any of them. Finally, the attribute type CDATA is the most general of all and broad enough to cover any attribute value; however, CDATA attributes will have most of their whitespace preserved, so the save attribute value literal may give different results.

For example, the following attribute definition is very strongly typed:

Original declaration (strongly typed)

```
<!ATTLIST para
   src ENTITY #REQUIRED>
```

The only valid value for the src attribute is the name of an unparsed entity (in full SGML, the name of any general entity) declared in the DTD. The following declaration is slightly less restrictive:

Backward-compatible change (less strongly typed)

```
<!ATTLIST para
   src NMTOKEN #REQUIRED>
```

The value of the `src` attribute must still be a single token, but the token no longer has to be the name of a declared attribute. Finally, the following declaration is the least restrictive of all:

Backward-compatible change (weakly typed)

```
<!ATTLIST para
  src CDATA #REQUIRED>
```

Now the value of the `src` attribute may contain any characters allowed in an attribute value and is not restricted to a single token.

6.1.7   *SGML: Structural Compatibility*

The additional facilities available in full SGML also have implications for structural compatibility, in the following areas:

1. ordering
2. repetition of data
3. CDATA and RCDATA declared content
4. inclusion and exclusion exceptions
5. additional SGML attribute types

6.1.7.1   Ordering

In addition to *repetition*, *alternation*, and *omissibility*, full SGML allows the property of **ordering** in a content model:

1. **ordered** content: the content tokens, if present, must appear in the specified order
2. **unordered** content: the content tokens, if present, may appear in any order

To make two or more content tokens unordered, you use the "&" connector between them. In the following example, the elements

name and **institution** are unordered, so the **author** element may include **name** followed by **institution,** or **institution** followed by **name**:

Unordered content model

```
<!ELEMENT author - - (name & institution)>
```

To make two or more content tokens ordered, you use the " , " connector between them. In the following example, the element types **name** and **institution** are ordered, so the author element may include only **name** followed by **institution**, *not* **institution** followed by **name**:

Ordered content model

```
<!ELEMENT author - - (name, institution)>
```

An unordered sequence of content tokens is always less **restrictive** than an ordered sequence. As a result, the following hold true:

- if you change ordering of a sequence from *ordered* to *unordered*, the change will be backward-compatible with existing documents
- if you change the ordering of a sequence from *unordered* to *ordered*, the change may not be backward-compatible with existing documents

For example, the ISO 12083 Book DTD currently contains the following declaration:

Original ISO 12083 declaration (unordered)

```
<!ELEMENT figgrp - - (title? & fig*)>
```

In this content model, both the **title** and (multiple) **fig** elements may appear, but the order is not specified. If you were to change the content model to enforce the order, it would become *more* restrictive, and the DTD would no longer be guaranteed compatible with existing documents:

Backward-incompatible change to ISO 12083 (ordered)

```
<!ELEMENT figgrp - - (title?, fig*)>
```

If any existing document places the **title** element after one or more **fig** elements, the document will not be valid with the new DTD.

At the root, the ISO 12083 Book DTD contains the following declaration (inclusion exceptions omitted):

Original ISO 12083 declaration (ordered)

```
<!ELEMENT book - - (front, body, appmat?, back?)>
```

If, for some reason, you wanted to allow these top-level elements to appear in any order, you could make this content model unordered. It would become *less* restrictive, and the DTD would remain compatible with existing documents:

Backward-compatible change to ISO 12083 (unordered)

```
<!ELEMENT book - - (front & body & appmat? & back?)>
```

Since existing documents will always have the elements in the original order, and the new version of the DTD allows the same elements in any order, there is no construction in the original DTD that would not also be valid with the new one.

Ordering of Data

Unlike XML, full SGML allows you to put #PCDATA in an ordered or unordered sequence; to avoid problems with mixed content, however, you should should always include #PCDATA alone or as part of a repeatable OR group. For more information, see Section 1.2.3.5, page 16.

6.1.7.2 Repetition of Data

Repetition does not apply directly to character data, since character data are inherently repeatable, but in full SGML it can apply to a group that contains mixed content. For example, consider the following declaration from TEI-Lite:

Declaration from TEI-Lite

```
<!ELEMENT label - - (#PCDATA | ident | code | kw | abbr |
  address | date | name | num | rs | time | add | corr | del
  |gap | orig | reg | sic | unclear | emph | foreign | gloss
  |hi | mentioned | soCalled | term | title | ptr | ref |
  xptr | xref | anchor | s | seg | gi | formula)*>
```

This is the *only* way that you are allowed to include mixed content in XML, but full SGML would allow you to remove the repetition, so that either character data or an instance of one of the element types could appear in **label**, but not both:

Backward-incompatible change to TEI-Lite

```
<!ELEMENT label - - (#PCDATA | ident | code | kw | abbr |
  address | date | name | num | rs | time | add | corr | del
  | gap | orig | reg | sic | unclear | emph | foreign | gloss
  | hi | mentioned | soCalled | term | title | ptr | ref |
  xptr | xref | anchor | s | seg | gi | formula)>
```

Nevertheless, it is essential that groups containing mixed content *always* be repeatable, or else unpredictable parsing errors may occur. For more information, see Section 1.2.3.5, page 16.

6.1.7.3 CDATA and RCDATA Declared Content

In full SGML, the declared content CDATA or RCDATA changes SGML's delimiter recognition:

- in CDATA content, SGML recognizes only the ETAGO(</) delimiter (when followed by a name character)

- in RCDATA content, SGML recognizes only the ETAGO (</), CRO (&#), and ERO (&) delimiters (when followed by a name character)
- In regular content, SGML recognizes the ETAGO (</ before a name character), CRO (&#), ERO (&), STAGO (< before a name character), MDO (<!), and PIO (<?) delimiters, together with the MSC (]]), NET (/), and SHORTREF in some circumstances

Any change in declared content—or a change between declared content and a content model—may cause the parser to interpret some delimiters as data or some data as delimiters.

6.1.7.4   Inclusion and Exclusion Exceptions

Full SGML inclusion and exclusion exceptions affect omissibility. An inclusion exception makes an element type optional anywhere within an element and its children, even where not explicitly allowed by the content model. Removing an inclusion exception is always a backward-incompatible change, since it changes the omissibility from *optional* to *forbidden*.

An exclusion exception makes an element type forbidden anywhere within an element and its children, even where explicitly allowed by a content model or by an inclusion exception. Removing an exclusion exception is *always* a backward-compatible change, because any content allowed before still is allowed.

6.1.7.5   Additional SGML Attribute Types

Full SGML allows the following additional repeatable attribute types:

1. NAMES
2. NUMBERS
3. NUTOKENS

These are all less restrictive than the non-repeatable equivalents, NAME, NUMBER, and NUTOKEN.

Overall, full SGML offers the additional attribute types NUMBER, NUMBERS, NAME, NAMES, NUTOKEN, and NUTOKENS—all of these are more restrictive equivalents of NMTOKEN.

6.2   Lexical Compatibility

The previous sections' guidelines for structural compatibility (Section 6.1, page 180) are not enough to guarantee that a new version of a DTD will be backwards-compatible with all documents, because documents may contain lexical features that interact with the (external) DTD:

1. XML and SGML documents can declare entities in their document-type declaration subsets

2. XML and SGML parsers treat whitespace differently in mixed content and in element content

6.2.1   *Entities*

Both XML and SGML documents may declare new entities (along with notations, elements, and attribute lists) in their document-type declaration subsets. Because entity declarations in the subset take precedence over entity declarations in the external DTD, the results may be unpredictable. For example, the following document-type declaration contains in its subset a parameter entity declaration for confidential:

Document type declaration with parameter entity

```
<!DOCTYPE book SYSTEM "doc.dtd" [
  <!ENTITY % confidential "INCLUDE">
]>
```

The declaration of the parameter entity `confidential` takes precedence over any declaration of the same parameter entity in the external DTD.

Sometimes DTD implementors deliberately use this mechanism to allow users to reconfigure a DTD (see Chapter 8); in that case, with luck and good documentation, there will be no compatibility problems. Unfortunately, DTDs also declare parameter entities for internal use only, and those parameter entities share the same name space.

For example, the ISO 12083 book DTD uses the parameter entity `pub` internally to group all element types that can appear in the **pubfront** element:

ISO 12083 sample

```
<!ENTITY % pub "sponsor | contract | reprint | cpyrt | date |
                pubname | location | confgrp | avail">
<!ELEMENT pubfront ((%pub;)|(%pub.ph;))* >
```

There is no standard way to prevent authors from inadvertently overriding this value in their internal subsets. If an author were to declare a parameter entity `pub` for another purpose, then its value would override the original declaration and would alter the content model for **pubfront** in the ISO 12083 book DTD:

Incompatibility in internal subset

```
<!DOCTYPE book PUBLIC "ISO 12083:1993//DTD Book//EN"
"book.dtd" [
  <!ENTITY % pub "INCLUDE">
]>
```

With luck, any such problems in existing documents will show up quickly. If, however, your new revision of the DTD contains any *new* entity declarations, there is no easy way to be certain that the entity name does not conflict with one already used by an existing document's subset. For example, after noticing the error, the author might have changed the above declaration by renaming pub to public:

Renamed parameter entity

```
<!DOCTYPE book PUBLIC "ISO 12083:1993//DTD Book//EN" [
  <!ENTITY % public "INCLUDE">
]>
```

This declaration will cause no problems, because the current version of the ISO 12083 book DTD uses no parameter entity called public; however, a new version of the DTD might introduce a parameter entity with the same name to hold a different type of information. In that case, the declaration in the existing document's subset would override the declaration in the new revision of the DTD, causing further problems. In general, *any* declaration of new entities can cause backward incompatibilities.

You might be able to prevent this problem by reserving a standard prefix for all of your parameter entities (such as book-). You can ask authors to avoid declaring any parameter entities beginning with that prefix, though there is no way to enforce the policy without designing customized software.

6.2.2   *Whitespace*

Normally, XML and SGML treat whitespace in element content as ignorable, but treat most whitespace in mixed content as significant (full SGML ignores some record ends). For example, consider the following element-type declaration (see also Figure 6–2):

Sample declaration with element content

```
<!DOCTYPE contacts (name|email)*>
```

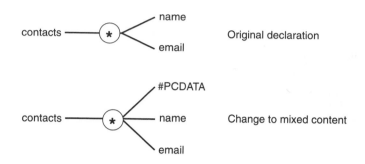

Figure 6–2 Whitespace Compatibility—Adding #PCDATA to a content model changes the treatment of whitespace in an existing document.

Because **contacts** can contain only elements, the following two samples will produce identical output from some XML and all SGML parsers:

Whitespace around subelement

```
<contacts>    <name>David Megginson</name>    </contacts>
```

No whitespace around subelement

```
<contacts><name>David Megginson</name></contacts>
```

Introducing #PCDATA in the same content model should be a backward-compatible change, because it allows everything that was allowed before; however, once an element type has mixed content, XML considers all of the whitespace in it to be significant (see Figure 6–2):

Sample declaration with mixed content

```
<!DOCTYPE contacts (#PCDATA|name|email)*>
```

Now, XML parsers will consider any whitespace that appears before and after elements within **contacts** to be significant, so the results of formating or otherwise processing the document could be surprisingly different, even though the parser will not report an error.

6.2.3   *SGML: Lexical Compatibility*

If you are working with full SGML instead of XML, you must also consider two other lexical compatibility problems:

1. full SGML documents can omit start and end tags in a DTD-dependent way
2. SGML uses different record-end handling in mixed content than it does in element content

6.2.3.1   Markup Minimization

If an SGML declaration specifies OMITTAG YES, and the element declaration's omitted tag minimization explicitly allows omission, then document authors may leave out start or end tags where the omission will not cause ambiguity. A small change to a DTD, however, can affect where omission will produce an error.

Start-Tag Omission

Authors may omit start tags if all of the following criteria apply (see ISO 8879:1986, clause 7.3.1.1):

1. exactly one element type is required at that point in the document, and all others (if any) are optional
2. the element type has no required attributes (you would have to specify a value in the start tag)
3. the element type does not have declared content, like CDATA
4. the element type is not declared EMPTY

Any change to your DTD that might alter one of these conditions may be backward-incompatible with existing documents that use markup minimization. For example, consider the following small DTD:

Original declarations

```
<!ELEMENT chapter - o (title, para+)>
<!ELEMENT title o o (#PCDATA)>
<!ELEMENT para - o (#PCDATA)>
```

Since a title must appear at the beginning of a chapter, and a paragraph must follow the title, it is permissible to omit the start and end tags for a title:

Title with omitted tags

```
<chapter>
This is the title
<para>First paragraph...</para>
</chapter>
```

According to the omissibility (Section 6.1.2, page 183) rules introduced earlier, a change in omissibility from *required* to *optional* should be backward-compatible, but because of the markup peculiarities in this document, it is not:

Backward-incompatible change

```
<!ELEMENT chapter - o (title?, para+)>
```

Now that the chapter title is optional, the SGML parser will assume that the missing start tag belongs to a **para** (which *is* required). When it finds the `</title>` end tag, it will report a parsing error.

Because of hidden dangers like this, tag omission is rarely a good idea in SGML, and XML quite rightly bans it.

End-Tag Omission

Authors may omit end tags if all of the following criteria apply (see ISO 8879:1986, clause 7.3.1.2):

1. the document has ended
2. the end tag for an ancestor element appears

3. an element begins that is not allowed in the current element

Any change to your DTD that might affect the third condition may be backward-incompatible with existing documents that use markup minimization. For example, consider the following declaration:

Original declaration

```
<!ELEMENT para - o (#PCDATA|quot|emph)*>
```

Since the element type **list** is not allowed in the content model of **para**, it is possible to omit the `</para>` end tag before the beginning of a list:

Omitted end tag for paragraph

```
<para>This is a paragraph
<list>
<item>item 1</item>
<item>item 2</item>
</list>
```

According to the alternation (Section 6.1.3, page 186) rules given earlier, the addition of an alternative should be backward-compatible, but because of the markup peculiarities in this document, it is not:

Backward-incompatible change

```
<!ELEMENT para - o (#PCDATA|quot|emph|list)*>
```

Now that a list is allowed *within* a paragraph, the start tag for the list will not end the **para** element. The parser will now (mistakenly) assume that the list is a child of the paragraph instead of a sibling and may generate an error (depending on what appears next in the document).

You can work around this problem by fully normalizing every existing document before using it for the first time with each new DTD revision, but such a process could be expensive to implement and difficult to maintain, especially outside of a small, tightly-controlled environment. Again, the best strategy is to design your original DTD so that it does not permit tag omission at all by always requiring start tags and always requiring end tags for non-EMPTY elements.

6.2.3.2   Record Ends

Normally, a full SGML parser will ignore record ends in certain locations:

1. immediately after a start tag in mixed content and element content
2. immediately before an end tag in mixed content and element content
3. between elements in element content only

As a result, from an SGML parser's point of view, the following two DocBook paragraphs will be identical:

DocBook paragraph

```
<Para>This is a paragraph.</Para>
```

DocBook paragraph (ignored record ends)

```
<Para>
This is a paragraph.
</Para>
```

In the second example, the parser will ignore the record end after the opening `<Para>` tag and before the closing `</Para>` tag, so the data will be identical to the data in the first example.

There is a difficulty, however (a known bug that is being fixed in the revision of ISO 8879): a full SGML parser decides whether a record end is data *before* it decides whether to ignore it (based on the content model):

1. if #PCDATA is allowed *anywhere* in the content model, the parser assumes that a record end is data (possibly to be ignored)
2. if #PCDATA is not allowed *anywhere* in the content model, the parser assumes that a record end is not data

These rules might cause compatibility problems, then, if you revise a DTD by adding #PCDATA to any content model that does not already have it. For example, consider the following element declaration from MIL-STD-38784:

Original declaration from MIL-STD-38784

```
<!ELEMENT acronym - - (def, term) -(acronym | %exclus;)>
```

Authors might ask you to modify the declaration so that they can enter the term directly without creating an element for it:

Backward-incompatible change to MIL-STD-38784

```
<!ELEMENT acronym - - (def?, (term|#PCDATA)) -(acronym |
                       %exclus;)>
```

According to the alternation (Section 6.1.3, page 186) rules introduced earlier, adding an alternative should be a backward-compatible change—after all, all existing documents will have a **def** element followed by a **term** element, and that sequence is still allowed by the new content model.

However, since #PCDATA is now allowed in the content model, the SGML parser will treat record ends as data. For example, an existing document might have the following markup:

Element content

```
<acronym>
 <def>Standard Generalized Markup Language</def>
 <term>SGML</term>
</acronym>
```

This is perfectly acceptable with the original declaration, because **acronym** has only element content, so the SGML parser will treat the record ends after the `<acronym>` start tag, between the **def** and **term** elements, and before the `</acronym>` end tag as insignificant whitespace.

With the new element declaration, however, these record ends all become data, and each one will cause a parsing error if `#PCDATA` is not allowed at that point. For more information on the problems associated with mixed content, see Section 1.2.3.5, page 16.

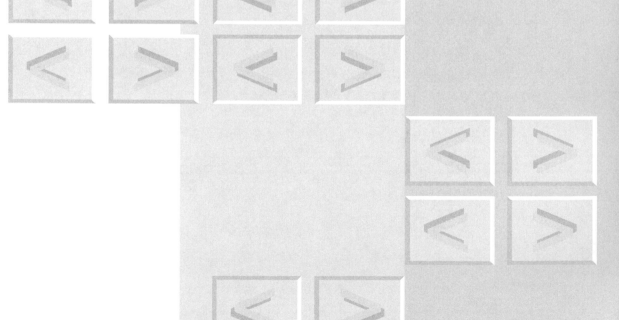

Exchanging Document Fragments

If you are an individual author working on a single text, you will often choose to edit your whole text as a single physical unit (such as a disk file—XML and full SGML call these units **external entities**, no matter how you store them). When you need more flexibility, you can break your document down into multiple entities (see Figure 7–1):

Document instance as a single entity

```
<!DOCTYPE book PUBLIC "-//Megginson//DTD Book//EN"
                       "book.dtd">

<book>
 <chapter>
  <title>Overview</title>
  [...]
 </chapter>
 <chapter>
  <title>Installation</title>
  [...]
 </chapter>
 <chapter>
  <title>Troubleshooting</title>
  [...]
 </chapter>
</book>
```

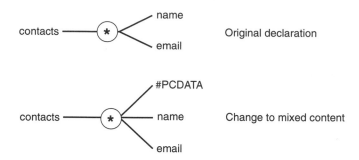

Figure 7–1   One Document as Multiple Entities—A single logical document may consist of many entities (the external DTD subset is actually an entity itself).

SGML document as multiple entities

```
<!DOCTYPE book PUBLIC "-//Megginson//DTD Book//EN"
"book.dtd" [
 <!ENTITY overview SYSTEM "overview.xml">
 <!ENTITY installation SYSTEM "install.xml">
 <!ENTITY troubleshooting SYSTEM "trouble.xml">
]>
<book>
 &overview;
 &installation;
 &troubleshooting;
</book>
```

In the second example, the chapters themselves reside in the entities named `overview.xml`, `install.xml`, and `trouble.xml`.

There are three important advantages to breaking the document down like this:

1. you can store each chapter separately in a revision management system
2. you can reuse the same chapter in another book, simply by including a reference to the same entity
3. you can exchange individual chapters with other people

For the author that I mentioned at the beginning of the chapter, the second and third considerations are not so important: if the author is writing a single, stand-alone text, then information reuse and entity exchange hardly matter.

Often, however, the second and third considerations—information reuse and information exchange—are exactly the reasons that a large organization chooses to use a structured document standard. Consider these users:

- an aircraft manufacturer that creates hundreds of thousands of pages of documentation for each model of aircraft, sharing the work among a team of dozens or hundreds of technical writers, each responsible for a specific part of a manual
- a scientific publisher that sends articles out to external writers and editors, then incorporates them back into a single journal
- a regulatory agency that collects regulations and reports from other organizations and assembles them into different publications

Each of these users needs to be able to pull large documents apart into smaller fragments, then to put the pieces back together again. Organizations such as these often purchase large, XML and/or SGML-aware document-management systems to handle this work internally (using proprietary techniques), but those systems cannot help if the fragments need to leave the premises; furthermore, the fact that the systems use proprietary techniques negates one of the greatest fundamental advantages of XML and SGML: the ability to exchange documents among different software packages running on different platforms.

Unfortunately, both XML and SGML define rules for parsing only complete documents, not for parsing individual text entities. Some commercial software tools provide work-arounds for this problem, but because they are not standardized, they do not allow free exchange.

In this chapter, I introduce three general strategies for exchanging fragments of XML or SGML documents:

1. treating the fragment as a stand-alone document
2. reparenting in a dummy document
3. constructing a document out of other complete documents

There are three areas that each approach must address:

ANCESTORS AND SIBLINGS
How will the recipient's software know the fragment's context in the document?

CROSS-REFERENCES
How will the recipient's software resolve cross-references to other parts of the document?

ENTITIES
How will the recipient's software know what entities are declared for the fragment's parent document?

This chapter will show how you can handle these problems using each of the approaches.

7.1   Editing Fragments as Stand-Alone Documents

If you deliver a fragment of an XML or SGML document to an author, the most obvious thing for the author to do is simply to add a new *document-type declaration* to the beginning and try parsing it with the original DTD.

For example, an author might receive a fragment of an ISO 12083 book:

ISO 12083 fragment

```
<chapter id="repell">
<title>Insect Repellants</title>
[...]
</chapter>
```

The document-type declaration for the entire document might have looked like this:

Original document-type declaration

```
<!DOCTYPE book PUBLIC "ISO 12083:1993//DTD Book//EN"
"book.dtd">
```

If the author simply creates a new document-type declaration with **chapter** as the document element, and prepends the declaration to the fragment, then the fragment *may* parse:

New document-type declaration for fragment

```
<!DOCTYPE chapter PUBLIC "ISO 12083:1993//DTD Book//EN"
"book.dtd">
<chapter id="repell">
<title>Insect Repellants</title>
[...]
</chapter>
```

To be more specific, the fragment will parse correctly as a stand-alone document only if the fragment meets the following conditions:

■ the fragment makes no cross-references—using IDREF attributes—to parts of the document outside of the fragment

■ the fragment does not include any references to entities
that are not declared in the external DTD

SGML Note: *In full SGML, this approach will also fail if
the fragment uses instances of any element types that were
declared as inclusion exceptions on an ancestor element, unless
they are also explicitly allowed by the content model (the ISO
12083 Book DTD declares the element types figgrp, footnote, and
note as inclusion exceptions on the root book element type, but not
on chapter).*

These are the types of caveats that give software engineers nervous
breakdowns: this approach might work correctly with the first 49
sample fragments and then fail on the 50th. In this section, I will
introduce strategies for dealing with these problems for stand-alone
fragments, and then in each of the following sections (for the other
approaches) I will discuss the same problems under the same
headings.

7.1.1   *Ancestors and Siblings*

The stand-alone approach provides no structural context for a fragment. The lack of context, in itself, will not bother the parser; however, authors will not know where or how their fragment fits into the
overall document. Is it the first chapter or the last? In a recursive
DTD, how deeply is it nested?

7.1.2   *Cross-References*

A more serious problem with stand-alone fragments appears for
cross-references. Most existing DTDs (HTML is an obvious

exception) manage internal cross-references using ID/IDREF pairs; however, individual divisions of a document (such as an article, chapter, or task) will frequently make cross-references to *other* divisions:

Cross-references in original document

```
<Chapter Id="disassembly">
 <Title>Disassembly of the Radio</Title>
 [...]
</Chapter>

<Chapter Id="reassembly">
 <Title>Reassembly of the Radio</Title>
 <Note>For information on disassembly, see <Xref
 Linkend="disassembly"/></Note>
 [...]
</Chapter>
```

In this example, using DocBook, the Linkend attribute for the **XRef** element is an IDREF pointing to the element with the ID "disassembly," which happens to be to a different chapter. Now, if you remove the second chapter and make it into a stand-alone fragment, the cross-reference will no longer be valid:

Unresolved cross-reference in fragment

```
<!DOCTYPE Chapter PUBLIC "-//Davenport//DTD Docbook 3.0//EN"
                         "docbook.dtd">

<Chapter Id="reassembly">
 <Title>Reassembly of the Radio</Title>
 <Note>For information on disassembly, see <XRef
 Linkend="disassembly"/></Note>
 [...]
</Chapter>
```

The parser will report a validation error because no element with the ID "disassembly" appears in the stand-alone fragment.

There are two solutions to this problem:

1. create a new version of the DTD, changing all IDREF attributes to NMTOKEN attributes (or NAMES in full SGML)

and all IDREFS attributes to NMTOKENS attributes (or NAMES in full SGML)

2. create a new EMPTY element type as a placeholder

7.1.2.1   Changing IDREFs

For the first solution, you simply edit the DTD to change the attribute types IDREF and IDREFS to NMTOKEN and NMTOKENS and then ship the modified DTD with the fragment.

 SGML Note: With full SGML, you can use NAME or NAMES to provide exactly the same lexical constraints as IDREF and IDREFS.

For example, your original DTD might have contained a declaration like this:

Original declaration

```
<!ATTLIST link
    target IDREF #REQUIRED>
```

For a stand-alone fragment, you would create a modified DTD with the following declaration:

Revised declaration for fragment

```
<!ATTLIST link
    target NMTOKEN #REQUIRED>
```

This approach has the advantage of not requiring changes to the fragment itself—you make the changes once, up front, by creating a modified version of each DTD. The disadvantages of this approach, however, are more serious:

1. if the author working on the fragment adds cross-references, the author will not know whether they actually point to ID values anywhere in the full document
2. if the author working on the fragment adds a new ID, the author will not know if that ID is already in use elsewhere in the full document

For example, an author might include a cross-reference to a chapter with the ID "catalogue" instead of "catalog", or the author might create a new section with the ID "troubleshooting" when a section with the same ID already exists in a different chapter that is not included in the fragment. These errors will not appear until you try to reincorporate the fragment into the parent document.

As a result, you should use this approach *only* when you know that the user will not be adding cross-references or IDs (preferably when you have designed an authoring tool that enforces that policy); otherwise, it will lead to serious problems that more than outweigh the ease of initial implementation.

7.1.2.2   Creating Placeholders

The second approach also involves modifying the DTD, this time to allow an EMPTY placeholder element type to hold existing IDs in the document. The element type for the empty placeholder might look something like this:

Placeholder for unresolved cross-references

```
<!ELEMENT bridge EMPTY>
<!ATTLIST bridge
  id ID #REQUIRED>
```

When you remove the fragment, you should arrange for a program to scan the full document and insert placeholder elements for all IDs found in other parts of the document:

Fragment with placeholders

```
<!DOCTYPE Chapter PUBLIC
                  "-//Megginson//DTD Modified DocBook//EN"
                  "modified-docbook.dtd">

<Chapter Id="reassembly">
 <Title>Reassembly of the Radio</Title>
 <Para>For information on disassembly, see <XRef
 Linkend="disassembly"/></Para>
 [...]
 <bridge id="disassembly"/>
 <bridge id="intro"/>
 <bridge id="partslist"/>
</Chapter>
```

When you reassemble the document, you can simply strip all of the **bridge** elements out again.

It might be tempting to include placeholders only for the IDs that have IDREFs already pointing to them from inside the fragment, but usually you should include *all* of the IDs in the document—that way, the author working on the fragment can create new IDREFs to other IDs without worrying that they are incorrect and can create new IDs without worrying about conflicts with existing IDs.

There are still dangers with this approach if two authors are working on different fragments at the same time, because both authors might add new IDs with the same names, or one author might delete an element that has a placeholder in the other author's fragment; again, the problems would not appear until you tried to reassemble the document. Generally, however, this is the best solution for the exchange of stand-alone fragments.

7.1.3 *Entities*

When you exchange document fragments, you will always need to deal with the problem of entities. If you use the same external DTD with the fragment as with its parent, then you will preserve the entity declarations from the external DTD itself, but you might lose the declarations from the internal subset. For example, consider the following document-type declaration for an ISO 12083 document:

Local entity declarations in original document

```
<!DOCTYPE book PUBLIC "ISO 12083:1993//DTD Book//EN"
"book.dtd" [
  <!ENTITY ph "Prentice-Hall">
  <!ENTITY authorphoto PUBLIC
      "-//Megginson//NDATA Picture of Me//EN"
      "david.tiff" NDATA tiff>
]>
```

If you were distributing a section as a stand-alone fragment, you would have to reproduce all of those entity declarations in the fragment's declaration:

Entity declarations reproduced for fragment

```
<!DOCTYPE section PUBLIC "ISO 12083:1993//DTD Book//EN"
"book.dtd" [
  <!ENTITY ph "Prentice-Hall">
  <!ENTITY authorphoto PUBLIC
      "-//Megginson//NDATA Picture of Me//EN"
      "david.tiff" NDATA tiff>
]>
```

At first glance, it might seem that you can save some effort by using two shortcuts:

1. include entity declarations only for the entities actually referenced in the fragment
2. include entity declarations only for general entities, since parameter entities are for use in DTDs rather than in document instances

In fact, neither of these will work unless you have tight control over the authors' software and working practices. If you include entity declarations only for the entities that the fragment currently references, the person working on the fragment might declare a new entity with the same name as one used elsewhere in the parent document; if you included declarations only for general entities, the author would not be able to use parameter entities to configure the DTD.

When you want to incorporate the fragment back into the parent document, you will have to check to see if the author has declared any new entities; if so, you will have to merge the declarations into those of the parent document. If two different authors have been working on different fragments, and each has declared a new entity with the same name and different values, you will have to rename one of them and replace all of the references in the fragment. Like IDs and IDREFs, entity declarations can make exchanging document fragments very messy.

7.1.4   *Summary*

In the end, then, exchanging stand-alone fragments is much more difficult than it might first appear, since it usually requires changes both to the fragment *and* to the DTD: you will still have to cope with the problems of entity declarations and ID resolution and with possible naming conflicts if two authors work on different fragments at the same time.

This approach, still, may be a good choice if you have a fair bit of control over your authors' environments. For example, if they are all using the same editing software, you might be able to customize the software to prevent them from declaring new entities or assigning new IDs, or you might be able to enforce a naming convention that will avoid conflicts.

7.1.5   *SGML: Stand-Alone Fragments*

There are two additional major considerations for exchanging full-SGML stand-alone fragments:

1. #CURRENT attributes

2. inclusion and exclusion exceptions

7.1.5.1   #CURRENT Attributes

The problem with #CURRENT attributes is that the attribute must be specified for the first instance of an element type, but need not be for the following ones (see Section 1.3.2, page 21). For example, the TEI-Lite DTD declares the attribute type as #CURRENT, so that something like this is legal:

#CURRENT attribute values

```
<div id="xx01" type="chapter">
 [...]
</div>
<div id="xx02">
 [...]
</div>
```

In this context, the second **div** element inherits the value "chapter" for its type attribute. If you were to remove the second **div** element and ship it as a stand-alone fragment, however, it would lose that value, and you would have to add it explicitly:

Stand-alone fragment with #CURRENT value supplied

```
<!DOCTYPE div PUBLIC "-//TEI//DTD TEI Lite 1.0//EN"
               "teilite.dtd">


<div id="xx02" type="chapter">
 [...]
</div>
```

This would require some sort of preprocessing.

7.1.5.2   Inclusion and Exclusion Exceptions

Inclusion Exceptions

You may find that your fragment will not parse at all because it includes an element that is an inclusion exception on the document root or another higher level element type. For example, the TEI-Lite DTD allows the element types **index**, **interp**, **interpGrp**, **lb**, **milestone**, and **pb** to appear as inclusion exceptions for the high-level **text** element. If you were exchanging a fragment containing a **div** element (say, at the chapter level), the following document-type declaration would *not* work if the fragment contained any of the elements listed above:

Document type declaration for fragment

```
<!DOCTYPE div PUBLIC "-//TEI//DTD TEI Lite 1.0//EN">
```

The problem is that the element-type declaration for **div** does not have any inclusion exceptions of its own, so if you start there, element types like **milestone** are never included:

TEI-Lite declaration

```
<!ELEMENT div - - ([...])>
```

The only solution to this problem, when it occurs, is to create a new version of the DTD, modifying the declaration for the *fragment's* root element type so that it repeats the inclusion exception:

Modified declaration for fragment

```
<!ELEMENT div - - ([...])
          +(index | interp | interpGrp | lb | milestone | pb)>
```

The designers of the DocBook and MIL-STD-38784 DTDs have already anticipated this problem. Those DTDs repeat all inclusion exceptions for each element type that they think could be exchanged or edited as a stand-alone fragment. In DocBook, for example, the following element types have the inclusion exceptions already attached: **Set**, **Book**, **Chapter**, **Appendix**, **Part**, **Preface**, **Reference**, **PartIntro**, **Sect1**, **SimpleSect**, **RefEntry**, and **Article**.

Exclusion Exceptions

A less obvious problem is that of exclusion exceptions. If a higher level element type contains an exclusion exception, you will also miss it when you begin at a lower level; in that case, however, your stand-alone fragment will still parse properly, and you might not suspect an error. The problem is that if the exclusion exception is missing, authors might be able to insert new elements into the fragment that are not allowed in the same place in the full document.

For example, consider a DTD with the following declarations:

DTD with exclusion exceptions

```
<!ELEMENT book - - (title, body)>

<!ELEMENT title - - (#PCDATA|publishing-note)*>

<!ELEMENT body - - (chapt+) -(publishing-note)>

<!ELEMENT chapt - - (title,[...])>
```

Here, publishing notes are not allowed in the main body of the book. If you made a **chapt** element into a stand-alone fragment, authors would be able to include **publishing-note** elements in the chapter title, because by starting at **chapt,** the parser misses the exclusion exception for **body.**

To solve this problem, you must rewrite the DTD so that the root element type of the fragment includes all accumulated exclusion exceptions as well as inclusion exceptions.

7.2   Reparenting in a Dummy Document

The second solution to exchanging SGML document fragments takes a slightly different approach: instead of distributing the fragment by itself, you distribute it in a skeleton document that provides the minimum context necessary for parsing.

For example, if the fragment were a section (**sect1**) in a DocBook document, you would place it in a skeleton document like this:

Fragment in skeleton document

```
<!DOCTYPE book PUBLIC "-//Davenport//DTD DocBook 3.0//EN"
                     "docbook.dtd" [
]>
<Book>
<Chapter>
<Title></Title>

<!-- Begin fragment -->

<Sect1>
<Title>Sample Section</Title>
<Para>This is the sample section.</Para>
</Sect1>

<!-- End fragment -->

</Chapter>
</Book>
```

The author should edit only the **Sect1** element, not its ancestors. When the author returns the skeleton document, you simply extract the fragment and put it back in its original place in the parent document.

This approach works especially well for DTDs like DocBook, where front matter (etc) are optional; MIL-STD-38784 or TEI-Lite, on the other hand, require extensive front matter, so the skeleton document would have to be much larger.

7.2.1 *Ancestors and Siblings*

The reparenting approach can provide context much more easily than the stand-alone approach (see Section 7.1.1, page 220); in fact, with the reparenting approach, you can provide as much ancestor and sibling information as you wish. For example, your skeleton document can contain empty placeholders for the surrounding chapters and as sections well as:

Skeleton DocBook document

```
<!DOCTYPE book PUBLIC "-//Davenport//DTD DocBook 3.0//EN"
                      "docbook.dtd" [
]>
<Book>
<Chapter>
<Title>First Chapter</Title>
<Para></Para>
</Chapter>

<Chapter>
<Title>Second Chapter</Title>

<Sect1>
<Title>Previous Section</Title>
<Para></Para>
</Sect1>

<!-- Begin fragment -->

<Sect1>
<Title>Sample Section</Title>
<Para>This is the sample section.</Para>
</Sect1>

<!-- End fragment -->

<Sect1>
<Title>Following Section</Title>
<Para></Para>
</Sect1>

</Chapter>
</Book>
```

Note that in this example I have filled in the titles for the surrounding sectioning elements. For the parser, there is no need to provide *any* character data in a skeleton, since #PCDATA in a content model can match zero characters. Sometimes, however, a little character data (such as section titles) will be helpful for the authors.

7.2.2   *Cross-References*

The reparenting method provides a simpler (if more verbose) method for resolving cross-references in a fragment. Instead of modifying the DTD to support a placeholder element for IDs outside of the fragment, as suggested for stand-alone fragments (see Section 7.1.2, page 220), you should simply include IDs in the correct places in your skeleton:

Cross-references in skeleton document

```
<!DOCTYPE book PUBLIC "-//Davenport//DTD DocBook 3.0//EN"
                      "docbook.dtd" [
]>
<Book>
<Chapter Id="first">
<Title>First Chapter</Title>
<Para></Para>
</Chapter>

<Chapter Id="second">
<Title>Second Chapter</Title>

<Sect1 Id="second.previous">
<Title>Previous Section</Title>
<Para></Para>
</Sect1>

<!-- Begin fragment -->

<Sect1 Id="second.sample">
<Title>Sample Section</Title>
<Para>This is the sample section, with a cross-reference
```

```
<XRef
Linkend="second.following"/>).</Para>
</Sect1>

<!-- End fragment -->

<Sect1 Id="second.following">
<Title>Following Section</Title>
<Para></Para>
</Sect1>

</Chapter>
</Book>
```

It might be tempting, at first, to include in the skeleton only the elements (and IDs) that the fragment currently refers to; if you did so, however, authors would run into two problems:

1. they would not be able to add new cross-references to other elements outside the fragment
2. they would not know what IDs are already used when they have to assign new ones within the fragment

To be safe, as with the reparenting approach, you should always include elements for *all* IDs, even though you will end up with a somewhat bloated fragment.

You will still face the problem of possible naming conflicts if two authors are working on different fragments and both add new elements with the same ID. If you can, you should enforce some sort of naming convention to help avoid these problems—for example, you might assign a unique prefix to each chapter, so that all IDs in the introduction must begin with "intr.", whereas all IDs in the chapter on configuration must begin with "conf."

With this system, if Mary were working on the introduction and John were working on the configuration chapter, and both wanted to create an ID called "install", Mary would name hers `intr.install` and John would name his `conf.install`; as a result, there would be no conflict.

7.2.3   *Entities*

Most of the difficulties with entities in the stand-alone approach (see Section 7.1.3, page 224) do not appear with the reparenting approach. Generally, when you create a dummy document, you should include the original document-type declaration verbatim. If you do so, then the dummy document will have all of the same entity declarations as its parent.

That said, there is still the possibility of name conflicts if two authors are working on separate fragments and both create new entities with the same names and different values. Your software must be capable of resolving these conflicts by renaming one of the new entities and all of its references.

7.2.4   *Summary*

With the reparenting approach, you are essentially delivering a copy of the parent document with most or all of the character data removed outside of the fragment itself, leaving a large structural skeleton. You can remove every element outside of the fragment that meets four criteria:

1. it is not an ancestor of the fragment
2. it is not required by its parent's content model (if its parent cannot be removed)
3. it does not have an ID value specified
4. it does not contain an element with an ID value specified

One disadvantage is that this type of document will usually be much larger than stand-alone fragments.

If you are choosing between the two approaches, you will have to decide which is more important: keeping the size of the fragment small, or saving work while extracting and reintegrating the fragment. The final section of this chapter will introduce a fundamentally different approach: treating each fragment as a separate document from the beginning.

7.2.5   *SGML: Reparenting*

For reparenting, the only additional SGML considerations are inclusion and exclusion exceptions.

7.2.5.1   Inclusion and Exclusion Exceptions

Inclusion and exclusion exceptions are where the reparenting method provides the greatest advantages over the stand-alone method. Because your dummy document uses the same document element type as the original document, it will automatically use all of the same inclusion and exclusion exceptions, and you can avoid the extra work necessary for stand-alone fragments (see Section 7.1.5.2, page 228).

7.3   Using Subdocuments

The first two approaches to exchanging document fragments— stand-alone fragments (Section 7.1, page 218) and reparenting in a dummy document (Section 7.2, page 230)—have many problems, but the most serious are related to name space. With these methods, there is no general, portable way to ensure that two authors working on separate fragments will not use conflicting names for entities or element IDs.

The third approach takes advantage of the fact that XML or SGML NDATA entities can contain *any* kind of data: not only graphics, video, audio, etc., but also other XML documents. You can create each chapter as an independent document, with its own document type declaration, then join them together using another XML master document.

First, you declare a notation for XML documents, then declare an NDATA entity for each chapter (or other subdocument) that you want to assemble:

Declaring subdocuments in XML

```
<!NOTATION XML SYSTEM "http://www.w3.org/XML/">
<!ENTITY chap01 SYSTEM "chap01.xml" NDATA XML>
<!ENTITY chap02 SYSTEM "chap02.xml" NDATA XML>
```

Next, declare an element type (usually empty) with an ENTITY attribute to act as a placeholder for the subdocument:

Declaring a placeholder for a subdocument

```
<!ELEMENT chapter-ptr EMPTY>
<!ATTLIST chapter-ptr
   source ENTITY #REQUIRED>
```

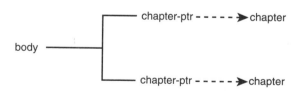

Figure 7–2 Assembling Subdocuments— Each of the **chapter-ptr** elements actually contains a pointer to a separate XML document holding the chapter.

In the document instance, you use the empty placeholders to show where the sub-documents should appear:

Placeholders for subdocuments

```
<body>
<chapter-ptr source="chap01"/>
<chapter-ptr source="chap02"/>
</body>
```

The subdocuments themselves are all independent XML documents, with their own DTDs. (They may use the same DTD or different ones, as appropriate.) As a result, although you have to do more initial setup, you will not have to do any extra work (or write any customized software) simply to extract, distribute, and reintegrate fragments.

Of course, this approach assumes that you are willing to write a short, separate DTD for the master document. It also assumes that you know in advance what parts of your document you might need to exchange as fragments. For many documentation projects, this last requirement is not too difficult: a magazine editor will always be exchanging articles, not paragraphs, and a book editor may be exchanging only chapters.

7.3.1 *Ancestors and Siblings*

Unlike arbitrary fragments, subdocuments can be processed as documents in their own right; however, like fragments, subdocuments contain no information about their context in the master document. Unless you communicate the information in another way (such as a separate document bundled with the subdocument), the author will have no way of determining how the fragment fits in the rest of the master document.

7.3.2   *Cross-References*

When you use subdocuments, you are actually dealing with two name spaces rather than one. Internally, each subdocument can use IDs and IDREFs for cross-references; to refer to other fragments, however, it must use extending linking facilities—like those provided by the HyTime standard or those proposed in XLL `<http://www.w3.org/TR/WD-xml-link>`—because the target appears in another XML document.

It may take a little more work to set up an external cross-referencing scheme, but once you have, you will not have to worry about name space conflicts: two authors can use the same ID name in different fragments without causing a conflict in the master document.

Imagine that you want to make a cross-reference to the following element in a separate XML document:

Target element (in separate document)

```
<div id="gls">
 <head>Glossary</head>


 [...]


</div>
```

This section introduces two schemes for creating the cross-document link:

1. the scheme used by HyTime
2. the scheme proposed in XLL

Note that both of these schemes allow much more sophisticated cross-reference schemes than the ones illustrated here; this section is concerned only with simple, unidirection, and untyped external links.

7.3.2.1   Simple External Reference: HyTime Scheme

For HyTime, you begin by declaring an external entity for the document containing the glossary:

Entity declaration for external SGML document

```
<!NOTATION XML SYSTEM "http://www.w3.org/XML/">
<!ENTITY gloss SYSTEM "glossary.xml" NDATA XML>
```

Next, you use three elements to make the external cross-reference, **clink, nameloc**, and **nmlist.** Because these element types use architectural forms (see Part Four), you can rename them in your own DTD; for the sake of the example, however, I will use the HyTime names.

Your cross-reference element **clink** uses an IDREF as usual:

HyTime clink

```
For more info, see <clink linkend="glossary">the
glossary</clink>
```

The IDREF, however, actually points to another element in *your* document, **nameloc**:

HyTime nameloc and nmlist

```
<nameloc id="glossary">
  <nmlist nametype="element" docorsub="gloss">gls</nmlist>
</nameloc>
```

The **nameloc** element is a placeholder in your document that points to a location in an external document. In this case, the **nmlist** element has the actual information: look for a cross-reference to an element (`nametype="element"`) in the external document or subdocument entity named **gloss** (`docorsub="gloss"`) with the ID "gls". This scheme may seem complicated, but it is very powerful: for example, a single cross-reference may include targets in several documents:

Multiple targets for a single cross-reference

```
<nameloc id="glossary">
  <nmlist nametype="element" docorsub="gloss">gls</nmlist>
  <nmlist nametype="element" docorsub="intro">usage</nmlist>
  <nmlist nametype="element" docorsub="install">prereq
    </nmlist>
</nameloc>
```

HyTime Value Reference

The HyTime standard includes another facility worth noting, even if you do not choose the HyTime scheme for external cross-references. HyTime defines a **value reference** (**valueref**) *attribute form* (clause 6.7.1), which can simplify the processing of subdocuments when you are using software designed to work with HyTime. The following element-type definition instructs a HyTime engine to treat the subdocument entity as if it appeared in the parent document:

HyTime VALUEREF example

```
<!ELEMENT chapter EMPTY>
<!ATTLIST chapter
  source ENTITY #REQUIRED
  valueref CDATA #FIXED "#ELEMENT source">
```

Since the valueref attribute is #FIXED, you do not have to specify a value for it in the document instance itself (you can also give it a different name, if desired). If you were using HyTime, you would also have to provide a value for the HyTime attribute—for more information on this and other HyTime facilities, see the HyTime web site, <http://www.hytime.org/>.

7.3.2.2   Simple External Reference: XLL Scheme

The XLL scheme is much simpler than HyTime: you use only one element, and you do not declare. Again, you may use any name for the link element type, but for the sake of these examples, this section uses the names given in the XLL specification.

You use the **SIMPLE** link type to make a straightforward, unidirectional external link and provide an Internet uniform resource locator (URL) directly in the link:

XLL cross-reference to an external SGML document

```
For more info, see
<SIMPLE HREF="glossary.xml#gls">the glossary</SIMPLE>.
```

Note that the URL has the ID in the target document appended to it after the "#" connector.

XLL also has provision for more complicated arrangements like HyTime's **nameloc**, but it does not require them. In general, you may find that it is a good idea to keep the information on your links in one place rather than scattered throughout your document: when URLs change, you will need to find and update the information easily. HyTime enforces this practice by requiring entities and **nameloc**, whereas XLL allows you to take (possibly costly) shortcuts if you wish.

7.3.3   *Entities*

Subdocuments do not inherit entity declarations from the documents that contain them. Sometimes the lack of inheritance will cause you difficulties, and sometimes it will help.

The work of reintegrating subdocuments is easier because you do not have to worry about entity naming conflicts, as you do for the stand-alone (Section 7.1.3, page 224) and reparenting (Section 7.2.3, page 234) approaches: each subdocument has its own name space, and a change that an author makes to one will not affect another.

Your work will be slightly harder if you *want* to declare document-wide entities. You could repeat the same entity declarations in the declaration subset of each subdocument, but it would be difficult to avoid errors or make changes later.

The problem is easy to solve, however: simply create a separate entity (such as a disk file) containing all of the document-wide entity declarations, then include a single reference to it in each subset:

Including common entity declarations

```
<!DOCTYPE chapter PUBLIC "-//Davenport//DTD DocBook 3.0//EN"
                         "docbook.dtd" [
  <!ENTITY % ents SYSTEM "global.ent">
  %ents;
]>
```

If you use this approach, you will have to distribute the `global.ent` file together with a fragment and to forbid authors from editing that file.

7.3.4   *Summary*

If you *can* use subdocuments, then you probably should—they solve many of the problems with the other approaches, at the cost of only a little extra setup work.

This approach will work, however, only if you know *in advance* where you will need to split off fragments. If you will always be distributing chapters, articles, tasks, or some predictable combination of these, then the subdocument approach will work well; if you might need to split off fragments at any arbitrary level, however, you will need to adopt one of the other, more complicated approaches.

7.3.5   *SGML: Subdocuments*

7.3.5.1   SUBDOC Entities

If you are using full SGML, you can declare the external entities for the subdocuments with the type SUBDOC and do not need to provide a notation. (The NDATA approach will still work, but it does not describe the relationship as accurately as SUBDOC does):

Subdocument entity declarations

```
<!ENTITY chap01 SYSTEM "chap01.sgm" SUBDOC>
<!ENTITY chap02 SYSTEM "chap02.sgm" SUBDOC>
```

In addition, some SGML tools will be able to process these automatically for you.

7.3.5.2   Inclusion and Exclusion Exceptions

Subdocuments are complete documents, so any inclusions or exclusions will be identical when they are distributed independently. None of the problems with the stand-alone (Section 7.1.5.2, page 228) or reparenting (Section 7.2.5.1, page 235) approaches appear with sub-document entities.

Exceptions may still cause difficulties, however, if you are adapting an existing DTD for use with fragments. In that case, the comments for stand-alone documents (Section 7.1.5.2, page 228) apply here as well. Some DTDs—such as DocBook and MIL-STD-38784—will work as is; others will require some minor modifications.

DTD Customization

Chapter

8

Over the past decade, many computer programmers have begun taking an object-oriented approach to programming, using languages such as Java, C++, or Smalltalk. One of the greatest advantages of the object-oriented approach is that, instead of starting from scratch, programmers can create new classes of objects that inherit from existing classes and then modify those new classes only where necessary.

For example, assume that a programmer needed to create an image map, where users could perform actions by clicking the mouse on different parts of a picture. An object-oriented programmer would find a class that displayed different types of images, then would derive a new class that inherited all of the functionality of the existing class but added the ability to handle mouse clicks. By using inheritance, the programmer would save all the work of writing, debugging, and documenting the existing image drawing routines.

The core XML and SGML standards contain no formal provisions for allowing one DTD to inherit from another. Inheritance has turned out to be so necessary, however, that DTD designers have devised ways to achieve some of the same effects by using existing syntax. In addition to the techniques described in this chapter, a standardized construct—architectural forms (Part Four)—provides a formal method for showing how one DTD may be derived from another.

The next part of this book is devoted entirely to architectural forms. This chapter examines other existing practices from two perspectives:

1. the types of customizations that people generally need to perform and the reasons for them

2. the actual mechanisms for customization in the five model DTDs

8.1   Types of Customization

If you find a DTD that already contains much of what you need, you may decide to start with that DTD rather than writing an entirely new one. You will often find, however, that the DTD in its current form does not meet *all* of your requirements; in that case, you will want to modify it. Typically, you need to do one or more of the following:

1. remove unnecessary element types and/or attributes to create a simpler version for authors to use (Section 8.1.1)

2. add new element types and/or attributes to create a specialized version for your subject matter (Section 8.1.2, page 249)

3. rearrange the element structure to accommodate the needs of your authors or the subject matter (Section 8.1.3, page 250)

8.1.1   *Simplifying a DTD for Authoring*

You may choose to simplify a DTD for either or both of the following reasons:

1. to save your authors work, by eliminating unnecessary choice (Section 8.1.1.1)
2. to help authors avoid markup errors, by removing element types or attributes that they should not use (Section 8.1.1.2, page 248)

8.1.1.1   Eliminating Unnecessary Choice

Authors often do not need to use all of the element types in large exchange DTDs such as the five model DTDs covered by this book. For example, your authors might write simple procedures like this in DocBook:

Simple procedure in DocBook

```
<Procedure>
 <Title>Opening the Computer Case</Title>
 <Caution>
  <Para>Always disconnect power before opening a computer
  case.</Para>
 </Caution>
 <Step>
  <Para>Grip the left and right sides of the case with your
  fingers.</Para>
 </Step>
 <Step>
  <Para>Press the button at the bottom right of the computer
  case with your right thumb.</Para>
 </Step>
 <Step>
  <Para>While holding the button depressed, slide top half of
  the case forward until it is completely detached from its
  base.</Para>
 </Step>
</Procedure>
```

The DocBook DTD currently requires at least one **step** within a procedure, but it also allows 46 other element types to appear optionally as siblings of the step. When an author simply wants to insert a new step in DocBook, the author will have to choose from the following list of alternatives:

Abstract Address Anchor AuthorBlurb BlockQuote Bridgehead CalloutList Caution CmdSynopsis Comment Epigraph Equation Example Figure FormalPara FuncSynopsis GlossList Graphic GraphicCO Highlights Important InformalEquation InformalExample InformalTable ItemizedList LiteralLayout MsgSet Note OrderedList Para Procedure ProgramListing ProgramListingCO Screen ScreenCO ScreenShot SegmentedList Sidebar SimPara SimpleList Step Synopsis Table Tip TitleAbbrev VariableList Warning

If you know that authors will never need to insert any element into a procedure but **Title**, **Step**, **Note**, **Important**, **Warning**, **Caution**, or **Tip**, then you will probably decide to do some extra work once, in the DTD itself, instead of requiring authors to do extra work over and over again for every procedure that they create. In this case, you could modify the DTD to remove all but these seven elements from the content of the **Procedure** element.

8.1.1.2   Avoiding Markup Errors

In complex document-production systems, authors do not create all of the content in a document; instead, they create only what needs to be written by hand, and various transformation and database processing software adds additional information before publishing.

For example, you might already have a relational database containing information about replacement parts, circuit breakers, bug tracking, and so on. If your authors typed this information in by hand, two problems could appear:

1. they might retype the information incorrectly

2. the information in the database and the information in the document might gradually get out-of-sync

To avoid these problems, you can design software to automatically generate the lists or tables from the database during each publishing run. There are other types of information that you can generate automatically, such as revision markup, a table of contents, a list of figures, various indexes, a glossary, and certain types of standard notes or cautions.

Authors will never enter this information by hand, so it makes no sense to include the corresponding element types in their version of the DTD—doing so could cause not only confusion among the authors but also errors during production as well, especially if your software mistakenly thought that it had added some of the information itself.

8.1.2   *Adding Element Types to a DTD*

In many cases, instead of (or in addition to) removing element types or attributes, you will want to add new ones to describe your information more precisely.

For example, the MIL-STD-38784 DTD contains a generic element **warning**. However, if authors were writing troubleshooting documentation for viewing on an on-board computer in an airplane cockpit, you might actually need to create three types of warnings:

1. routine warnings that simply appear on the computer display
2. moderately important warnings that appear on the computer display and generate a beep to draw the flight crew's attention
3. critical warnings that the computer should read aloud to the flight crew through a voice synthesizer

You could specify these either by adding a new attribute to the **warning** element type or by creating three different element types for warnings and adding them to the appropriate content models in the DTD (these examples are simplified slightly):

New element types for warnings

```
<!ELEMENT warning (icon?, para*)>
<!ATTLIST warning %chgatt; >


<!ELEMENT important-warning (icon?, para*)>
<!ATTLIST important-warning %chgatt; >


<!ELEMENT urgent-warning (icon?, para*)>
<!ATTLIST urgent-warning %chgatt; >
```

New attributes for warnings

```
<!ELEMENT warning (icon?, para*)>
<!ATTLIST warning
  %chgatt;
  urgency (regular|important|urgent) "regular">
```

8.1.3   *Restructuring a DTD's Components*

Finally, in addition to adding or removing element types, you will often need to change a DTD's structure, usually to make the DTD more restrictive.

The model DTDs are loosely structured so that they can accommodate many different approaches to writing. The ISO 12083 book DTD, for example, allows the front matter to contain a title group, author group, optional date, and optional publication front-matter, followed by any combination of zero or more forewords, introductions, prefaces, acknowledgments, dedications, abstracts, or supplementary material, followed by an optional table of contents (see Figure 8–1):

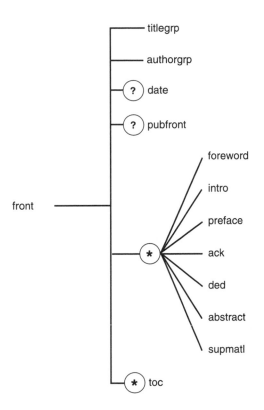

Figure 8–1 Customizing a DTD for Authors (Original)—The original ISO 12083 frontmatter provides much flexibility, even when authors do not need it.

Original ISO 12083 frontmatter

```
<!ELEMENT front (titlegrp, authgrp, date?, pubfront?,
            (foreword|intro|preface|ack|ded|abstract|
            supmatl)*, toc?)>
```

If you were preparing the DTD for authors in a book series, and the series editor decided that all books must have only the title, author, date, introduction, and acknowledgments—in that order—followed by an optional table of contents you might want to modify the ISO 12083 DTD to enforce the policy (see Figure 8–2):

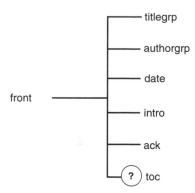

Figure 8–2   Customizing a DTD for Authors (Modified)—A modified version of the ISO 12083 frontmatter eliminates element types that authors do not use, and makes some others (like **date**) mandatory. All documents will still be compatible with the original DTD.

Modified ISO 12083 front matter

```
<!ELEMENT front (titlegrp, authgrp, date, intro, ack, toc?)>
```

Documents created with the modified declaration would still work with the original one, but authors would not have the same opportunity to make mistakes.

8.2   Extension Mechanisms in the Model DTDs

You can modify any DTD simply by editing the physical entity (such as a disk file) that contains it; however, once you have done so, you have severed your ties with the original DTD—your new DTD will not keep pace with changes in new versions of the original—and you have to take on the work of editing, maintaining, and documenting a large DTD yourself rather than simply maintaining a few short extensions.

Despite these problems, physically changing the original DTD is usually the best choice, because it guarantees stability and complete control—you do not have to worry that your authors might some day have newer versions of the base DTD that are incompatible with your modifications. No matter what approach you choose, however, you should *always* assign a new public identifier to your customized DTD to avoid confusion.

The alternative method for customizing DTDs—using parameter entities and other declarations in the internal DTD subset to supplement or override declarations in the external DTD subset—is a practice of questionable value, precisely because it creates a new DTD masquerading as the old one. Processing software may not work correctly with the modified DTD, and existing documentation may be inaccurate or even misleading.

Nevertheless, there are circumstances where it makes sense to allow some configuration: For example, you might want to generate authoring and publishing DTDs from the same source, using parameter entities and marked sections for configuration, or you might want to create different levels of the same DTD for different authors.

It is worthwhile, then, to examine the extension mechanisms in the five model DTDs. Two of the model DTDs—DocBook and full TEI (but not TEI-Lite)—contain explicit mechanisms for customization; the others do not, but they do use parameter entities in their content models, so you can override at least parts of them.

Each of the following subsections provides the following:

1. a brief overview of the extension mechanisms available (if any) in one of the model DTDs
2. an example of how you could use declarations in the document-type declaration subset to modify that DTD to include a new inline element type **slang** in the mixed content of paragraphs and other similar element types

8.2.1   *Customizing the DocBook DTD*

The DocBook DTD, like the full TEI (Section 8.2.2, page 257) DTD, is designed so that you can customize it on many different levels by using parameter entities. The parameter entities use an elaborate naming scheme:

*.CLASS

A group of related element types that tend to appear together in content models, such as list.class for list-like element types:

DocBook class entity

```
<!ENTITY % local.list.class "">
<!ENTITY % list.class
  "CalloutList|GlossList|ItemizedList|OrderedList|
   SegmentedList|SimpleList|VariableList
     %local.list.class;">
```

*.MIX

An OR group of element types that can appear together as a repeatable list in a content model, such as local.footnote.mix for the contents of footnotes:

DocBook mix entity

```
<!ENTITY % local.footnote.mix "">
<!ENTITY % footnote.mix
  "%list.class;|%linespecific.class;|%synop.class;|
   %para.class;|%informal.class;%local.footnote.mix;">
```

Note how the *.mix parameter entities are often built out of *.class parameter entities.

*.CONTENT

Other, nonrepeatable fragments of content models, such as div.title.content for the title information at the beginning of a sectioning element:

DocBook content entity

```
<!ENTITY % div.title.content "Title, TitleAbbrev?">
```

*.ATTRIB

Reusable sets of attribute declarations, such as `status.attrib` for the editorial or publication status of the element:

DocBook attrib entity

```
<!ENTITY % local.status.attrib "">
<!ENTITY % status.attrib
 "Status CDATA #IMPLIED
  %local.status.attrib;"
>
```

*.MODULE

Parameter entities for marked sections in the DTD, controlling which element-type declarations (or groups of declarations) will be included and which will be ignored:

DocBook module entity

```
<!ENTITY % title.module "INCLUDE">
<![%title.module;[
<!ENTITY % local.title.attrib "">
<!ENTITY % title.role.attrib "%role.attrib;">
<!ELEMENT Title (%title.char.mix;)+>
<!ATTLIST Title
  %pagenum.attrib;
  %common.attrib;
  %title.role.attrib;
  %local.title.attrib;>
]]>
```

If an author were to declare the parameter entity `title.module` with the value "IGNORE" in the document-type declaration subset, thereby overriding the declaration shown here, then the element-type declaration for the **Title** element would be omitted from the DTD.

If you override the values of any of these, you can alter content modules or attribute declarations in the DocBook DTD. Often, however, you will not need to override the entire parameter entity value; instead, use the `local.*` variant to extend the existing value.

For example, the content model of a paragraph in DocBook is equivalent to the following:

DocBook paragraph

```
<!ELEMENT Para (%para.char.mix; | %para.mix;)*>
```

The `para.char.mix` parameter entity that makes up part of its content model is declared as follows:

DocBook paragraph content

```
<!ENTITY % local.para.char.mix "">
<!ENTITY % para.char.mix
  "#PCDATA|%xref.char.class;|%gen.char.class;|
  %link.char.class;|%tech.char.class;|%base.char.class;|
  %docinfo.char.class;|%other.char.class;|
  %inlineobj.char.class;|%synop.class;|
  %local.para.char.mix;">
```

You could extend the content model of **Para** (and other related elements) to include the **slang** element type by redeclaring the entire `para.char.mix` parameter entity, but it is usually easier simply to provide a value for `local.para.char.mix`:

Extension to DocBook

```
<!DOCTYPE book [
  <!ENTITY % docbook PUBLIC
                  "-//Davenport//DTD DocBook 3.0//EN"
                  "docbook.dtd">
  <!ENTITY % local.para.char.mix "|slang">
  <!ELEMENT slang (#PCDATA)>
  %docbook;
]>
```

8.2.2 *Customizing the TEI DTDs*

The TEI-Lite DTD was generated from the full TEI DTDs with all parameter entities expanded; as a result, there is no way to customize it without physically altering the DTD file.

For example, the TEI-Lite DTD declaration for a paragraph element is equivalent to the following:

TEI-Lite paragraph

```
<!ELEMENT p (#PCDATA|ident|code|kw|abbr|address|date|
             name|num|rs|time|add|corr|del|gap|orig|reg|
             sic|unclear|emph|foreign|gloss|hi|mentioned|
             soCalled|term|title|ptr|ref|xptr|xref|anchor|
             s|seg|gi|formula|eg|bibl|biblFull|cit|q|label|
             list|listBibl|note|figure|stage|table|text)*>
```

There is nothing here that you can override to add a new **slang** element type to the content model. On the other hand, the full TEI declaration for the same element type uses parameter entities extensively:

Full TEI Declaration

```
<!ENTITY % p "INCLUDE">
<![%p;[
<!ELEMENT %n.p; %paraContent;>
<!ATTLIST %n.p;
  %a.global;
  TEIform CDATA "p">
]]>
```

As with DocBook (Section 8.2.1, page 254), there is a parameter entity that determines whether the declaration is included at all (p), a parameter entity for the content (paraContent), and a parameter entity for reusable attribute declarations (a.global). The full TEI DTDs actually go further than DocBook, by allowing the renaming of element types as well: if you preferred the name **para** to **p**, you could simply declare the parameter entity n.p with a new value:

Parameter entity for element type name

```
<!ENTITY % n.p "para">
```

All element types in the full TEI DTDs have an `n.*` parameter entity for renaming, and the DTD always refers to them using this entity. If you wanted to rename **table**, for example, you would simply declare a new value for the parameter entity `n.table`.

The main purpose of this mechanism is to allow internationalization of the DTD—non-English speakers can rename the element types for their own languages. To simplify processing, all TEI element types have a #FIXED attribute `TEIform` that indicates the normative name for the element. Processing software should work from the attribute value rather than from the element-type name. (This scheme is similar to architectural forms.)

To customize the full TEI DTD, it would be necessary to add the **slang** element type to the **paraContent** parameter entity that appears in the content model for **p**. The parameter entity has the following declaration:

TEI paragraph content

```
<!ENTITY % paraContent "(#PCDATA|%m.phrase;|%m.inter;)*">
```

There is no hook here for adding new declarations. However, because **slang** is, in effect, a type of phrase, you should look at the `m.phrase` parameter entity:

TEI phrasal content

```
<!ENTITY % x.phrase "">
<!ENTITY % m.phrase "%x.phrase;%m.data;|%m.edit;|
                    %m.formPointers;|%m.hqphrase;|%m.loc;|
                    %m.phrase.verse;|%m.seg;|
                    %m.sgmlKeywords;|
                    %n.formula;|%n.fw;|%n.handShift;">
```

This declaration does contain the empty parameter entity `x.phrase`. If you supply a value for it, that value will automatically be included in the value of the `m.phrase` parameter entity, and eventually, in the content model for paragraphs. To add the **slang** element type, include the following in the document-type declaration subset:

Extending TEI phrasal content

```
<!ENTITY % x.phrase "slang |">
<!ELEMENT slang (#PCDATA)>
```

8.2.2.1   Base and Auxiliary Tagsets

Full TEI also provides a higher level configuration mechanism. There is a series of what the TEI refers to as *base tagsets*, including (but not limited to) the following:

1. prose
2. verse
3. drama
4. transcription of the spoken word
5. dictionaries
6. terminology

Every full TEI document must activate one of these base tagsets by declaring the appropriate parameter entity with the value "INCLUDE". (There are also special provisions for allowing more than one base.) For example, if your authors were working on screenplays, you would want to enable the TEI.drama base tagset in your document-type declaration subset as follows:

Including the TEI drama base tagset

```
<!ENTITY % TEI.drama "INCLUDE">
```

(These configuration entities do not apply to TEI-Lite.)

In addition to the required base tagset, you may activate one or more auxiliary tagsets for special requirements, such as feature set descriptions, advanced linking, phonetic transcription, and textual criticism. For example, if you wanted to enable attributes for describing certainty and uncertainty for element types in the full TEI DTD, you would declare the following parameter entity in your document-type declaration subset:

Including a TEI auxiliary tagset

```
<!ENTITY % TEI.certainty "INCLUDE">
```

8.2.3 *Customizing the HTML DTD*

The HTML DTD—like the MIL-STD-38784 (Section 8.2.4, page 261) and ISO 12083 (Section 8.2.5, page 262) DTDs—was not designed for customization: It contains no general extension mechanisms similar to those found in DocBook or full TEI. Because HTML is designed only for display in browsers hard-coded for the DTD, there would be little point in ever extending it. If you wish to design a DTD that can map to HTML easily, you would be better off using architectural forms (Part Four).

However, the DTD does use parameter entities for some content models, so it is possible to override these to add a new element type. The HTML DTD declares the **P** (paragraph) element type as follows:

HTML paragraph element type

```
<!ELEMENT P (%inline;)*>
```

The `inline` parameter entity references, among others, the `phrase` parameter entity, which has the following declaration:

HTML phrasal content

```
<!ENTITY % phrase "EM | STRONG | DFN | CODE |
                SAMP | KBD | VAR | CITE | ABBR | ACRONYM" >
```

You cannot extend this, but you can override it in the document-type declaration subset:

Modifying a content model in HTML

```
<!ENTITY % phrase "EM | STRONG | DFN | CODE |
                SAMP | KBD | VAR | CITE | ABBR | ACRONYM |
                SLANG" >
<!ELEMENT SLANG (#PCDATA)>
```

8.2.4 *Customizing the MIL-STD-38784 DTD*

Like the HTML and ISO 12083 (Section 8.2.5, page 262) DTDs, the MIL-STD-38784 DTD contains no specialized extension mechanisms; it does, however, use parameter entities in content models, so it is often possible to add a new element by overriding one of the entities.

For MIL-STD-38784, a declaration equivalent to the following appears for the **para** element type:

MIL-STD-38784 paragraph element type

```
<!ELEMENT para %paracon;>
<!ATTLIST para
  id ID #IMPLIED
  xrefid IDREF #IMPLIED
  %chgatt;
  %secur;>
```

The `paracon` parameter entity refers the **text** parameter entity, which contains the actual mixed content:

MIL-STD-38784 original phrasal content

```
<!ENTITY % text "(#PCDATA|change|tabmat|ftnref|xref|verbatim
             |emphasis| applicbil|graphic|extref|dataiden|
             hcp|esds|nsp|acronym)*" >
```

To add the **slang** element type to mixed content in a paragraph, simply override this declaration in the document-type declaration subset:

MIL-STD-38784 modified phrasal content

```
<!DOCTYPE doc PUBLIC "-//USA-DOD//DTD MIL-STD-38784 AMEND1//
EN" "mil-std-38784-a1.dtd" [
  <!ENTITY % text "(#PCDATA|change|tabmat|ftnref|xref|
             verbatim|emphasis|applicabil
             |graphic|extref|dataiden|
             hcp|esds|nsp|acronym|slang)*" >
  <!ELEMENT slang (#PCDATA)>
]>
```

8.2.5   *Customizing the ISO 12083 DTDs*

Like the HTML and MIL-STD-38784 (Section 8.2.4, page 261) DTDs, the ISO 12083 book DTD has no special mechanisms for customization, but it does use parameter entities in its content models.

These parameter entities use special prefixes, depending on their use:

P.*

Content allowed in paragraphs (and possibly phrases)

S.*

Content allowed in sections

I.*

Content allowed in inclusion exceptions

M.*

A content model or declared content

A.*

An attribute definition

There are also special suffixes allowed:

*.PH

Phrasal content

*.D

Default content model

*.ZZ

Subelements

For example, the parameter entity `p.form` refers to formula element types that can appear in paragraphs, and the parameter entity `ade.ph` refers to address element types that can appear in phrases.

In the ISO 12083 DTD, the **p** (paragraph) element type has the following declaration:

ISO 12083 paragraph element type

```
<!ELEMENT p (#PCDATA|%p.zz.ph;|%p.zz;)*>
```

Following the naming scheme given above, the `p.zz.ph` parameter entity refers to phrasal subelements that can appear within a paragraph, and the `p.zz` parameter entity refers to other subelements that can appear within a paragraph.

The `p.zz.ph` parameter entity has the following declaration:

ISO 12083 phrasal content

```
<!ENTITY % p.zz.ph "q|pages|%p.em.ph;|%p.rf.ph;">
```

Unfortunately, neither the `p.em.ph` (emphasized phrases) nor the `p.rf.ph` (references) parameter entity is suitable for the new **slang** element type, and you cannot redeclare the `p.zz.ph` parameter entity itself, because it refers to other parameter entities that would not exist until *after* the parser has read the ISO 12083 DTD (at which point, it would be too late to override `p.zz.ph`).

There are two possible solutions to this problem. The first is to cheat a little and add **slang** to **p.em.ph**, which has the following original declaration:

ISO 12083 emphasized phrases

```
<!ENTITY % p.em.ph  "emph">
```

To replace it, you would use the following document-type declaration:

Modifying a content model in ISO 12083

```
<!DOCTYPE book PUBLIC "ISO 12083:1993//DTD Book//EN"
                      "docbook.dtd" [
  <!ENTITY % p.em.ph "emph|slang">
  <!ELEMENT slang (#PCDATA)>
]>
```

The declaration of **p.em.ph** would override that in the ISO 12083 DTD, because the parser would read it first.

The second method is to add **slang** directly to `p.zz.ph`, but only after duplicating the declarations for the **p.em.ph** and **p.rf.ph** parameter entities:

Modifying the ISO 12083 phrasal content

```
<!DOCTYPE book PUBLIC "ISO 12083:1993//DTD Book//EN"
                      "book.dtd" [
  <!ENTITY % p.em.ph "emph">
  <!ENTITY % p.rf.ph "noteref|fnoteref
                     |figref|tableref|artref|
                     appref|citeref|secref|formref|glosref
                     |indexref">
  <!ENTITY % p.zz.ph "slang|q|pages|%p.em.ph;|%p.rf.ph;">
  <!ELEMENT slang (#PCDATA)>
]>
```

This second solution, however, would make it more difficult to maintain the document, because any changes to `p.em.ph` or `p.rf.ph` in future versions of the DTD would be ignored. (Your declarations would override them.)

Part Four

The final part of this book introduces the new extended facility for architectural forms, which allows XML or SGML documents to conform simultaneously to more than one DTD. The next three chapters contain enough information for you to understand architectural forms and to start using them in your own DTDs:

■ Chapter 9 introduces the general concepts behind architectural forms and provides a series of examples of how (and when) they can be used

■ Chapter 10 introduces the most important syntax for architectural forms

■ Chapter 11 introduces advanced architectural-form syntax that you can use for difficult requirements and other special situations

DTD Design
with
Architectural
Forms

Architectural Forms: Concepts

XML and SGML define a common syntax for adding structured markup to documents and providing an schema (the DTD) for that markup; unfortunately, whereas the common markup syntax ensures that two users can parse or edit the same document, it does not ensure that they can actually share the information contained within that document—normally, to share information, two users must agree to use the same DTD.

For example, take a look at the following two short sample documents (which use two different DTDs; see also Figure 9–1):

Sample document #1

```
<!DOCTYPE doc1 PUBLIC
                "-//Megginson//DTD Document Type 1//EN"
                "doc1.dtd">

<doc1>
 <front>
  <title>Sample Document</title>
 </front>
 <body>
  <para>This is the first paragraph.</para>
  <para>This is the second paragraph.</para>
 </body>
</doc1>
```

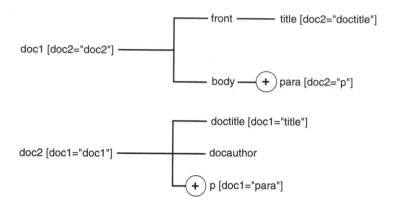

Figure 9–1 Deriving DTDs—Even though they use different element type names, each of the DTDs for the two sample documents can be derived mostly from the other.

Sample document #2

```
<!DOCTYPE doc2 PUBLIC
                "-//Megginson//DTD Document Type 2//EN"
                "doc2.dtd">
<doc2>
 <doctitle>Sample Document</doctitle>
 <docauthor>David Megginson</docauthor>
 <p>This is the first paragraph.</p>
 <p>This is the second paragraph.</p>
</doc2>
```

To a human reader, it is obvious that these two examples represent almost exactly the same document, containing the same information. To an XML parser or other processing software, however, these are entirely different documents, simply because they conform to different DTDs.

The presence of two different DTDs might cause problems such as the following:

■   a company designs a typesetting system for the doc1 document type but cannot use the system when it receives documents conforming to the doc2 DTD

■ two suppliers order the same specification, but the first one requires information conforming to the doc1 DTD, while the other requires information conforming to the doc2 DTD

Typically, if a company or organization has to exchange documents with one that uses a different DTD, the company is forced to create and maintain customized processing software to transform the document from one type to the other—whenever *either* of the DTDs changes, the company has to modify or even rewrite the transformation software.

This process is unnecessarily time-consuming, expensive, and risky; obviously, it would be much better if you could put some kind of information in the DTDs themselves to show how the element types correspond to each other:

- **doc1** corresponds to **doc2**
- **title** corresponds to **doctitle**
- **para** corresponds to **p**

Software designed for doc1 documents could then process any document similar to the doc1 DTD, even if the document being processed actually conformed to a different DTD.

Annex A.3 to the second edition of the HyTime standard (ISO/IEC 10744:1997) introduces *architectural forms* to provide exactly this sort of information for SGML and XML documents. The document that introduces them is called the *Architectural Form Definition Requirements* (**AFDR**). (See the HyTime web site <http://www.hytime.org/> for details.)

You implement architectural forms by using standard XML or SGML syntax that follows certain special rules (see Chapter 10 and Chapter 11)—this way, you can use your existing XML or SGML software to create and edit documents that use architectural forms.

The rest of this chapter provides more detail about architectural-form concepts and uses but without introducing any of the actual XML or SGML syntax required to support them. If you are eager to know the technical details, you can skip ahead to the next chapter now and return later if you need more background information; otherwise, you can read any or all of the following sections:

1. the role of *meta-DTDs* in defining and validating architectural forms
2. the creation of derived documents that conform both to their own DTD and to one or more meta-DTDs
3. some practical uses of architectural forms, with examples
4. a summary of the terminology associated with architectural forms

9.1   Meta-DTDs

With architectural forms, you can have more than one DTD associated with your document:

- your document's DTD is called the **client**, or the **derived DTD**
- the additional DTDs from which the document is derived are called the **meta-DTDs**, each of which defines a single **base architecture**

In other words, if you had a regular XML document conforming to a DTD called doc1, and if the DTD's architectural forms derived the document from a second DTD called doc2, then the doc2 DTD would be the **meta-DTD** and the doc1 DTD would be its **client DTD**.

It is important to understand that, in nearly all cases, these terms refer only to how you use the DTD—they represent nothing intrinsic to the DTDs themselves. The same DTD can even be a client DTD and a meta-DTD at the same time.

The client DTD represents a document's **encompassing architecture**—it defines everything that can appear in the document. A document must have exactly one encompassing architecture, and if anything that appears in the document is not part of that architecture, the document is invalid.

The meta-DTD(s), if present, represent a document's **enabling architecture(s)**—they define some of what will appear in the document. A document may have zero or more enabling architectures, and those architectures are not required to cover everything in the document.

9.2   Documents

As shown in the examples in Chapter 10, you will usually define your architectural forms within the client DTD itself. Nevertheless, an architectural engine parses your document, not your client DTD, against the meta-DTD. A document that conforms to a meta-DTD is called a **client document** of the meta-DTD's architecture.

For example, imagine that you had a document conforming to a DTD named doc1, and you derived some of the document's contents from the DTD named doc2. The following would then be true:

- doc2 is a *meta-DTD* for your document, defining a *base architecture* (possibly one of many)
- your document is a *client document* of the doc2 architecture

9.2.1   *Types of Architectural Forms*

A client document (or, more often, the client DTD) uses *architectural forms* to derive its markup components from the base architecture defined by a meta-DTD. The following types of forms exist:

ELEMENT FORM

The element type in a meta-DTD from which you have derived an element in your client document

ATTRIBUTE FORM

The attribute in a meta-DTD from which you have derived an attribute in your client document

NOTATION FORM

The notation in a meta-DTD from which you have derived a notation in your client document

In other words, you can derive elements, element attributes, and notations from the base architecture defined by the meta-DTD.

SGML Note: *In full SGML, you may also use a data attribute form.*

Here are some typical types of derivations:

- the element **cite** in the client document conforms to the element type **title** in the meta-DTD (an *element form*)
- the attribute **key** for the element **chapter** in the client document conforms to the attribute id in the meta-DTD (an *attribute form*)
- the notation gif in the client document conforms to the notation graphic in the meta-DTD (a *notation form*)

9.2.2 *The Architectural Document*

Taken together, all of the elements, attributes, and character data in a document that are derived from architectural forms make up another, virtual document, the **architectural document**. Consider the following sample document (excluding its document-type declaration):

Client document

```
<order>
 <shipper>SGML Smelting Inc</shipper>
 <receiver>Tags-R-Us</receiver>
 <item>
  <description>Start tags</description>
  <catalog-no>258-627-99</catalog-no>
  <quantity>18</quantity>
  <unit-price>$1.99</unit-price>
  <total-price>$35.82</total-price>
 </item>
</order>
```

For this document, you might specify the following derivations of a base architecture defined by an `invoice` meta-DTD (the syntax for specifying these associations appears in Chapter 10 and Chapter 11):

- the **order** element is derived from the **invoice** architectural form
- the **receiver** element is derived from the **customer** architectural form
- the **item** element is derived from the **item** architectural form
- the **catalog-no** element is derived from the **catno** architectural form
- the **quantity** element is derived from the **num** architectural form
- the **total-price** element is derived from the **billable** architectural form.

If you actually applied all of these derivations, you would end up with a different document, called the *architectural document*:

Architectural document

```
<invoice>
 <customer>Tags-R-Us</customer>
 <item>
  <catno>258-627-99</catno>
  <num>18</num>
  <billable>$35.82</billable>
 </item>
</invoice>
```

9.3   Practical Uses of Architectural Forms

This section introduces four practical uses of architectural forms for document design and management:

1. DTD extension
2. software reusability
3. multi-use documents
4. extended validation of structure and business rules

9.3.1   *DTD Extension*

Normally, when people design XML or SGML processing software, they create it to work with documents conforming to a specific DTD: for example, they might design a program for converting DocBook documents to Postscript, for extracting database information from a MIL-STD-38784 document, or for generating bibliographical records from TEI documents.

Normally, this dependence on the DTD can be costly, because every time you add new element types to the DTD, the software will have to be modified or even entirely rewritten—otherwise, it might report an error, or worse, produce unpredictable output.

With a careful use of architectural forms, however, and properly designed processing software, you can often add element types to a DTD without requiring software changes: simply use the original version of the DTD as a meta-DTD and derive later versions from it. If your software works from the base architecture (the original version) instead of the derived DTD (the new version), it will never see unexpected element types.

When deriving the new version of the DTD from the old one, you choose between two different actions for each new element type that you create:

1. derive it from a similar (usually more general) element type in the old version of the DTD
2. omit it from architectural processing altogether (either merging its character data into that of a higher level element or skipping the character data as well)

For example, imagine that you have an element type **emphasis**—for general emphasized phrases—in the old version of the DTD, and that you are adding an element type **foreign**—for foreign words and phrases—in the new version of the DTD. If you decide that a foreign phrase is simply a more specialized type of emphasized phrase (formatting software, for example, might render both in italics), then you can derive the **foreign** element type from the **emphasis** element form.

The **foreign** element type did not exist when you designed the formatting software; nevertheless, because your software can determine (and recognize) the architectural form of all **foreign** elements, it can make reasonable assumptions about how to process them.

Of course, major changes to the DTD will still require changes to your processing software, but when you use architectural forms for

DTD extension, the software will not be quite so tightly linked to a specific DTD version, and you will not incur high software-maintenance costs every time you make a minor revision to your DTD.

9.3.2   *Software Reusability*

Typically, processing software depends heavily on the names of element types in a specific DTD—for example, software might enter the contents of every **city** element into a database, format every **paragraph** element as a separate block of text preceded by 6 points of vertical whitespace, or follow hyperlinks from every **link** element.

As a result, very little processing software is capable of dealing with more than one DTD. If another DTD had element types named **ville** instead of **city**, **para** instead of **paragraph**, or **a** instead of **link**, the software would not be able to process the elements, even if they were used in exactly the same way.

Fortunately, architectural forms allow you to break the overdependence on names and instead to process elements based on classes. Processing software designed to work with a base architecture can process any document that conforms to that architecture, no matter what DTD the document uses.

For example, the processing software might recognize an architectural form named **location** and know that the contents of any element derived from this architectural form should be inserted into a database. If the first DTD derived its **city** element type from this architectural form, and the second derived its **ville** element type from this architectural form, the software would be capable of processing both correctly, despite the difference in element-type names.

9.3.2.1   A Common Book Architecture?

This approach could be especially valuable for developing XML formatting or browsing software. The five model DTDs, for example, have a great deal of structure in common, despite the fact that their element type names often differ:

Table 9.1   Sample common element types in the five model DTDs

Item	ISO 12083	DocBook	TEI-Lite	MIL-STD-38784	HTML
a paragraph	p	Para	p	para	P
an emphasized phrase	emph	Emphasis	emph	emphasis	EM
a list item	item	ListItem	item	item	LI
a table cell	cell	Entry	cell	entry	TD

Of course, there are also significant differences among the DTDs, such as the recursive sectioning element types in TEI-Lite or the total lack of sectioning element types in HTML; but even allowing for those, a software tool like an online browser could make a reasonable attempt at displaying a formatted version of any of these five document types if they derived some of the more important elements from a simple, common base architecture.

This idea becomes even more powerful if a set of DTDs is designed from the start to share a more detailed base architecture—in that case, a single piece of software could perform useful processing on a unlimited number of document types. Base architectures could include models for book-oriented documents, electronic commerce, technical specifications, and many other applications. Since XML is very young, there is a good opportunity right now to work with base architectures like these.

9.3.3   *Multiuse Documents*

The previous section explained how architectural forms could allow
one piece of processing software to deal with many different document types; in fact, it is also possible to allow a single document type
to be processed by many different pieces of software, by deriving the
document type from more than one base architecture at the same
time.

For example, imagine that you had to provide data for three different applications:

1. a bibliographical database
2. an inventory of parts
3. print formatting

Each of these requires its own view of a document. The bibliographical database might require basic cataloging information about a
publication:

Bibliographical Information

```
<document>
 <title>Widget Assembly Instructions</title>
 <author>David Megginson</author>
 <date>1 July 1997</date>
 <version>3.0</version>
</document>
```

The parts inventory might require a list of all parts required for a
procedure:

Parts Inventory

```
<parts-list>
 <part>gizmo</part>
 <part>sprocket</part>
 <part>gear</part>
</parts-list>
```

And finally, the formatting software might require lists and paragraphs for display:

Formatting

```
<sheet>
 <front>
  <title>Widget Assembly Instructions</title>
  <author>David Megginson</author>
 </front>
 <body>
  <section>
   <title>Parts Required</title>
   <list>
    <item>gizmo</item>
    <item>sprocket</item>
    <item>gear</item>
   </list>
  </section>
  <section>
   <heading>Procedure</heading>
   <para>Use the gizmo to connect the gear to the sprocket,
    then stand back at a safe distance before applying
    power.</para>
  </section>
 </body>
</sheet>
```

With architectural forms, you can represent each of these as a different base architecture within the *same SGML document*. The bibliographical database, for example, can look for any element type with the architectural form **title** and process it appropriately, no matter what DTD the document uses.

Multiuse documents save you from either producing a large amount of customized software to transform your document, or (worse) from creating several different documents with the same information—architectural forms can show, unambiguously, how an architecture-aware program should process a document's contents simply by deriving those contents from the program's architecture.

9.3.4   *Extended Validation*

Many companies work with an entire family of DTDs rather than just one, and in most cases, each company has a set of business rules that should apply all documents. Here are some typical examples:

- every document must have a preface and a copyright notice
- notes, warnings, and cautions must always appear before the first paragraph in a section
- all chapters and sections are required to have an attribute specifying security status

Each individual DTD must enforce these rules, as far as XML or SGML syntax allows. If there are dozens of different DTDs, however, errors might creep in—in that case, it might be worth creating a base architecture specifically for validating that every document follows these business rules, no matter what DTD it uses. Using architectural forms will help you catch design errors quickly and maintain consistent standards across all of your document types.

9.4   Summary of Terminology

Architectural forms use new terminology that might not be familiar even to experienced SGML users. This section summarizes the new terminology introduced in this chapter and used throughout this part of the book.

AFDR

The *Architectural Form Definition Requirements*, the document describing architectural forms (Annex A.3, ISO/IEC 10744, 2nd ed.). (See the HyTime web site `<http://www.hytime.org/>` for access to an online copy.)

ARCHITECTURAL DOCUMENT
   The virtual document consisting only of the parts of a document
   that conform to a base architecture

ARCHITECTURAL ENGINE
   Software specially designed for processing architectural forms in an
   SGML document. (It is often possible to handle architectural forms
   with no specialized software.)

ARCHITECTURAL FORMS
   Rules for creating and processing components of documents

ATTRIBUTE FORM
   The attribute in a meta-DTD from which you have derived an
   attribute in your client document

BASE ARCHITECTURE
   A collection of architectural forms that may apply to a document,
   as defined by a single *meta-DTD*

CLIENT DOCUMENT
   A document that uses architectural forms

CLIENT DTD
   The DTD of a document that uses architectural forms (see also
   derived DTD)

DATA ATTRIBUTE FORM
   The data attribute in a meta-DTD from which you have derived a
   data attribute in your client document (SGML only)

DERIVED DTD
   The DTD of a document that uses architectural forms (see also *client DTD*)

ELEMENT FORM
   The element in a meta-DTD from which you have derived an element in your client document

ENABLING ARCHITECTURE
An architecture from which you have derived your document's DTD

ENCOMPASSING ARCHITECTURE
A document's regular DTD

META-DTD
A DTD that defines (some of) the architectural forms that may appear in a document (see also *base architecture*)

NOTATION FORM
The notation in a meta-DTD from which you have derived a notation in your client document.

Basic Architectural Forms Syntax

hapter 9 introduced the concepts and terminology associated with architectural forms. This chapter introduces the XML and SGML syntax for the most common facilities of architectural-form markup, and Chapter 11 will introduce various advanced topics.

If you are reading about architectural forms for the first time, you might want to start experimenting with them as soon as you have finished this chapter, turning to Chapter 11 only if you run into problems. (The free SP parser <http://www.jclark.com/sp/>, available on the CD-ROM inclued with this book, comes with a complete architectural engine that you can use.)

For architectural forms, you need to think of two logically separate processes operating on your XML or SGML document:

1. the regular parser
2. the architectural engine

The markup described in this chapter has no special meaning to the regular XML or SGML parser, which will see only processing instructions, attribute values, and so on. It is the **architectural engine** that attaches special meanings to the syntax described in this chapter and the next. (The architectural engine may be as simple as a few extra subroutines that examine attribute values, or it may be a complex piece of software in its own right, as required.)

When you look at a typical client (or derived) DTD, you will see that most of the additional markup for architectural forms involves nothing more than special attributes declared with #FIXED values:

- the name of the #FIXED attribute is usually the same as the name of the architecture (i.e., HyTime or DSSSL)
- the value of the #FIXED attribute is the name of the *architectural form*—the corresponding element type in the meta-DTD.

For example, imagine a client DTD that refers to a base architecture named biblio. The client DTD might have an element type named **doctitle**, whereas the meta-DTD might have an element type named **title**. To show that these two are equivalent, the client DTD will use the following attribute definition for the **doctitle** element type:

Specifying an architectural form in the client DTD

```
<!ATTLIST doctitle
  biblio NMTOKEN #FIXED "title">
```

The architecture is named biblio (like the attribute), the client DTD's element-type name is **doctitle**; and the meta-DTD's element-type name is **title**. Because this is a fixed attribute, the parser will automatically assign it this value for every **doctitle** element, even if the author does not specify it. The following would work just as well:

Specifying an architectural form in the document

```
<doctitle biblio="title">Title</doctitle>
```

However, declaring a #FIXED value saves typing, avoids errors, and hides the architectural-form markup from the authors.

On a less-trivial level, architectural processing is configurable. Sometimes, for example, you will want to specify how to deal with character data and when to enable or disable architectural processing (see Chapter 11); you will want to derive attributes as well as elements from the base architecture; and, most importantly, you will want to let the architectural engine know what attributes represent architectural forms and how to find the meta-DTDs for their base architectures. This chapter covers basic architectural-form syntax in two parts:

1. setup and configuration for using architectural forms
2. basic forms for elements, attributes, unparsed entities, and data-content notations

10.1   Setup and Configuration

Before you can use architectural forms, you must add two types of information to your DTD (or to the document-type-declaration subset):

1. the names of the base architectures you are using
2. information about each base architecture

You can provide all of this information using standard XML or SGML syntactic constructions.

For example, imagine that you wanted to derive your document from a base architecture for bibliographic headers. To declare this architecture, you can use a simple processing instruction such as the following:

Architecture use declaration processing instruction

```
<?IS10744:arch name="biblio"
  public-id="-//Megginson//NOTATION AFDR ARCBASE
Bibliographic Header//EN"
  dtd-system-id="biblio.dtd"?>
```

The "`IS10744:arch`" (or "`IS10744 arch`") at the beginning identifies this as an **architecture use declaration**. The form with the colon is recommended for XML; the form with the space is chiefly for full SGML.

Following that comes an attribute specification list for the architecture; in this example, the declaration provides the name of the base architecture ("`biblio`"), a public identifier for the base architecture ("`"-//Megginson//NOTATION AFDR ARCBASE Bibliographic Header//EN"`"), and a system identifier for the meta-DTD ("`biblio.dtd`").

Because this declaration is a processing instruction, it will cause no difficulties with XML or SGML parsers that are not aware of architectural forms.

10.1.1 *Architecture Use Declaration Attributes*

You may specify any of the following **architecture use declaration attributes** in the architecture use declaration:

name
> The name of the base architecture (required)

public-id
> A public identifier for the architecture (as a notation) (You should normally include this, so that the architectural engine knows what architecture it is working with.)

dtd-public-id
> The public identifier for the meta-DTD

dtd-system-id

The system identifier for the meta-DTD (You should normally specify this, so that the architectural engine can find the meta-DTD.)

form-att

The name of an element attribute used for deriving elements from the base architecture (defaults to the name of the architecture)

renamer-att

The name of an element attribute used to rename other attributes to match the attributes in the base architecture (by default, there is no renaming)

suppressor-att

The name of an element attribute that you can use to selectively suppress architectural-form processing in parts of a document (by default, there is no suppression)

ignore-data-att

The name of an element attribute that you can use to specify how the architectural engine should handle data (by default, data is recognized where it is allowed by the base architecture and ignored where it is not)

doc-elem-form

The name of the document element in the base architecture (by default, it is the same as the base architecture name)

bridge-form

The name of a default architectural form for elements that have an ID but no architectural form of their own

data-form

The name of a default architectural notation for unparsed entities in your document that have no corresponding notation in the base architecture

auto
A flag controlling whether element-type names and notations are derived automatically when their names are the same in the base architecture (automatically derived by default)

options
The names of additional, optional support attributes for this architecture

10.1.2 *SGML: Original Syntax*

The architecture use declaration processing instruction can be used with full SGML as well as XML. Alteratively, the original syntax for declaring a base architecture in full SGML can still be used, although is a little more involved, as the following example shows:

Declaring a base architecture in SGML

```
<!-- Architecture Base Declaration -->
<?IS10744 ArcBase biblio>

<!-- Architecture Notation Declaration -->
<!NOTATION biblio PUBLIC
  "-//Megginson//NOTATION AFDR ARCBASE Bibliographic
  Header// EN">

<!-- Architecture Support Attribute Declarations -->
<!ATTLIST #NOTATION biblio
  ArcDtd CDATA #FIXED "biblioDtd">

<!-- Architecture Entity Declaration -->
<!NOTATION SGML PUBLIC
    "ISO 8879:1986//NOTATION Standard Generalized Markup
    Language//EN">
<!ENTITY biblioDtd PUBLIC
    "-//Megginson//DTD Bibliographic Header//EN"
    CDATA SGML>
```

There are four types of declarations in the example above:

1. **ARCHITECTURE BASE DECLARATION**

   A processing instruction that names the architectures used by the document:

   Architecture base declaration

   ```
   <?IS10744 ArcBase biblio>
   ```

   In this case, the document will use a single base architecture named `biblio`. This corresponds to the `name` attribute in the architecture use declaration.

2. **ARCHITECTURE NOTATION DECLARATION**

   A notation declaration for a single architecture:

   Architecture notation declaration

   ```
   <!NOTATION biblio PUBLIC
       "-//Megginson//NOTATION AFDR ARCBASE Bibliographic
        Header//EN">
   ```

   The `biblio` architecture is represented by the `biblio` notation (the two must always have the same name). This notation's public identifier corresponds to `public-id` in the architecture use declaration.

3. **ARCHITECTURE SUPPORT ATTRIBUTES**

   Data attributes attached to each *architecture notation declaration*, providing configuration information for each architecture:

   Architecture support attributes

   ```
   <!ATTLIST #NOTATION biblio
     ArcDtd CDATA #FIXED "biblioDtd">
   ```

   In this case, the `biblio` architecture is defined by the meta-DTD contained in the entity named `biblioDtd`.

4. **ARCHITECTURE ENTITY DECLARATION**

   An external entity (possibly accompanied by a notation) indicating the actual meta-DTD for each base architecture:

Architecture entity declaration

```
<!NOTATION SGML PUBLIC

   "ISO 8879:1986//NOTATION Standard Generalized Markup
     Language//EN">

<!ENTITY biblioDtd PUBLIC
              "-//Megginson//DTD Bibliographic Header//EN"

     CDATA SGML>
```

In this case, the entity containing the meta-DTD for the `biblio` base architecture uses the public identifier "`-//Megginson//DTD Bibliographic Header//EN`". The entity's public and system identifiers correspond to `dtd-public-id` and `dtd-system-id` in the architecture use declaration.

These declarations add no new syntax to SGML; instead, they use existing constructions like processing-instructions, notation declarations, entity declarations, and data attributes to mark up all of the necessary information. As a result, you can create client DTDs and documents with any existing, fully-conformant SGML tools, and the markup will cause no problems with SGML tools that are not aware of base architectures.

10.1.2.1   Architecture Base Declaration

The first declaration that has to appear in a client DTD is the **architecture base declaration**, which lists all of the architectures to which your document conforms. This declaration is nothing more than a processing instruction beginning with the words "`IS10744 ArcBase`" and followed by a whitespace-separated list of base-architecture names (each corresponding to `name` in a separate architecture use declaration):

Architecture base declaration

```
<?IS10744 ArcBase biblio HyTime>
```

In this example, the document conforms to both the `biblio` and `HyTime` architectures. This is equivalent to the following architecture use declarations:

Equivalent architecture use declarations

```
<?IS10744 arch name="biblio">
<?IS10744 arch name="HyTime">
```

You could also use two separate architecture base declarations with exactly the same effect:

Multiple architecture base declarations

```
<?IS10744 ArcBase biblio>
<?IS10744 ArcBase HyTime>
```

Usually, you will find it most convenient to put the architecture base declaration in the DTD itself, usually in the external portion; it is important to remember, however, that the declaration applies to documents, not to DTDs—if your DTD allows documents to conform to the base architectures but does not *require* them to, then you should include the declaration in the (conforming) documents themselves or in the internal declaration subset:

ArcBase declaration in subset

```
<!DOCTYPE doc PUBLIC
    "-//Megginson//DTD Generic Document//EN" [
  <?IS10744 ArcBase biblio>
]>
```

10.1.2.2 Architecture Notation Declaration

Now that the architecture base declaration has let the architectural engine know what base architecture(s) are available, you need to provide one **architecture notation declaration** for each base architecture:

Architecture notation declaration

```
<!NOTATION biblio PUBLIC
    "-//Megginson//NOTATION AFDR ARCBASE Bibliographic
    Header//EN">
```

This notation *must* have the same name as the base architecture itself. You may choose any public identifier you wish (your architectural engine may impose some limits), but the AFDR specification recommends beginning the public text description with the words "AFDR ARCBASE", as in the example above. The notation's public identifier corresponds to public-id in the architecture use declaration.

At first, it might seem strange that you declare base architectures as notations; however, there is a certain consistent logic to the choice (other than the need not to introduce any new SGML syntax). Just as you declare a notation for an image format like JPEG or PNG to tell your processing software how to interpret certain graphics, you can declare a notation for a base architecture to tell your architectural engine how to interpret the architectural forms in your document.

10.1.2.3   Architecture Entity Declaration

You need to declare an external entity for each base architecture (This is the entity name that you supplied for the ArcDtd architecture support attribute), to show where the meta-DTD is actually located. Ideally, you should declare an external CDATA entity with the notation "ISO 8879:1986//NOTATION Standard Generalized Markup Language//EN":

Architecture entity declaration

```
<!NOTATION SGML PUBLIC
    "ISO 8879:1986//NOTATION Standard Generalized Markup
    Language//EN">
<!ENTITY biblioDtd PUBLIC
    "-//Megginson//DTD Bibliographic Header//EN"
    CDATA SGML>
```

Neither the CDATA nor the notation is required, however. The following would work just as well (though it would not be as clear to people reading your DTD):

Architecture entity declaration without notation

```
<!ENTITY biblioDtd PUBLIC
    "-//Megginson//DTD Bibliographic Header//EN">
```

You may use any entity name that you want, since you provide the name to the architectural engine using the ArcDtd support attribute. The entity's public and system identifiers correspond to dtd-public-id and dtd-system-id in the architecture use declaration.

10.1.2.4   Architecture Support Attributes

Like element types, notations in full SGML can have attributes (typically, these provide extra information, like the dimensions of a graphic or the sampling rate of an audio clip). Since you declare base architectures as notations using the architecture notation declarations, it makes sense that you would use these attributes to specify how your document will be implementing the architecture:

Architecture support attribute declarations

```
<!-- Architecture Support Attribute Declarations -->
<!ATTLIST #NOTATION biblio
  ArcDtd CDATA #FIXED "biblioDtd">
```

The ArcDtd data attribute is the most important, and it is the only one that is required: it tells the architectural engine what entity to look at for the meta-DTD. These correspond to the dtd-public-id and/or dtd-system-id architecture use declaration attributes in an architecture use declaration processing instruction.

Though the ArcDtd attribute is the only one that you *must* provide, there are eleven other, optional support attributes that might find useful for certain requirements, most of which correspond to attributes available in the architecture use declaration:

ArcDTD

The name of an entity pointing to the DTD for the base architecture. If the entity is a parameter entity, include the PERO delimiter ("%") before the name—note, however, that you cannot declare a parameter entity as CDATA and provide a notation, as you can with a general entity. The entity's public and system identifiers correspond to `dtd-public-id` and `dtd-system-id` in the architecture use declaration.

ArcFormA

Corresponds to `form-att` in the architecture use declaration

ArcNamrA

Corresponds to `renamer-att` in the architecture use declaration

ArcSuprA

Corresponds to `suppressor-att` in the architecture use declaration

ArcIgnDA

Corresponds to `ignore-data-att` in the architecture use declaration

ArcDocF

Corresponds to `doc-elem-form` in the architecture use declaration

ArcBridF

Corresponds to `bridge-form` in the architecture use declaration

ArcDataF

Corresponds to `data-form` in the architecture use declaration

ArcAuto

Corresponds to `auto` in the architecture use declaration

ArcOptSA

Corresponds to `options` in the architecture use declaration

In addition to these, there are two more architecture use declarations available in full SGML:

ArcQuant

Variant quantities necessary to parse the DTD for the base architecture, if it uses a different SGML declaration than the current document (Section 11.5.2, page 328)

ArcOpt

The names of parameter entities in the meta-DTD that should be set to INCLUDE. You may use this support attribute only if its name appears in the value of the ArcOptSA support attribute (Section 11.5.1, page 327). This could also be useful in XML.

10.2 Basic Forms

Once you have set up a base architecture, simply use attributes to describe the relationship between the element types and attributes in your client DTD and the architectural forms defined by the meta-DTD.

This section introduces three types of basic forms possible in XML:

1. element forms
2. attribute forms
3. notation forms

Once you are comfortable with the material in this section, you can read Chapter 11 for information on more advanced architectural markup.

10.2.1 Deriving Elements

You use attributes to derive elements in your client DTD from element types in a meta-DTD—the element types in the meta-DTD are called **element forms**. For each base architecture used by your document, there is an **architectural form attribute** name (form-att) reserved exclusively for this purpose.

By default, the architectural form attribute has the same name as the base architecture—if your base architecture is named biblio, the architectural engine will look for a reserved attribute named biblio on elements and notations—but if you need to, you can choose a different name using form-att in the architecture use declaration. The following example sets the name of the architectural form attribute for the biblio architecture to "bib" rather than to the default "biblio":

Renaming the *architectural form attribute*

```
<?IS10744:arch name="biblio" form-att="bib"?>
```

Normally, there will be no need to rename the architecture support attribute, but this mechanism is available to help avoid naming conflicts if you are attempting to fit architectural forms into an existing DTD.

For an example of the architectural form attribute in use, imagine a base architecture defined by the following *meta-DTD*:

Meta-DTD

```
<!-- A simple bibliographic record -->
<!ELEMENT biblio (title,author,date,copyright)>
<!ELEMENT title (#PCDATA)>
<!ELEMENT author (#PCDATA)>
<!ELEMENT date (#PCDATA)>
<!ELEMENT copyright (#PCDATA)>
```

Because the document element of the meta-DTD is named biblio, you will likely give the base architecture the name biblio as well (though it can be called anything in your client DTD).

If the base architecture is named biblio, then by default the *architectural form attribute* name is biblio as well. The following example

uses the attribute to derive elements in your client document from the
element forms defined by the meta-DTD:

Client document (explicit attribute values)

```
<doc biblio="biblio">
 <header>
  <doctitle biblio="title">Title</doctitle>
  <byline biblio="author">Author</byline>
  <pubdate biblio="date">Publication Date</pubdate>
  <cpyrt biblio="copyright">Copyright</cpyrt>
  <notes>These are some notes</notes>
 </header>
 <body>
  <chapter>
   <title>First Chapter</title>
   [...]
  </chapter>
 </body>
</doc>
```

Here is an English description of the meanings of these attributes:

- the **doc** element corresponds to the `biblio` architectural
  form (you always have to derive the document element)
- the **header** element is not derived an architectural form
  (it has no `biblio` attribute), so the architectural engine
  will ignore it
- the **doctitle** element corresponds to the `title`
  architectural form
- the **byline** element corresponds to the `author`
  architectural form
- the **pubdate** element corresponds to the `date`
  architectural form
- the **cpyrt** element corresponds to the `copyright`
  architectural form
- the **notes, body, chapter,** and **title** elements are not
  derived from architectural forms. (They have no `biblio`
  attributes.)

The architectural engine will see only the architectural elements whose forms are specified by the `biblio` attribute, ignoring nonarchitectural elements altogether. The architectural elements together form a virtual document, the *architectural document*, although there is no need for an architectural engine to construct this explicitly:

Architectural document
```
<biblio>
 <title>Title</title>
 <author>Author</author>
 <date>Publication Date</date>
 <copyright>Copyright</copyright>
</biblio>
```

To avoid always having to specify values for the attribute you may provide a default value in the DTD; if you don't want users to be able to override it, you can make the value #FIXED:

Sample architectural forms
```
<!ATTLIST doc
   biblio NMTOKEN #FIXED "biblio">
<!ATTLIST doctitle
   biblio NMTOKEN #FIXED "title">
<!ATTLIST byline
   biblio NMTOKEN #FIXED "author">
<!ATTLIST pubdate
   biblio NMTOKEN #FIXED "pubdate">
<!ATTLIST cpyrt
   biblio NMTOKEN #FIXED "copyright">
```

Document authors do not even need to know that they are using architectural forms, because the forms are hidden away in the DTD:

Client document (defaulted attribute values)
```
<doc>
 <header>
  <doctitle>Title</doctitle>
  <byline>Author</byline>
  <pubdate>Publication Date</pubdate>
  <cpyrt>Copyright</cpyrt>
```

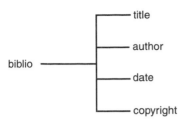

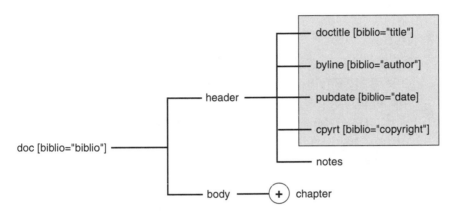

Figure 10–1 Deriving a DTD from the biblio Architecture—The doc DTD uses the biblio architecture to represent one type of embedded information in its documents.

```
 <notes>These are some notes</notes>
</header>
<body>
 <chapter>
  <title>First Chapter</title>
  [...]
 </chapter>
</body>
</doc>
```

10.2.1.1 Element Form Strategies

An architectural engine will not care how you specify the value for an architectural form attribute. As a result, you can use several strategies for providing or obtaining a value:

- You can leave the attribute #IMPLIED, so that the element is derived from an architectural form only when authors provide an explicit value:

Preventing derivation with an #IMPLIED attribute

```
<!ATTLIST doctitle
  biblio NMTOKEN #IMPLIED>
```

In this example, the **doctitle** element will have an architectural form in the biblio architecture only if the author specifies a value; otherwise, it will not be part of the architectural document. Users can specify any arbitrary NMTOKEN value, so it is not possible to prevent authors from creating invalid derived elements in their documents.

- You can make the attribute #REQUIRED, so that users always have to provide an explicit form:

Requiring the user to specify the form

```
<!ATTLIST doctitle
  biblio NMTOKEN #REQUIRED>
```

In this example, the **doctitle** element will always have *some* architectural form in the biblio architecture, and the author will have to specify which one. Since users can specify any arbitrary NMTOKEN value, it is not possible to prevent authors from creating invalid derived elements in their documents.

- You can provide a default value, so that the element is usually derived from a default architectural form unless the author explicitly provides a value:

Providing a default form

```
<!ATTLIST doctitle
  biblio NMTOKEN "title">
```

In this example, the **doctitle** element will have the `title` architectural form in the `biblio` architecture by default, but authors can override the form. Because users can specify any arbitrary NMTOKEN value, it is not possible to prevent authors from creating invalid derived elements in their documents.

- You can provide a #FIXED default value (the most common approach), so that the element is always derived from the same architectural form:

Providing a #FIXED form

```
<!ATTLIST doctitle
  biblio NMTOKEN #FIXED "title">
```

In this example, the **doctitle** element will always have the `title` architectural form in the `biblio` architecture, and authors cannot override the form.

- With any of the first three approaches, you can use a name token list for the attribute type, to require authors to select an architectural form only from a fixed range of choices:

Providing a choice of forms

```
<!ATTLIST doctitle
  biblio (title|subtitle) "title">
```

In this example, the **doctitle** element will always have either a `title` or a `subtitle` architectural form in the `biblio` architecture; if the author does not specify a value, the architectural form will default to `title`.

It is also possible to allow automatic derivation of some elements without specifying the architectural form attribute (see Section 11.1, page 312).

10.2.2 *Deriving Attributes*

Normally, an architectural engine will derive attributes automatically, if they have the same name in the base architecture and in the client DTD, and it will always derive an ID attribute from another ID attribute, no matter what the names are. For example, consider the following declaration from the meta-DTD:

Meta-DTD excerpt

```
<!ATTLIST para
  id ID #IMPLIED
  type CDATA #IMPLIED>
```

By default, any attribute of a **para** element with the name id or type in the client document will be directly derived from the id or type attribute in the base architecture.

There are several cases where this default behavior is not desirable:

- if the same attribute has different names in the base architecture and the client DTD, the architectural engine will fail to associate them
- if semantically different attributes happen to have the same name in the base architecture and the client DTD, the architectural engine will incorrectly assume that it should associate them
- if an attribute's type in the client DTD is a token group, the tokens may not correspond exactly with the tokens (if any) in the base architecture
- if an attribute value corresponds to an element's content in the meta-DTD, the element's content may correspond to an attribute value in the meta-DTD

If any of these complications appears in your client DTD, then declare an **architectural attribute renamer attribute** using renamer-att in the architecture use declaration:

Declaring an architectural attribute renamer

```
<?IS10744:arch name="doc" renamer-att="doc-atts"?>
```

Following this example, if any element has an attribute named doc-atts, the architectural engine will use it as the architectural attribute renamer to determine how to derive attributes from the base architecture.

The most basic use of the *architectural attribute renamer* is simply to derive attributes in the client document from attributes with different names in the base architecture. For example, your client DTD might use the attributes role and rev for the same purpose as the attributes type and version in the base architecture.

You can specify this association simply by listing the names in a whitespace-delimited list (put the architectural attribute name first, followed by the attribute name in your client DTD):

Renaming attributes

```
<!ATTLIST p
  doc NMTOKEN #FIXED "para"
  doc-atts CDATA #FIXED "type role version rev"
  role CDATA #IMPLIED
  rev CDATA #IMPLIED>
```

In this example, the doc-atts attribute is the architectural attribute renamer, deriving role from the attribute form type and rev from the attribute form version.

For more advanced uses of the architectural attribute renamer, see Section 11.3, page 318.

10.2.3 *Deriving Notations*

In XML, notations do not have attributes, so you cannot supply an explicit architectural form for them; however, notations will be derived automatically from notations in your meta-DTD unless you specify `nArcAuto` for the value of the `auto` architecture variable (see Section 11.1, page 312).

10.2.4   *SGML: Basic Forms*

Since SGML allows data attributes for notations, it is also possible to derive notations in the client document from notations in the meta-DTD explicitly, using *notation forms*.

10.2.4.1   Notation Forms

An SGML architectural engine will recognize references to external data entities (*unparsed entities*: CDATA, SDATA, or NDATA) only if it can find an architectural notation for them; otherwise, it simply ignores the references.

As a result, it is notations rather than entities that you have to derive from the meta-DTD; in fact, you derive notations exactly the same way as elements, using the *architectural form attribute* in the notation's data attributes.

For example, consider the following notation declaration from a meta-DTD for an architecture named `doc`:

Meta-DTD excerpt

```
<!NOTATION tiff-notation PUBLIC
    "ISO 12083:1993//NOTATION TIFF-1//EN">
```

If you want to derive your own notation `tiff` from this, you can simply provide the association with the data attribute `doc`:

Client DTD excerpt

```
<!NOTATION tiff PUBLIC "ISO 12083:1993//NOTATION TIFF-1//
EN">
<!ATTLIST #NOTATION tiff
  doc NAME #FIXED "tiff-notation">
```

Now, your document can declare an unparsed entity that uses the tiff notation:

Entity declaration for client document

```
<!ENTITY pic SYSTEM "pic.tif" NDATA tiff>
```

Because this entity uses a notation tiff that *does* have an equivalent in the meta-DTD, the architectural engine will recognize any references to it; otherwise, it simply would have skipped them.

Advanced Architectural Forms Syntax

Chapter

11

If the information in this book is your first exposure to architectural forms, you might want to stop now and try applying the basic syntax for architectural forms (Chapter 10)—you may find that it is sufficient for all of your requirements.

Sometimes, however, you will discover special situations when you cannot provide a simple, one-to-one association between your client DTD and the base architecture represented by the meta-DTD; in other situations, you might want to use shortcuts to minimize the number of extra declarations in the DTD. In these cases, you can use some of the special, advanced facilities available for architectural forms, as described in this chapter under the following topics:

1. automatic derivation of elements and attributes
2. suppressing architectural processing for elements and data
3. obtaining architectural attribute values from various sources
4. providing default information for a base architecture
5. the meta-DTD.

11.1 Automatic Derivation

By default, an architectural engine will derive elements and notations from architectural forms with the same name *even if you do not
provide an architectural form attribute* for the elements. For example, if
your client DTD has an element type **caution**, and the meta-DTD
has an element type with the same name, the architectural engine
would automatically associate the two.

This behavior will not always be what you want—for example,
your client DTD might use the element type **name** as part of an
address structure, whereas the meta-DTD might use it to tag people's
names within paragraphs:

Meta-DTD excerpt

```
<!ELEMENT para (#PCDATA|emphasis|link|name)*>
```

Client DTD excerpt

```
<!ELEMENT address (name, street1, street2,
                   city, postal-code)>
```

If the architectural engine tries to derive the one **name** element
from the other, it will generate an error, because each occurs in places
where the other is not allowed.

Fortunately, there are three ways to prevent this kind of automatic
derivation:

1. derive **name** explicitly from something else, if there is an
   appropriate architectural form (in XML, for elements
   only)
2. provide **name** with an architectural form attribute with
   an #IMPLIED value (in XML, for elements only)
3. set the architecture use declaration attribute auto in the
   architecture use declaration to the value "nArcAuto" (elements or notations)

Of these three solutions, the third is the best—if you make a habit of setting `auto` to nArcAuto, you will avoid many nasty surprises and make your DTD somewhat more self-documenting as well (since every architectural element and notation will have to have an explicit architectural form attribute):

Disabling automatic derivation
```
<?IS10744:arch name="biblio" auto="nArcAuto"?>
```

Note that this declaration will *not* prevent the architectural engine from deriving attributes automatically, but it will prevent automatic derivation of elements and notations. (see Section 11.3, page 318.)

11.1.1 *SGML: Automatic Derivation*

In full SGML, you can also use the `ArcAuto` architectural support attribute to disable automatic derivation:

Disabling automatic derivation
```
<!ATTLIST #NOTATION biblio
  ArcAuto NMTOKEN #FIXED "nArcAuto"
  [...]>
```

11.2 Suppressing Architectural Processing

This subsection describes the special facilities available for suppressing architectural processing in two ways:

1. suppressing the recognition of elements and their content (including character data)
2. suppressing the recognition of character data by itself

11.2.1   *Suppressing Elements*

In some situations, it can be useful selectively to turn architectural processing on or off. For example, consider the following declarations in a meta-DTD:

Meta-DTD excerpt

```
<!ELEMENT para (#PCDATA)>
<!ELEMENT list (list-item+)>
<!ELEMENT item (#PCDATA)>
```

The meta-DTD allows only #PCDATA within list items. Your client DTD, on the other hand, might require paragraphs to appear within a list item:

Client DTD excerpt (incorrect)

```
<!ELEMENT p (#PCDATA)>
<!ATTLIST p
  doc NMTOKEN #FIXED "para">
<!ELEMENT ol (li+)>
<!ATTLIST ol
  doc NMTOKEN #FIXED "list">
<!ELEMENT li (p+)>
<!ATTLIST li
  doc NMTOKEN #FIXED "list-item">
```

This arrangement will fail because the architectural engine will see the para architectural form within list items, where it is not allowed, and may report an error or produce incorrect output.

To solve this problem, use the suppressor-att architecture use declaration attribute to declare a new **architecture suppressor attribute** for suppressing or enabling architectural-form processing:

Enabling an architecture suppressor attribute

```
<?IS10744:arch name="doc" suppressor-att="doc-processing"?>
```

Once you have included this declaration, if an attribute named **doc-processing** appears for any element, the architectural engine can take action based on the following attribute values:

sArcForm
Suppress architectural processing until the parser finds a descendant with a non-implied value for the architecture-suppressor attribute (the element itself will still be processed, unless sArcAll is already in force).

sArcNone
Do not suppress architectural processing; if architectural processing is conditionally suppressed, restore it. (The element itself will also be processed, unless sArcAll is already in force.)

sArcAll
Unconditionally stop all architectural processing for the descendants of this element, even if one of them specifies the value "sArc-None" for the architecture-suppressor attribute. (The element itself will still be processed, unless an ancestor has already specified sArc-None.)

#IMPLIED
Inherit the current behavior.

The solution to the list item problem, then, is simply to suppress architectural processing within the list item:

Client DTD excerpt (correct)

```
<!ELEMENT p (#PCDATA)>
<!ATTLIST p
  doc NMTOKEN #FIXED "para">
<!ELEMENT ol (li+)>
<!ATTLIST ol
  doc NMTOKEN #FIXED "list">
<!ELEMENT li (p+)>
<!ATTLIST li
  doc NMTOKEN #FIXED "list-item"
  doc-processing NMTOKEN #FIXED "sArcForm">
```

11.2.2 *Suppressing Data*

It is also possible to instruct the architectural engine to ignore character data under different circumstances. For example, consider the following document excerpt:

Client document excerpt

```
<item>This is the only option
available<elaboration>In fact, you could also
consider erasing the hard drive.</elaboration>.</item>
```

If **item** were architectural and **elaboration** were not, by default the architectural engine would merge the data of **elaboration** with the data of its parent:

Architectural document excerpt (incorrect)

```
<item>This is the only option
available.In fact, you could also
consider erasing the hard drive..</item>
```

While the default behavior is often useful, it is obviously inappropriate here; instead, you might prefer that the architectural engine simply ignore the data of **elaboration** altogether.

To control data recognition, you start with the `ignore-data-att` architecture use declaration attribute:

Enabling an ignore data attribute

```
<?IS10744:arch name="doc" ignore-data-att="data-flag"?>
```

This declaration tells the architectural engine that any attribute named `data-flag` will contain special instructions for data recognition.

If `data-flag` is not `#IMPLIED`, it must have one of the following three values:

ArcIgnD
Always ignore data.

cArcIgnD

Conditionally ignore data if it occurs where the meta-DTD does not allow it (the default behavior).

nArcIgnD

Never ignore data: report an error if there is data where the meta-DTD does not allow it.

An element inherits its parent's behavior if the attribute's value is #IMPLIED.

In this example, the architectural engine should always ignore the data in the **elaboration** element, so you should specify the value ArcIgnD:

Suppressing data for an element type

```
<!ATTLIST elaboration
  data-flag NMTOKEN #FIXED "ArcIgnD">
```

Now the architectural engine will correctly ignore the data within the **elaboration** element:

Architectural document excerpt (correct)

```
<item>This is the only option
available.</item>
```

11.2.3 *SGML: Suppressing Architectural Processing*

In full SGML, instead of the architecture use declaration attributes suppressor-att and ignore-data-att, the you can use architectural support attributes ArcSupr and ArcIgnDA:

Declaring an architecture suppressor attribute

```
<!ATTLIST #NOTATION doc
  ArcSupr NAME #FIXED "doc-processing"
  [...]>
```

Declaring an ignore data attribute

```
<!ATTLIST #NOTATION doc
  ArcIgnDA NAME #FIXED "data-flag"
  [...]>
```

11.3 Architectural Attribute Values

Sometimes, you need to do more than derive attributes in your client document directly from attributes in the meta-DTD. This section introduces four special facilities available for more complicated architectural attribute requirements:

1. forcing an architectural attribute to take its default value
2. renaming tokens when they differ between the client DTD and the meta-DTD
3. deriving content in the client document from an attribute value in the architectural document
4. deriving an attribute value in the client document from content in the architectural document

For any of these, you need to assign a value to the `renamer-att` architecture use declaration attribute, just as you do for simple attribute renaming (Section 10.2.2, page 306):

Enabling an architectural attribute renamer attribute

```
<?IS10744:arch name="doc" renamer-att="doc-atts"?>
```

11.3.1 *Attribute Defaulting*

If you want the architectural engine to ignore an attribute value altogether (even if it has the same name as an attribute form in the base architecture), you can rename it to the value #DEFAULT using the *architectural attribute renamer attribute*:

Client DTD excerpt

```
<!ATTLIST p
  doc NMTOKEN #FIXED "para"
  doc-atts CDATA #FIXED "version rev type #DEFAULT"
  rev CDATA #IMPLIED
  type CDATA #IMPLIED>
```

In this example, the architectural engine will derive the attribute rev from the attribute form version, but ignore any values specified for type in the client document.

11.3.2   *Tokens*

Name token groups provide a convenient way to require authors to choose from a list of preselected attribute values; however, there can be problems if the meta-DTD requires different tokens than the client DTD.

For example, imagine that the following appears in your meta-DTD:

Meta-DTD excerpt

```
<!ATTLIST para
  status (draft|final) #IMPLIED>
```

The status attribute form must have one of the values draft or final. The client DTD, however, might use different tokens for the same concept:

Client DTD excerpt (incorrect)

```
<!ATTLIST p
  doc NMTOKEN #FIXED "para"
  revstat (initial|approved) #IMPLIED
  doc-atts CDATA #FIXED "status revstat">
```

This derivation will fail, because the revstat attribute will always have the value initial or approved, whereas the meta-DTD requires draft or final.

Fortunately, the AFDR allows you to rename the token names by using #MAPTOKEN:

Client DTD excerpt with tokens mapped

```
<!ATTLIST p
  doc NMTOKEN #FIXED "para"
  revstat (initial|approved) #IMPLIED
  doc-atts CDATA #FIXED "status revstat
                        #MAPTOKEN draft initial
                        #MAPTOKEN final approved">
```

This declaration instructs the architectural engine to map the token initial in the client document to the token draft in the base architecture and to map the token approved in the client document to the token final in the base architecture.

These declarations will work even with a CDATA attribute in the client architecture—a full architectural engine will simply split it into tokens before applying the mappings.

11.3.3 *Deriving Content from Attribute Values*

Some DTDs put information in attribute values, while other DTDs put the same information in content. For example, consider the following element-type definition:

Meta-DTD excerpt

```
<!ELEMENT phone EMPTY>
<!ATTLIST phone
  num CDATA #REQUIRED>
```

This definition uses the attribute num to hold a phone number, rather than allowing the number as content. If you were deriving a client DTD from this base architecture, and your client DTD included the phone number as content, an element form alone would not work:

Client DTD excerpt (incorrect)

```
<!ELEMENT phone (#PCDATA)>
<!ATTLIST phone
  docarc NMTOKEN #FIXED "phone">
```

There are two problems here: the client **phone** element may have content, but the architectural form may not; and the architectural form requires an attribute num, which the client element does not provide.

To solve this problem, map the architectural attribute num to the token #CONTENT, rather than to another attribute:

Client DTD excerpt (correct)

```
<!ELEMENT phone (#PCDATA)>
<!ATTLIST phone
  doc NMTOKEN #FIXED "phone"
  doc-atts CDATA #FIXED "num #CONTENT">
```

This token instructs the architectural engine to use the element's content as the value for the architectural attribute.

Now, your client document might have the following markup:

Client document excerpt

```
<phone>(212) 555-1212</phone>
```

When it sees this, the architectural engine will make the content into an attribute value:

Architectural document excerpt

```
<phone num="(212) 555-1212"/>
```

11.3.4 Deriving Attribute Values from Content

The problem described in the previous section can also occur in reverse: the meta-DTD might require content where the client DTD has an attribute. For example, the meta-DTD might model an internal link as follows:

Meta-DTD excerpt

```
<!ELEMENT link (#PCDATA)>
<!ATTLIST link
  target IDREF #REQUIRED>
```

In this example, the text (etc) that the user should select appears as the element's content. Your client DTD, on the other hand, might put the text in a second attribute:

Client DTD excerpt (incorrect)

```
<!ELEMENT link EMPTY>
<!ATTLIST link
  doc NMTOKEN #FIXED "link"
  target IDREF #REQUIRED
  label CDATA #REQUIRED>
```

The derivation will not work as expected, because the descriptive text in the label attribute will not appear in the architectural document.

In this case, you need to map the attribute label to the token #ARCCONT:

Client DTD excerpt (correct)

```
<!ELEMENT link EMPTY>
<!ATTLIST link
  doc NMTOKEN #FIXED "link"
  doc-atts CDATA #FIXED "#ARCCONT label"
  target IDREF #REQUIRED
  label CDATA #REQUIRED>
```

Note that #ARCCONT stands in place of the architectural attribute, not the client attribute.

Now, your client document might have the following markup:

Client document excerpt

```
<link target="intro" label="Introduction"/>
```

When the architectural engine sees this markup, it will treat the value of the label attribute as if it were content:

Architectural document excerpt

```
<link target="intro">Introduction</link>
```

11.3.5 *SGML: Architectural Attributes*

In SGML, you may use the ArcNamrA support attribute instead of renamer-att:

Enabling a renamer attribute

```
<!ATTLIST #NOTATION doc
  ArcNamrA NAME #FIXED "doc-atts"
  [...]>
```

11.4 Default Architectural Information

There are two situations where it is useful to provide default architectural forms in your client DTD:

1. there are unparsed entities that use non-architectural notations (Section 11.4.1, page 324)

2. if there are non-architectural elements that may take IDs
   (Section 11.4.2)

In both situations, something that *is* architectural—an unparsed
entity in the first case, or an element with an IDREF, in the second
case—might refer to something that would not otherwise be part of
the architectural document.

11.4.1 *Creating a Default Notation*

For many types of architectural processing, one does not really need
to know the specific notations for individual unparsed entities,
because the architectural engine will not try to process the data in
them.

To avoid the extra work of deriving every notation in your client
DTD from one in the meta-DTD, you can use the data-form architecture declaration attribute (Section 10.1.1, page 290) to declare a
default notation in the meta-DTD: All notations in your client DTD
without explicit notation forms will automatically be derived from
the default notation.

For example, your meta-DTD might contain a generic notation
similar to the following:

Meta-DTD Excerpt

```
<!NOTATION data PUBLIC
    "-//Megginson//NOTATION AFDR ARCBASE General Data//EN">
```

You could declare this as the default notation in the doc architecture using the data-form architecture use declaration attribute:

Client DTD Excerpt

```
<?IS10744:arch name="doc" data-form="data"?>
```

Now, *all* unparsed entities will be recognized by the architectural engine—any that use notations without their own notation forms will have the architectural `data` notation by default.

In XML, always specify this attribute if you have set `auto` to `nArcAuto`, since there is no other way to derive notations.

11.4.2 *Resolving* IDREF*s*

DTDs often allow many different types of elements—chapters, tables, paragraphs, graphics, or even inline phrases—to have ID attributes. An element with an IDREF may point to any of these, anywhere in the document.

The problem is that the element with the IDREF might be architectural, whereas the element with the target ID might not; as a result, the architectural document seen by the architectural engine will have an unresolved IDREF. For example, consider the following excerpt from a client document:

Client document excerpt

```
<note id="xaa">This is a note.</note>

<para>This is a <link linkend="xaa">reference to a note
</link>.</para>
```

If **para** and **link** are architectural, but **note** is not, the architectural document will look like this:

Architectural document excerpt (incorrect)

```
<para>This is a <link linkend="xaa">reference to a note
</link>.</para>
```

Unfortunately, there is now no element with the ID "xaa", so the architectural engine may report a validation error.

The solution to this problem is to declare an **architecture bridge form name** using the `bridge-form` architecture use declaration attribute:

Defining a bridge for elements with IDs

```
<?IS10744:arch name="biblio" bridge-form="bridge"?>
```

The architectural engine will automatically derive any otherwise non-architectural elements with an ID from the architectural form **bridge**:

Architectural document excerpt (correct)

```
<bridge id="xaa">This is a note.</bridge>

<para>This is a <link linkend="xaa">reference to a note
</link>.</para>
```

This is a very useful technique for situations where you need only a placeholder for the target of an IDREF.

11.4.3   SGML: Default Architectural Information

In full SGML, you can also use the architecture support attributes `ArcDataF` and `ArcBridF`:

Client DTD Excerpt

```
<!ATTLIST #NOTATION doc
  ArcDataF NAME #FIXED "data"
  [...]>
```

Defining a bridge for elements with IDs

```
<!ATTLIST #NOTATION biblio
  ArcBridF NAME "bridge" #FIXED
  [...]>
```

11.5 Meta-DTDs

Most of the time, meta-DTDs are simply regular XML or SGML DTDs being used in a special way: existing DTDs can be used as meta-DTDs with no modification. There are, however, some special issues involved with meta-DTDs.

This section covers three topics related to meta-DTDs:

1. meta-DTD configuration
2. special SGML considerations

11.5.1 *Meta-DTD Configuration*

As described in detail in Chapter 8, DTDs often allow customization by using parameter entities. In the following example, the element **note** will have a different content model, depending on whether the parameter entity authoring has the value IGNORE or INCLUDE:

Configurable DTD

```
<![%authoring;[
  <!ENTITY % note.CONTENT "(#PCDATA)">
>
<!ENTITY % note.CONTENT "(para+)">

<!ELEMENT note %note.CONTENT;>
```

If the parameter entity authoring is set to INCLUDE, the parser will use the first entity declaration and skip the second; otherwise, it will skip the first and use the second.

There is a problem, however, if your meta-DTD uses this kind of configuration. Normally, you would set the parameter entity in the document type declaration subset:

Configuring a regular DTD

```
<!DOCTYPE doc SYSTEM "doc.dtd" [
  <!ENTITY % authoring "INCLUDE">
]>
```

However, the entities that you declare in your regular document and DTD do not affect the meta-DTD, so there is no obvious way to set the value of the `authoring` parameter entity, except by using the `options` architecture use declaration attribute:

Declaring a New Architecture Use Declaration Attribute

```
<?IS10744:arch name="doc" options="included"
included="authoring"?>
```

The `options` attribute provides a list of names of additional attributes. The values of each of those attributes are the names of parameter entities that should be set to `INCLUDE`.

11.5.1.1   SGML: Meta-DTD Configuration

In full SGML, you may also use the `ArcOptSA` architecture support attribute (Section 10.1.1, page 290) in the same way:

Setting a parameter entity for the meta-DTD

```
<!ATTLIST #NOTATION doc
 ArcOptSA NMTOKENS #FIXED "authoring">
```

For a meta-DTD, this has exactly the same effect as providing an entity declaration in the document-type declaration subset for a regular DTD.

It is important to note, however, that this is an additional, optional support attribute. The `ArcOpt` support attribute contains the names of all additional support attributes recognized by the architectural engine. By default, its value is `ArcOptSA`—if you provide a different value, then the `ArcOptSA` support attribute may not be available.

11.5.2   *SGML: Meta-DTDs*

There are two further considerations for meta-DTDs in full SGML:

1. quantities
2. general NAMECASE substitution

11.5.2.1   Meta-DTD Quantities

In full SGML, the SGML declaration determines the delimiters, quantities, character sets, and facilities used by a specific SGML document (and, by extension, by its DTD). The architectural engine will use the same declaration for parsing the meta-DTD, so you cannot use a meta-DTD that requires different delimiters or facilities than your client DTD and client document require.

There is, however, one exception to this rule. If the only difference between the requirements is in the quantities specified in the QUANTITY set of the SGML declaration, you may use the ArcQuant architecture support attribute (Section 10.1.1, page 290) to change specific quantities.

For example, your client DTD and document might use a declaration with the following quantities:

Client SGML declaration quantities

```
QUANTITY SGMLREF
  ATTCNT 48
  NAMELEN 12
  LITLEN 360
```

This quantity set uses the SGML defaults, except that elements may have up to 48 attributes (instead of 40), names may be up to 12 characters long (instead of eight), and literals may be up to 360 characters long (instead of 240).

The meta-DTD, however, might require longer names and literals; if so, you can declare them as follows:

Meta-DTD quantities

```
<!ATTLIST #NOTATION doc
  ArcQuant NMTOKENS #FIXED "NAMELEN 24 LITLEN 1024"
  [...]>
```

Now, the meta-DTD may have names up to 24 character long and literals up to 1024 characters long.

11.5.2.2   General NAMECASE Substitution

In addition to placing constraints on the meta-DTD itself (see Section 11.5.2.1, page 329), the SGML declaration may allow or forbid case substitution.

If your SGML declaration enables general name-case substitution (as do the reference concrete syntax and the SGML declarations for all five of this book's model DTDs), then the word `ArcBase` and the names of the architecture support attributes will be case-insensitive. An SGML declaration that allows general name-case substitution will contain something similar to the following:

Name-case substitution enabled

```
NAMECASE
   GENERAL YES
```

If your SGML declaration makes this specification, then the architectural engine will consider `ARCBASE`, `arcbase`, and `aRcBaSe`, or `ArcDtd` and `arcdtD`, to be equivalent.

If you are using a variant SGML declaration that forbids general name-case substitution (as with the SGML declaration used for XML compatibility), all of the attribute names and keywords for architectural forms support *will* be case-sensitive:

Name-case substitution disabled

```
NAMECASE
   GENERAL NO
```

In this case, the architectural engine would consider `arcdtd`, `ARCDTD`, and `ArcDtd` to be distinct attributes.

Part Five

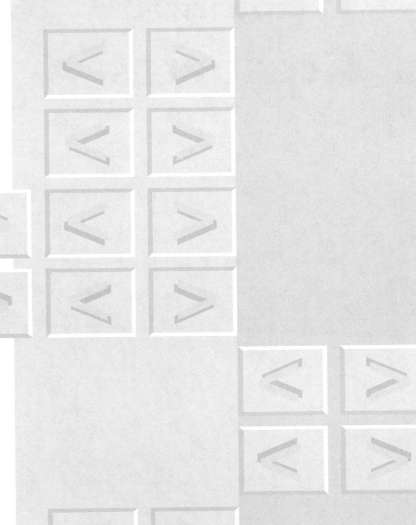

Back Matter

Model DTDs: Index of Element Types and Attributes

Appendix

This index lists all of the element type names and attribute names used in the book's five model DTDs. Note that although the examples in the book use the original case of the DTDs, all names are normalized to lower-case in this index for ease of access.

a (ELEMENT: HTML)

abbr (ATTRIBUTE: HTML)
    elements: td (HTML), th (HTML)

abbr (ELEMENT: HTML, TEI-Lite)

abbrev (ELEMENT: DocBook)

abbrsect (ELEMENT: MIL-STD-38784)

abbrtitle (ELEMENT: MIL-STD-38784)

abstract (ELEMENT: DocBook, ISO 12083)

accel (ELEMENT: DocBook)

accept (ATTRIBUTE: HTML)
    elements: input (HTML)

accept-charset (ATTRIBUTE: HTML)
    elements: form (HTML)

accesskey (ATTRIBUTE: HTML)
    elements: a (HTML), area (HTML), button (HTML), input (HTML), label (HTML),
    legend (HTML), textarea (HTML)

acidfree (ELEMENT: ISO 12083)

ack (ELEMENT: ISO 12083)

ackno   (ELEMENT: DocBook)

acqno   (ELEMENT: ISO 12083)

acronym   (ELEMENT: DocBook, HTML, MIL-STD-38784)

acronymlist   (ELEMENT: MIL-STD-38784)

action   (ATTRIBUTE: DocBook, HTML, MIL-STD-38784)
elements: form (HTML), keycombo (DocBook), mrchgtxt (MIL-STD-38784), shortcut (DocBook)

action   (ELEMENT: DocBook)

activity   (ELEMENT: MIL-STD-38784)

add   (ELEMENT: TEI-Lite)

address   (ATTRIBUTE: MIL-STD-38784)
elements: contents (MIL-STD-38784)

address   (ELEMENT: DocBook, HTML, MIL-STD-38784, TEI-Lite)

addrline   (ELEMENT: TEI-Lite)

aff   (ELEMENT: ISO 12083)

affiliation   (ELEMENT: DocBook)

afterwrd   (ELEMENT: ISO 12083)

agent   (ATTRIBUTE: TEI-Lite)
elements: gap (TEI-Lite), unclear (TEI-Lite)

aggloc   (ATTRIBUTE: ISO 12083)
elements: nameloc (ISO 12083)

align   (ATTRIBUTE: DocBook, HTML, ISO 12083, MIL-STD-38784)
elements: bottom (ISO 12083), col (HTML), colgroup (HTML), colspec (DocBook), colspec (MIL-STD-38784), dformgrp (ISO 12083), dformula (ISO 12083), entry (DocBook), entry (MIL-STD-38784), entrytbl (DocBook), entrytbl (MIL-STD-38784), fraction (ISO 12083), graphic (DocBook), inlinegraphic (DocBook), middle (ISO 12083), spanspec (DocBook), spanspec (MIL-STD-38784), tbody (HTML), td (HTML), tfoot (HTML), tgroup (DocBook), tgroup (MIL-STD-38784), th (HTML), thead (HTML), top (ISO 12083), tr (HTML)

allowbrk   (ATTRIBUTE: MIL-STD-38784)
elements: verbatim (MIL-STD-38784)

alphabet   (ATTRIBUTE: ISO 12083)
elements: dformula (ISO 12083), formula (ISO 12083), p (ISO 12083), q (ISO 12083), title (ISO 12083)

alt   (ATTRIBUTE: HTML)
elements: area (HTML), img (HTML), input (HTML)

alt   (ELEMENT: DocBook)

ana   (ATTRIBUTE: TEI-Lite)
elements: abbr (TEI-Lite), add (TEI-Lite), address (TEI-Lite), addrline (TEI-Lite), argument (TEI-Lite), author (TEI-Lite), authority (TEI-Lite), availability (TEI-Lite), back (TEI-Lite), bibl (TEI-Lite), biblfull (TEI-Lite), biblscope (TEI-Lite), body (TEI-Lite), byline (TEI-Lite), catdesc (TEI-Lite), category (TEI-Lite), catref (TEI-Lite), cell (TEI-Lite), change (TEI-Lite), cit. (TEI-Lite), classcode (TEI-Lite), classdecl (TEI-Lite), closer (TEI-Lite), code (TEI-Lite), corr (TEI-Lite), creation (TEI-Lite), date (TEI-Lite), dateline (TEI-Lite), distributor (TEI-Lite), div (TEI-Lite), div0 (TEI-Lite), div1 (TEI-Lite), div2 (TEI-Lite), div3 (TEI-Lite), div4 (TEI-Lite), div5 (TEI-Lite), div6 (TEI-Lite), div7 (TEI-Lite), divgen (TEI-Lite), docauthor (TEI-Lite), docdate (TEI-

Lite), docedition (TEI-Lite), docimprint (TEI-Lite), doctitle (TEI-Lite), edition (TEI-Lite), editionstmt (TEI-Lite), editor (TEI-Lite), editorialdecl (TEI-Lite), eg (TEI-Lite), emph (TEI-Lite), encodingdesc (TEI-Lite), epigraph (TEI-Lite), extent (TEI-Lite), figdesc (TEI-Lite), figure (TEI-Lite), filedesc (TEI-Lite), formula (TEI-Lite), front (TEI-Lite), funder (TEI-Lite), gap (TEI-Lite), gi (TEI-Lite), gloss (TEI-Lite), group (TEI-Lite), head (TEI-Lite), ident (TEI-Lite), idno (TEI-Lite), imprint (TEI-Lite), index (TEI-Lite), interp (TEI-Lite), interpgrp (TEI-Lite), keywords (TEI-Lite), kw (TEI-Lite), l (TEI-Lite), label (TEI-Lite), langusage (TEI-Lite), lg (TEI-Lite), list (TEI-Lite), listbibl (TEI-Lite), mentioned (TEI-Lite), name (TEI-Lite), notesstmt (TEI-Lite), num (TEI-Lite), opener (TEI-Lite), orig (TEI-Lite), p (TEI-Lite), principal (TEI-Lite), profiledesc (TEI-Lite), projectdesc (TEI-Lite), ptr (TEI-Lite), publicationstmt (TEI-Lite), publisher (TEI-Lite), pubplace (TEI-Lite), q (TEI-Lite), ref (TEI-Lite), refsdecl (TEI-Lite), reg (TEI-Lite), rendition (TEI-Lite), resp (TEI-Lite), respstmt (TEI-Lite), revisiondesc (TEI-Lite), row (TEI-Lite), rs (TEI-Lite), s (TEI-Lite), salute (TEI-Lite), samplingdecl (TEI-Lite), seg (TEI-Lite), seriesstmt (TEI-Lite), sic (TEI-Lite), signed (TEI-Lite), socalled (TEI-Lite), sourcedesc (TEI-Lite), sp (TEI-Lite), speaker (TEI-Lite), sponsor (TEI-Lite), stage (TEI-Lite), table (TEI-Lite), tagsdecl (TEI-Lite), tagusage (TEI-Lite), taxonomy (TEI-Lite), tei.2 (TEI-Lite), teiheader (TEI-Lite), term (TEI-Lite), text (TEI-Lite), textclass (TEI-Lite), time (TEI-Lite), title (TEI-Lite), titlepage (TEI-Lite), titlepart (TEI-Lite), titlestmt (TEI-Lite), trailer (TEI-Lite), unclear (TEI-Lite), xptr (TEI-Lite), xref (TEI-Lite)

anchor   (ELEMENT: DocBook, TEI-Lite)
anchored   (ATTRIBUTE: TEI-Lite)
    elements: note (TEI-Lite)
appendix   (ELEMENT: DocBook, ISO 12083, MIL-STD-38784)
applic   (ELEMENT: MIL-STD-38784)
applicabil   (ELEMENT: MIL-STD-38784)
application   (ATTRIBUTE: DocBook)
    elements: modespec (DocBook)
application   (ELEMENT: DocBook)
applicdef   (ELEMENT: MIL-STD-38784)
applichd   (ELEMENT: MIL-STD-38784)
applicref   (ATTRIBUTE: MIL-STD-38784)
    elements: abbrsect (MIL-STD-38784), applicabil (MIL-STD-38784), applicdef (MIL-STD-38784), dddesc (MIL-STD-38784), ddindex (MIL-STD-38784), figure (MIL-STD-38784), foldout (MIL-STD-38784), lrp (MIL-STD-38784), para0 (MIL-STD-38784), ratd (MIL-STD-38784), safesum (MIL-STD-38784), step1 (MIL-STD-38784), step2 (MIL-STD-38784), step3 (MIL-STD-38784), step4 (MIL-STD-38784), subpara1 (MIL-STD-38784), subpara2 (MIL-STD-38784), subpara3 (MIL-STD-38784), symsect (MIL-STD-38784), table (MIL-STD-38784), tabmat (MIL-STD-38784), tctolist (MIL-STD-38784), tmimprep (MIL-STD-38784)
appltitle   (ELEMENT: MIL-STD-38784)
appmat   (ELEMENT: ISO 12083)
appref   (ELEMENT: ISO 12083)
arch   (ATTRIBUTE: DocBook)
    elements: abbrev (DocBook), abstract (DocBook), accel (DocBook), ackno (DocBook), acronym (DocBook), action (DocBook), address (DocBook), affiliation

(DocBook), alt (DocBook), anchor (DocBook), appendix (DocBook), application (DocBook), area (DocBook), areaset (DocBook), areaspec (DocBook), arg (DocBook), artheader (DocBook), article (DocBook), artpagenums (DocBook), attribution (DocBook), author (DocBook), authorblurb (DocBook), authorgroup (DocBook), authorinitials (DocBook), beginpage (DocBook), bibliodiv (DocBook), biblioentry (DocBook), bibliography (DocBook), bibliomisc (DocBook), bibliomixed (DocBook), bibliomset (DocBook), biblioset (DocBook), blockquote (DocBook), book (DocBook), bookbiblio (DocBook), bookinfo (DocBook), bridgehead (DocBook), callout (DocBook), calloutlist (DocBook), caution (DocBook), chapter (DocBook), citation (DocBook), citerefentry (DocBook), citetitle (DocBook), city (DocBook), classname (DocBook), cmdsynopsis (DocBook), co (DocBook), collab (DocBook), collabname (DocBook), command (DocBook), comment (DocBook), computeroutput (DocBook), confdates (DocBook), confgroup (DocBook), confnum (DocBook), confsponsor (DocBook), conftitle (DocBook), contractnum (DocBook), contractsponsor (DocBook), contrib (DocBook), copyright (DocBook), corpauthor (DocBook), corpname (DocBook), country (DocBook), database (DocBook), date (DocBook), dedication (DocBook), docinfo (DocBook), edition (DocBook), editor (DocBook), email (DocBook), emphasis (DocBook), entry (DocBook), entrytbl (DocBook), envar (DocBook), epigraph (DocBook), equation (DocBook), errorcode (DocBook), errorname (DocBook), errortype (DocBook), example (DocBook), fax (DocBook), figure (DocBook), filename (DocBook), firstname (DocBook), firstterm (DocBook), footnote (DocBook), footnoteref (DocBook), foreignphrase (DocBook), formalpara (DocBook), funcdef (DocBook), funcparams (DocBook), funcprototype (DocBook), funcsynopsis (DocBook), funcsynopsisinfo (DocBook), function (DocBook), glossary (DocBook), glossdef (DocBook), glossdiv (DocBook), glossentry (DocBook), glosslist (DocBook), glosssee (DocBook), glossseealso (DocBook), glossterm (DocBook), graphic (DocBook), graphicco (DocBook), group (DocBook), guibutton (DocBook), guiicon (DocBook), guilabel (DocBook), guimenu (DocBook), guimenuitem (DocBook), guisubmenu (DocBook), hardware (DocBook), highlights (DocBook), holder (DocBook), honorific (DocBook), important (DocBook), index (DocBook), indexdiv (DocBook), indexentry (DocBook), indexterm (DocBook), informalequation (DocBook), informalexample (DocBook), informaltable (DocBook), inlineequation (DocBook), inlinegraphic (DocBook), interface (DocBook), interfacedefinition (DocBook), invpartnumber (DocBook), isbn (DocBook), issn (DocBook), issuenum (DocBook), itemizedlist (DocBook), itermset (DocBook), jobtitle (DocBook), keycap (DocBook), keycode (DocBook), keycombo (DocBook), keysym (DocBook), keyword (DocBook), keywordset (DocBook), legalnotice (DocBook), lineage (DocBook), lineannotation (DocBook), link (DocBook), listitem (DocBook), literal (DocBook), literallayout (DocBook), lot (DocBook), lotentry (DocBook), manvolnum (DocBook), markup (DocBook), medialabel (DocBook), member (DocBook), menuchoice (DocBook), modespec (DocBook), mousebutton (DocBook), msg (DocBook), msgaud (DocBook), msgentry (DocBook), msgexplan (DocBook), msginfo (DocBook), msglevel (DocBook), msgmain (DocBook), msgorig (DocBook), msgrel (DocBook), msgset (DocBook), msgsub (DocBook), msgtext (DocBook), note (DocBook), olink (DocBook), option (DocBook), optional (DocBook), orderedlist (DocBook), orgdiv (DocBook), orgname (DocBook), otheraddr (DocBook), othercredit (DocBook), othername (DocBook), pagenums (DocBook), para (DocBook), paramdef (DocBook), parameter (DocBook), part (DocBook), partintro (DocBook), phone (DocBook), phrase (DocBook), pob (DocBook), postcode (DocBook), preface (DocBook), primary (DocBook), primaryie (DocBook), printhistory (DocBook), procedure (DocBook), productname (DocBook), productnumber (DocBook), programlisting (DocBook), programlistingco (DocBook), prompt (DocBook), property (DocBook), pubdate (DocBook), publisher (DocBook), publishername (DocBook), pubsnumber (DocBook), quote (DocBook), refclass (DocBook), refdescriptor (DocBook), refentry (DocBook), refentrytitle (DocBook), reference (DocBook), refmeta (DocBook), refmiscinfo (DocBook), refname (DocBook), refnamediv (DocBook), refpurpose (DocBook), refsect1 (DocBook), refsect1info (DocBook), refsect2 (DocBook), refsect2info (DocBook), refsect3 (DocBook), refsect3info (DocBook), refsynopsisdiv (DocBook), refsynopsisdivinfo (DocBook), releaseinfo (DocBook), replaceable (DocBook), returnvalue (DocBook), revhistory (DocBook), revision (DocBook), revnumber (DocBook), revremark (DocBook), row (DocBook), sbr (DocBook), screen (DocBook), screenco (DocBook), screeninfo (DocBook), screenshot (DocBook), secondary (DocBook), secondaryie (DocBook), sect1 (DocBook), sect1info (DocBook), sect2 (DocBook), sect2info (DocBook), sect3 (DocBook), sect3info (DocBook), sect4 (DocBook), sect4info (DocBook), sect5 (DocBook), sect5info (DocBook), see (DocBook), seealso (DocBook), seealsoie (DocBook), seeie (DocBook), seg (DocBook), seglistitem (DocBook), segmentedlist (DocBook), segtitle (DocBook), seriesinfo (DocBook), seriesvolnums (DocBook), set (DocBook), setindex (DocBook), setinfo (DocBook), sgmltag (DocBook), shortaffil (DocBook), shortcut (DocBook), sidebar (DocBook), simpara (DocBook), simplelist (DocBook), simplesect (DocBook), state (DocBook), step (DocBook), street (DocBook), structfield (DocBook), structname (DocBook), subject (DocBook), subjectset (DocBook), subjectterm (DocBook), subscript (DocBook), substeps (DocBook), subtitle (DocBook), superscript (DocBook), surname (DocBook), symbol (DocBook), synopfragment (DocBook), synopfragmentref (DocBook), synopsis (DocBook), systemitem (DocBook), table (DocBook), tbody (DocBook), term (DocBook), tertiary (DocBook), tertiaryie (DocBook), tfoot (DocBook), tgroup (DocBook), thead (DocBook), tip (DocBook), title (DocBook), titleabbrev (DocBook), toc (DocBook), tocback (DocBook), tocchap (DocBook), tocentry (DocBook), tocfront (DocBook), toclevel1 (DocBook), toclevel2 (DocBook), toclevel3 (DocBook), toclevel4 (DocBook), toclevel5 (DocBook), tocpart (DocBook), token (DocBook), trademark (DocBook), type (DocBook), ulink (DocBook), userinput (DocBook), varargs (DocBook), variablelist (DocBook), varlistentry (DocBook), void (DocBook), volumenum (DocBook), warning (DocBook), wordasword (DocBook), xref (DocBook), year (DocBook)

archive   (ATTRIBUTE: HTML)
    elements: object (HTML)
area   (ELEMENT: DocBook, HTML)
arearefs   (ATTRIBUTE: DocBook)
    elements: callout (DocBook)
areaset   (ELEMENT: DocBook)
areaspec   (ELEMENT: DocBook)
arg   (ELEMENT: DocBook)

argument   (ELEMENT: TEI-Lite)

arrange   (ATTRIBUTE: ISO 12083)
   elements: inf (ISO 12083), sup (ISO 12083)

array   (ELEMENT: ISO 12083)

arraycel   (ELEMENT: ISO 12083)

arraycol   (ELEMENT: ISO 12083)

arrayrow   (ELEMENT: ISO 12083)

artheader   (ELEMENT: DocBook)

article   (ELEMENT: DocBook)

artpagenums   (ELEMENT: DocBook)

artref   (ELEMENT: ISO 12083)

artwork   (ELEMENT: ISO 12083)

assocfig   (ATTRIBUTE: MIL-STD-38784)
   elements: abbrsect (MIL-STD-38784), appendix (MIL-STD-38784), applicdef (MIL-STD-38784), chapter (MIL-STD-38784), ddchapter (MIL-STD-38784), dddesc (MIL-STD-38784), ddindex (MIL-STD-38784), docpart (MIL-STD-38784), figtable (MIL-STD-38784), figure (MIL-STD-38784), foldout (MIL-STD-38784), legend (MIL-STD-38784), lrp (MIL-STD-38784), para0 (MIL-STD-38784), ratd (MIL-STD-38784), safesum (MIL-STD-38784), section (MIL-STD-38784), step1 (MIL-STD-38784), step2 (MIL-STD-38784), step3 (MIL-STD-38784), step4 (MIL-STD-38784), subpara1 (MIL-STD-38784), subpara2 (MIL-STD-38784), subpara3 (MIL-STD-38784), symsect (MIL-STD-38784), table (MIL-STD-38784), tabmat (MIL-STD-38784), tctolist (MIL-STD-38784), tctotbl (MIL-STD-38784), tmimprep (MIL-STD-38784), volume (MIL-STD-38784)

assoctab   (ATTRIBUTE: MIL-STD-38784)
   elements: abbrsect (MIL-STD-38784), appendix (MIL-STD-38784), applicdef (MIL-STD-38784), chapter (MIL-STD-38784), ddchapter (MIL-STD-38784), dddesc (MIL-STD-38784), ddindex (MIL-STD-38784), docpart (MIL-STD-38784), figure (MIL-STD-38784), foldout (MIL-STD-38784), lrp (MIL-STD-38784), para0 (MIL-STD-38784), ratd (MIL-STD-38784), safesum (MIL-STD-38784), section (MIL-STD-38784), step1 (MIL-STD-38784), step2 (MIL-STD-38784), step3 (MIL-STD-38784), step4 (MIL-STD-38784), subpara1 (MIL-STD-38784), subpara2 (MIL-STD-38784), subpara3 (MIL-STD-38784), symsect (MIL-STD-38784), table (MIL-STD-38784), tabmat (MIL-STD-38784), tctolist (MIL-STD-38784), tctotbl (MIL-STD-38784), tmimprep (MIL-STD-38784), volume (MIL-STD-38784)

attribution   (ELEMENT: DocBook)

authgrp   (ELEMENT: ISO 12083)

authnot   (ELEMENT: MIL-STD-38784)

author   (ELEMENT: DocBook, ISO 12083, TEI-Lite)

authorblurb   (ELEMENT: DocBook)

authorgroup   (ELEMENT: DocBook)

authorinitials   (ELEMENT: DocBook)

authority   (ELEMENT: TEI-Lite)

autobuild   (ATTRIBUTE: MIL-STD-38784)
   elements: contents (MIL-STD-38784), lepcontents (MIL-STD-38784)

autogen   (ATTRIBUTE: MIL-STD-38784)
   elements: acronymlist (MIL-STD-38784)

auxfront   (ELEMENT: MIL-STD-38784)
avail   (ELEMENT: ISO 12083)
availability   (ELEMENT: TEI-Lite)
axis   (ATTRIBUTE: HTML)
    elements: td (HTML), th (HTML)
b   (ELEMENT: HTML)
back   (ELEMENT: ISO 12083, TEI-Lite)
base   (ELEMENT: HTML)
baseform   (ATTRIBUTE: DocBook)
    elements: glossterm (DocBook)
bdo   (ELEMENT: HTML)
beginpage   (ELEMENT: DocBook)
bibl   (ELEMENT: TEI-Lite)
biblfull   (ELEMENT: TEI-Lite)
bibliodiv   (ELEMENT: DocBook)
biblioentry   (ELEMENT: DocBook)
bibliography   (ELEMENT: DocBook)
bibliomisc   (ELEMENT: DocBook)
bibliomixed   (ELEMENT: DocBook)
bibliomset   (ELEMENT: DocBook)
biblioset   (ELEMENT: DocBook)
biblist   (ELEMENT: ISO 12083)
biblscope   (ELEMENT: TEI-Lite)
big   (ELEMENT: HTML)
blockquote   (ELEMENT: DocBook, HTML)
boardno   (ATTRIBUTE: MIL-STD-38784)
    elements: graphic (MIL-STD-38784)
body   (ELEMENT: HTML, ISO 12083, MIL-STD-38784, TEI-Lite)
bold   (ELEMENT: ISO 12083)
book   (ELEMENT: DocBook, ISO 12083)
bookbiblio   (ELEMENT: DocBook)
bookinfo   (ELEMENT: DocBook)
border   (ATTRIBUTE: HTML)
    elements: table (HTML)
botmar   (ATTRIBUTE: MIL-STD-38784)
    elements: colspec (MIL-STD-38784), table (MIL-STD-38784), tabmat (MIL-STD-38784), tgroup (MIL-STD-38784)
bottom   (ELEMENT: ISO 12083)
box   (ELEMENT: ISO 12083)
boxterm   (ATTRIBUTE: MIL-STD-38784)
    elements: applicdef (MIL-STD-38784)
bq   (ELEMENT: ISO 12083)
br   (ELEMENT: HTML)
break   (ELEMENT: ISO 12083)
bridgehead   (ELEMENT: DocBook)
brk   (ELEMENT: MIL-STD-38784)
button   (ELEMENT: HTML)

by   (ATTRIBUTE: MIL-STD-38784)
    elements: modreq (MIL-STD-38784)
byline   (ELEMENT: TEI-Lite)
calendar   (ATTRIBUTE: TEI-Lite)
    elements: date (TEI-Lite)
callout   (ELEMENT: DocBook, MIL-STD-38784)
calloutlist   (ELEMENT: DocBook)
caption   (ELEMENT: HTML)
catalog   (ELEMENT: ISO 12083)
catdesc   (ELEMENT: TEI-Lite)
category   (ATTRIBUTE: MIL-STD-38784)
    elements: modreq (MIL-STD-38784)
category   (ELEMENT: TEI-Lite)
catref   (ELEMENT: TEI-Lite)
caution   (ELEMENT: DocBook, MIL-STD-38784)
cell   (ELEMENT: ISO 12083, TEI-Lite)
cellcont   (ATTRIBUTE: MIL-STD-38784)
    elements: table (MIL-STD-38784), tabmat (MIL-STD-38784), tctotbl (MIL-STD-38784)
cellpadding   (ATTRIBUTE: HTML)
    elements: table (HTML)
cellspacing   (ATTRIBUTE: HTML)
    elements: table (HTML)
cert   (ATTRIBUTE: TEI-Lite)
    elements: abbr (TEI-Lite), add (TEI-Lite), corr (TEI-Lite), del (TEI-Lite), sic (TEI-Lite), unclear (TEI-Lite)
certainty   (ATTRIBUTE: TEI-Lite)
    elements: date (TEI-Lite)
change   (ATTRIBUTE: MIL-STD-38784)
    elements: change (MIL-STD-38784)
change   (ELEMENT: MIL-STD-38784, TEI-Lite)
chapter   (ELEMENT: DocBook, ISO 12083, MIL-STD-38784)
char   (ATTRIBUTE: DocBook, HTML, MIL-STD-38784)
    elements: col (HTML), colgroup (HTML), colspec (DocBook), colspec (MIL-STD-38784), entry (DocBook), entry (MIL-STD-38784), entrytbl (DocBook), entrytbl (MIL-STD-38784), spanspec (DocBook), spanspec (MIL-STD-38784), tbody (HTML), td (HTML), tfoot (HTML), tgroup (DocBook), tgroup (MIL-STD-38784), th (HTML), thead (HTML), tr (HTML)
charoff   (ATTRIBUTE: DocBook, HTML, MIL-STD-38784)
    elements: col (HTML), colgroup (HTML), colspec (DocBook), colspec (MIL-STD-38784), entry (DocBook), entry (MIL-STD-38784), entrytbl (DocBook), entrytbl (MIL-STD-38784), spanspec (DocBook), spanspec (MIL-STD-38784), tbody (HTML), td (HTML), tfoot (HTML), tgroup (DocBook), tgroup (MIL-STD-38784), th (HTML), thead (HTML), tr (HTML)
charset   (ATTRIBUTE: HTML)
    elements: a (HTML), link (HTML), script (HTML)
checked   (ATTRIBUTE: HTML)

elements: input (HTML)

chgdate   (ELEMENT: MIL-STD-38784)

chghist   (ELEMENT: MIL-STD-38784)

chginssht   (ELEMENT: MIL-STD-38784)

chglen   (ATTRIBUTE: MIL-STD-38784)
elements: mrchgtxt (MIL-STD-38784)

chglevel   (ATTRIBUTE: MIL-STD-38784)
elements: pgbrk (MIL-STD-38784)

chglist   (ELEMENT: MIL-STD-38784)

chgloc   (ATTRIBUTE: MIL-STD-38784)
elements: mrchgtxt (MIL-STD-38784)

chgnum   (ELEMENT: MIL-STD-38784)

chgpara   (ELEMENT: MIL-STD-38784)

chgrec   (ELEMENT: MIL-STD-38784)

choice   (ATTRIBUTE: DocBook)
elements: arg (DocBook), group (DocBook)

cit   (ELEMENT: TEI-Lite)

citation   (ELEMENT: DocBook, ISO 12083)

cite   (ATTRIBUTE: HTML)
elements: blockquote (HTML), del (HTML), ins (HTML), q (HTML)

cite   (ELEMENT: HTML)

citeref   (ELEMENT: ISO 12083)

citerefentry   (ELEMENT: DocBook)

citetitle   (ELEMENT: DocBook)

city   (ELEMENT: DocBook, ISO 12083)

class   (ATTRIBUTE: DocBook, HTML)
elements: a (HTML), abbr (HTML), acronym (HTML), address (HTML), application (DocBook), area (HTML), article (DocBook), b (HTML), bdo (HTML), big (HTML), blockquote (HTML), body (HTML), br (HTML), button (HTML), caption (HTML), cite (HTML), code (HTML), col (HTML), colgroup (HTML), database (DocBook), dd (HTML), del (HTML), dfn (HTML), div (HTML), dl (HTML), dt (HTML), em (HTML), fieldset (HTML), filename (DocBook), form (HTML), h1 (HTML), h2 (HTML), h3 (HTML), h4 (HTML), h5 (HTML), h6 (HTML), hr (HTML), i (HTML), img (HTML), indexterm (DocBook), input (HTML), ins (HTML), interface (DocBook), kbd (HTML), label (HTML), legend (HTML), li (HTML), link (HTML), map (HTML), medialabel (DocBook), noscript (HTML), object (HTML), ol (HTML), optgroup (HTML), option (HTML), p (HTML), parameter (DocBook), pre (HTML), productname (DocBook), q (HTML), refmiscinfo (DocBook), replaceable (DocBook), samp (HTML), select (HTML), sgmltag (DocBook), small (HTML), span (HTML), strong (HTML), sub (HTML), sup (HTML), symbol (DocBook), systemitem (DocBook), table (HTML), tbody (HTML), td (HTML), textarea (HTML), tfoot (HTML), th (HTML), thead (HTML), tr (HTML), trademark (DocBook), tt (HTML), ul (HTML), var (HTML)

classcode   (ELEMENT: TEI-Lite)

classdecl   (ELEMENT: TEI-Lite)

classid   (ATTRIBUTE: HTML)
elements: object (HTML)

classname   (ELEMENT: DocBook)
cline   (ELEMENT: ISO 12083)
closer   (ELEMENT: TEI-Lite)
cmdsynopsis   (ELEMENT: DocBook)
cmntrcat   (ATTRIBUTE: MIL-STD-38784)
    elements: modreq (MIL-STD-38784)
cnycode   (ATTRIBUTE: ISO 12083)
    elements: country (ISO 12083)
co   (ELEMENT: DocBook)
code   (ELEMENT: HTML, TEI-Lite)
codebase   (ATTRIBUTE: HTML)
    elements: object (HTML)
coden   (ELEMENT: ISO 12083)
codetype   (ATTRIBUTE: HTML)
    elements: object (HTML)
col   (ELEMENT: HTML)
colalign   (ATTRIBUTE: ISO 12083)
    elements: array (ISO 12083)
colgroup   (ELEMENT: HTML)
collab   (ELEMENT: DocBook)
collabname   (ELEMENT: DocBook)
colname   (ATTRIBUTE: DocBook, MIL-STD-38784)
    elements: colspec (DocBook), colspec (MIL-STD-38784), entry (DocBook), entry
    (MIL-STD-38784), entrytbl (DocBook), entrytbl (MIL-STD-38784)
colnum   (ATTRIBUTE: DocBook, MIL-STD-38784)
    elements: colspec (DocBook), colspec (MIL-STD-38784)
color   (ATTRIBUTE: MIL-STD-38784)
    elements: emphasis (MIL-STD-38784), graphic (MIL-STD-38784)
cols   (ATTRIBUTE: DocBook, HTML, MIL-STD-38784, TEI-Lite)
    elements: cell (TEI-Lite), entrytbl (DocBook), entrytbl (MIL-STD-38784), table (TEI-
    Lite), textarea (HTML), tgroup (DocBook), tgroup (MIL-STD-38784)
colsep   (ATTRIBUTE: DocBook, ISO 12083, MIL-STD-38784)
    elements: array (ISO 12083), colspec (DocBook), colspec (MIL-STD-38784), entry
    (DocBook), entry (MIL-STD-38784), entrytbl (DocBook), entrytbl (MIL-STD-
    38784), figtable (MIL-STD-38784), informaltable (DocBook), spanspec (DocBook),
    spanspec (MIL-STD-38784), table (DocBook), table (MIL-STD-38784), tabmat
    (MIL-STD-38784), tctotbl (MIL-STD-38784), tgroup (DocBook), tgroup (MIL-STD-
    38784)
colspan   (ATTRIBUTE: HTML)
    elements: td (HTML), th (HTML)
colspec   (ELEMENT: DocBook, MIL-STD-38784)
columns   (ATTRIBUTE: DocBook)
    elements: simplelist (DocBook)
colwidth   (ATTRIBUTE: DocBook, MIL-STD-38784)
    elements: colspec (DocBook), colspec (MIL-STD-38784), legend (MIL-STD-
    38784)
command   (ELEMENT: DocBook)

comment   (ELEMENT: DocBook)

compon   (ATTRIBUTE: MIL-STD-38784)

elements: abbrsect (MIL-STD-38784), appendix (MIL-STD-38784), applicdef (MIL-STD-38784), chapter (MIL-STD-38784), ddchapter (MIL-STD-38784), dddesc (MIL-STD-38784), ddindex (MIL-STD-38784), docpart (MIL-STD-38784), figure (MIL-STD-38784), foldout (MIL-STD-38784), lrp (MIL-STD-38784), para0 (MIL-STD-38784), ratd (MIL-STD-38784), safesum (MIL-STD-38784), section (MIL-STD-38784), step1 (MIL-STD-38784), step2 (MIL-STD-38784), step3 (MIL-STD-38784), step4 (MIL-STD-38784), subpara1 (MIL-STD-38784), subpara2 (MIL-STD-38784), subpara3 (MIL-STD-38784), symsect (MIL-STD-38784), table (MIL-STD-38784), tabmat (MIL-STD-38784), tctolist (MIL-STD-38784), tctotbl (MIL-STD-38784), tmimprep (MIL-STD-38784), volume (MIL-STD-38784)

computeroutput   (ELEMENT: DocBook)

confdates   (ELEMENT: DocBook)

confgroup   (ELEMENT: DocBook)

confgrp   (ELEMENT: ISO 12083)

confname   (ELEMENT: ISO 12083)

confnum   (ELEMENT: DocBook)

conformance   (ATTRIBUTE: DocBook)

elements: abbrev (DocBook), abstract (DocBook), accel (DocBook), ackno (DocBook), acronym (DocBook), action (DocBook), address (DocBook), affiliation (DocBook), alt (DocBook), anchor (DocBook), appendix (DocBook), application (DocBook), area (DocBook), areaset (DocBook), areaspec (DocBook), arg (DocBook), artheader (DocBook), article (DocBook), artpagenums (DocBook), attribution (DocBook), author (DocBook), authorblurb (DocBook), authorgroup (DocBook), authorinitials (DocBook), beginpage (DocBook), bibliodiv (DocBook), biblioentry (DocBook), bibliography (DocBook), bibliomisc (DocBook), bibliomixed (DocBook), bibliomset (DocBook), biblioset (DocBook), blockquote (DocBook), book (DocBook), bookbiblio (DocBook), bookinfo (DocBook), bridgehead (DocBook), callout (DocBook), calloutlist (DocBook), caution (DocBook), chapter (DocBook), citation (DocBook), citerefentry (DocBook), citetitle (DocBook), city (DocBook), classname (DocBook), cmdsynopsis (DocBook), co (DocBook), collab (DocBook), collabname (DocBook), command (DocBook), comment (DocBook), computeroutput (DocBook), confdates (DocBook), confgroup (DocBook), confnum (DocBook), confsponsor (DocBook), conftitle (DocBook), contractnum (DocBook), contractsponsor (DocBook), contrib (DocBook), copyright (DocBook), corpauthor (DocBook), corpname (DocBook), country (DocBook), database (DocBook), date (DocBook), dedication (DocBook), docinfo (DocBook), edition (DocBook), editor (DocBook), email (DocBook), emphasis (DocBook), entry (DocBook), entrytbl (DocBook), envar (DocBook), epigraph (DocBook), equation (DocBook), errorcode (DocBook), errorname (DocBook), errortype (DocBook), example (DocBook), fax (DocBook), figure (DocBook), filename (DocBook), firstname (DocBook), firstterm (DocBook), footnote (DocBook), footnoteref (DocBook), foreignphrase (DocBook), formalpara (DocBook), funcdef (DocBook), funcparams (DocBook), funcprototype (DocBook), funcsynopsis (DocBook), funcsynopsisinfo (DocBook), function (DocBook), glossary (DocBook), glossdef (DocBook), glossdiv (DocBook), glossentry (DocBook), glosslist (DocBook), glosssee (DocBook), glossseealso

(DocBook), glossterm (DocBook), graphic (DocBook), graphicco (DocBook), group (DocBook), guibutton (DocBook), guiicon (DocBook), guilabel (DocBook), guimenu (DocBook), guimenuitem (DocBook), guisubmenu (DocBook), hardware (DocBook), highlights (DocBook), holder (DocBook), honorific (DocBook), important (DocBook), index (DocBook), indexdiv (DocBook), indexentry (DocBook), indexterm (DocBook), informalequation (DocBook), informalexample (DocBook), informaltable (DocBook), inlineequation (DocBook), inlinegraphic (DocBook), interface (DocBook), interfacedefinition (DocBook), invpartnumber (DocBook), isbn (DocBook), issn (DocBook), issuenum (DocBook), itemizedlist (DocBook), itermset (DocBook), jobtitle (DocBook), keycap (DocBook), keycode (DocBook), keycombo (DocBook), keysym (DocBook), keyword (DocBook), keywordset (DocBook), legalnotice (DocBook), lineage (DocBook), lineannotation (DocBook), link (DocBook), listitem (DocBook), literal (DocBook), literallayout (DocBook), lot (DocBook), lotentry (DocBook), manvolnum (DocBook), markup (DocBook), medialabel (DocBook), member (DocBook), menuchoice (DocBook), modespec (DocBook), mousebutton (DocBook), msg (DocBook), msgaud (DocBook), msgentry (DocBook), msgexplan (DocBook), msginfo (DocBook), msglevel (DocBook), msgmain (DocBook), msgorig (DocBook), msgrel (DocBook), msgset (DocBook), msgsub (DocBook), msgtext (DocBook), note (DocBook), olink (DocBook), option (DocBook), optional (DocBook), orderedlist (DocBook), orgdiv (DocBook), orgname (DocBook), otheraddr (DocBook), othercredit (DocBook), othername (DocBook), pagenums (DocBook), para (DocBook), paramdef (DocBook), parameter (DocBook), part (DocBook), partintro (DocBook), phone (DocBook), phrase (DocBook), pob (DocBook), postcode (DocBook), preface (DocBook), primary (DocBook), primaryie (DocBook), printhistory (DocBook), procedure (DocBook), productname (DocBook), productnumber (DocBook), programlisting (DocBook), programlistingco (DocBook), prompt (DocBook), property (DocBook), pubdate (DocBook), publisher (DocBook), publishername (DocBook), pubsnumber (DocBook), quote (DocBook), refclass (DocBook), refdescriptor (DocBook), refentry (DocBook), refentrytitle (DocBook), reference (DocBook), refmeta (DocBook), refmiscinfo (DocBook), refname (DocBook), refnamediv (DocBook), refpurpose (DocBook), refsect1 (DocBook), refsect1info (DocBook), refsect2 (DocBook), refsect2info (DocBook), refsect3 (DocBook), refsect3info (DocBook), refsynopsisdiv (DocBook), refsynopsisdivinfo (DocBook), releaseinfo (DocBook), replaceable (DocBook), returnvalue (DocBook), revhistory (DocBook), revision (DocBook), revnumber (DocBook), revremark (DocBook), row (DocBook), sbr (DocBook), screen (DocBook), screenco (DocBook), screeninfo (DocBook), screenshot (DocBook), secondary (DocBook), secondaryie (DocBook), sect1 (DocBook), sect1info (DocBook), sect2 (DocBook), sect2info (DocBook), sect3 (DocBook), sect3info (DocBook), sect4 (DocBook), sect4info (DocBook), sect5 (DocBook), sect5info (DocBook), see (DocBook), seealso (DocBook), seealsoie (DocBook), seeie (DocBook), seg (DocBook), seglistitem (DocBook), segmentedlist (DocBook), segtitle (DocBook), seriesinfo (DocBook), seriesvolnums (DocBook), set (DocBook), setindex (DocBook), setinfo (DocBook), sgmltag (DocBook), shortaffil (DocBook), shortcut (DocBook), sidebar (DocBook), simpara (DocBook), simplelist (DocBook), simplesect (DocBook), state (DocBook), step (DocBook), street (DocBook), structfield (DocBook), structname (DocBook), subject (DocBook), subjectset (DocBook), subjectterm (DocBook), subscript (DocBook), substeps (DocBook), subtitle (DocBook), superscript (DocBook), surname (DocBook), symbol (DocBook), synopfragment (DocBook), synopfragmentref (DocBook), synopsis (DocBook), systemitem (DocBook), table (DocBook), tbody (DocBook), term (DocBook), tertiary (DocBook), tertiaryie (DocBook), tfoot (DocBook), tgroup (DocBook), thead (DocBook), tip (DocBook), title (DocBook), titleabbrev (DocBook), toc (DocBook), tocback (DocBook), tocchap (DocBook), tocentry (DocBook), tocfront (DocBook), toclevel1 (DocBook), toclevel2 (DocBook), toclevel3 (DocBook), toclevel4 (DocBook), toclevel5 (DocBook), tocpart (DocBook), token (DocBook), trademark (DocBook), type (DocBook), ulink (DocBook), userinput (DocBook), varargs (DocBook), variablelist (DocBook), varlistentry (DocBook), void (DocBook), volumenum (DocBook), warning (DocBook), wordasword (DocBook), xref (DocBook), year (DocBook)

confsponsor   (ELEMENT: DocBook)
conftitle   (ELEMENT: DocBook)
content   (ATTRIBUTE: HTML)
 elements: meta (HTML)
contents   (ATTRIBUTE: DocBook)
 elements: bookinfo (DocBook), setinfo (DocBook)
contents   (ELEMENT: MIL-STD-38784)
continuation   (ATTRIBUTE: DocBook)
 elements: orderedlist (DocBook)
contract   (ELEMENT: ISO 12083)
contractno   (ELEMENT: MIL-STD-38784)
contractnum   (ELEMENT: DocBook)
contractsponsor   (ELEMENT: DocBook)
contrib   (ELEMENT: DocBook)
contype   (ATTRIBUTE: MIL-STD-38784)
 elements: abbrsect (MIL-STD-38784), appendix (MIL-STD-38784), applicdef (MIL-STD-38784), chapter (MIL-STD-38784), ddchapter (MIL-STD-38784), dddesc (MIL-STD-38784), ddindex (MIL-STD-38784), docpart (MIL-STD-38784), figure (MIL-STD-38784), foldout (MIL-STD-38784), lrp (MIL-STD-38784), para0 (MIL-STD-38784), ratd (MIL-STD-38784), safesum (MIL-STD-38784), section (MIL-STD-38784), step1 (MIL-STD-38784), step2 (MIL-STD-38784), step3 (MIL-STD-38784), step4 (MIL-STD-38784), subpara1 (MIL-STD-38784), subpara2 (MIL-STD-38784), subpara3 (MIL-STD-38784), symsect (MIL-STD-38784), table (MIL-STD-38784), tabmat (MIL-STD-38784), tctolist (MIL-STD-38784), tctotbl (MIL-STD-38784), tmimprep (MIL-STD-38784), volume (MIL-STD-38784)
coordend   (ATTRIBUTE: MIL-STD-38784)
 elements: graphic (MIL-STD-38784)
coords   (ATTRIBUTE: DocBook, HTML)
 elements: a (HTML), area (DocBook), area (HTML), areaset (DocBook)
coordst   (ATTRIBUTE: MIL-STD-38784)
 elements: figtable (MIL-STD-38784), graphic (MIL-STD-38784), legend (MIL-STD-38784)
copyright   (ELEMENT: DocBook, MIL-STD-38784)
corpauth   (ELEMENT: ISO 12083)

corpauthor   (ELEMENT: DocBook)

corpname   (ELEMENT: DocBook)

corr   (ATTRIBUTE: TEI-Lite)
 elements: sic (TEI-Lite)

corr   (ELEMENT: TEI-Lite)

corresp   (ATTRIBUTE: TEI-Lite)
 elements: abbr (TEI-Lite), add (TEI-Lite), address (TEI-Lite), addrline (TEI-Lite), argument (TEI-Lite), author (TEI-Lite), authority (TEI-Lite), availability (TEI-Lite), back (TEI-Lite), bibl (TEI-Lite), biblfull (TEI-Lite), biblscope (TEI-Lite), body (TEI-Lite), byline (TEI-Lite), catdesc (TEI-Lite), category (TEI-Lite), catref (TEI-Lite), cell (TEI-Lite), change (TEI-Lite), cit (TEI-Lite), classcode (TEI-Lite), classdecl (TEI-Lite), closer (TEI-Lite), code (TEI-Lite), corr (TEI-Lite), creation (TEI-Lite), date (TEI-Lite), dateline (TEI-Lite), distributor (TEI-Lite), div (TEI-Lite), div0 (TEI-Lite), div1 (TEI-Lite), div2 (TEI-Lite), div3 (TEI-Lite), div4 (TEI-Lite), div5 (TEI-Lite), div6 (TEI-Lite), div7 (TEI-Lite), divgen (TEI-Lite), docauthor (TEI-Lite), docdate (TEI-Lite), docedition (TEI-Lite), docimprint (TEI-Lite), doctitle (TEI-Lite), edition (TEI-Lite), editionstmt (TEI-Lite), editor (TEI-Lite), editorialdecl (TEI-Lite), eg (TEI-Lite), emph (TEI-Lite), encodingdesc (TEI-Lite), epigraph (TEI-Lite), extent (TEI-Lite), figdesc (TEI-Lite), figure (TEI-Lite), filedesc (TEI-Lite), formula (TEI-Lite), front (TEI-Lite), funder (TEI-Lite), gap (TEI-Lite), gi (TEI-Lite), gloss (TEI-Lite), group (TEI-Lite), head (TEI-Lite), ident (TEI-Lite), idno (TEI-Lite), imprint (TEI-Lite), index (TEI-Lite), interp (TEI-Lite), interpgrp (TEI-Lite), keywords (TEI-Lite), kw (TEI-Lite), l (TEI-Lite), label (TEI-Lite), langusage (TEI-Lite), lg (TEI-Lite), list (TEI-Lite), listbibl (TEI-Lite), mentioned (TEI-Lite), name (TEI-Lite), notesstmt (TEI-Lite), num (TEI-Lite), opener (TEI-Lite), orig (TEI-Lite), p (TEI-Lite), principal (TEI-Lite), profiledesc (TEI-Lite), projectdesc (TEI-Lite), ptr (TEI-Lite), publicationstmt (TEI-Lite), publisher (TEI-Lite), pubplace (TEI-Lite), q (TEI-Lite), ref (TEI-Lite), refsdecl (TEI-Lite), reg (TEI-Lite), rendition (TEI-Lite), resp (TEI-Lite), respstmt (TEI-Lite), revisiondesc (TEI-Lite), row (TEI-Lite), rs (TEI-Lite), s (TEI-Lite), salute (TEI-Lite), samplingdecl (TEI-Lite), seg (TEI-Lite), seriesstmt (TEI-Lite), sic (TEI-Lite), signed (TEI-Lite), socalled (TEI-Lite), sourcedesc (TEI-Lite), sp (TEI-Lite), speaker (TEI-Lite), sponsor (TEI-Lite), stage (TEI-Lite), table (TEI-Lite), tagsdecl (TEI-Lite), tagusage (TEI-Lite), taxonomy (TEI-Lite), tei.2 (TEI-Lite), teiheader (TEI-Lite), term (TEI-Lite), text (TEI-Lite), textclass (TEI-Lite), time (TEI-Lite), title (TEI-Lite), titlepage (TEI-Lite), titlepart (TEI-Lite), titlestmt (TEI-Lite), trailer (TEI-Lite), unclear (TEI-Lite), xptr (TEI-Lite), xref (TEI-Lite)

country   (ELEMENT: DocBook, ISO 12083)

cover   (ATTRIBUTE: MIL-STD-38784)
 elements: doc (MIL-STD-38784)

cowidth   (ATTRIBUTE: MIL-STD-38784)
 elements: legend (MIL-STD-38784)

cpyrt   (ELEMENT: ISO 12083)

cpyrtclr   (ELEMENT: ISO 12083)

cpyrtnme   (ELEMENT: ISO 12083)

crdate   (ATTRIBUTE: TEI-Lite)
 elements: ptr (TEI-Lite), ref (TEI-Lite), xptr (TEI-Lite), xref (TEI-Lite)

creation   (ELEMENT: TEI-Lite)

creator   (ATTRIBUTE: TEI-Lite)
 elements: teiheader (TEI-Lite)
data   (ATTRIBUTE: HTML)
 elements: object (HTML)
database   (ELEMENT: DocBook)
dataiden   (ELEMENT: MIL-STD-38784)
datapagesize   (ATTRIBUTE: HTML)
 elements: table (HTML)
date   (ATTRIBUTE: MIL-STD-38784)
 elements: modreq (MIL-STD-38784)
date   (ELEMENT: DocBook, ISO 12083, MIL-STD-38784, TEI-Lite)
date.created   (ATTRIBUTE: TEI-Lite)
 elements: teiheader (TEI-Lite)
date.updated   (ATTRIBUTE: TEI-Lite)
 elements: teiheader (TEI-Lite)
dateinc   (ELEMENT: MIL-STD-38784)
dateline   (ELEMENT: TEI-Lite)
datetime   (ATTRIBUTE: HTML)
 elements: del (HTML), ins (HTML)
dd   (ELEMENT: HTML, ISO 12083)
ddchapter   (ELEMENT: MIL-STD-38784)
dddesc   (ELEMENT: MIL-STD-38784)
ddhd   (ELEMENT: ISO 12083)
ddindex   (ELEMENT: MIL-STD-38784)
ddlist   (ELEMENT: MIL-STD-38784)
ddsheet   (ELEMENT: MIL-STD-38784)
declare   (ATTRIBUTE: HTML)
 elements: object (HTML)
decls   (ATTRIBUTE: TEI-Lite)
 elements: back (TEI-Lite), body (TEI-Lite), div (TEI-Lite), div0 (TEI-Lite), div1 (TEI-Lite), div2 (TEI-Lite), div3 (TEI-Lite), div4 (TEI-Lite), div5 (TEI-Lite), div6 (TEI-Lite), div7 (TEI-Lite), front (TEI-Lite), group (TEI-Lite), text (TEI-Lite)
ded   (ELEMENT: ISO 12083)
dedication   (ELEMENT: DocBook)
def   (ELEMENT: MIL-STD-38784)
default   (ATTRIBUTE: TEI-Lite)
 elements: bibl (TEI-Lite), biblfull (TEI-Lite), editorialdecl (TEI-Lite), langusage (TEI-Lite), listbibl (TEI-Lite), projectdesc (TEI-Lite), samplingdecl (TEI-Lite), sourcedesc (TEI-Lite), textclass (TEI-Lite)
defer   (ATTRIBUTE: HTML)
 elements: script (HTML)
defhd   (ELEMENT: MIL-STD-38784)
deflist   (ELEMENT: ISO 12083, MIL-STD-38784)
degree   (ELEMENT: ISO 12083)
del   (ELEMENT: HTML, TEI-Lite)
delchlvl   (ATTRIBUTE: MIL-STD-38784)
 elements: abbrsect (MIL-STD-38784), appendix (MIL-STD-38784), applicdef (MIL-

STD-38784), caution (MIL-STD-38784), chapter (MIL-STD-38784), ddchapter (MIL-STD-38784), dddesc (MIL-STD-38784), ddindex (MIL-STD-38784), deflist (MIL-STD-38784), docpart (MIL-STD-38784), figtable (MIL-STD-38784), figure (MIL-STD-38784), foldout (MIL-STD-38784), glossary (MIL-STD-38784), internatlstd (MIL-STD-38784), line (MIL-STD-38784), lrp (MIL-STD-38784), note (MIL-STD-38784), para (MIL-STD-38784), para0 (MIL-STD-38784), randlist (MIL-STD-38784), ratd (MIL-STD-38784), safesum (MIL-STD-38784), section (MIL-STD-38784), seqlist (MIL-STD-38784), serno (MIL-STD-38784), step1 (MIL-STD-38784), step2 (MIL-STD-38784), step3 (MIL-STD-38784), step4 (MIL-STD-38784), subfig (MIL-STD-38784), subpara1 (MIL-STD-38784), subpara2 (MIL-STD-38784), subpara3 (MIL-STD-38784), symsect (MIL-STD-38784), table (MIL-STD-38784), tabmat (MIL-STD-38784), tctolist (MIL-STD-38784), tctono (MIL-STD-38784), tctorow (MIL-STD-38784), tctotbl (MIL-STD-38784), tmidno (MIL-STD-38784), tmimprep (MIL-STD-38784), volume (MIL-STD-38784), warning (MIL-STD-38784), warnpage (MIL-STD-38784), wpgentry (MIL-STD-38784)

deltype   (ATTRIBUTE: MIL-STD-38784)
elements: abbrsect (MIL-STD-38784), appendix (MIL-STD-38784), applicdef (MIL-STD-38784), caution (MIL-STD-38784), chapter (MIL-STD-38784), ddchapter (MIL-STD-38784), dddesc (MIL-STD-38784), ddindex (MIL-STD-38784), deflist (MIL-STD-38784), docpart (MIL-STD-38784), figtable (MIL-STD-38784), figure (MIL-STD-38784), foldout (MIL-STD-38784), glossary (MIL-STD-38784), internatlstd (MIL-STD-38784), line (MIL-STD-38784), lrp (MIL-STD-38784), note (MIL-STD-38784), para (MIL-STD-38784), para0 (MIL-STD-38784), randlist (MIL-STD-38784), ratd (MIL-STD-38784), safesum (MIL-STD-38784), section (MIL-STD-38784), seqlist (MIL-STD-38784), serno (MIL-STD-38784), step1 (MIL-STD-38784), step2 (MIL-STD-38784), step3 (MIL-STD-38784), step4 (MIL-STD-38784), subfig (MIL-STD-38784), subpara1 (MIL-STD-38784), subpara2 (MIL-STD-38784), subpara3 (MIL-STD-38784), symsect (MIL-STD-38784), table (MIL-STD-38784), tabmat (MIL-STD-38784), tctolist (MIL-STD-38784), tctono (MIL-STD-38784), tctorow (MIL-STD-38784), tctotbl (MIL-STD-38784), tmidno (MIL-STD-38784), tmimprep (MIL-STD-38784), volume (MIL-STD-38784), warning (MIL-STD-38784), warnpage (MIL-STD-38784), wpgentry (MIL-STD-38784)

den   (ELEMENT: ISO 12083)
depth   (ATTRIBUTE: DocBook)
elements: graphic (DocBook), inlinegraphic (DocBook)
desc   (ATTRIBUTE: TEI-Lite)
elements: gap (TEI-Lite)
destr   (ELEMENT: MIL-STD-38784)
dfn   (ELEMENT: HTML)
dformgrp   (ELEMENT: ISO 12083)
dformula   (ELEMENT: ISO 12083)
dir   (ATTRIBUTE: HTML)
elements: a (HTML), abbr (HTML), acronym (HTML), address (HTML), area (HTML), b (HTML), bdo (HTML), big (HTML), blockquote (HTML), body (HTML), button (HTML), caption (HTML), cite (HTML), code (HTML), col (HTML), colgroup (HTML), dd (HTML), del (HTML), dfn (HTML), div (HTML), dl (HTML), dt (HTML), em (HTML), fieldset (HTML), form (HTML), h1 (HTML), h2 (HTML), h3 (HTML), h4

(HTML), h5 (HTML), h6 (HTML), head (HTML), html (HTML), i (HTML), img (HTML), input (HTML), ins (HTML), kbd (HTML), label (HTML), legend (HTML), li (HTML), link (HTML), map (HTML), meta (HTML), noscript (HTML), object (HTML), ol (HTML), optgroup (HTML), option (HTML), p (HTML), pre (HTML), q (HTML), samp (HTML), select (HTML), small (HTML), span (HTML), strong (HTML), style (HTML), sub (HTML), sup (HTML), table (HTML), tbody (HTML), td (HTML), textarea (HTML), tfoot (HTML), th (HTML), thead (HTML), title (HTML), tr (HTML), tt (HTML), ul (HTML), var (HTML)

direct   (ATTRIBUTE: ISO 12083, TEI-Lite)
    elements: markref (ISO 12083), q (TEI-Lite)

disabled   (ATTRIBUTE: HTML)
    elements: button (HTML), input (HTML), optgroup (HTML), option (HTML), select (HTML), textarea (HTML)

discl   (ELEMENT: MIL-STD-38784)

disclos1   (ATTRIBUTE: MIL-STD-38784)
    elements: discl (MIL-STD-38784)

disposn   (ATTRIBUTE: MIL-STD-38784)
    elements: mrrespns (MIL-STD-38784)

distrib   (ELEMENT: MIL-STD-38784)

distributor   (ELEMENT: TEI-Lite)

div   (ELEMENT: HTML, TEI-Lite)

div0   (ELEMENT: TEI-Lite)

div1   (ELEMENT: TEI-Lite)

div2   (ELEMENT: TEI-Lite)

div3   (ELEMENT: TEI-Lite)

div4   (ELEMENT: TEI-Lite)

div5   (ELEMENT: TEI-Lite)

div6   (ELEMENT: TEI-Lite)

div7   (ELEMENT: TEI-Lite)

divgen   (ELEMENT: TEI-Lite)

dl   (ELEMENT: HTML)

doc   (ATTRIBUTE: TEI-Lite)
    elements: xptr (TEI-Lite), xref (TEI-Lite)

doc   (ELEMENT: MIL-STD-38784)

docauthor   (ELEMENT: TEI-Lite)

docdate   (ELEMENT: TEI-Lite)

docedition   (ELEMENT: TEI-Lite)

docid   (ATTRIBUTE: MIL-STD-38784)
    elements: doc (MIL-STD-38784)

docimprint   (ELEMENT: TEI-Lite)

docinfo   (ELEMENT: DocBook)

docpart   (ELEMENT: MIL-STD-38784)

docpartn   (ELEMENT: MIL-STD-38784)

docstat   (ATTRIBUTE: MIL-STD-38784)
    elements: doc (MIL-STD-38784)

doctitle   (ELEMENT: TEI-Lite)

doctype   (ATTRIBUTE: TEI-Lite)

elements: refsdecl (TEI-Lite)

doctype   (ELEMENT: MIL-STD-38784)

downgrd   (ELEMENT: MIL-STD-38784)

dt   (ELEMENT: HTML)

ecpno   (ELEMENT: MIL-STD-38784)

ed   (ATTRIBUTE: TEI-Lite)
elements: lb (TEI-Lite), milestone (TEI-Lite), pb (TEI-Lite)

edition   (ELEMENT: DocBook, ISO 12083, TEI-Lite)

editionstmt   (ELEMENT: TEI-Lite)

editor   (ELEMENT: DocBook, TEI-Lite)

editorialdecl   (ELEMENT: TEI-Lite)

effdatenot   (ELEMENT: MIL-STD-38784)

eg   (ELEMENT: TEI-Lite)

em   (ELEMENT: HTML)

email   (ELEMENT: DocBook, ISO 12083)

emergency   (ATTRIBUTE: MIL-STD-38784)
elements: abbrsect (MIL-STD-38784), appendix (MIL-STD-38784), applicdef (MIL-STD-38784), chapter (MIL-STD-38784), ddchapter (MIL-STD-38784), dddesc (MIL-STD-38784), ddindex (MIL-STD-38784), lrp (MIL-STD-38784), para0 (MIL-STD-38784), pgbrk (MIL-STD-38784), ratd (MIL-STD-38784), safesum (MIL-STD-38784), section (MIL-STD-38784), step1 (MIL-STD-38784), step2 (MIL-STD-38784), step3 (MIL-STD-38784), step4 (MIL-STD-38784), subpara1 (MIL-STD-38784), subpara2 (MIL-STD-38784), subpara3 (MIL-STD-38784), symsect (MIL-STD-38784), tctolist (MIL-STD-38784), tmimprep (MIL-STD-38784)

emph   (ELEMENT: ISO 12083, TEI-Lite)

emphasis   (ELEMENT: DocBook, MIL-STD-38784)

encodingdesc   (ELEMENT: TEI-Lite)

enctype   (ATTRIBUTE: HTML)
elements: form (HTML)

end   (ATTRIBUTE: ISO 12083)
elements: overline (ISO 12083), undrline (ISO 12083)

endterm   (ATTRIBUTE: DocBook)
elements: link (DocBook), xref (DocBook)

enjamb   (ATTRIBUTE: TEI-Lite)
elements: l (TEI-Lite)

entity   (ATTRIBUTE: TEI-Lite)
elements: figure (TEI-Lite)

entityref   (ATTRIBUTE: DocBook)
elements: graphic (DocBook), inlinegraphic (DocBook)

entry   (ELEMENT: DocBook, MIL-STD-38784)

entrytbl   (ELEMENT: DocBook, MIL-STD-38784)

envar   (ELEMENT: DocBook)

epigraph   (ELEMENT: DocBook, TEI-Lite)

equation   (ELEMENT: DocBook)

errorcode   (ELEMENT: DocBook)

errorname   (ELEMENT: DocBook)

errortype   (ELEMENT: DocBook)

esds   (ATTRIBUTE: MIL-STD-38784)
   elements: abbrsect (MIL-STD-38784), applicdef (MIL-STD-38784), dddesc (MIL-STD-38784), ddindex (MIL-STD-38784), lrp (MIL-STD-38784), para0 (MIL-STD-38784), ratd (MIL-STD-38784), safesum (MIL-STD-38784), step1 (MIL-STD-38784), step2 (MIL-STD-38784), step3 (MIL-STD-38784), step4 (MIL-STD-38784), subpara1 (MIL-STD-38784), subpara2 (MIL-STD-38784), subpara3 (MIL-STD-38784), symsect (MIL-STD-38784), tctolist (MIL-STD-38784), tmimprep (MIL-STD-38784)
esds   (ELEMENT: MIL-STD-38784)
evaluate   (ATTRIBUTE: TEI-Lite)
   elements: ptr (TEI-Lite), ref (TEI-Lite), xptr (TEI-Lite), xref (TEI-Lite)
event   (ATTRIBUTE: HTML)
   elements: script (HTML)
example   (ELEMENT: DocBook)
expan   (ATTRIBUTE: TEI-Lite)
   elements: abbr (TEI-Lite)
expcont   (ELEMENT: MIL-STD-38784)
extent   (ATTRIBUTE: TEI-Lite)
   elements: gap (TEI-Lite)
extent   (ELEMENT: ISO 12083, TEI-Lite)
externalid   (ATTRIBUTE: MIL-STD-38784)
   elements: extref (MIL-STD-38784)
extref   (ELEMENT: MIL-STD-38784)
fax   (ELEMENT: DocBook, ISO 12083)
fence   (ELEMENT: ISO 12083)
fieldset   (ELEMENT: HTML)
fig   (ELEMENT: ISO 12083)
figdesc   (ELEMENT: TEI-Lite)
figgrp   (ELEMENT: ISO 12083)
figref   (ELEMENT: ISO 12083)
figtable   (ELEMENT: MIL-STD-38784)
figure   (ELEMENT: DocBook, MIL-STD-38784, TEI-Lite)
file   (ATTRIBUTE: ISO 12083)
   elements: biblist (ISO 12083)
filedesc   (ELEMENT: TEI-Lite)
filename   (ELEMENT: DocBook)
fileref   (ATTRIBUTE: DocBook)
   elements: graphic (DocBook), inlinegraphic (DocBook)
firstname   (ELEMENT: DocBook)
firstterm   (ELEMENT: DocBook)
float   (ATTRIBUTE: DocBook)
   elements: figure (DocBook)
fname   (ELEMENT: ISO 12083)
fnoteref   (ELEMENT: ISO 12083)
foldout   (ELEMENT: MIL-STD-38784)
foldsect   (ELEMENT: MIL-STD-38784)
fontsize   (ATTRIBUTE: MIL-STD-38784)

elements: emphasis (MIL-STD-38784)

footnote   (ELEMENT: DocBook, ISO 12083)

footnoteref   (ELEMENT: DocBook)

footnotes   (ATTRIBUTE: MIL-STD-38784)
elements: table (MIL-STD-38784), tabmat (MIL-STD-38784)

for   (ATTRIBUTE: HTML)
elements: label (HTML), script (HTML)

foreign   (ELEMENT: TEI-Lite)

foreignphrase   (ELEMENT: DocBook)

foreword   (ELEMENT: ISO 12083, MIL-STD-38784)

form   (ELEMENT: HTML)

formalpara   (ELEMENT: DocBook)

format   (ATTRIBUTE: DocBook)
elements: address (DocBook), funcsynopsisinfo (DocBook), graphic (DocBook), inlinegraphic (DocBook), literallayout (DocBook), programlisting (DocBook), screen (DocBook), synopsis (DocBook)

formref   (ELEMENT: ISO 12083)

formula   (ELEMENT: ISO 12083, TEI-Lite)

fpi   (ATTRIBUTE: DocBook)
elements: book (DocBook), set (DocBook)

fraction   (ELEMENT: ISO 12083)

frame   (ATTRIBUTE: DocBook, HTML, MIL-STD-38784)
elements: figtable (MIL-STD-38784), informaltable (DocBook), table (DocBook), table (HTML), table (MIL-STD-38784), tabmat (MIL-STD-38784), tctotbl (MIL-STD-38784)

from   (ATTRIBUTE: TEI-Lite)
elements: xptr (TEI-Lite), xref (TEI-Lite)

front   (ELEMENT: ISO 12083, MIL-STD-38784, TEI-Lite)

ftnote   (ELEMENT: MIL-STD-38784)

ftnref   (ELEMENT: MIL-STD-38784)

funcdef   (ELEMENT: DocBook)

funcparams   (ELEMENT: DocBook)

funcprototype   (ELEMENT: DocBook)

funcsynopsis   (ELEMENT: DocBook)

funcsynopsisinfo   (ELEMENT: DocBook)

function   (ATTRIBUTE: TEI-Lite)
elements: anchor (TEI-Lite), s (TEI-Lite), seg (TEI-Lite)

function   (ELEMENT: DocBook)

funder   (ELEMENT: TEI-Lite)

gap   (ELEMENT: TEI-Lite)

gi   (ATTRIBUTE: TEI-Lite)
elements: tagusage (TEI-Lite)

gi   (ELEMENT: TEI-Lite)

glosref   (ELEMENT: ISO 12083)

gloss   (ELEMENT: TEI-Lite)

glossary   (ELEMENT: DocBook, ISO 12083, MIL-STD-38784)

glossdef   (ELEMENT: DocBook)

glossdiv   (ELEMENT: DocBook)
glossentry   (ELEMENT: DocBook)
glosslist   (ELEMENT: DocBook)
glosssee   (ELEMENT: DocBook)
glossseealso   (ELEMENT: DocBook)
glossterm   (ELEMENT: DocBook)
graphic   (ELEMENT: DocBook, MIL-STD-38784)
graphicco   (ELEMENT: DocBook)
graphsty   (ATTRIBUTE: MIL-STD-38784)
    elements: graphic (MIL-STD-38784)
group   (ELEMENT: DocBook, TEI-Lite)
guibutton   (ELEMENT: DocBook)
guiicon   (ELEMENT: DocBook)
guilabel   (ELEMENT: DocBook)
guimenu   (ELEMENT: DocBook)
guimenuitem   (ELEMENT: DocBook)
guisubmenu   (ELEMENT: DocBook)
h1   (ELEMENT: HTML)
h2   (ELEMENT: HTML)
h3   (ELEMENT: HTML)
h4   (ELEMENT: HTML)
h5   (ELEMENT: HTML)
h6   (ELEMENT: HTML)
hand   (ATTRIBUTE: TEI-Lite)
    elements: add (TEI-Lite), del (TEI-Lite), gap (TEI-Lite), unclear (TEI-Lite)
hardware   (ELEMENT: DocBook)
hazmat   (ELEMENT: MIL-STD-38784)
hcp   (ATTRIBUTE: MIL-STD-38784)
    elements: abbrsect (MIL-STD-38784), applicdef (MIL-STD-38784), dddesc (MIL-STD-38784), ddindex (MIL-STD-38784), lrp (MIL-STD-38784), para0 (MIL-STD-38784), ratd (MIL-STD-38784), safesum (MIL-STD-38784), step1 (MIL-STD-38784), step2 (MIL-STD-38784), step3 (MIL-STD-38784), step4 (MIL-STD-38784), subpara1 (MIL-STD-38784), subpara2 (MIL-STD-38784), subpara3 (MIL-STD-38784), symsect (MIL-STD-38784), tctolist (MIL-STD-38784), tmimprep (MIL-STD-38784)
hcp   (ELEMENT: MIL-STD-38784)
head   (ELEMENT: HTML, ISO 12083, TEI-Lite)
headers   (ATTRIBUTE: HTML)
    elements: td (HTML), th (HTML)
height   (ATTRIBUTE: HTML)
    elements: img (HTML), object (HTML)
hi   (ELEMENT: TEI-Lite)
highlights   (ELEMENT: DocBook)
holder   (ELEMENT: DocBook)
honorific   (ELEMENT: DocBook)
horrefpt   (ATTRIBUTE: MIL-STD-38784)
    elements: figtable (MIL-STD-38784), legend (MIL-STD-38784)

hplace   (ATTRIBUTE: MIL-STD-38784)
    elements: graphic (MIL-STD-38784)
hr   (ELEMENT: HTML)
href   (ATTRIBUTE: HTML)
    elements: a (HTML), area (HTML), base (HTML), link (HTML)
hreflang   (ATTRIBUTE: HTML)
    elements: a (HTML), link (HTML)
hscale   (ATTRIBUTE: MIL-STD-38784)
    elements: graphic (MIL-STD-38784)
hspace   (ELEMENT: ISO 12083)
html   (ELEMENT: HTML)
http-equiv   (ATTRIBUTE: HTML)
    elements: meta (HTML)
hynames   (ATTRIBUTE: ISO 12083)
    elements: appref (ISO 12083), artref (ISO 12083), citeref (ISO 12083), figref (ISO 12083), fnoteref (ISO 12083), formref (ISO 12083), glosref (ISO 12083), indexref (ISO 12083), noteref (ISO 12083), secref (ISO 12083), tableref (ISO 12083)
hyphflag   (ATTRIBUTE: MIL-STD-38784)
    elements: pgbrk (MIL-STD-38784)
hytime   (ATTRIBUTE: ISO 12083)
    elements: appref (ISO 12083), artref (ISO 12083), book (ISO 12083), citation (ISO 12083), citeref (ISO 12083), figref (ISO 12083), fnoteref (ISO 12083), formref (ISO 12083), glosref (ISO 12083), indexref (ISO 12083), nameloc (ISO 12083), nmlist (ISO 12083), noteref (ISO 12083), secref (ISO 12083), tableref (ISO 12083)
i   (ELEMENT: HTML)
icon   (ELEMENT: MIL-STD-38784)
id   (ATTRIBUTE: DocBook, HTML, ISO 12083, MIL-STD-38784, TEI-Lite)
    elements: a (HTML), abbr (HTML), abbr (TEI-Lite), abbrev (DocBook), abbrsect (MIL-STD-38784), abstract (DocBook), abstract (ISO 12083), accel (DocBook), ack (ISO 12083), ackno (DocBook), acronym (DocBook), acronym (HTML), action (DocBook), add (TEI-Lite), address (DocBook), address (HTML), address (TEI-Lite), addrline (TEI-Lite), aff (ISO 12083), affiliation (DocBook), afterwrd (ISO 12083), alt (DocBook), anchor (DocBook), anchor (TEI-Lite), appendix (DocBook), appendix (ISO 12083), appendix (MIL-STD-38784), applic (MIL-STD-38784), application (DocBook), applicdef (MIL-STD-38784), appref (ISO 12083), area (DocBook), area (HTML), areaset (DocBook), areaspec (DocBook), arg (DocBook), argument (TEI-Lite), artheader (DocBook), article (DocBook), artpagenums (DocBook), artref (ISO 12083), artwork (ISO 12083), attribution (DocBook), author (DocBook), author (TEI-Lite), authorblurb (DocBook), authorgroup (DocBook), authorinitials (DocBook), authority (TEI-Lite), availability (TEI-Lite), b (HTML), back (TEI-Lite), bdo (HTML), beginpage (DocBook), bibl (TEI-Lite), biblfull (TEI-Lite), bibliodiv (DocBook), biblioentry (DocBook), bibliography (DocBook), bibliomisc (DocBook), bibliomixed (DocBook), bibliomset (DocBook), biblioset (DocBook), biblscope (TEI-Lite), big (HTML), blockquote (DocBook), blockquote (HTML), body (HTML), body (TEI-Lite), book (DocBook), book (ISO 12083), bookbiblio (DocBook), bookinfo (DocBook), br (HTML), bridgehead (DocBook), button (HTML), byline (TEI-Lite), callout (DocBook),

calloutlist (DocBook), caption (HTML), catdesc (TEI-Lite), category (TEI-Lite), catref (TEI-Lite), caution (DocBook), cell (TEI-Lite), change (TEI-Lite), chapter (DocBook), chapter (ISO 12083), chapter (MIL-STD-38784), cit (TEI-Lite), citation (DocBook), citation (ISO 12083), cite (HTML), citeref (ISO 12083), citerefentry (DocBook), citetitle (DocBook), city (DocBook), classcode (TEI-Lite), classdecl (TEI-Lite), classname (DocBook), closer (TEI-Lite), cmdsynopsis (DocBook), co (DocBook), code (HTML), code (TEI-Lite), col (HTML), colgroup (HTML), collab (DocBook), collabname (DocBook), command (DocBook), comment (DocBook), computeroutput (DocBook), confdates (DocBook), confgroup (DocBook), confnum (DocBook), confsponsor (DocBook), conftitle (DocBook), contractnum (DocBook), contractsponsor (DocBook), contrib (DocBook), copyright (DocBook), corpauth (ISO 12083), corpauthor (DocBook), corpname (DocBook), corr (TEI-Lite), country (DocBook), creation (TEI-Lite), database (DocBook), date (DocBook), date (TEI-Lite), dateline (TEI-Lite), dd (HTML), dd (ISO 12083), ddchapter (MIL-STD-38784), dddesc (MIL-STD-38784), ddindex (MIL-STD-38784), ded (ISO 12083), dedication (DocBook), deflist (ISO 12083), del (HTML), del (TEI-Lite), dfn (HTML), dformgrp (ISO 12083), dformula (ISO 12083), distributor (TEI-Lite), div (HTML), div (TEI-Lite), div0 (TEI-Lite), div1 (TEI-Lite), div2 (TEI-Lite), div3 (TEI-Lite), div4 (TEI-Lite), div5 (TEI-Lite), div6 (TEI-Lite), div7 (TEI-Lite), divgen (TEI-Lite), dl (HTML), docauthor (TEI-Lite), docdate (TEI-Lite), docedition (TEI-Lite), docimprint (TEI-Lite), docinfo (DocBook), doctitle (TEI-Lite), dt (HTML), edition (DocBook), edition (TEI-Lite), editionstmt (TEI-Lite), editor (DocBook), editor (TEI-Lite), editorialdecl (TEI-Lite), eg (TEI-Lite), em (HTML), email (DocBook), emph (TEI-Lite), emphasis (DocBook), encodingdesc (TEI-Lite), entry (DocBook), entry (MIL-STD-38784), entrytbl (DocBook), envar (DocBook), epigraph (DocBook), epigraph (TEI-Lite), equation (DocBook), errorcode (DocBook), errorname (DocBook), errortype (DocBook), example (DocBook), extent (TEI-Lite), fax (DocBook), fieldset (HTML), fig (ISO 12083), figdesc (TEI-Lite), figgrp (ISO 12083), figref (ISO 12083), figure (DocBook), figure (MIL-STD-38784), figure (TEI-Lite), filedesc (TEI-Lite), filename (DocBook), firstname (DocBook), firstterm (DocBook), fnoteref (ISO 12083), foldout (MIL-STD-38784), footnote (DocBook), footnote (ISO 12083), footnoteref (DocBook), foreign (TEI-Lite), foreignphrase (DocBook), foreword (ISO 12083), form (HTML), formalpara (DocBook), formref (ISO 12083), formula (ISO 12083), formula (TEI-Lite), front (TEI-Lite), ftnote (MIL-STD-38784), funcdef (DocBook), funcparams (DocBook), funcprototype (DocBook), funcsynopsis (DocBook), funcsynopsisinfo (DocBook), function (DocBook), funder (TEI-Lite), gap (TEI-Lite), gi (TEI-Lite), glosref (ISO 12083), gloss (TEI-Lite), glossary (DocBook), glossary (ISO 12083), glossdef (DocBook), glossdiv (DocBook), glossentry (DocBook), glosslist (DocBook), glosssee (DocBook), glossseealso (DocBook), glossterm (DocBook), graphic (DocBook), graphicco (DocBook), group (DocBook), group (TEI-Lite), guibutton (DocBook), guiicon (DocBook), guilabel (DocBook), guimenu (DocBook), guimenuitem (DocBook), guisubmenu (DocBook), h1 (HTML), h2 (HTML), h3 (HTML), h4 (HTML), h5 (HTML), h6 (HTML), hardware (DocBook), head (TEI-Lite), hi (TEI-Lite), highlights (DocBook), holder (DocBook), honorific (DocBook), hr (HTML), i (HTML), icon (MIL-STD-38784), ident (TEI-Lite), idno (TEI-Lite), img (HTML), important (DocBook), imprint (TEI-Lite), index (DocBook), index (ISO 12083), index (MIL-STD-38784), index (TEI-Lite), indexdiv (DocBook), indexentry (DocBook), indexref (ISO 12083), indexterm (DocBook), informalequation (DocBook), informalexample (DocBook), informaltable (DocBook), inlineequation (DocBook), inlinegraphic (DocBook), input (HTML), ins (HTML), interface (DocBook), interfacedefinition (DocBook), interp (TEI-Lite), interpgrp (TEI-Lite), intro (ISO 12083), invpartnumber (DocBook), isbn (DocBook), issn (DocBook), issuenum (DocBook), item (ISO 12083), item (TEI-Lite), itemizedlist (DocBook), itermset (DocBook), jobtitle (DocBook), kbd (HTML), keycap (DocBook), keycode (DocBook), keycombo (DocBook), keysym (DocBook), keyword (DocBook), keywords (TEI-Lite), keywordset (DocBook), kw (TEI-Lite), l (TEI-Lite), label (HTML), label (TEI-Lite), language (TEI-Lite), langusage (TEI-Lite), lb (TEI-Lite), legalnotice (DocBook), legend (HTML), lg (TEI-Lite), li (HTML), lineage (DocBook), lineannotation (DocBook), link (DocBook), link (HTML), list (ISO 12083), list (TEI-Lite), listbibl (TEI-Lite), listitem (DocBook), literal (DocBook), literallayout (DocBook), lot (DocBook), lotentry (DocBook), lrp (MIL-STD-38784), lrpentry (MIL-STD-38784), manvolnum (DocBook), map (HTML), mark (ISO 12083), markup (DocBook), medialabel (DocBook), member (DocBook), mentioned (TEI-Lite), menuchoice (DocBook), milestone (TEI-Lite), modespec (DocBook), modreq (MIL-STD-38784), mousebutton (DocBook), msg (DocBook), msgaud (DocBook), msgentry (DocBook), msgexplan (DocBook), msginfo (DocBook), msglevel (DocBook), msgmain (DocBook), msgorig (DocBook), msgrel (DocBook), msgset (DocBook), msgsub (DocBook), msgtext (DocBook), name (TEI-Lite), nameloc (ISO 12083), noscript (HTML), note (DocBook), note (ISO 12083), note (TEI-Lite), noteref (ISO 12083), notesstmt (TEI-Lite), num (TEI-Lite), object (HTML), ol (HTML), olink (DocBook), opener (TEI-Lite), optgroup (HTML), option (DocBook), option (HTML), optional (DocBook), orderedlist (DocBook), orgdiv (DocBook), orgname (DocBook), orig (TEI-Lite), otheraddr (DocBook), othercredit (DocBook), othername (DocBook), p (HTML), p (ISO 12083), p (TEI-Lite), pagenums (DocBook), para (DocBook), para (MIL-STD-38784), para0 (MIL-STD-38784), param (HTML), paramdef (DocBook), parameter (DocBook), part (DocBook), partintro (DocBook), pb (TEI-Lite), phone (DocBook), phrase (DocBook), pob (DocBook), postcode (DocBook), pre (HTML), preface (DocBook), preface (ISO 12083), primary (DocBook), primaryie (DocBook), principal (TEI-Lite), printhistory (DocBook), procedure (DocBook), productname (DocBook), productnumber (DocBook), profiledesc (TEI-Lite), programlisting (DocBook), programlistingco (DocBook), projectdesc (TEI-Lite), prompt (DocBook), property (DocBook), ptr (TEI-Lite), pubdate (DocBook), publicationstmt (TEI-Lite), publisher (DocBook), publisher (TEI-Lite), publishername (DocBook), pubplace (TEI-Lite), pubsnumber (DocBook), q (HTML), q (ISO 12083), q (TEI-Lite), quote (DocBook), ratd (MIL-STD-38784), ref (TEI-Lite), refclass (DocBook), refdescriptor (DocBook), refentry (DocBook), refentrytitle (DocBook), reference (DocBook), refmeta (DocBook), refmiscinfo (DocBook), refname (DocBook), refnamediv (DocBook), refpurpose (DocBook), refsdecl (TEI-Lite), refsect1 (DocBook), refsect1info (DocBook), refsect2 (DocBook), refsect2info (DocBook), refsect3 (DocBook), refsect3info (DocBook), refsynopsisdiv (DocBook), refsynopsisdivinfo (DocBook), reg (TEI-Lite), releaseinfo (DocBook), rendition (TEI-Lite), replaceable (DocBook), resp (TEI-Lite), respstmt (TEI-Lite), returnvalue (DocBook), revhistory (DocBook), revision (DocBook), revisiondesc (TEI-Lite), revnumber (DocBook), revremark (DocBook), row (DocBook), row (TEI-Lite), rs (TEI-Lite), s (TEI-Lite), safesum (MIL-STD-38784), salute (TEI-Lite), samp (HTML), samplingdecl (TEI-Lite), sbr (DocBook), screen (DocBook), screenco (DocBook), screeninfo (DocBook), screenshot (DocBook), secondary (DocBook), secondaryie (DocBook), secref (ISO 12083), sect1 (DocBook), sect1info (DocBook), sect2 (DocBook), sect2info (DocBook), sect3 (DocBook), sect3info (DocBook), sect4 (DocBook), sect4info (DocBook), sect5 (DocBook), sect5info (DocBook), section (ISO 12083), section (MIL-STD-38784), see (DocBook), seealso (DocBook), seealsoie (DocBook), seeie (DocBook), seg (DocBook), seg (TEI-Lite), seglistitem (DocBook), segmentedlist (DocBook), segtitle (DocBook), select (HTML), seriesinfo (DocBook), seriesstmt (TEI-Lite), seriesvolnums (DocBook), set (DocBook), setindex (DocBook), setinfo (DocBook), sgmltag (DocBook), shortaffil (DocBook), shortcut (DocBook), sic (TEI-Lite), sidebar (DocBook), signed (TEI-Lite), simpara (DocBook), simplelist (DocBook), simplesect (DocBook), small (HTML), socalled (TEI-Lite), sourcedesc (TEI-Lite), sp (TEI-Lite), span (HTML), speaker (TEI-Lite), sponsor (TEI-Lite), stage (TEI-Lite), state (DocBook), step (DocBook), step1 (MIL-STD-38784), step2 (MIL-STD-38784), step3 (MIL-STD-38784), step4 (MIL-STD-38784), street (DocBook), strong (HTML), structfield (DocBook), structname (DocBook), sub (HTML), subfig (MIL-STD-38784), subject (DocBook), subjectset (DocBook), subjectterm (DocBook), subpara1 (MIL-STD-38784), subpara2 (MIL-STD-38784), subpara3 (MIL-STD-38784), subscript (DocBook), subsect1 (ISO 12083), subsect2 (ISO 12083), subsect3 (ISO 12083), subsect4 (ISO 12083), subsect5 (ISO 12083), subsect6 (ISO 12083), substeps (DocBook), subtitle (DocBook), sup (HTML), superscript (DocBook), surname (DocBook), symbol (DocBook), symsect (MIL-STD-38784), synopfragment (DocBook), synopfragmentref (DocBook), synopsis (DocBook), systemitem (DocBook), table (DocBook), table (HTML), table (ISO 12083), table (MIL-STD-38784), table (TEI-Lite), tableref (ISO 12083), tabmat (MIL-STD-38784), tagsdecl (TEI-Lite), tagusage (TEI-Lite), taxonomy (TEI-Lite), tbody (DocBook), tbody (HTML), tctolist (MIL-STD-38784), tctotbl (MIL-STD-38784), td (HTML), tei.2 (TEI-Lite), teiheader (TEI-Lite), term (DocBook), term (ISO 12083), term (TEI-Lite), tertiary (DocBook), tertiaryie (DocBook), text (TEI-Lite), textarea (HTML), textclass (TEI-Lite), tfnid (MIL-STD-38784), tfoot (DocBook), tfoot (HTML), tgroup (DocBook), th (HTML), thead (DocBook), thead (HTML), time (TEI-Lite), tip (DocBook), title (DocBook), title (TEI-Lite), titleabbrev (DocBook), titlepage (TEI-Lite), titlepart (TEI-Lite), titlestmt (TEI-Lite), tmimprep (MIL-STD-38784), toc (DocBook), tocback (DocBook), tocchap (DocBook), tocentry (DocBook), tocfront (DocBook), toclevel1 (DocBook), toclevel2 (DocBook), toclevel3 (DocBook), toclevel4 (DocBook), toclevel5 (DocBook), tocpart (DocBook), token (DocBook), tr (HTML), trademark (DocBook), trailer (TEI-Lite), tt (HTML), type (DocBook), ul (HTML), ulink (DocBook), unclear (TEI-Lite), userinput (DocBook), var (HTML), varargs (DocBook), variablelist (DocBook), varlistentry (DocBook), void (DocBook), volumenum (DocBook), warning (DocBook), wordasword (DocBook), xptr (TEI-Lite), xref (DocBook), xref (TEI-Lite), year (DocBook)

ident   (ATTRIBUTE: TEI-Lite)
       elements: tagusage (TEI-Lite)

ident   (ELEMENT: TEI-Lite)
idinfo   (ELEMENT: MIL-STD-38784)
idno   (ELEMENT: TEI-Lite)
illuslist   (ELEMENT: MIL-STD-38784)
img   (ELEMENT: HTML)
important   (ELEMENT: DocBook)
imprint   (ELEMENT: TEI-Lite)
indaddr   (ELEMENT: ISO 12083)
indent   (ATTRIBUTE: MIL-STD-38784)
     elements: line (MIL-STD-38784)
index   (ATTRIBUTE: TEI-Lite)
     elements: index (TEI-Lite)
index   (ELEMENT: DocBook, ISO 12083, MIL-STD-38784, TEI-Lite)
indexdiv   (ELEMENT: DocBook)
indexentry   (ELEMENT: DocBook)
indexid   (ATTRIBUTE: MIL-STD-38784)
     elements: abbrsect (MIL-STD-38784), appendix (MIL-STD-38784), applicdef (MIL-STD-38784), chapter (MIL-STD-38784), ddchapter (MIL-STD-38784), dddesc (MIL-STD-38784), ddindex (MIL-STD-38784), docpart (MIL-STD-38784), figure (MIL-STD-38784), foldout (MIL-STD-38784), lrp (MIL-STD-38784), para0 (MIL-STD-38784), ratd (MIL-STD-38784), safesum (MIL-STD-38784), section (MIL-STD-38784), subpara1 (MIL-STD-38784), subpara2 (MIL-STD-38784), subpara3 (MIL-STD-38784), symsect (MIL-STD-38784), table (MIL-STD-38784), tabmat (MIL-STD-38784), tctolist (MIL-STD-38784), tctotbl (MIL-STD-38784), tmimprep (MIL-STD-38784), volume (MIL-STD-38784)
indexref   (ELEMENT: ISO 12083)
indexterm   (ELEMENT: DocBook)
indxflag   (ELEMENT: ISO 12083)
indxname   (ELEMENT: ISO 12083)
indxsubj   (ELEMENT: ISO 12083)
inf   (ELEMENT: ISO 12083)
infolwr   (ATTRIBUTE: MIL-STD-38784)
     elements: subjinfo (MIL-STD-38784)
informalequation   (ELEMENT: DocBook)
informalexample   (ELEMENT: DocBook)
informaltable   (ELEMENT: DocBook)
infoup   (ATTRIBUTE: MIL-STD-38784)
     elements: subjinfo (MIL-STD-38784)
inheritnum   (ATTRIBUTE: DocBook)
     elements: orderedlist (DocBook)
inlineequation   (ELEMENT: DocBook)
inlinegraphic   (ELEMENT: DocBook)
input   (ELEMENT: HTML)
ins   (ELEMENT: HTML)
inschlvl   (ATTRIBUTE: MIL-STD-38784)
     elements: abbrsect (MIL-STD-38784), appendix (MIL-STD-38784), applicdef (MIL-STD-38784), caution (MIL-STD-38784), chapter (MIL-STD-38784), ddchapter

(MIL-STD-38784), dddesc (MIL-STD-38784), ddindex (MIL-STD-38784), deflist (MIL-STD-38784), docpart (MIL-STD-38784), figtable (MIL-STD-38784), figure (MIL-STD-38784), foldout (MIL-STD-38784), glossary (MIL-STD-38784), internatlstd (MIL-STD-38784), line (MIL-STD-38784), lrp (MIL-STD-38784), note (MIL-STD-38784), para (MIL-STD-38784), para0 (MIL-STD-38784), randlist (MIL-STD-38784), ratd (MIL-STD-38784), safesum (MIL-STD-38784), section (MIL-STD-38784), seqlist (MIL-STD-38784), serno (MIL-STD-38784), step1 (MIL-STD-38784), step2 (MIL-STD-38784), step3 (MIL-STD-38784), step4 (MIL-STD-38784), subfig (MIL-STD-38784), subpara1 (MIL-STD-38784), subpara2 (MIL-STD-38784), subpara3 (MIL-STD-38784), symsect (MIL-STD-38784), table (MIL-STD-38784), tabmat (MIL-STD-38784), tctolist (MIL-STD-38784), tctono (MIL-STD-38784), tctorow (MIL-STD-38784), tctotbl (MIL-STD-38784), tmidno (MIL-STD-38784), tmimprep (MIL-STD-38784), volume (MIL-STD-38784), warning (MIL-STD-38784), warnpage (MIL-STD-38784), wpgentry (MIL-STD-38784)

insertpg   (ELEMENT: MIL-STD-38784)
inst   (ATTRIBUTE: TEI-Lite)
     elements: interp (TEI-Lite), interpgrp (TEI-Lite)
interface   (ELEMENT: DocBook)
interfacedefinition   (ELEMENT: DocBook)
internatlstd   (ELEMENT: MIL-STD-38784)
interp   (ELEMENT: TEI-Lite)
interpgrp   (ELEMENT: TEI-Lite)
intlstd1   (ATTRIBUTE: MIL-STD-38784)
     elements: internatlstd (MIL-STD-38784)
intlstd2   (ATTRIBUTE: MIL-STD-38784)
     elements: internatlstd (MIL-STD-38784)
intro   (ELEMENT: ISO 12083, MIL-STD-38784)
invpartnumber   (ELEMENT: DocBook)
isbn   (ELEMENT: DocBook, ISO 12083)
ismap   (ATTRIBUTE: HTML)
     elements: img (HTML)
issn   (ELEMENT: DocBook)
issuenum   (ELEMENT: DocBook)
italic   (ELEMENT: ISO 12083)
item   (ELEMENT: ISO 12083, MIL-STD-38784, TEI-Lite)
itemizedlist   (ELEMENT: DocBook)
itermset   (ELEMENT: DocBook)
jobtitle   (ELEMENT: DocBook)
kbd   (ELEMENT: HTML)
key   (ATTRIBUTE: TEI-Lite)
     elements: name (TEI-Lite), pubplace (TEI-Lite), rs (TEI-Lite)
keycap   (ELEMENT: DocBook)
keycode   (ELEMENT: DocBook)
keycombo   (ELEMENT: DocBook)
keyphras   (ELEMENT: ISO 12083)
keysym   (ELEMENT: DocBook)
keyword   (ELEMENT: DocBook, ISO 12083)

keywords   (ELEMENT: TEI-Lite)
keywordset   (ELEMENT: DocBook)
kw   (ELEMENT: TEI-Lite)
l   (ELEMENT: TEI-Lite)
label   (ATTRIBUTE: DocBook, HTML, MIL-STD-38784)
  elements: abbrsect (MIL-STD-38784), appendix (DocBook), appendix (MIL-STD-38784), applicdef (MIL-STD-38784), area (DocBook), areaset (DocBook), book (DocBook), chapter (DocBook), chapter (MIL-STD-38784), cmdsynopsis (DocBook), co (DocBook), ddchapter (MIL-STD-38784), dddesc (MIL-STD-38784), ddindex (MIL-STD-38784), docpart (MIL-STD-38784), equation (DocBook), example (DocBook), figure (DocBook), figure (MIL-STD-38784), foldout (MIL-STD-38784), footnote (DocBook), footnoteref (DocBook), funcsynopsis (DocBook), informaltable (DocBook), item (MIL-STD-38784), lot (DocBook), lrp (MIL-STD-38784), optgroup (HTML), option (HTML), para0 (MIL-STD-38784), part (DocBook), partintro (DocBook), ratd (MIL-STD-38784), reference (DocBook), safesum (MIL-STD-38784), sect1 (DocBook), sect2 (DocBook), sect3 (DocBook), sect4 (DocBook), sect5 (DocBook), section (MIL-STD-38784), step1 (MIL-STD-38784), step2 (MIL-STD-38784), step3 (MIL-STD-38784), step4 (MIL-STD-38784), subfig (MIL-STD-38784), subpara1 (MIL-STD-38784), subpara2 (MIL-STD-38784), subpara3 (MIL-STD-38784), symsect (MIL-STD-38784), synopsis (DocBook), table (DocBook), table (MIL-STD-38784), tabmat (MIL-STD-38784), tctolist (MIL-STD-38784), tctotbl (MIL-STD-38784), tmimprep (MIL-STD-38784), tocback (DocBook), tocchap (DocBook), tocfront (DocBook), volume (MIL-STD-38784)
label   (ELEMENT: HTML, TEI-Lite)
lacrwidth   (ATTRIBUTE: MIL-STD-38784)
  elements: acronymlist (MIL-STD-38784)
lang   (ATTRIBUTE: DocBook, HTML, TEI-Lite)
  elements: a (HTML), abbr (HTML), abbr (TEI-Lite), abbrev (DocBook), abstract (DocBook), accel (DocBook), ackno (DocBook), acronym (DocBook), acronym (HTML), action (DocBook), add (TEI-Lite), address (DocBook), address (HTML), address (TEI-Lite), addrline (TEI-Lite), affiliation (DocBook), alt (DocBook), anchor (TEI-Lite), appendix (DocBook), application (DocBook), area (DocBook), area (HTML), areaset (DocBook), areaspec (DocBook), arg (DocBook), argument (TEI-Lite), artheader (DocBook), article (DocBook), artpagenums (DocBook), attribution (DocBook), author (DocBook), author (TEI-Lite), authorblurb (DocBook), authorgroup (DocBook), authorinitials (DocBook), authority (TEI-Lite), availability (TEI-Lite), b (HTML), back (TEI-Lite), bdo (HTML), beginpage (DocBook), bibl (TEI-Lite), biblfull (TEI-Lite), bibliodiv (DocBook), biblioentry (DocBook), bibliography (DocBook), bibliomisc (DocBook), bibliomixed (DocBook), bibliomset (DocBook), biblioset (DocBook), biblscope (TEI-Lite), big (HTML), blockquote (DocBook), blockquote (HTML), body (HTML), body (TEI-Lite), book (DocBook), bookbiblio (DocBook), bookinfo (DocBook), bridgehead (DocBook), button (HTML), byline (TEI-Lite), callout (DocBook), calloutlist (DocBook), caption (HTML), catdesc (TEI-Lite), category (TEI-Lite), catref (TEI-Lite), caution (DocBook), cell (TEI-Lite), change (TEI-Lite), chapter (DocBook), cit (TEI-Lite), citation (DocBook), cite (HTML), citerefentry (DocBook), citetitle (DocBook), city

(DocBook), classcode (TEI-Lite), classdecl (TEI-Lite), classname (DocBook), closer (TEI-Lite), cmdsynopsis (DocBook), co (DocBook), code (HTML), code (TEI-Lite), col (HTML), colgroup (HTML), collab (DocBook), collabname (DocBook), command (DocBook), comment (DocBook), computeroutput (DocBook), confdates (DocBook), confgroup (DocBook), confnum (DocBook), confsponsor (DocBook), conftitle (DocBook), contractnum (DocBook), contractsponsor (DocBook), contrib (DocBook), copyright (DocBook), corpauthor (DocBook), corpname (DocBook), corr (TEI-Lite), country (DocBook), creation (TEI-Lite), database (DocBook), date (DocBook), date (TEI-Lite), dateline (TEI-Lite), dd (HTML), dedication (DocBook), del (HTML), del (TEI-Lite), dfn (HTML), distributor (TEI-Lite), div (HTML), div (TEI-Lite), div0 (TEI-Lite), div1 (TEI-Lite), div2 (TEI-Lite), div3 (TEI-Lite), div4 (TEI-Lite), div5 (TEI-Lite), div6 (TEI-Lite), div7 (TEI-Lite), divgen (TEI-Lite), dl (HTML), docauthor (TEI-Lite), docdate (TEI-Lite), docedition (TEI-Lite), docimprint (TEI-Lite), docinfo (DocBook), doctitle (TEI-Lite), dt (HTML), edition (DocBook), edition (TEI-Lite), editionstmt (TEI-Lite), editor (DocBook), editor (TEI-Lite), editorialdecl (TEI-Lite), eg (TEI-Lite), em (HTML), email (DocBook), emph (TEI-Lite), emphasis (DocBook), encodingdesc (TEI-Lite), entry (DocBook), entrytbl (DocBook), envar (DocBook), epigraph (DocBook), epigraph (TEI-Lite), equation (DocBook), errorcode (DocBook), errorname (DocBook), errortype (DocBook), example (DocBook), extent (TEI-Lite), fax (DocBook), fieldset (HTML), figdesc (TEI-Lite), figure (DocBook), figure (TEI-Lite), filedesc (TEI-Lite), filename (DocBook), firstname (DocBook), firstterm (DocBook), footnote (DocBook), footnoteref (DocBook), foreign (TEI-Lite), foreignphrase (DocBook), form (HTML), formalpara (DocBook), formula (TEI-Lite), front (TEI-Lite), funcdef (DocBook), funcparams (DocBook), funcprototype (DocBook), funcsynopsis (DocBook), funcsynopsisinfo (DocBook), function (DocBook), funder (TEI-Lite), gap (TEI-Lite), gi (TEI-Lite), gloss (TEI-Lite), glossary (DocBook), glossdef (DocBook), glossdiv (DocBook), glossentry (DocBook), glosslist (DocBook), glosssee (DocBook), glossseealso (DocBook), glossterm (DocBook), graphic (DocBook), graphicco (DocBook), group (DocBook), group (TEI-Lite), guibutton (DocBook), guiicon (DocBook), guilabel (DocBook), guimenu (DocBook), guimenuitem (DocBook), guisubmenu (DocBook), h1 (HTML), h2 (HTML), h3 (HTML), h4 (HTML), h5 (HTML), h6 (HTML), hardware (DocBook), head (HTML), head (TEI-Lite), hi (TEI-Lite), highlights (DocBook), holder (DocBook), honorific (DocBook), html (HTML), i (HTML), ident (TEI-Lite), idno (TEI-Lite), img (HTML), important (DocBook), imprint (TEI-Lite), index (DocBook), index (TEI-Lite), indexdiv (DocBook), indexentry (DocBook), indexterm (DocBook), informalequation (DocBook), informalexample (DocBook), informaltable (DocBook), inlineequation (DocBook), inlinegraphic (DocBook), input (HTML), ins (HTML), interface (DocBook), interfacedefinition (DocBook), interp (TEI-Lite), interpgrp (TEI-Lite), invpartnumber (DocBook), isbn (DocBook), issn (DocBook), issuenum (DocBook), item (TEI-Lite), itemizedlist (DocBook), itermset (DocBook), jobtitle (DocBook), kbd (HTML), keycap (DocBook), keycode (DocBook), keycombo (DocBook), keysym (DocBook), keyword (DocBook), keywords (TEI-Lite), keywordset (DocBook), kw (TEI-Lite), l (TEI-Lite), label (HTML), label (TEI-Lite), language (TEI-Lite), langusage (TEI-Lite), lb (TEI-Lite), legalnotice (DocBook), legend (HTML), lg (TEI-Lite), li (HTML), lineage (DocBook), lineannotation (DocBook), link (DocBook), link (HTML), list

(TEI-Lite), listbibl (TEI-Lite), listitem (DocBook), literal (DocBook), literallayout (DocBook), lot (DocBook), lotentry (DocBook), manvolnum (DocBook), map (HTML), markup (DocBook), medialabel (DocBook), member (DocBook), mentioned (TEI-Lite), menuchoice (DocBook), meta (HTML), milestone (TEI-Lite), modespec (DocBook), mousebutton (DocBook), msg (DocBook), msgaud (DocBook), msgentry (DocBook), msgexplan (DocBook), msginfo (DocBook), msglevel (DocBook), msgmain (DocBook), msgorig (DocBook), msgrel (DocBook), msgset (DocBook), msgsub (DocBook), msgtext (DocBook), name (TEI-Lite), noscript (HTML), note (DocBook), note (TEI-Lite), notesstmt (TEI-Lite), num (TEI-Lite), object (HTML), ol (HTML), olink (DocBook), opener (TEI-Lite), optgroup (HTML), option (DocBook), option (HTML), optional (DocBook), orderedlist (DocBook), orgdiv (DocBook), orgname (DocBook), orig (TEI-Lite), otheraddr (DocBook), othercredit (DocBook), othername (DocBook), p (HTML), p (TEI-Lite), pagenums (DocBook), para (DocBook), paramdef (DocBook), parameter (DocBook), part (DocBook), partintro (DocBook), pb (TEI-Lite), phone (DocBook), phrase (DocBook), pob (DocBook), postcode (DocBook), pre (HTML), preface (DocBook), primary (DocBook), primaryie (DocBook), principal (TEI-Lite), printhistory (DocBook), procedure (DocBook), productname (DocBook), productnumber (DocBook), profiledesc (TEI-Lite), programlisting (DocBook), programlistingco (DocBook), projectdesc (TEI-Lite), prompt (DocBook), property (DocBook), ptr (TEI-Lite), pubdate (DocBook), publicationstmt (TEI-Lite), publisher (DocBook), publisher (TEI-Lite), publishername (DocBook), pubplace (TEI-Lite), pubsnumber (DocBook), q (HTML), q (TEI-Lite), quote (DocBook), ref (TEI-Lite), refclass (DocBook), refdescriptor (DocBook), refentry (DocBook), refentrytitle (DocBook), reference (DocBook), refmeta (DocBook), refmiscinfo (DocBook), refname (DocBook), refnamediv (DocBook), refpurpose (DocBook), refsdecl (TEI-Lite), refsect1 (DocBook), refsect1info (DocBook), refsect2 (DocBook), refsect2info (DocBook), refsect3 (DocBook), refsect3info (DocBook), refsynopsisdiv (DocBook), refsynopsisdivinfo (DocBook), reg (TEI-Lite), releaseinfo (DocBook), rendition (TEI-Lite), replaceable (DocBook), resp (TEI-Lite), respstmt (TEI-Lite), returnvalue (DocBook), revhistory (DocBook), revision (DocBook), revisiondesc (TEI-Lite), revnumber (DocBook), revremark (DocBook), row (DocBook), row (TEI-Lite), rs (TEI-Lite), s (TEI-Lite), salute (TEI-Lite), samp (HTML), samplingdecl (TEI-Lite), sbr (DocBook), screen (DocBook), screenco (DocBook), screeninfo (DocBook), screenshot (DocBook), secondary (DocBook), secondaryie (DocBook), sect1 (DocBook), sect1info (DocBook), sect2 (DocBook), sect2info (DocBook), sect3 (DocBook), sect3info (DocBook), sect4 (DocBook), sect4info (DocBook), sect5 (DocBook), sect5info (DocBook), see (DocBook), seealso (DocBook), seealsoie (DocBook), seeie (DocBook), seg (DocBook), seg (TEI-Lite), seglistitem (DocBook), segmentedlist (DocBook), segtitle (DocBook), select (HTML), seriesinfo (DocBook), seriesstmt (TEI-Lite), seriesvolnums (DocBook), set (DocBook), setindex (DocBook), setinfo (DocBook), sgmltag (DocBook), shortaffil (DocBook), shortcut (DocBook), sic (TEI-Lite), sidebar (DocBook), signed (TEI-Lite), simpara (DocBook), simplelist (DocBook), simplesect (DocBook), small (HTML), socalled (TEI-Lite), sourcedesc (TEI-Lite), sp (TEI-Lite), span (HTML), speaker (TEI-Lite), sponsor (TEI-Lite), stage (TEI-Lite), state (DocBook), step (DocBook), street (DocBook), strong (HTML), structfield (DocBook), structname (DocBook), style (HTML), sub (HTML), subject (DocBook), subjectset (DocBook), subjectterm (DocBook), subscript (DocBook), substeps (DocBook), subtitle (DocBook), sup (HTML), superscript (DocBook), surname (DocBook), symbol (DocBook), synopfragment (DocBook), synopfragmentref (DocBook), synopsis (DocBook), systemitem (DocBook), table (DocBook), table (HTML), table (TEI-Lite), tagsdecl (TEI-Lite), tagusage (TEI-Lite), taxonomy (TEI-Lite), tbody (DocBook), tbody (HTML), td (HTML), tei.2 (TEI-Lite), teiheader (TEI-Lite), term (DocBook), term (TEI-Lite), tertiary (DocBook), tertiaryie (DocBook), text (TEI-Lite), textarea (HTML), textclass (TEI-Lite), tfoot (DocBook), tfoot (HTML), tgroup (DocBook), th (HTML), thead (DocBook), thead (HTML), time (TEI-Lite), tip (DocBook), title (DocBook), title (HTML), title (TEI-Lite), titleabbrev (DocBook), titlepage (TEI-Lite), titlepart (TEI-Lite), titlestmt (TEI-Lite), toc (DocBook), tocback (DocBook), tocchap (DocBook), tocentry (DocBook), tocfront (DocBook), toclevel1 (DocBook), toclevel2 (DocBook), toclevel3 (DocBook), toclevel4 (DocBook), toclevel5 (DocBook), tocpart (DocBook), token (DocBook), tr (HTML), trademark (DocBook), trailer (TEI-Lite), tt (HTML), type (DocBook), ul (HTML), ulink (DocBook), unclear (TEI-Lite), userinput (DocBook), var (HTML), varargs (DocBook), variablelist (DocBook), varlistentry (DocBook), void (DocBook), volumenum (DocBook), warning (DocBook), wordasword (DocBook), xptr (TEI-Lite), xref (DocBook), xref (TEI-Lite), year (DocBook)

language   (ATTRIBUTE: HTML)
  elements: script (HTML)
language   (ELEMENT: TEI-Lite)
langusage   (ELEMENT: TEI-Lite)
lb   (ELEMENT: TEI-Lite)
lccardno   (ELEMENT: ISO 12083)
leftind   (ATTRIBUTE: MIL-STD-38784)
  elements: table (MIL-STD-38784), tabmat (MIL-STD-38784), tgroup (MIL-STD-38784)
leftmar   (ATTRIBUTE: MIL-STD-38784)
  elements: colspec (MIL-STD-38784), table (MIL-STD-38784), tabmat (MIL-STD-38784), tgroup (MIL-STD-38784)
legalnotice   (ELEMENT: DocBook)
legend   (ELEMENT: HTML, MIL-STD-38784)
lep   (ELEMENT: MIL-STD-38784)
lepchg   (ELEMENT: MIL-STD-38784)
lepcontents   (ELEMENT: MIL-STD-38784)
lepentry   (ELEMENT: MIL-STD-38784)
leppage   (ELEMENT: MIL-STD-38784)
level   (ATTRIBUTE: MIL-STD-38784, TEI-Lite)
  elements: change (MIL-STD-38784), title (TEI-Lite)
level1   (ATTRIBUTE: TEI-Lite)
  elements: index (TEI-Lite)
level2   (ATTRIBUTE: TEI-Lite)
  elements: index (TEI-Lite)
level3   (ATTRIBUTE: TEI-Lite)
  elements: index (TEI-Lite)

level4   (ATTRIBUTE: TEI-Lite)
    elements: index (TEI-Lite)
lg   (ELEMENT: TEI-Lite)
li   (ELEMENT: HTML)
line   (ATTRIBUTE: MIL-STD-38784)
    elements: wpgentry (MIL-STD-38784)
line   (ELEMENT: MIL-STD-38784)
lineage   (ELEMENT: DocBook)
lineannotation   (ELEMENT: DocBook)
link   (ELEMENT: DocBook, HTML)
linkend   (ATTRIBUTE: DocBook)
    elements: firstterm (DocBook), footnoteref (DocBook), glossterm (DocBook), link (DocBook), seeie (DocBook), synopfragmentref (DocBook), tocback (DocBook), tocentry (DocBook), tocfront (DocBook), xref (DocBook)
linkends   (ATTRIBUTE: DocBook)
    elements: area (DocBook), co (DocBook), primaryie (DocBook), secondaryie (DocBook), seealsoie (DocBook), tertiaryie (DocBook)
linkmode   (ATTRIBUTE: DocBook)
    elements: olink (DocBook)
list   (ELEMENT: ISO 12083, TEI-Lite)
listbibl   (ELEMENT: TEI-Lite)
listitem   (ELEMENT: DocBook)
lit   (ELEMENT: ISO 12083)
literal   (ELEMENT: DocBook)
literallayout   (ELEMENT: DocBook)
llcordra   (ATTRIBUTE: MIL-STD-38784)
    elements: graphic (MIL-STD-38784)
localinfo   (ATTRIBUTE: DocBook)
    elements: olink (DocBook)
location   (ATTRIBUTE: ISO 12083)
    elements: inf (ISO 12083), sup (ISO 12083)
location   (ELEMENT: ISO 12083, MIL-STD-38784)
longdesc   (ATTRIBUTE: HTML)
    elements: img (HTML)
lot   (ELEMENT: DocBook)
lotentry   (ELEMENT: DocBook)
lpost   (ATTRIBUTE: ISO 12083)
    elements: fence (ISO 12083)
lrp   (ELEMENT: MIL-STD-38784)
lrpentry   (ELEMENT: MIL-STD-38784)
lru   (ATTRIBUTE: MIL-STD-38784)
    elements: abbrsect (MIL-STD-38784), appendix (MIL-STD-38784), applicdef (MIL-STD-38784), chapter (MIL-STD-38784), ddchapter (MIL-STD-38784), dddesc (MIL-STD-38784), ddindex (MIL-STD-38784), docpart (MIL-STD-38784), figure (MIL-STD-38784), foldout (MIL-STD-38784), lrp (MIL-STD-38784), para0 (MIL-STD-38784), ratd (MIL-STD-38784), safesum (MIL-STD-38784), section (MIL-STD-38784), step1 (MIL-STD-38784), step2 (MIL-STD-38784), step3 (MIL-STD-

38784), step4 (MIL-STD-38784), subpara1 (MIL-STD-38784), subpara2 (MIL-STD-38784), subpara3 (MIL-STD-38784), symsect (MIL-STD-38784), table (MIL-STD-38784), tabmat (MIL-STD-38784), tctolist (MIL-STD-38784), tctotbl (MIL-STD-38784), tmimprep (MIL-STD-38784), volume (MIL-STD-38784)

ltermwidth   (ATTRIBUTE: MIL-STD-38784)
elements: applicdef (MIL-STD-38784), deflist (MIL-STD-38784), symsect (MIL-STD-38784)

ltmidwidth   (ATTRIBUTE: MIL-STD-38784)
elements: lrp (MIL-STD-38784)

maintlvl   (ELEMENT: MIL-STD-38784)

manvolnum   (ELEMENT: DocBook)

map   (ELEMENT: HTML)

mark   (ATTRIBUTE: DocBook, MIL-STD-38784)
elements: change (MIL-STD-38784), ftnref (MIL-STD-38784), itemizedlist (DocBook)

mark   (ELEMENT: ISO 12083)

markref   (ELEMENT: ISO 12083)

markup   (ELEMENT: DocBook)

maxlength   (ATTRIBUTE: HTML)
elements: input (HTML)

media   (ATTRIBUTE: HTML)
elements: link (HTML), style (HTML)

medialabel   (ELEMENT: DocBook)

member   (ELEMENT: DocBook)

mentioned   (ELEMENT: TEI-Lite)

menuchoice   (ELEMENT: DocBook)

met   (ATTRIBUTE: TEI-Lite)
elements: l (TEI-Lite), lg (TEI-Lite)

meta   (ELEMENT: HTML)

method   (ATTRIBUTE: HTML)
elements: form (HTML)

mfr   (ELEMENT: MIL-STD-38784)

middle   (ELEMENT: ISO 12083)

milestone   (ELEMENT: TEI-Lite)

mindepth   (ATTRIBUTE: MIL-STD-38784)
elements: colspec (MIL-STD-38784), table (MIL-STD-38784), tabmat (MIL-STD-38784), tgroup (MIL-STD-38784)

modelno   (ELEMENT: MIL-STD-38784)

modespec   (ELEMENT: DocBook)

modreq   (ELEMENT: MIL-STD-38784)

module   (ATTRIBUTE: MIL-STD-38784)
elements: abbrsect (MIL-STD-38784), appendix (MIL-STD-38784), applicdef (MIL-STD-38784), chapter (MIL-STD-38784), ddchapter (MIL-STD-38784), dddesc (MIL-STD-38784), ddindex (MIL-STD-38784), docpart (MIL-STD-38784), figure (MIL-STD-38784), foldout (MIL-STD-38784), lrp (MIL-STD-38784), para0 (MIL-STD-38784), ratd (MIL-STD-38784), safesum (MIL-STD-38784), section (MIL-STD-38784), step1 (MIL-STD-38784), step2 (MIL-STD-38784), step3 (MIL-STD-

38784), step4 (MIL-STD-38784), subpara1 (MIL-STD-38784), subpara2 (MIL-STD-38784), subpara3 (MIL-STD-38784), symsect (MIL-STD-38784), table (MIL-STD-38784), tabmat (MIL-STD-38784), tctolist (MIL-STD-38784), tctotbl (MIL-STD-38784), tmimprep (MIL-STD-38784), volume (MIL-STD-38784)

moreinfo   (ATTRIBUTE: DocBook)
elements: action (DocBook), application (DocBook), command (DocBook), computeroutput (DocBook), database (DocBook), errorcode (DocBook), filename (DocBook), function (DocBook), guibutton (DocBook), guiicon (DocBook), guilabel (DocBook), guimenu (DocBook), guimenuitem (DocBook), guisubmenu (DocBook), hardware (DocBook), interface (DocBook), interfacedefinition (DocBook), keycap (DocBook), keycombo (DocBook), literal (DocBook), menuchoice (DocBook), mousebutton (DocBook), parameter (DocBook), prompt (DocBook), property (DocBook), shortcut (DocBook), systemitem (DocBook), userinput (DocBook)

morerows   (ATTRIBUTE: DocBook, MIL-STD-38784)
elements: entry (DocBook), entry (MIL-STD-38784)

mousebutton   (ELEMENT: DocBook)

mrchgtxt   (ELEMENT: MIL-STD-38784)

mrgenmod   (ELEMENT: MIL-STD-38784)

mrinfo   (ELEMENT: MIL-STD-38784)

mrinstr   (ELEMENT: MIL-STD-38784)

mritem   (ELEMENT: MIL-STD-38784)

mrlist   (ELEMENT: MIL-STD-38784)

mrmod   (ELEMENT: MIL-STD-38784)

mrpara   (ELEMENT: MIL-STD-38784)

mrreason   (ELEMENT: MIL-STD-38784)

mrrespns   (ELEMENT: MIL-STD-38784)

msg   (ELEMENT: DocBook)

msgaud   (ELEMENT: DocBook)

msgentry   (ELEMENT: DocBook)

msgexplan   (ELEMENT: DocBook)

msginfo   (ELEMENT: DocBook)

msglevel   (ELEMENT: DocBook)

msgmain   (ELEMENT: DocBook)

msgorig   (ELEMENT: DocBook)

msgrel   (ELEMENT: DocBook)

msgset   (ELEMENT: DocBook)

msgsub   (ELEMENT: DocBook)

msgtext   (ELEMENT: DocBook)

msn   (ELEMENT: ISO 12083)

multiple   (ATTRIBUTE: HTML)
elements: select (HTML)

n   (ATTRIBUTE: TEI-Lite)
elements: abbr (TEI-Lite), add (TEI-Lite), address (TEI-Lite), addrline (TEI-Lite), anchor (TEI-Lite), argument (TEI-Lite), author (TEI-Lite), authority (TEI-Lite), availability (TEI-Lite), back (TEI-Lite), bibl (TEI-Lite), biblfull (TEI-Lite), biblscope (TEI-Lite), body (TEI-Lite), byline (TEI-Lite), catdesc (TEI-Lite), category (TEI-Lite),

catref (TEI-Lite), cell (TEI-Lite), change (TEI-Lite), cit (TEI-Lite), classcode (TEI-Lite), classdecl (TEI-Lite), closer (TEI-Lite), code (TEI-Lite), corr (TEI-Lite), creation (TEI-Lite), date (TEI-Lite), dateline (TEI-Lite), del (TEI-Lite), distributor (TEI-Lite), div (TEI-Lite), div0 (TEI-Lite), div1 (TEI-Lite), div2 (TEI-Lite), div3 (TEI-Lite), div4 (TEI-Lite), div5 (TEI-Lite), div6 (TEI-Lite), div7 (TEI-Lite), divgen (TEI-Lite), docauthor (TEI-Lite), docdate (TEI-Lite), docedition (TEI-Lite), docimprint (TEI-Lite), doctitle (TEI-Lite), edition (TEI-Lite), editionstmt (TEI-Lite), editor (TEI-Lite), editorialdecl (TEI-Lite), eg (TEI-Lite), emph (TEI-Lite), encodingdesc (TEI-Lite), epigraph (TEI-Lite), extent (TEI-Lite), figdesc (TEI-Lite), figure (TEI-Lite), filedesc (TEI-Lite), foreign (TEI-Lite), formula (TEI-Lite), front (TEI-Lite), funder (TEI-Lite), gap (TEI-Lite), gi (TEI-Lite), gloss (TEI-Lite), group (TEI-Lite), head (TEI-Lite), hi (TEI-Lite), ident (TEI-Lite), idno (TEI-Lite), imprint (TEI-Lite), index (TEI-Lite), interp (TEI-Lite), interpgrp (TEI-Lite), item (TEI-Lite), keywords (TEI-Lite), kw (TEI-Lite), l (TEI-Lite), label (TEI-Lite), language (TEI-Lite), langusage (TEI-Lite), lb (TEI-Lite), lg (TEI-Lite), list (TEI-Lite), listbibl (TEI-Lite), mentioned (TEI-Lite), milestone (TEI-Lite), name (TEI-Lite), note (TEI-Lite), notesstmt (TEI-Lite), num (TEI-Lite), opener (TEI-Lite), orig (TEI-Lite), p (TEI-Lite), pb (TEI-Lite), principal (TEI-Lite), profiledesc (TEI-Lite), projectdesc (TEI-Lite), ptr (TEI-Lite), publicationstmt (TEI-Lite), publisher (TEI-Lite), pubplace (TEI-Lite), q (TEI-Lite), ref (TEI-Lite), refsdecl (TEI-Lite), reg (TEI-Lite), rendition (TEI-Lite), resp (TEI-Lite), respstmt (TEI-Lite), revisiondesc (TEI-Lite), row (TEI-Lite), rs (TEI-Lite), s (TEI-Lite), salute (TEI-Lite), samplingdecl (TEI-Lite), seg (TEI-Lite), seriesstmt (TEI-Lite), sic (TEI-Lite), signed (TEI-Lite), socalled (TEI-Lite), sourcedesc (TEI-Lite), sp (TEI-Lite), speaker (TEI-Lite), sponsor (TEI-Lite), stage (TEI-Lite), table (TEI-Lite), tagsdecl (TEI-Lite), tagusage (TEI-Lite), taxonomy (TEI-Lite), tei.2 (TEI-Lite), teiheader (TEI-Lite), term (TEI-Lite), text (TEI-Lite), textclass (TEI-Lite), time (TEI-Lite), title (TEI-Lite), titlepage (TEI-Lite), titlepart (TEI-Lite), titlestmt (TEI-Lite), trailer (TEI-Lite), unclear (TEI-Lite), xptr (TEI-Lite), xref (TEI-Lite))

name   (ATTRIBUTE: HTML, ISO 12083)
     elements: a (HTML), artwork (ISO 12083), button (HTML), fig (ISO 12083), input (HTML), map (HTML), meta (HTML), object (HTML), param (HTML), select (HTML), textarea (HTML)

name   (ELEMENT: TEI-Lite)

nameend   (ATTRIBUTE: DocBook, MIL-STD-38784)
     elements: entry (DocBook), entrytbl (DocBook), spanspec (DocBook), spanspec (MIL-STD-38784)

nameloc   (ELEMENT: ISO 12083)

namest   (ATTRIBUTE: DocBook, MIL-STD-38784)
     elements: entry (DocBook), entrytbl (DocBook), spanspec (DocBook), spanspec (MIL-STD-38784)

nametype   (ATTRIBUTE: ISO 12083)
     elements: nmlist (ISO 12083)

next   (ATTRIBUTE: TEI-Lite)
     elements: abbr (TEI-Lite), add (TEI-Lite), address (TEI-Lite), addrline (TEI-Lite), argument (TEI-Lite), author (TEI-Lite), authority (TEI-Lite), availability (TEI-Lite), back (TEI-Lite), bibl (TEI-Lite), biblfull (TEI-Lite), biblscope (TEI-Lite), body (TEI-Lite), byline (TEI-Lite), catdesc (TEI-Lite), category (TEI-Lite), catref (TEI-Lite), cell

(TEI-Lite), change (TEI-Lite), cit (TEI-Lite), classcode (TEI-Lite), classdecl (TEI-Lite), closer (TEI-Lite), code (TEI-Lite), corr (TEI-Lite), creation (TEI-Lite), date (TEI-Lite), dateline (TEI-Lite), distributor (TEI-Lite), div (TEI-Lite), div0 (TEI-Lite), div1 (TEI-Lite), div2 (TEI-Lite), div3 (TEI-Lite), div4 (TEI-Lite), div5 (TEI-Lite), div6 (TEI-Lite), div7 (TEI-Lite), divgen (TEI-Lite), docauthor (TEI-Lite), docdate (TEI-Lite), docedition (TEI-Lite), docimprint (TEI-Lite), doctitle (TEI-Lite), edition (TEI-Lite), editionstmt (TEI-Lite), editor (TEI-Lite), editorialdecl (TEI-Lite), eg (TEI-Lite), emph (TEI-Lite), encodingdesc (TEI-Lite), epigraph (TEI-Lite), extent (TEI-Lite), figdesc (TEI-Lite), figure (TEI-Lite), filedesc (TEI-Lite), formula (TEI-Lite), front (TEI-Lite), funder (TEI-Lite), gap (TEI-Lite), gi (TEI-Lite), gloss (TEI-Lite), group (TEI-Lite), head (TEI-Lite), ident (TEI-Lite), idno (TEI-Lite), imprint (TEI-Lite), index (TEI-Lite), interp (TEI-Lite), interpgrp (TEI-Lite), keywords (TEI-Lite), kw (TEI-Lite), l (TEI-Lite), label (TEI-Lite), langusage (TEI-Lite), lg (TEI-Lite), list (TEI-Lite), listbibl (TEI-Lite), mentioned (TEI-Lite), name (TEI-Lite), notesstmt (TEI-Lite), num (TEI-Lite), opener (TEI-Lite), orig (TEI-Lite), p (TEI-Lite), principal (TEI-Lite), profiledesc (TEI-Lite), projectdesc (TEI-Lite), ptr (TEI-Lite), publicationstmt (TEI-Lite), publisher (TEI-Lite), pubplace (TEI-Lite), q (TEI-Lite), ref (TEI-Lite), refsdecl (TEI-Lite), reg (TEI-Lite), rendition (TEI-Lite), resp (TEI-Lite), respstmt (TEI-Lite), revisiondesc (TEI-Lite), row (TEI-Lite), rs (TEI-Lite), s (TEI-Lite), salute (TEI-Lite), samplingdecl (TEI-Lite), seg (TEI-Lite), seriesstmt (TEI-Lite), sic (TEI-Lite), signed (TEI-Lite), socalled (TEI-Lite), sourcedesc (TEI-Lite), sp (TEI-Lite), speaker (TEI-Lite), sponsor (TEI-Lite), stage (TEI-Lite), table (TEI-Lite), tagsdecl (TEI-Lite), tagusage (TEI-Lite), taxonomy (TEI-Lite), tei.2 (TEI-Lite), teiheader (TEI-Lite), term (TEI-Lite), text (TEI-Lite), textclass (TEI-Lite), time (TEI-Lite), title (TEI-Lite), titlepage (TEI-Lite), titlepart (TEI-Lite), titlestmt (TEI-Lite), trailer (TEI-Lite), unclear (TEI-Lite), xptr (TEI-Lite), xref (TEI-Lite)

nmlist   (ELEMENT: ISO 12083)

no   (ELEMENT: ISO 12083)

nohref   (ATTRIBUTE: HTML)
elements: area (HTML)

nomen   (ELEMENT: MIL-STD-38784)

noscript   (ELEMENT: HTML)

notation   (ATTRIBUTE: TEI-Lite)
elements: formula (TEI-Lite)

note   (ELEMENT: DocBook, ISO 12083, MIL-STD-38784, TEI-Lite)

noteref   (ELEMENT: ISO 12083)

notes   (ELEMENT: ISO 12083)

notesstmt   (ELEMENT: TEI-Lite)

nsn   (ELEMENT: MIL-STD-38784)

nsp   (ATTRIBUTE: MIL-STD-38784)
elements: abbrsect (MIL-STD-38784), applicdef (MIL-STD-38784), dddesc (MIL-STD-38784), ddindex (MIL-STD-38784), lrp (MIL-STD-38784), para0 (MIL-STD-38784), ratd (MIL-STD-38784), safesum (MIL-STD-38784), step1 (MIL-STD-38784), step2 (MIL-STD-38784), step3 (MIL-STD-38784), step4 (MIL-STD-38784), subpara1 (MIL-STD-38784), subpara2 (MIL-STD-38784), subpara3 (MIL-STD-38784), symsect (MIL-STD-38784), tctolist (MIL-STD-38784), tmimprep (MIL-STD-38784)

nsp (ELEMENT: MIL-STD-38784)

num (ATTRIBUTE: ISO 12083)
> elements: dformgrp (ISO 12083), dformula (ISO 12083)

num (ELEMENT: ISO 12083, TEI-Lite)

numcols (ATTRIBUTE: MIL-STD-38784)
> elements: index (MIL-STD-38784), legend (MIL-STD-38784)

numeration (ATTRIBUTE: DocBook)
> elements: orderedlist (DocBook)

numstyle (ATTRIBUTE: MIL-STD-38784)
> elements: seqlist (MIL-STD-38784)

oadr (ELEMENT: MIL-STD-38784)

object (ELEMENT: HTML)

obnames (ATTRIBUTE: ISO 12083)
> elements: nmlist (ISO 12083)

occurs (ATTRIBUTE: TEI-Lite)
> elements: tagusage (TEI-Lite)

ol (ELEMENT: HTML)

olink (ELEMENT: DocBook)

onblur (ATTRIBUTE: HTML)
> elements: a (HTML), area (HTML), button (HTML), input (HTML), label (HTML), select (HTML), textarea (HTML)

onchange (ATTRIBUTE: HTML)
> elements: input (HTML), select (HTML), textarea (HTML)

onclick (ATTRIBUTE: HTML)
> elements: a (HTML), abbr (HTML), acronym (HTML), address (HTML), area (HTML), b (HTML), big (HTML), blockquote (HTML), body (HTML), button (HTML), caption (HTML), cite (HTML), code (HTML), col (HTML), colgroup (HTML), dd (HTML), del (HTML), dfn (HTML), div (HTML), dl (HTML), dt (HTML), em (HTML), fieldset (HTML), form (HTML), h1 (HTML), h2 (HTML), h3 (HTML), h4 (HTML), h5 (HTML), h6 (HTML), hr (HTML), i (HTML), img (HTML), input (HTML), ins (HTML), kbd (HTML), label (HTML), legend (HTML), li (HTML), link (HTML), map (HTML), noscript (HTML), object (HTML), ol (HTML), optgroup (HTML), option (HTML), p (HTML), pre (HTML), q (HTML), samp (HTML), select (HTML), small (HTML), span (HTML), strong (HTML), sub (HTML), sup (HTML), table (HTML), tbody (HTML), td (HTML), textarea (HTML), tfoot (HTML), th (HTML), thead (HTML), tr (HTML), tt (HTML), ul (HTML), var (HTML)

ondblclick (ATTRIBUTE: HTML)
> elements: a (HTML), abbr (HTML), acronym (HTML), address (HTML), area (HTML), b (HTML), big (HTML), blockquote (HTML), body (HTML), button (HTML), caption (HTML), cite (HTML), code (HTML), col (HTML), colgroup (HTML), dd (HTML), del (HTML), dfn (HTML), div (HTML), dl (HTML), dt (HTML), em (HTML), fieldset (HTML), form (HTML), h1 (HTML), h2 (HTML), h3 (HTML), h4 (HTML), h5 (HTML), h6 (HTML), hr (HTML), i (HTML), img (HTML), input (HTML), ins (HTML), kbd (HTML), label (HTML), legend (HTML), li (HTML), link (HTML), map (HTML), noscript (HTML), object (HTML), ol (HTML), optgroup (HTML), option (HTML), p (HTML), pre (HTML), q (HTML), samp (HTML), select (HTML), small (HTML), span (HTML), strong (HTML), sub (HTML), sup (HTML), table (HTML), tbody (HTML), td

(HTML), textarea (HTML), tfoot (HTML), th (HTML), thead (HTML), tr (HTML), tt (HTML), ul (HTML), var (HTML)

onfocus (ATTRIBUTE: HTML)
elements: a (HTML), area (HTML), button (HTML), input (HTML), label (HTML), select (HTML), textarea (HTML)

onkeydown (ATTRIBUTE: HTML)
elements: a (HTML), abbr (HTML), acronym (HTML), address (HTML), area (HTML), b (HTML), big (HTML), blockquote (HTML), body (HTML), button (HTML), caption (HTML), cite (HTML), code (HTML), col (HTML), colgroup (HTML), dd (HTML), del (HTML), dfn (HTML), div (HTML), dl (HTML), dt (HTML), em (HTML), fieldset (HTML), form (HTML), h1 (HTML), h2 (HTML), h3 (HTML), h4 (HTML), h5 (HTML), h6 (HTML), hr (HTML), i (HTML), img (HTML), input (HTML), ins (HTML), kbd (HTML), label (HTML), legend (HTML), li (HTML), link (HTML), map (HTML), noscript (HTML), object (HTML), ol (HTML), optgroup (HTML), option (HTML), p (HTML), pre (HTML), q (HTML), samp (HTML), select (HTML), small (HTML), span (HTML), strong (HTML), sub (HTML), sup (HTML), table (HTML), tbody (HTML), td (HTML), textarea (HTML), tfoot (HTML), th (HTML), thead (HTML), tr (HTML), tt (HTML), ul (HTML), var (HTML)

onkeypress (ATTRIBUTE: HTML)
elements: a (HTML), abbr (HTML), acronym (HTML), address (HTML), area (HTML), b (HTML), big (HTML), blockquote (HTML), body (HTML), button (HTML), caption (HTML), cite (HTML), code (HTML), col (HTML), colgroup (HTML), dd (HTML), del (HTML), dfn (HTML), div (HTML), dl (HTML), dt (HTML), em (HTML), fieldset (HTML), form (HTML), h1 (HTML), h2 (HTML), h3 (HTML), h4 (HTML), h5 (HTML), h6 (HTML), hr (HTML), i (HTML), img (HTML), input (HTML), ins (HTML), kbd (HTML), label (HTML), legend (HTML), li (HTML), link (HTML), map (HTML), noscript (HTML), object (HTML), ol (HTML), optgroup (HTML), option (HTML), p (HTML), pre (HTML), q (HTML), samp (HTML), select (HTML), small (HTML), span (HTML), strong (HTML), sub (HTML), sup (HTML), table (HTML), tbody (HTML), td (HTML), textarea (HTML), tfoot (HTML), th (HTML), thead (HTML), tr (HTML), tt (HTML), ul (HTML), var (HTML)

onkeyup (ATTRIBUTE: HTML)
elements: a (HTML), abbr (HTML), acronym (HTML), address (HTML), area (HTML), b (HTML), big (HTML), blockquote (HTML), body (HTML), button (HTML), caption (HTML), cite (HTML), code (HTML), col (HTML), colgroup (HTML), dd (HTML), del (HTML), dfn (HTML), div (HTML), dl (HTML), dt (HTML), em (HTML), fieldset (HTML), form (HTML), h1 (HTML), h2 (HTML), h3 (HTML), h4 (HTML), h5 (HTML), h6 (HTML), hr (HTML), i (HTML), img (HTML), input (HTML), ins (HTML), kbd (HTML), label (HTML), legend (HTML), li (HTML), link (HTML), map (HTML), noscript (HTML), object (HTML), ol (HTML), optgroup (HTML), option (HTML), p (HTML), pre (HTML), q (HTML), samp (HTML), select (HTML), small (HTML), span (HTML), strong (HTML), sub (HTML), sup (HTML), table (HTML), tbody (HTML), td (HTML), textarea (HTML), tfoot (HTML), th (HTML), thead (HTML), tr (HTML), tt (HTML), ul (HTML), var (HTML)

onload (ATTRIBUTE: HTML)
elements: body (HTML)

onmousedown (ATTRIBUTE: HTML)

elements: a (HTML), abbr (HTML), acronym (HTML), address (HTML), area (HTML), b (HTML), big (HTML), blockquote (HTML), body (HTML), button (HTML), caption (HTML), cite (HTML), code (HTML), col (HTML), colgroup (HTML), dd (HTML), del (HTML), dfn (HTML), div (HTML), dl (HTML), dt (HTML), em (HTML), fieldset (HTML), form (HTML), h1 (HTML), h2 (HTML), h3 (HTML), h4 (HTML), h5 (HTML), h6 (HTML), hr (HTML), i (HTML), img (HTML), input (HTML), ins (HTML), kbd (HTML), label (HTML), legend (HTML), li (HTML), link (HTML), map (HTML), noscript (HTML), object (HTML), ol (HTML), optgroup (HTML), option (HTML), p (HTML), pre (HTML), q (HTML), samp (HTML), select (HTML), small (HTML), span (HTML), strong (HTML), sub (HTML), sup (HTML), table (HTML), tbody (HTML), td (HTML), textarea (HTML), tfoot (HTML), th (HTML), thead (HTML), tr (HTML), tt (HTML), ul (HTML), var (HTML)

onmousemove   (ATTRIBUTE: HTML)

elements: a (HTML), abbr (HTML), acronym (HTML), address (HTML), area (HTML), b (HTML), big (HTML), blockquote (HTML), body (HTML), button (HTML), caption (HTML), cite (HTML), code (HTML), col (HTML), colgroup (HTML), dd (HTML), del (HTML), dfn (HTML), div (HTML), dl (HTML), dt (HTML), em (HTML), fieldset (HTML), form (HTML), h1 (HTML), h2 (HTML), h3 (HTML), h4 (HTML), h5 (HTML), h6 (HTML), hr (HTML), i (HTML), img (HTML), input (HTML), ins (HTML), kbd (HTML), label (HTML), legend (HTML), li (HTML), link (HTML), map (HTML), noscript (HTML), object (HTML), ol (HTML), optgroup (HTML), option (HTML), p (HTML), pre (HTML), q (HTML), samp (HTML), select (HTML), small (HTML), span (HTML), strong (HTML), sub (HTML), sup (HTML), table (HTML), tbody (HTML), td (HTML), textarea (HTML), tfoot (HTML), th (HTML), thead (HTML), tr (HTML), tt (HTML), ul (HTML), var (HTML)

onmouseout   (ATTRIBUTE: HTML)

elements: a (HTML), abbr (HTML), acronym (HTML), address (HTML), area (HTML), b (HTML), big (HTML), blockquote (HTML), body (HTML), button (HTML), caption (HTML), cite (HTML), code (HTML), col (HTML), colgroup (HTML), dd (HTML), del (HTML), dfn (HTML), div (HTML), dl (HTML), dt (HTML), em (HTML), fieldset (HTML), form (HTML), h1 (HTML), h2 (HTML), h3 (HTML), h4 (HTML), h5 (HTML), h6 (HTML), hr (HTML), i (HTML), img (HTML), input (HTML), ins (HTML), kbd (HTML), label (HTML), legend (HTML), li (HTML), link (HTML), map (HTML), noscript (HTML), object (HTML), ol (HTML), optgroup (HTML), option (HTML), p (HTML), pre (HTML), q (HTML), samp (HTML), select (HTML), small (HTML), span (HTML), strong (HTML), sub (HTML), sup (HTML), table (HTML), tbody (HTML), td (HTML), textarea (HTML), tfoot (HTML), th (HTML), thead (HTML), tr (HTML), tt (HTML), ul (HTML), var (HTML)

onmouseover   (ATTRIBUTE: HTML)

elements: a (HTML), abbr (HTML), acronym (HTML), address (HTML), area (HTML), b (HTML), big (HTML), blockquote (HTML), body (HTML), button (HTML), caption (HTML), cite (HTML), code (HTML), col (HTML), colgroup (HTML), dd (HTML), del (HTML), dfn (HTML), div (HTML), dl (HTML), dt (HTML), em (HTML), fieldset (HTML), form (HTML), h1 (HTML), h2 (HTML), h3 (HTML), h4 (HTML), h5 (HTML), h6 (HTML), hr (HTML), i (HTML), img (HTML), input (HTML), ins (HTML), kbd (HTML), label (HTML), legend (HTML), li (HTML), link (HTML), map (HTML), noscript (HTML), object (HTML), ol (HTML), optgroup (HTML), option (HTML), p

(HTML), pre (HTML), q (HTML), samp (HTML), select (HTML), small (HTML), span (HTML), strong (HTML), sub (HTML), sup (HTML), table (HTML), tbody (HTML), td (HTML), textarea (HTML), tfoot (HTML), th (HTML), thead (HTML), tr (HTML), tt (HTML), ul (HTML), var (HTML)

onmouseup   (ATTRIBUTE: HTML)
    elements: a (HTML), abbr (HTML), acronym (HTML), address (HTML), area (HTML), b (HTML), big (HTML), blockquote (HTML), body (HTML), button (HTML), caption (HTML), cite (HTML), code (HTML), col (HTML), colgroup (HTML), dd (HTML), del (HTML), dfn (HTML), div (HTML), dl (HTML), dt (HTML), em (HTML), fieldset (HTML), form (HTML), h1 (HTML), h2 (HTML), h3 (HTML), h4 (HTML), h5 (HTML), h6 (HTML), hr (HTML), i (HTML), img (HTML), input (HTML), ins (HTML), kbd (HTML), label (HTML), legend (HTML), li (HTML), link (HTML), map (HTML), noscript (HTML), object (HTML), ol (HTML), optgroup (HTML), option (HTML), p (HTML), pre (HTML), q (HTML), samp (HTML), select (HTML), small (HTML), span (HTML), strong (HTML), sub (HTML), sup (HTML), table (HTML), tbody (HTML), td (HTML), textarea (HTML), tfoot (HTML), th (HTML), thead (HTML), tr (HTML), tt (HTML), ul (HTML), var (HTML)

onreset   (ATTRIBUTE: HTML)
    elements: form (HTML)

onselect   (ATTRIBUTE: HTML)
    elements: input (HTML), textarea (HTML)

onsubmit   (ATTRIBUTE: HTML)
    elements: form (HTML)

onunload   (ATTRIBUTE: HTML)
    elements: body (HTML)

opener   (ELEMENT: TEI-Lite)

optgroup   (ELEMENT: HTML)

option   (ELEMENT: DocBook, HTML)

optional   (ELEMENT: DocBook)

orderedlist   (ELEMENT: DocBook)

ordering   (ATTRIBUTE: ISO 12083)
    elements: nameloc (ISO 12083)

org   (ATTRIBUTE: TEI-Lite)
    elements: div (TEI-Lite), div0 (TEI-Lite), div1 (TEI-Lite), div2 (TEI-Lite), div3 (TEI-Lite), div4 (TEI-Lite), div5 (TEI-Lite), div6 (TEI-Lite), div7 (TEI-Lite), lg (TEI-Lite)

orgaddr   (ELEMENT: ISO 12083)

organiz   (ATTRIBUTE: MIL-STD-38784)
    elements: modreq (MIL-STD-38784)

orgcat   (ATTRIBUTE: MIL-STD-38784)
    elements: modreq (MIL-STD-38784)

orgdiv   (ELEMENT: DocBook, ISO 12083)

orgname   (ELEMENT: DocBook, ISO 12083)

orient   (ATTRIBUTE: DocBook, MIL-STD-38784)
    elements: figure (MIL-STD-38784), foldout (MIL-STD-38784), informaltable (DocBook), subfig (MIL-STD-38784), table (DocBook), table (MIL-STD-38784), tabmat (MIL-STD-38784)

orig   (ATTRIBUTE: TEI-Lite)

elements: reg (TEI-Lite)

orig   (ELEMENT: TEI-Lite)

os   (ATTRIBUTE: DocBook)

elements: abbrev (DocBook), abstract (DocBook), accel (DocBook), ackno (DocBook), acronym (DocBook), action (DocBook), address (DocBook), affiliation (DocBook), alt (DocBook), anchor (DocBook), appendix (DocBook), application (DocBook), area (DocBook), areaset (DocBook), areaspec (DocBook), arg (DocBook), artheader (DocBook), article (DocBook), artpagenums (DocBook), attribution (DocBook), author (DocBook), authorblurb (DocBook), authorgroup (DocBook), authorinitials (DocBook), beginpage (DocBook), bibliodiv (DocBook), biblioentry (DocBook), bibliography (DocBook), bibliomisc (DocBook), bibliomixed (DocBook), bibliomset (DocBook), biblioset (DocBook), blockquote (DocBook), book (DocBook), bookbiblio (DocBook), bookinfo (DocBook), bridgehead (DocBook), callout (DocBook), calloutlist (DocBook), caution (DocBook), chapter (DocBook), citation (DocBook), citerefentry (DocBook), citetitle (DocBook), city (DocBook), classname (DocBook), cmdsynopsis (DocBook), co (DocBook), collab (DocBook), collabname (DocBook), command (DocBook), comment (DocBook), computeroutput (DocBook), confdates (DocBook), confgroup (DocBook), confnum (DocBook), confsponsor (DocBook), conftitle (DocBook), contractnum (DocBook), contractsponsor (DocBook), contrib (DocBook), copyright (DocBook), corpauthor (DocBook), corpname (DocBook), country (DocBook), database (DocBook), date (DocBook), dedication (DocBook), docinfo (DocBook), edition (DocBook), editor (DocBook), email (DocBook), emphasis (DocBook), entry (DocBook), entrytbl (DocBook), envar (DocBook), epigraph (DocBook), equation (DocBook), errorcode (DocBook), errorname (DocBook), errortype (DocBook), example (DocBook), fax (DocBook), figure (DocBook), filename (DocBook), firstname (DocBook), firstterm (DocBook), footnote (DocBook), footnoteref (DocBook), foreignphrase (DocBook), formalpara (DocBook), funcdef (DocBook), funcparams (DocBook), funcprototype (DocBook), funcsynopsis (DocBook), funcsynopsisinfo (DocBook), function (DocBook), glossary (DocBook), glossdef (DocBook), glossdiv (DocBook), glossentry (DocBook), glosslist (DocBook), glosssee (DocBook), glossseealso (DocBook), glossterm (DocBook), graphic (DocBook), graphicco (DocBook), group (DocBook), guibutton (DocBook), guiicon (DocBook), guilabel (DocBook), guimenu (DocBook), guimenuitem (DocBook), guisubmenu (DocBook), hardware (DocBook), highlights (DocBook), holder (DocBook), honorific (DocBook), important (DocBook), index (DocBook), indexdiv (DocBook), indexentry (DocBook), indexterm (DocBook), informalequation (DocBook), informalexample (DocBook), informaltable (DocBook), inlineequation (DocBook), inlinegraphic (DocBook), interface (DocBook), interfacedefinition (DocBook), invpartnumber (DocBook), isbn (DocBook), issn (DocBook), issuenum (DocBook), itemizedlist (DocBook), itermset (DocBook), jobtitle (DocBook), keycap (DocBook), keycode (DocBook), keycombo (DocBook), keysym (DocBook), keyword (DocBook), keywordset (DocBook), legalnotice (DocBook), lineage (DocBook), lineannotation (DocBook), link (DocBook), listitem (DocBook), literal (DocBook), literallayout (DocBook), lot (DocBook), lotentry (DocBook), manvolnum (DocBook), markup (DocBook), medialabel (DocBook), member (DocBook), menuchoice (DocBook), modespec (DocBook), mousebutton (DocBook), msg (DocBook), msgaud

(DocBook), msgentry (DocBook), msgexplan (DocBook), msginfo (DocBook), msglevel (DocBook), msgmain (DocBook), msgorig (DocBook), msgrel (DocBook), msgset (DocBook), msgsub (DocBook), msgtext (DocBook), note (DocBook), olink (DocBook), option (DocBook), optional (DocBook), orderedlist (DocBook), orgdiv (DocBook), orgname (DocBook), otheraddr (DocBook), othercredit (DocBook), othername (DocBook), pagenums (DocBook), para (DocBook), paramdef (DocBook), parameter (DocBook), part (DocBook), partintro (DocBook), phone (DocBook), phrase (DocBook), pob (DocBook), postcode (DocBook), preface (DocBook), primary (DocBook), primaryie (DocBook), printhistory (DocBook), procedure (DocBook), productname (DocBook), productnumber (DocBook), programlisting (DocBook), programlistingco (DocBook), prompt (DocBook), property (DocBook), pubdate (DocBook), publisher (DocBook), publishername (DocBook), pubsnumber (DocBook), quote (DocBook), refclass (DocBook), refdescriptor (DocBook), refentry (DocBook), refentrytitle (DocBook), reference (DocBook), refmeta (DocBook), refmiscinfo (DocBook), refname (DocBook), refnamediv (DocBook), refpurpose (DocBook), refsect1 (DocBook), refsect1info (DocBook), refsect2 (DocBook), refsect2info (DocBook), refsect3 (DocBook), refsect3info (DocBook), refsynopsisdiv (DocBook), refsynopsisdivinfo (DocBook), releaseinfo (DocBook), replaceable (DocBook), returnvalue (DocBook), revhistory (DocBook), revision (DocBook), revnumber (DocBook), revremark (DocBook), row (DocBook), sbr (DocBook), screen (DocBook), screenco (DocBook), screeninfo (DocBook), screenshot (DocBook), secondary (DocBook), secondaryie (DocBook), sect1 (DocBook), sect1info (DocBook), sect2 (DocBook), sect2info (DocBook), sect3 (DocBook), sect3info (DocBook), sect4 (DocBook), sect4info (DocBook), sect5 (DocBook), sect5info (DocBook), see (DocBook), seealso (DocBook), seealsoie (DocBook), seeie (DocBook), seg (DocBook), seglistitem (DocBook), segmentedlist (DocBook), segtitle (DocBook), seriesinfo (DocBook), seriesvolnums (DocBook), set (DocBook), setindex (DocBook), setinfo (DocBook), sgmltag (DocBook), shortaffil (DocBook), shortcut (DocBook), sidebar (DocBook), simpara (DocBook), simplelist (DocBook), simplesect (DocBook), state (DocBook), step (DocBook), street (DocBook), structfield (DocBook), structname (DocBook), subject (DocBook), subjectset (DocBook), subjectterm (DocBook), subscript (DocBook), substeps (DocBook), subtitle (DocBook), superscript (DocBook), surname (DocBook), symbol (DocBook), synopfragment (DocBook), synopfragmentref (DocBook), synopsis (DocBook), systemitem (DocBook), table (DocBook), tbody (DocBook), term (DocBook), tertiary (DocBook), tertiaryie (DocBook), tfoot (DocBook), tgroup (DocBook), thead (DocBook), tip (DocBook), title (DocBook), titleabbrev (DocBook), toc (DocBook), tocback (DocBook), tocchap (DocBook), tocentry (DocBook), tocfront (DocBook), toclevel1 (DocBook), toclevel2 (DocBook), toclevel3 (DocBook), toclevel4 (DocBook), toclevel5 (DocBook), tocpart (DocBook), token (DocBook), trademark (DocBook), type (DocBook), ulink (DocBook), userinput (DocBook), varargs (DocBook), variablelist (DocBook), varlistentry (DocBook), void (DocBook), volumenum (DocBook), warning (DocBook), wordasword (DocBook), xref (DocBook), year (DocBook))

otheraction   (ATTRIBUTE: DocBook)
elements: keycombo (DocBook), shortcut (DocBook)

otheraddr   (ELEMENT: DocBook)

othercredit   (ELEMENT: DocBook)
othername   (ELEMENT: DocBook)
otherterm   (ATTRIBUTE: DocBook)
    elements: glosssee (DocBook), glossseealso (DocBook)
otherunits   (ATTRIBUTE: DocBook)
    elements: area (DocBook), areaset (DocBook), areaspec (DocBook)
othinfo   (ELEMENT: ISO 12083)
overline   (ELEMENT: ISO 12083)
override   (ATTRIBUTE: DocBook)
    elements: listitem (DocBook)
p   (ELEMENT: HTML, ISO 12083, TEI-Lite)
package   (ELEMENT: ISO 12083)
pagenum   (ATTRIBUTE: DocBook)
    elements: anchor (DocBook), beginpage (DocBook), indexterm (DocBook),
    lotentry (DocBook), title (DocBook), toc (DocBook), tocback (DocBook), tocentry
    (DocBook), tocfront (DocBook)
pagenums   (ELEMENT: DocBook)
pages   (ELEMENT: ISO 12083)
para   (ELEMENT: DocBook, MIL-STD-38784)
para0   (ELEMENT: MIL-STD-38784)
paraflag   (ATTRIBUTE: MIL-STD-38784)
    elements: pgbrk (MIL-STD-38784)
param   (ELEMENT: HTML)
paramdef   (ELEMENT: DocBook)
parameter   (ELEMENT: DocBook)
paratitle   (ELEMENT: MIL-STD-38784)
parentbook   (ATTRIBUTE: DocBook)
    elements: article (DocBook)
part   (ATTRIBUTE: TEI-Lite)
    elements: div (TEI-Lite), div0 (TEI-Lite), div1 (TEI-Lite), div2 (TEI-Lite), div3 (TEI-
    Lite), div4 (TEI-Lite), div5 (TEI-Lite), div6 (TEI-Lite), div7 (TEI-Lite), l (TEI-Lite), lg
    (TEI-Lite), seg (TEI-Lite)
part   (ELEMENT: DocBook, ISO 12083)
partintro   (ELEMENT: DocBook)
partno   (ATTRIBUTE: MIL-STD-38784)
    elements: abbrsect (MIL-STD-38784), appendix (MIL-STD-38784), applicdef (MIL-
    STD-38784), chapter (MIL-STD-38784), ddchapter (MIL-STD-38784), dddesc
    (MIL-STD-38784), ddindex (MIL-STD-38784), docpart (MIL-STD-38784), figure
    (MIL-STD-38784), foldout (MIL-STD-38784), lrp (MIL-STD-38784), para0 (MIL-
    STD-38784), ratd (MIL-STD-38784), safesum (MIL-STD-38784), section (MIL-
    STD-38784), step1 (MIL-STD-38784), step2 (MIL-STD-38784), step3 (MIL-STD-
    38784), step4 (MIL-STD-38784), subpara1 (MIL-STD-38784), subpara2 (MIL-
    STD-38784), subpara3 (MIL-STD-38784), symsect (MIL-STD-38784), table (MIL-
    STD-38784), tabmat (MIL-STD-38784), tctolist (MIL-STD-38784), tctotbl (MIL-
    STD-38784), tmimprep (MIL-STD-38784), volume (MIL-STD-38784)
partno   (ELEMENT: MIL-STD-38784)
path   (ATTRIBUTE: DocBook)

elements: filename (DocBook)

pb   (ELEMENT: TEI-Lite)

performance   (ATTRIBUTE: DocBook)
elements: step (DocBook), substeps (DocBook)

pgbrk   (ELEMENT: MIL-STD-38784)

pgdeep   (ATTRIBUTE: MIL-STD-38784)
elements: table (MIL-STD-38784), tabmat (MIL-STD-38784)

pgnumber   (ATTRIBUTE: MIL-STD-38784)
elements: pgbrk (MIL-STD-38784)

pgnumber   (ELEMENT: MIL-STD-38784)

pgstyle   (ATTRIBUTE: MIL-STD-38784)
elements: foldout (MIL-STD-38784)

pgwide   (ATTRIBUTE: DocBook, MIL-STD-38784)
elements: figure (MIL-STD-38784), foldout (MIL-STD-38784), informaltable (DocBook), table (DocBook), table (MIL-STD-38784), tabmat (MIL-STD-38784)

phone   (ELEMENT: DocBook, ISO 12083)

phrase   (ELEMENT: DocBook, MIL-STD-38784)

place   (ATTRIBUTE: MIL-STD-38784, TEI-Lite)
elements: add (TEI-Lite), figtable (MIL-STD-38784), figure (MIL-STD-38784), foldout (MIL-STD-38784), note (TEI-Lite)

pob   (ELEMENT: DocBook)

poem   (ELEMENT: ISO 12083)

poemline   (ELEMENT: ISO 12083)

post   (ATTRIBUTE: ISO 12083)
elements: post (ISO 12083)

post   (ELEMENT: ISO 12083)

postbox   (ELEMENT: ISO 12083)

postcode   (ELEMENT: DocBook, ISO 12083)

postspace   (ATTRIBUTE: MIL-STD-38784)
elements: figure (MIL-STD-38784), foldout (MIL-STD-38784), line (MIL-STD-38784)

pre   (ELEMENT: HTML)

precaut   (ELEMENT: MIL-STD-38784)

preface   (ELEMENT: DocBook, ISO 12083, MIL-STD-38784)

prefix   (ATTRIBUTE: MIL-STD-38784)
elements: randlist (MIL-STD-38784)

prespace   (ATTRIBUTE: MIL-STD-38784)
elements: figure (MIL-STD-38784), foldout (MIL-STD-38784), line (MIL-STD-38784)

pretmidno   (ELEMENT: MIL-STD-38784)

prev   (ATTRIBUTE: TEI-Lite)
elements: abbr (TEI-Lite), add (TEI-Lite), address (TEI-Lite), addrline (TEI-Lite), argument (TEI-Lite), author (TEI-Lite), authority (TEI-Lite), availability (TEI-Lite), back (TEI-Lite), bibl (TEI-Lite), biblfull (TEI-Lite), biblscope (TEI-Lite), body (TEI-Lite), byline (TEI-Lite), catdesc (TEI-Lite), category (TEI-Lite), catref (TEI-Lite), cell (TEI-Lite), change (TEI-Lite), cit (TEI-Lite), classcode (TEI-Lite), classdecl (TEI-Lite), closer (TEI-Lite), code (TEI-Lite), corr (TEI-Lite), creation (TEI-Lite), date

(TEI-Lite), dateline (TEI-Lite), distributor (TEI-Lite), div (TEI-Lite), div0 (TEI-Lite), div1 (TEI-Lite), div2 (TEI-Lite), div3 (TEI-Lite), div4 (TEI-Lite), div5 (TEI-Lite), div6 (TEI-Lite), div7 (TEI-Lite), divgen (TEI-Lite), docauthor (TEI-Lite), docdate (TEI-Lite), docedition (TEI-Lite), docimprint (TEI-Lite), doctitle (TEI-Lite), edition (TEI-Lite), editionstmt (TEI-Lite), editor (TEI-Lite), editorialdecl (TEI-Lite), eg (TEI-Lite), emph (TEI-Lite), encodingdesc (TEI-Lite), epigraph (TEI-Lite), extent (TEI-Lite), figdesc (TEI-Lite), figure (TEI-Lite), filedesc (TEI-Lite), formula (TEI-Lite), front (TEI-Lite), funder (TEI-Lite), gap (TEI-Lite), gi (TEI-Lite), gloss (TEI-Lite), group (TEI-Lite), head (TEI-Lite), ident (TEI-Lite), idno (TEI-Lite), imprint (TEI-Lite), index (TEI-Lite), interp (TEI-Lite), interpgrp (TEI-Lite), keywords (TEI-Lite), kw (TEI-Lite), l (TEI-Lite), label (TEI-Lite), langusage (TEI-Lite), lg (TEI-Lite), list (TEI-Lite), listbibl (TEI-Lite), mentioned (TEI-Lite), name (TEI-Lite), notesstmt (TEI-Lite), num (TEI-Lite), opener (TEI-Lite), orig (TEI-Lite), p (TEI-Lite), principal (TEI-Lite), profiledesc (TEI-Lite), projectdesc (TEI-Lite), ptr (TEI-Lite), publicationstmt (TEI-Lite), publisher (TEI-Lite), pubplace (TEI-Lite), q (TEI-Lite), ref (TEI-Lite), refsdecl (TEI-Lite), reg (TEI-Lite), rendition (TEI-Lite), resp (TEI-Lite), respstmt (TEI-Lite), revisiondesc (TEI-Lite), row (TEI-Lite), rs (TEI-Lite), s (TEI-Lite), salute (TEI-Lite), samplingdecl (TEI-Lite), seg (TEI-Lite), seriesstmt (TEI-Lite), sic (TEI-Lite), signed (TEI-Lite), socalled (TEI-Lite), sourcedesc (TEI-Lite), sp (TEI-Lite), speaker (TEI-Lite), sponsor (TEI-Lite), stage (TEI-Lite), table (TEI-Lite), tagsdecl (TEI-Lite), tagusage (TEI-Lite), taxonomy (TEI-Lite), tei.2 (TEI-Lite), teiheader (TEI-Lite), term (TEI-Lite), text (TEI-Lite), textclass (TEI-Lite), time (TEI-Lite), title (TEI-Lite), titlepage (TEI-Lite), titlepart (TEI-Lite), titlestmt (TEI-Lite), trailer (TEI-Lite), unclear (TEI-Lite), xptr (TEI-Lite), xref (TEI-Lite)
price   (ELEMENT: ISO 12083)
primary   (ELEMENT: DocBook)
primaryie   (ELEMENT: DocBook)
principal   (ELEMENT: TEI-Lite)
printhistory   (ELEMENT: DocBook)
priority   (ATTRIBUTE: MIL-STD-38784)
     elements: modreq (MIL-STD-38784)
procedure   (ELEMENT: DocBook)
productname   (ELEMENT: DocBook)
productnumber   (ELEMENT: DocBook)
profile   (ATTRIBUTE: HTML)
     elements: head (HTML)
profiledesc   (ELEMENT: TEI-Lite)
programlisting   (ELEMENT: DocBook)
programlistingco   (ELEMENT: DocBook)
projectdesc   (ELEMENT: TEI-Lite)
prompt   (ELEMENT: DocBook)
property   (ELEMENT: DocBook)
prtitle   (ELEMENT: MIL-STD-38784)
pslist   (ELEMENT: MIL-STD-38784)
ptr   (ELEMENT: TEI-Lite)
pubdate   (ELEMENT: DocBook, MIL-STD-38784)
pubfront   (ELEMENT: ISO 12083)

pubid   (ELEMENT: ISO 12083)
publicationstmt   (ELEMENT: TEI-Lite)
publisher   (ELEMENT: DocBook, TEI-Lite)
publishername   (ELEMENT: DocBook)
pubname   (ELEMENT: ISO 12083)
pubplace   (ELEMENT: TEI-Lite)
pubsnumber   (ELEMENT: DocBook)
pubwork   (ATTRIBUTE: DocBook)
    elements: citetitle (DocBook)
purpose   (ATTRIBUTE: ISO 12083)
    elements: title (ISO 12083)
q   (ELEMENT: HTML, ISO 12083, TEI-Lite)
quad   (ATTRIBUTE: MIL-STD-38784)
    elements: line (MIL-STD-38784)
quote   (ELEMENT: DocBook)
racrwidth   (ATTRIBUTE: MIL-STD-38784)
    elements: acronymlist (MIL-STD-38784)
radical   (ELEMENT: ISO 12083)
radicand   (ELEMENT: ISO 12083)
radix   (ELEMENT: ISO 12083)
randlist   (ELEMENT: MIL-STD-38784)
ratd   (ELEMENT: MIL-STD-38784)
readonly   (ATTRIBUTE: HTML)
    elements: input (HTML), textarea (HTML)
real   (ATTRIBUTE: TEI-Lite)
    elements: l (TEI-Lite), lg (TEI-Lite)
rear   (ELEMENT: MIL-STD-38784)
reason   (ATTRIBUTE: TEI-Lite)
    elements: gap (TEI-Lite), unclear (TEI-Lite)
ref   (ELEMENT: TEI-Lite)
ref1   (ATTRIBUTE: ISO 12083)
    elements: indxflag (ISO 12083)
ref2   (ATTRIBUTE: ISO 12083)
    elements: indxflag (ISO 12083)
ref3   (ATTRIBUTE: ISO 12083)
    elements: indxflag (ISO 12083)
ref4   (ATTRIBUTE: ISO 12083)
    elements: indxflag (ISO 12083)
refclass   (ELEMENT: DocBook)
refdes   (ATTRIBUTE: MIL-STD-38784)
    elements: abbrsect (MIL-STD-38784), appendix (MIL-STD-38784), applicdef (MIL-STD-38784), chapter (MIL-STD-38784), ddchapter (MIL-STD-38784), dddesc (MIL-STD-38784), ddindex (MIL-STD-38784), docpart (MIL-STD-38784), figure (MIL-STD-38784), foldout (MIL-STD-38784), lrp (MIL-STD-38784), para0 (MIL-STD-38784), ratd (MIL-STD-38784), safesum (MIL-STD-38784), section (MIL-STD-38784), step1 (MIL-STD-38784), step2 (MIL-STD-38784), step3 (MIL-STD-38784), step4 (MIL-STD-38784), subpara1 (MIL-STD-38784), subpara2 (MIL-

STD-38784), subpara3 (MIL-STD-38784), symsect (MIL-STD-38784), table (MIL-STD-38784), tabmat (MIL-STD-38784), tctolist (MIL-STD-38784), tctotbl (MIL-STD-38784), tmimprep (MIL-STD-38784), volume (MIL-STD-38784)

refdescriptor   (ELEMENT: DocBook)

refentry   (ELEMENT: DocBook)

refentrytitle   (ELEMENT: DocBook)

reference   (ELEMENT: DocBook)

refid   (ATTRIBUTE: ISO 12083)
   elements: markref (ISO 12083)

refmeta   (ELEMENT: DocBook)

refmiscinfo   (ELEMENT: DocBook)

refname   (ELEMENT: DocBook)

refnamediv   (ELEMENT: DocBook)

refpos   (ATTRIBUTE: MIL-STD-38784)
   elements: modreq (MIL-STD-38784)

refpurpose   (ELEMENT: DocBook)

refsdecl   (ELEMENT: TEI-Lite)

refsect1   (ELEMENT: DocBook)

refsect1info   (ELEMENT: DocBook)

refsect2   (ELEMENT: DocBook)

refsect2info   (ELEMENT: DocBook)

refsect3   (ELEMENT: DocBook)

refsect3info   (ELEMENT: DocBook)

refsynopsisdiv   (ELEMENT: DocBook)

refsynopsisdivinfo   (ELEMENT: DocBook)

reg   (ATTRIBUTE: TEI-Lite)
   elements: name (TEI-Lite), orig (TEI-Lite), pubplace (TEI-Lite), rs (TEI-Lite)

reg   (ELEMENT: TEI-Lite)

rel   (ATTRIBUTE: HTML)
   elements: a (HTML), link (HTML)

relation   (ATTRIBUTE: DocBook)
   elements: bibliomset (DocBook), biblioset (DocBook)

releaseinfo   (ELEMENT: DocBook)

remap   (ATTRIBUTE: DocBook)
   elements: abbrev (DocBook), abstract (DocBook), accel (DocBook), ackno (DocBook), acronym (DocBook), action (DocBook), address (DocBook), affiliation (DocBook), alt (DocBook), anchor (DocBook), appendix (DocBook), application (DocBook), area (DocBook), areaset (DocBook), areaspec (DocBook), arg (DocBook), artheader (DocBook), article (DocBook), artpagenums (DocBook), attribution (DocBook), author (DocBook), authorblurb (DocBook), authorgroup (DocBook), authorinitials (DocBook), beginpage (DocBook), bibliodiv (DocBook), biblioentry (DocBook), bibliography (DocBook), bibliomisc (DocBook), bibliomixed (DocBook), bibliomset (DocBook), biblioset (DocBook), blockquote (DocBook), book (DocBook), bookbiblio (DocBook), bookinfo (DocBook), bridgehead (DocBook), callout (DocBook), calloutlist (DocBook), caution (DocBook), chapter (DocBook), citation (DocBook), citerefentry (DocBook), citetitle (DocBook), city (DocBook), classname (DocBook), cmdsynopsis (DocBook), co (DocBook), collab

(DocBook), collabname (DocBook), command (DocBook), comment (DocBook), computeroutput (DocBook), confdates (DocBook), confgroup (DocBook), confnum (DocBook), confsponsor (DocBook), conftitle (DocBook), contractnum (DocBook), contractsponsor (DocBook), contrib (DocBook), copyright (DocBook), corpauthor (DocBook), corpname (DocBook), country (DocBook), database (DocBook), date (DocBook), dedication (DocBook), docinfo (DocBook), edition (DocBook), editor (DocBook), email (DocBook), emphasis (DocBook), entry (DocBook), entrytbl (DocBook), envar (DocBook), epigraph (DocBook), equation (DocBook), errorcode (DocBook), errorname (DocBook), errortype (DocBook), example (DocBook), fax (DocBook), figure (DocBook), filename (DocBook), firstname (DocBook), firstterm (DocBook), footnote (DocBook), footnoteref (DocBook), foreignphrase (DocBook), formalpara (DocBook), funcdef (DocBook), funcparams (DocBook), funcprototype (DocBook), funcsynopsis (DocBook), funcsynopsisinfo (DocBook), function (DocBook), glossary (DocBook), glossdef (DocBook), glossdiv (DocBook), glossentry (DocBook), glosslist (DocBook), glosssee (DocBook), glossseealso (DocBook), glossterm (DocBook), graphic (DocBook), graphicco (DocBook), group (DocBook), guibutton (DocBook), guiicon (DocBook), guilabel (DocBook), guimenu (DocBook), guimenuitem (DocBook), guisubmenu (DocBook), hardware (DocBook), highlights (DocBook), holder (DocBook), honorific (DocBook), important (DocBook), index (DocBook), indexdiv (DocBook), indexentry (DocBook), indexterm (DocBook), informalequation (DocBook), informalexample (DocBook), informaltable (DocBook), inlineequation (DocBook), inlinegraphic (DocBook), interface (DocBook), interfacedefinition (DocBook), invpartnumber (DocBook), isbn (DocBook), issn (DocBook), issuenum (DocBook), itemizedlist (DocBook), itermset (DocBook), jobtitle (DocBook), keycap (DocBook), keycode (DocBook), keycombo (DocBook), keysym (DocBook), keyword (DocBook), keywordset (DocBook), legalnotice (DocBook), lineage (DocBook), lineannotation (DocBook), link (DocBook), listitem (DocBook), literal (DocBook), literallayout (DocBook), lot (DocBook), lotentry (DocBook), manvolnum (DocBook), markup (DocBook), medialabel (DocBook), member (DocBook), menuchoice (DocBook), modespec (DocBook), mousebutton (DocBook), msg (DocBook), msgaud (DocBook), msgentry (DocBook), msgexplan (DocBook), msginfo (DocBook), msglevel (DocBook), msgmain (DocBook), msgorig (DocBook), msgrel (DocBook), msgset (DocBook), msgsub (DocBook), msgtext (DocBook), note (DocBook), olink (DocBook), option (DocBook), optional (DocBook), orderedlist (DocBook), orgdiv (DocBook), orgname (DocBook), otheraddr (DocBook), othercredit (DocBook), othername (DocBook), pagenums (DocBook), para (DocBook), paramdef (DocBook), parameter (DocBook), part (DocBook), partintro (DocBook), phone (DocBook), phrase (DocBook), pob (DocBook), postcode (DocBook), preface (DocBook), primary (DocBook), primaryie (DocBook), printhistory (DocBook), procedure (DocBook), productname (DocBook), productnumber (DocBook), programlisting (DocBook), programlistingco (DocBook), prompt (DocBook), property (DocBook), pubdate (DocBook), publisher (DocBook), publishername (DocBook), pubsnumber (DocBook), quote (DocBook), refclass (DocBook), refdescriptor (DocBook), refentry (DocBook), refentrytitle (DocBook), reference (DocBook), refmeta (DocBook), refmiscinfo (DocBook), refname (DocBook), refnamediv (DocBook), refpurpose (DocBook), refsect1 (DocBook), refsect1info

(DocBook), refsect2 (DocBook), refsect2info (DocBook), refsect3 (DocBook), refsect3info (DocBook), refsynopsisdiv (DocBook), refsynopsisdivinfo (DocBook), releaseinfo (DocBook), replaceable (DocBook), returnvalue (DocBook), revhistory (DocBook), revision (DocBook), revnumber (DocBook), revremark (DocBook), row (DocBook), sbr (DocBook), screen (DocBook), screenco (DocBook), screeninfo (DocBook), screenshot (DocBook), secondary (DocBook), secondaryie (DocBook), sect1 (DocBook), sect1info (DocBook), sect2 (DocBook), sect2info (DocBook), sect3 (DocBook), sect3info (DocBook), sect4 (DocBook), sect4info (DocBook), sect5 (DocBook), sect5info (DocBook), see (DocBook), seealso (DocBook), seealsoie (DocBook), seeie (DocBook), seg (DocBook), seglistitem (DocBook), segmentedlist (DocBook), segtitle (DocBook), seriesinfo (DocBook), seriesvolnums (DocBook), set (DocBook), setindex (DocBook), setinfo (DocBook), sgmltag (DocBook), shortaffil (DocBook), shortcut (DocBook), sidebar (DocBook), simpara (DocBook), simplelist (DocBook), simplesect (DocBook), state (DocBook), step (DocBook), street (DocBook), structfield (DocBook), structname (DocBook), subject (DocBook), subjectset (DocBook), subjectterm (DocBook), subscript (DocBook), substeps (DocBook), subtitle (DocBook), superscript (DocBook), surname (DocBook), symbol (DocBook), synopfragment (DocBook), synopfragmentref (DocBook), synopsis (DocBook), systemitem (DocBook), table (DocBook), tbody (DocBook), term (DocBook), tertiary (DocBook), tertiaryie (DocBook), tfoot (DocBook), tgroup (DocBook), thead (DocBook), tip (DocBook), title (DocBook), titleabbrev (DocBook), toc (DocBook), tocback (DocBook), tocchap (DocBook), tocentry (DocBook), tocfront (DocBook), toclevel1 (DocBook), toclevel2 (DocBook), toclevel3 (DocBook), toclevel4 (DocBook), toclevel5 (DocBook), tocpart (DocBook), token (DocBook), trademark (DocBook), type (DocBook), ulink (DocBook), userinput (DocBook), varargs (DocBook), variablelist (DocBook), varlistentry (DocBook), void (DocBook), volumenum (DocBook), warning (DocBook), wordasword (DocBook), xref (DocBook), year (DocBook)

remarks   (ELEMENT: MIL-STD-38784)
removepg   (ELEMENT: MIL-STD-38784)
rend   (ATTRIBUTE: TEI-Lite)
elements: abbr (TEI-Lite), add (TEI-Lite), address (TEI-Lite), addrline (TEI-Lite), anchor (TEI-Lite), argument (TEI-Lite), author (TEI-Lite), authority (TEI-Lite), availability (TEI-Lite), back (TEI-Lite), bibl (TEI-Lite), biblfull (TEI-Lite), biblscope (TEI-Lite), body (TEI-Lite), byline (TEI-Lite), catdesc (TEI-Lite), category (TEI-Lite), catref (TEI-Lite), cell (TEI-Lite), change (TEI-Lite), cit (TEI-Lite), classcode (TEI-Lite), classdecl (TEI-Lite), closer (TEI-Lite), code (TEI-Lite), corr (TEI-Lite), creation (TEI-Lite), date (TEI-Lite), dateline (TEI-Lite), del (TEI-Lite), distributor (TEI-Lite), div (TEI-Lite), div0 (TEI-Lite), div1 (TEI-Lite), div2 (TEI-Lite), div3 (TEI-Lite), div4 (TEI-Lite), div5 (TEI-Lite), div6 (TEI-Lite), div7 (TEI-Lite), divgen (TEI-Lite), docauthor (TEI-Lite), docdate (TEI-Lite), docedition (TEI-Lite), docimprint (TEI-Lite), doctitle (TEI-Lite), edition (TEI-Lite), editionstmt (TEI-Lite), editor (TEI-Lite), editorialdecl (TEI-Lite), eg (TEI-Lite), emph (TEI-Lite), encodingdesc (TEI-Lite), epigraph (TEI-Lite), extent (TEI-Lite), figdesc (TEI-Lite), figure (TEI-Lite), filedesc (TEI-Lite), foreign (TEI-Lite), formula (TEI-Lite), front (TEI-Lite), funder (TEI-Lite), gap (TEI-Lite), gi (TEI-Lite), gloss (TEI-Lite), group (TEI-Lite), head (TEI-Lite), hi (TEI-Lite), ident (TEI-Lite), idno (TEI-Lite), imprint (TEI-Lite), index

(TEI-Lite), interp (TEI-Lite), interpgrp (TEI-Lite), item (TEI-Lite), keywords (TEI-Lite), kw (TEI-Lite), l (TEI-Lite), label (TEI-Lite), language (TEI-Lite), langusage (TEI-Lite), lb (TEI-Lite), lg (TEI-Lite), list (TEI-Lite), listbibl (TEI-Lite), mentioned (TEI-Lite), milestone (TEI-Lite), name (TEI-Lite), note (TEI-Lite), notesstmt (TEI-Lite), num (TEI-Lite), opener (TEI-Lite), orig (TEI-Lite), p (TEI-Lite), pb (TEI-Lite), principal (TEI-Lite), profiledesc (TEI-Lite), projectdesc (TEI-Lite), ptr (TEI-Lite), publicationstmt (TEI-Lite), publisher (TEI-Lite), pubplace (TEI-Lite), q (TEI-Lite), ref (TEI-Lite), refsdecl (TEI-Lite), reg (TEI-Lite), rendition (TEI-Lite), resp (TEI-Lite), respstmt (TEI-Lite), revisiondesc (TEI-Lite), row (TEI-Lite), rs (TEI-Lite), s (TEI-Lite), salute (TEI-Lite), samplingdecl (TEI-Lite), seg (TEI-Lite), seriesstmt (TEI-Lite), sic (TEI-Lite), signed (TEI-Lite), socalled (TEI-Lite), sourcedesc (TEI-Lite), sp (TEI-Lite), speaker (TEI-Lite), sponsor (TEI-Lite), stage (TEI-Lite), table (TEI-Lite), tagsdecl (TEI-Lite), tagusage (TEI-Lite), taxonomy (TEI-Lite), tei.2 (TEI-Lite), teiheader (TEI-Lite), term (TEI-Lite), text (TEI-Lite), textclass (TEI-Lite), time (TEI-Lite), title (TEI-Lite), titlepage (TEI-Lite), titlepart (TEI-Lite), titlestmt (TEI-Lite), trailer (TEI-Lite), unclear (TEI-Lite), xptr (TEI-Lite), xref (TEI-Lite)

render   (ATTRIBUTE: TEI-Lite)
elements: tagusage (TEI-Lite)

renderas   (ATTRIBUTE: DocBook)
elements: bridgehead (DocBook), sect1 (DocBook), sect2 (DocBook), sect3 (DocBook), sect4 (DocBook), sect5 (DocBook)

rendition   (ELEMENT: TEI-Lite)

rep   (ATTRIBUTE: DocBook)
elements: arg (DocBook), group (DocBook)

replaceable   (ELEMENT: DocBook)

reportid   (ELEMENT: ISO 12083)

reprint   (ELEMENT: ISO 12083)

reprodep   (ATTRIBUTE: MIL-STD-38784)
elements: graphic (MIL-STD-38784)

reprowid   (ATTRIBUTE: MIL-STD-38784)
elements: graphic (MIL-STD-38784)

resp   (ATTRIBUTE: TEI-Lite)
elements: abbr (TEI-Lite), add (TEI-Lite), corr (TEI-Lite), del (TEI-Lite), gap (TEI-Lite), interp (TEI-Lite), interpgrp (TEI-Lite), note (TEI-Lite), orig (TEI-Lite), ptr (TEI-Lite), ref (TEI-Lite), reg (TEI-Lite), sic (TEI-Lite), unclear (TEI-Lite), xptr (TEI-Lite), xref (TEI-Lite)

resp   (ELEMENT: TEI-Lite)

respstmt   (ELEMENT: TEI-Lite)

returnvalue   (ELEMENT: DocBook)

rev   (ATTRIBUTE: HTML)
elements: a (HTML), link (HTML)

revchg   (ATTRIBUTE: MIL-STD-38784)
elements: abbrsect (MIL-STD-38784), appendix (MIL-STD-38784), applicdef (MIL-STD-38784), caution (MIL-STD-38784), change (MIL-STD-38784), chapter (MIL-STD-38784), ddchapter (MIL-STD-38784), dddesc (MIL-STD-38784), ddindex (MIL-STD-38784), deflist (MIL-STD-38784), docpart (MIL-STD-38784), figtable (MIL-STD-38784), figure (MIL-STD-38784), foldout (MIL-STD-38784), glossary

(MIL-STD-38784), internatlstd (MIL-STD-38784), line (MIL-STD-38784), lrp (MIL-STD-38784), note (MIL-STD-38784), para (MIL-STD-38784), para0 (MIL-STD-38784), randlist (MIL-STD-38784), ratd (MIL-STD-38784), safesum (MIL-STD-38784), section (MIL-STD-38784), seqlist (MIL-STD-38784), serno (MIL-STD-38784), step1 (MIL-STD-38784), step2 (MIL-STD-38784), step3 (MIL-STD-38784), step4 (MIL-STD-38784), subfig (MIL-STD-38784), subpara1 (MIL-STD-38784), subpara2 (MIL-STD-38784), subpara3 (MIL-STD-38784), symsect (MIL-STD-38784), table (MIL-STD-38784), tabmat (MIL-STD-38784), tctolist (MIL-STD-38784), tctono (MIL-STD-38784), tctorow (MIL-STD-38784), tctotbl (MIL-STD-38784), tmidno (MIL-STD-38784), tmimprep (MIL-STD-38784), volume (MIL-STD-38784), warning (MIL-STD-38784), warnpage (MIL-STD-38784), wpgentry (MIL-STD-38784)

revhistory   (ELEMENT: DocBook)
revision   (ATTRIBUTE: DocBook)
elements: abbrev (DocBook), abstract (DocBook), accel (DocBook), ackno (DocBook), acronym (DocBook), action (DocBook), address (DocBook), affiliation (DocBook), alt (DocBook), anchor (DocBook), appendix (DocBook), application (DocBook), area (DocBook), areaset (DocBook), areaspec (DocBook), arg (DocBook), artheader (DocBook), article (DocBook), artpagenums (DocBook), attribution (DocBook), author (DocBook), authorblurb (DocBook), authorgroup (DocBook), authorinitials (DocBook), beginpage (DocBook), bibliodiv (DocBook), biblioentry (DocBook), bibliography (DocBook), bibliomisc (DocBook), bibliomixed (DocBook), bibliomset (DocBook), biblioset (DocBook), blockquote (DocBook), book (DocBook), bookbiblio (DocBook), bookinfo (DocBook), bridgehead (DocBook), callout (DocBook), calloutlist (DocBook), caution (DocBook), chapter (DocBook), citation (DocBook), citerefentry (DocBook), citetitle (DocBook), city (DocBook), classname (DocBook), cmdsynopsis (DocBook), co (DocBook), collab (DocBook), collabname (DocBook), command (DocBook), comment (DocBook), computeroutput (DocBook), confdates (DocBook), confgroup (DocBook), confnum (DocBook), confsponsor (DocBook), conftitle (DocBook), contractnum (DocBook), contractsponsor (DocBook), contrib (DocBook), copyright (DocBook), corpauthor (DocBook), corpname (DocBook), country (DocBook), database (DocBook), date (DocBook), dedication (DocBook), docinfo (DocBook), edition (DocBook), editor (DocBook), email (DocBook), emphasis (DocBook), entry (DocBook), entrytbl (DocBook), envar (DocBook), epigraph (DocBook), equation (DocBook), errorcode (DocBook), errorname (DocBook), errortype (DocBook), example (DocBook), fax (DocBook), figure (DocBook), filename (DocBook), firstname (DocBook), firstterm (DocBook), footnote (DocBook), footnoteref (DocBook), foreignphrase (DocBook), formalpara (DocBook), funcdef (DocBook), funcparams (DocBook), funcprototype (DocBook), funcsynopsis (DocBook), funcsynopsisinfo (DocBook), function (DocBook), glossary (DocBook), glossdef (DocBook), glossdiv (DocBook), glossentry (DocBook), glosslist (DocBook), glosssee (DocBook), glossseealso (DocBook), glossterm (DocBook), graphic (DocBook), graphicco (DocBook), group (DocBook), guibutton (DocBook), guiicon (DocBook), guilabel (DocBook), guimenu (DocBook), guimenuitem (DocBook), guisubmenu (DocBook), hardware (DocBook), highlights (DocBook), holder (DocBook), honorific (DocBook), important (DocBook), index (DocBook), indexdiv (DocBook), indexentry

(DocBook), indexterm (DocBook), informalequation (DocBook), informalexample (DocBook), informaltable (DocBook), inlineequation (DocBook), inlinegraphic (DocBook), interface (DocBook), interfacedefinition (DocBook), invpartnumber (DocBook), isbn (DocBook), issn (DocBook), issuenum (DocBook), itemizedlist (DocBook), itermset (DocBook), jobtitle (DocBook), keycap (DocBook), keycode (DocBook), keycombo (DocBook), keysym (DocBook), keyword (DocBook), keywordset (DocBook), legalnotice (DocBook), lineage (DocBook), lineannotation (DocBook), link (DocBook), listitem (DocBook), literal (DocBook), literallayout (DocBook), lot (DocBook), lotentry (DocBook), manvolnum (DocBook), markup (DocBook), medialabel (DocBook), member (DocBook), menuchoice (DocBook), modespec (DocBook), mousebutton (DocBook), msg (DocBook), msgaud (DocBook), msgentry (DocBook), msgexplan (DocBook), msginfo (DocBook), msglevel (DocBook), msgmain (DocBook), msgorig (DocBook), msgrel (DocBook), msgset (DocBook), msgsub (DocBook), msgtext (DocBook), note (DocBook), olink (DocBook), option (DocBook), optional (DocBook), orderedlist (DocBook), orgdiv (DocBook), orgname (DocBook), otheraddr (DocBook), othercredit (DocBook), othername (DocBook), pagenums (DocBook), para (DocBook), paramdef (DocBook), parameter (DocBook), part (DocBook), partintro (DocBook), phone (DocBook), phrase (DocBook), pob (DocBook), postcode (DocBook), preface (DocBook), primary (DocBook), primaryie (DocBook), printhistory (DocBook), procedure (DocBook), productname (DocBook), productnumber (DocBook), programlisting (DocBook), programlistingco (DocBook), prompt (DocBook), property (DocBook), pubdate (DocBook), publisher (DocBook), publishername (DocBook), pubsnumber (DocBook), quote (DocBook), refclass (DocBook), refdescriptor (DocBook), refentry (DocBook), refentrytitle (DocBook), reference (DocBook), refmeta (DocBook), refmiscinfo (DocBook), refname (DocBook), refnamediv (DocBook), refpurpose (DocBook), refsect1 (DocBook), refsect1info (DocBook), refsect2 (DocBook), refsect2info (DocBook), refsect3 (DocBook), refsect3info (DocBook), refsynopsisdiv (DocBook), refsynopsisdivinfo (DocBook), releaseinfo (DocBook), replaceable (DocBook), returnvalue (DocBook), revhistory (DocBook), revision (DocBook), revnumber (DocBook), revremark (DocBook), row (DocBook), sbr (DocBook), screen (DocBook), screenco (DocBook), screeninfo (DocBook), screenshot (DocBook), secondary (DocBook), secondaryie (DocBook), sect1 (DocBook), sect1info (DocBook), sect2 (DocBook), sect2info (DocBook), sect3 (DocBook), sect3info (DocBook), sect4 (DocBook), sect4info (DocBook), sect5 (DocBook), sect5info (DocBook), see (DocBook), seealso (DocBook), seealsoie (DocBook), seeie (DocBook), seg (DocBook), seglistitem (DocBook), segmentedlist (DocBook), segtitle (DocBook), seriesinfo (DocBook), seriesvolnums (DocBook), set (DocBook), setindex (DocBook), setinfo (DocBook), sgmltag (DocBook), shortaffil (DocBook), shortcut (DocBook), sidebar (DocBook), simpara (DocBook), simplelist (DocBook), simplesect (DocBook), state (DocBook), step (DocBook), street (DocBook), structfield (DocBook), structname (DocBook), subject (DocBook), subjectset (DocBook), subjectterm (DocBook), subscript (DocBook), substeps (DocBook), subtitle (DocBook), superscript (DocBook), surname (DocBook), symbol (DocBook), synopfragment (DocBook), synopfragmentref (DocBook), synopsis (DocBook), systemitem (DocBook), table (DocBook), tbody (DocBook), term (DocBook), tertiary (DocBook), tertiaryie

(DocBook), tfoot (DocBook), tgroup (DocBook), thead (DocBook), tip (DocBook), title (DocBook), titleabbrev (DocBook), toc (DocBook), tocback (DocBook), tocchap (DocBook), tocentry (DocBook), tocfront (DocBook), toclevel1 (DocBook), toclevel2 (DocBook), toclevel3 (DocBook), toclevel4 (DocBook), toclevel5 (DocBook), tocpart (DocBook), token (DocBook), trademark (DocBook), type (DocBook), ulink (DocBook), userinput (DocBook), varargs (DocBook), variablelist (DocBook), varlistentry (DocBook), void (DocBook), volumenum (DocBook), warning (DocBook), wordasword (DocBook), xref (DocBook), year (DocBook)

revision   (ELEMENT: DocBook)

revisiondesc   (ELEMENT: TEI-Lite)

revisionflag   (ATTRIBUTE: DocBook)

elements: abbrev (DocBook), abstract (DocBook), accel (DocBook), ackno (DocBook), acronym (DocBook), action (DocBook), address (DocBook), affiliation (DocBook), alt (DocBook), anchor (DocBook), appendix (DocBook), application (DocBook), area (DocBook), areaset (DocBook), areaspec (DocBook), arg (DocBook), artheader (DocBook), article (DocBook), artpagenums (DocBook), attribution (DocBook), author (DocBook), authorblurb (DocBook), authorgroup (DocBook), authorinitials (DocBook), beginpage (DocBook), bibliodiv (DocBook), biblioentry (DocBook), bibliography (DocBook), bibliomisc (DocBook), bibliomixed (DocBook), bibliomset (DocBook), biblioset (DocBook), blockquote (DocBook), book (DocBook), bookbiblio (DocBook), bookinfo (DocBook), bridgehead (DocBook), callout (DocBook), calloutlist (DocBook), caution (DocBook), chapter (DocBook), citation (DocBook), citerefentry (DocBook), citetitle (DocBook), city (DocBook), classname (DocBook), cmdsynopsis (DocBook), co (DocBook), collab (DocBook), collabname (DocBook), command (DocBook), comment (DocBook), computeroutput (DocBook), confdates (DocBook), confgroup (DocBook), confnum (DocBook), confsponsor (DocBook), conftitle (DocBook), contractnum (DocBook), contractsponsor (DocBook), contrib (DocBook), copyright (DocBook), corpauthor (DocBook), corpname (DocBook), country (DocBook), database (DocBook), date (DocBook), dedication (DocBook), docinfo (DocBook), edition (DocBook), editor (DocBook), email (DocBook), emphasis (DocBook), entry (DocBook), entrytbl (DocBook), envar (DocBook), epigraph (DocBook), equation (DocBook), errorcode (DocBook), errorname (DocBook), errortype (DocBook), example (DocBook), fax (DocBook), figure (DocBook), filename (DocBook), firstname (DocBook), firstterm (DocBook), footnote (DocBook), footnoteref (DocBook), foreignphrase (DocBook), formalpara (DocBook), funcdef (DocBook), funcparams (DocBook), funcprototype (DocBook), funcsynopsis (DocBook), funcsynopsisinfo (DocBook), function (DocBook), glossary (DocBook), glossdef (DocBook), glossdiv (DocBook), glossentry (DocBook), glosslist (DocBook), glosssee (DocBook), glossseealso (DocBook), glossterm (DocBook), graphic (DocBook), graphicco (DocBook), group (DocBook), guibutton (DocBook), guiicon (DocBook), guilabel (DocBook), guimenu (DocBook), guimenuitem (DocBook), guisubmenu (DocBook), hardware (DocBook), highlights (DocBook), holder (DocBook), honorific (DocBook), important (DocBook), index (DocBook), indexdiv (DocBook), indexentry (DocBook), indexterm (DocBook), informalequation (DocBook), informalexample (DocBook), informaltable (DocBook), inlineequation (DocBook), inlinegraphic (DocBook), interface (DocBook), interfacedefinition (DocBook), invpartnumber

(DocBook), isbn (DocBook), issn (DocBook), issuenum (DocBook), itemizedlist (DocBook), itermset (DocBook), jobtitle (DocBook), keycap (DocBook), keycode (DocBook), keycombo (DocBook), keysym (DocBook), keyword (DocBook), keywordset (DocBook), legalnotice (DocBook), lineage (DocBook), lineannotation (DocBook), link (DocBook), listitem (DocBook), literal (DocBook), literallayout (DocBook), lot (DocBook), lotentry (DocBook), manvolnum (DocBook), markup (DocBook), medialabel (DocBook), member (DocBook), menuchoice (DocBook), modespec (DocBook), mousebutton (DocBook), msg (DocBook), msgaud (DocBook), msgentry (DocBook), msgexplan (DocBook), msginfo (DocBook), msglevel (DocBook), msgmain (DocBook), msgorig (DocBook), msgrel (DocBook), msgset (DocBook), msgsub (DocBook), msgtext (DocBook), note (DocBook), olink (DocBook), option (DocBook), optional (DocBook), orderedlist (DocBook), orgdiv (DocBook), orgname (DocBook), otheraddr (DocBook), othercredit (DocBook), othername (DocBook), pagenums (DocBook), para (DocBook), paramdef (DocBook), parameter (DocBook), part (DocBook), partintro (DocBook), phone (DocBook), phrase (DocBook), pob (DocBook), postcode (DocBook), preface (DocBook), primary (DocBook), primaryie (DocBook), printhistory (DocBook), procedure (DocBook), productname (DocBook), productnumber (DocBook), programlisting (DocBook), programlistingco (DocBook), prompt (DocBook), property (DocBook), pubdate (DocBook), publisher (DocBook), publishername (DocBook), pubsnumber (DocBook), quote (DocBook), refclass (DocBook), refdescriptor (DocBook), refentry (DocBook), refentrytitle (DocBook), reference (DocBook), refmeta (DocBook), refmiscinfo (DocBook), refname (DocBook), refnamediv (DocBook), refpurpose (DocBook), refsect1 (DocBook), refsect1info (DocBook), refsect2 (DocBook), refsect2info (DocBook), refsect3 (DocBook), refsect3info (DocBook), refsynopsisdiv (DocBook), refsynopsisdivinfo (DocBook), releaseinfo (DocBook), replaceable (DocBook), returnvalue (DocBook), revhistory (DocBook), revision (DocBook), revnumber (DocBook), revremark (DocBook), row (DocBook), sbr (DocBook), screen (DocBook), screenco (DocBook), screeninfo (DocBook), screenshot (DocBook), secondary (DocBook), secondaryie (DocBook), sect1 (DocBook), sect1info (DocBook), sect2 (DocBook), sect2info (DocBook), sect3 (DocBook), sect3info (DocBook), sect4 (DocBook), sect4info (DocBook), sect5 (DocBook), sect5info (DocBook), see (DocBook), seealso (DocBook), seealsoie (DocBook), seeie (DocBook), seg (DocBook), seglistitem (DocBook), segmentedlist (DocBook), segtitle (DocBook), seriesinfo (DocBook), seriesvolnums (DocBook), set (DocBook), setindex (DocBook), setinfo (DocBook), sgmltag (DocBook), shortaffil (DocBook), shortcut (DocBook), sidebar (DocBook), simpara (DocBook), simplelist (DocBook), simplesect (DocBook), state (DocBook), step (DocBook), street (DocBook), structfield (DocBook), structname (DocBook), subject (DocBook), subjectset (DocBook), subjectterm (DocBook), subscript (DocBook), substeps (DocBook), subtitle (DocBook), superscript (DocBook), surname (DocBook), symbol (DocBook), synopfragment (DocBook), synopfragmentref (DocBook), synopsis (DocBook), systemitem (DocBook), table (DocBook), tbody (DocBook), term (DocBook), tertiary (DocBook), tertiaryie (DocBook), tfoot (DocBook), tgroup (DocBook), thead (DocBook), tip (DocBook), title (DocBook), titleabbrev (DocBook), toc (DocBook), tocback (DocBook), tocchap (DocBook), tocentry (DocBook), tocfront (DocBook), toclevel1 (DocBook), toclevel2 (DocBook), toclevel3 (DocBook), toclevel4 (DocBook), toclevel5 (DocBook), tocpart (DocBook), token (DocBook), trademark (DocBook), type (DocBook), ulink (DocBook), userinput (DocBook), varargs (DocBook), variablelist (DocBook), varlistentry (DocBook), void (DocBook), volumenum (DocBook), warning (DocBook), wordasword (DocBook), xref (DocBook), year (DocBook)

revnum   (ELEMENT: MIL-STD-38784)

revnumber   (ELEMENT: DocBook)

revremark   (ELEMENT: DocBook)

rhyme   (ATTRIBUTE: TEI-Lite)
    elements: l (TEI-Lite), lg (TEI-Lite)

rid   (ATTRIBUTE: ISO 12083)
    elements: appref (ISO 12083), artref (ISO 12083), citeref (ISO 12083), figref (ISO 12083), fnoteref (ISO 12083), formref (ISO 12083), glosref (ISO 12083), indexref (ISO 12083), noteref (ISO 12083), secref (ISO 12083), tableref (ISO 12083)

rids   (ATTRIBUTE: ISO 12083)
    elements: author (ISO 12083)

rightind   (ATTRIBUTE: MIL-STD-38784)
    elements: table (MIL-STD-38784), tabmat (MIL-STD-38784), tgroup (MIL-STD-38784)

rightmar   (ATTRIBUTE: MIL-STD-38784)
    elements: colspec (MIL-STD-38784), table (MIL-STD-38784), tabmat (MIL-STD-38784), tgroup (MIL-STD-38784)

role   (ATTRIBUTE: DocBook, TEI-Lite)
    elements: abbrev (DocBook), abstract (DocBook), accel (DocBook), ackno (DocBook), acronym (DocBook), action (DocBook), address (DocBook), affiliation (DocBook), alt (DocBook), anchor (DocBook), appendix (DocBook), application (DocBook), area (DocBook), areaset (DocBook), areaspec (DocBook), arg (DocBook), artheader (DocBook), article (DocBook), artpagenums (DocBook), attribution (DocBook), author (DocBook), authorblurb (DocBook), authorgroup (DocBook), authorinitials (DocBook), beginpage (DocBook), bibliodiv (DocBook), biblioentry (DocBook), bibliography (DocBook), bibliomisc (DocBook), bibliomixed (DocBook), bibliomset (DocBook), biblioset (DocBook), blockquote (DocBook), book (DocBook), bookbiblio (DocBook), bookinfo (DocBook), bridgehead (DocBook), callout (DocBook), calloutlist (DocBook), caution (DocBook), cell (TEI-Lite), chapter (DocBook), citation (DocBook), citerefentry (DocBook), citetitle (DocBook), city (DocBook), classname (DocBook), cmdsynopsis (DocBook), co (DocBook), collab (DocBook), collabname (DocBook), command (DocBook), comment (DocBook), computeroutput (DocBook), confdates (DocBook), confgroup (DocBook), confnum (DocBook), confsponsor (DocBook), conftitle (DocBook), contractnum (DocBook), contractsponsor (DocBook), contrib (DocBook), copyright (DocBook), corpauthor (DocBook), corpname (DocBook), country (DocBook), database (DocBook), date (DocBook), dedication (DocBook), docinfo (DocBook), edition (DocBook), editor (DocBook), editor (TEI-Lite), email (DocBook), emphasis (DocBook), entry (DocBook), entrytbl (DocBook), envar (DocBook), epigraph (DocBook), equation (DocBook), errorcode (DocBook), errorname (DocBook), errortype (DocBook), example (DocBook), fax (DocBook), figure (DocBook), filename (DocBook), firstname (DocBook), firstterm (DocBook),

footnote (DocBook), footnoteref (DocBook), foreignphrase (DocBook), formalpara (DocBook), funcdef (DocBook), funcparams (DocBook), funcprototype (DocBook), funcsynopsis (DocBook), funcsynopsisinfo (DocBook), function (DocBook), glossary (DocBook), glossdef (DocBook), glossdiv (DocBook), glossentry (DocBook), glosslist (DocBook), glosssee (DocBook), glossseealso (DocBook), glossterm (DocBook), graphic (DocBook), graphicco (DocBook), group (DocBook), guibutton (DocBook), guiicon (DocBook), guilabel (DocBook), guimenu (DocBook), guimenuitem (DocBook), guisubmenu (DocBook), hardware (DocBook), highlights (DocBook), holder (DocBook), honorific (DocBook), important (DocBook), index (DocBook), indexdiv (DocBook), indexentry (DocBook), indexterm (DocBook), informalequation (DocBook), informalexample (DocBook), informaltable (DocBook), inlineequation (DocBook), inlinegraphic (DocBook), interface (DocBook), interfacedefinition (DocBook), invpartnumber (DocBook), isbn (DocBook), issn (DocBook), issuenum (DocBook), itemizedlist (DocBook), itermset (DocBook), jobtitle (DocBook), keycap (DocBook), keycode (DocBook), keycombo (DocBook), keysym (DocBook), keyword (DocBook), keywordset (DocBook), legalnotice (DocBook), lineage (DocBook), lineannotation (DocBook), link (DocBook), listitem (DocBook), literal (DocBook), literallayout (DocBook), lot (DocBook), lotentry (DocBook), manvolnum (DocBook), markup (DocBook), medialabel (DocBook), member (DocBook), menuchoice (DocBook), modespec (DocBook), mousebutton (DocBook), msg (DocBook), msgaud (DocBook), msgentry (DocBook), msgexplan (DocBook), msginfo (DocBook), msglevel (DocBook), msgmain (DocBook), msgorig (DocBook), msgrel (DocBook), msgset (DocBook), msgsub (DocBook), msgtext (DocBook), note (DocBook), olink (DocBook), option (DocBook), optional (DocBook), orderedlist (DocBook), orgdiv (DocBook), orgname (DocBook), otheraddr (DocBook), othercredit (DocBook), othername (DocBook), pagenums (DocBook), para (DocBook), paramdef (DocBook), parameter (DocBook), part (DocBook), partintro (DocBook), phone (DocBook), phrase (DocBook), pob (DocBook), postcode (DocBook), preface (DocBook), primary (DocBook), primaryie (DocBook), printhistory (DocBook), procedure (DocBook), productname (DocBook), productnumber (DocBook), programlisting (DocBook), programlistingco (DocBook), prompt (DocBook), property (DocBook), pubdate (DocBook), publisher (DocBook), publishername (DocBook), pubsnumber (DocBook), quote (DocBook), refclass (DocBook), refdescriptor (DocBook), refentry (DocBook), refentrytitle (DocBook), reference (DocBook), refmeta (DocBook), refmiscinfo (DocBook), refname (DocBook), refnamediv (DocBook), refpurpose (DocBook), refsect1 (DocBook), refsect1info (DocBook), refsect2 (DocBook), refsect2info (DocBook), refsect3 (DocBook), refsect3info (DocBook), refsynopsisdiv (DocBook), refsynopsisdivinfo (DocBook), releaseinfo (DocBook), replaceable (DocBook), returnvalue (DocBook), revhistory (DocBook), revision (DocBook), revnumber (DocBook), revremark (DocBook), row (DocBook), row (TEI-Lite), sbr (DocBook), screen (DocBook), screenco (DocBook), screeninfo (DocBook), screenshot (DocBook), secondary (DocBook), secondaryie (DocBook), sect1 (DocBook), sect1info (DocBook), sect2 (DocBook), sect2info (DocBook), sect3 (DocBook), sect3info (DocBook), sect4 (DocBook), sect4info (DocBook), sect5 (DocBook), sect5info (DocBook), see (DocBook), seealso (DocBook), seealsoie (DocBook), seeie (DocBook), seg (DocBook), seglistitem (DocBook), segmentedlist (DocBook), segtitle (DocBook), seriesinfo (DocBook), seriesvolnums (DocBook), set (DocBook), setindex (DocBook), setinfo (DocBook), sgmltag (DocBook), shortaffil (DocBook), shortcut (DocBook), sidebar (DocBook), simpara (DocBook), simplelist (DocBook), simplesect (DocBook), state (DocBook), step (DocBook), street (DocBook), structfield (DocBook), structname (DocBook), subject (DocBook), subjectset (DocBook), subjectterm (DocBook), subscript (DocBook), substeps (DocBook), subtitle (DocBook), superscript (DocBook), surname (DocBook), symbol (DocBook), synopfragment (DocBook), synopfragmentref (DocBook), synopsis (DocBook), systemitem (DocBook), table (DocBook), tbody (DocBook), term (DocBook), tertiary (DocBook), tertiaryie (DocBook), tfoot (DocBook), tgroup (DocBook), thead (DocBook), tip (DocBook), title (DocBook), titleabbrev (DocBook), toc (DocBook), tocback (DocBook), tocchap (DocBook), tocentry (DocBook), tocfront (DocBook), toclevel1 (DocBook), toclevel2 (DocBook), toclevel3 (DocBook), toclevel4 (DocBook), toclevel5 (DocBook), tocpart (DocBook), token (DocBook), trademark (DocBook), type (DocBook), ulink (DocBook), userinput (DocBook), varargs (DocBook), variablelist (DocBook), varlistentry (DocBook), void (DocBook), volumenum (DocBook), warning (DocBook), wordasword (DocBook), xref (DocBook), year (DocBook)

role   (ELEMENT: ISO 12083)

roman   (ELEMENT: ISO 12083)

rotate   (ATTRIBUTE: DocBook, MIL-STD-38784)
   elements: entry (DocBook), entry (MIL-STD-38784)

row   (ELEMENT: DocBook, ISO 12083, MIL-STD-38784, TEI-Lite)

rowalign   (ATTRIBUTE: ISO 12083)
   elements: array (ISO 12083)

rows   (ATTRIBUTE: HTML, TEI-Lite)
   elements: cell (TEI-Lite), table (TEI-Lite), textarea (HTML)

rowsep   (ATTRIBUTE: DocBook, ISO 12083, MIL-STD-38784)
   elements: array (ISO 12083), colspec (DocBook), colspec (MIL-STD-38784), entry (DocBook), entry (MIL-STD-38784), entrytbl (DocBook), entrytbl (MIL-STD-38784), figtable (MIL-STD-38784), informaltable (DocBook), row (DocBook), row (MIL-STD-38784), spanspec (DocBook), spanspec (MIL-STD-38784), table (DocBook), table (MIL-STD-38784), tabmat (MIL-STD-38784), tctotbl (MIL-STD-38784), tgroup (DocBook), tgroup (MIL-STD-38784)

rowspan   (ATTRIBUTE: HTML)
   elements: td (HTML), th (HTML)

rpost   (ATTRIBUTE: ISO 12083)
   elements: fence (ISO 12083)

rs   (ELEMENT: TEI-Lite)

rtermwidth   (ATTRIBUTE: MIL-STD-38784)
   elements: applicdef (MIL-STD-38784), deflist (MIL-STD-38784), symsect (MIL-STD-38784)

rtmidwidth   (ATTRIBUTE: MIL-STD-38784)
   elements: lrp (MIL-STD-38784)

rucordra   (ATTRIBUTE: MIL-STD-38784)
   elements: graphic (MIL-STD-38784)

rules   (ATTRIBUTE: HTML)

elements: table (HTML)

s　(ELEMENT: TEI-Lite)

safesum　(ELEMENT: MIL-STD-38784)

salute　(ELEMENT: TEI-Lite)

samp　(ELEMENT: HTML)

sample　(ATTRIBUTE: TEI-Lite)
elements: div (TEI-Lite), div0 (TEI-Lite), div1 (TEI-Lite), div2 (TEI-Lite), div3 (TEI-Lite), div4 (TEI-Lite), div5 (TEI-Lite), div6 (TEI-Lite), div7 (TEI-Lite), lg (TEI-Lite)

samplingdecl　(ELEMENT: TEI-Lite)

san　(ELEMENT: ISO 12083)

sansser　(ELEMENT: ISO 12083)

sbr　(ELEMENT: DocBook)

scale　(ATTRIBUTE: DocBook, ISO 12083)
elements: fig (ISO 12083), graphic (DocBook), inlinegraphic (DocBook)

scalefit　(ATTRIBUTE: DocBook, MIL-STD-38784)
elements: graphic (DocBook), graphic (MIL-STD-38784), inlinegraphic (DocBook)

scheme　(ATTRIBUTE: DocBook, HTML, TEI-Lite)
elements: catref (TEI-Lite), classcode (TEI-Lite), keywords (TEI-Lite), meta (HTML), subjectset (DocBook)

school　(ELEMENT: ISO 12083)

scope　(ATTRIBUTE: DocBook, HTML)
elements: indexterm (DocBook), td (HTML), th (HTML)

screen　(ELEMENT: DocBook)

screenco　(ELEMENT: DocBook)

screeninfo　(ELEMENT: DocBook)

screenshot　(ELEMENT: DocBook)

script　(ELEMENT: HTML)

sdabdy　(ATTRIBUTE: ISO 12083)
elements: chapter (ISO 12083), section (ISO 12083), subsect1 (ISO 12083), subsect2 (ISO 12083), subsect3 (ISO 12083), subsect4 (ISO 12083), subsect5 (ISO 12083), subsect6 (ISO 12083)

sdaform　(ATTRIBUTE: ISO 12083)
elements: acidfree (ISO 12083), acqno (ISO 12083), appref (ISO 12083), artref (ISO 12083), artwork (ISO 12083), author (ISO 12083), avail (ISO 12083), biblist (ISO 12083), book (ISO 12083), bq (ISO 12083), catalog (ISO 12083), cell (ISO 12083), citeref (ISO 12083), coden (ISO 12083), confgrp (ISO 12083), confname (ISO 12083), contract (ISO 12083), corpauth (ISO 12083), cpyrt (ISO 12083), cpyrtclr (ISO 12083), dd (ISO 12083), ddhd (ISO 12083), deflist (ISO 12083), edition (ISO 12083), email (ISO 12083), extent (ISO 12083), fax (ISO 12083), figref (ISO 12083), fnoteref (ISO 12083), footnote (ISO 12083), formref (ISO 12083), glosref (ISO 12083), head (ISO 12083), indaddr (ISO 12083), indexref (ISO 12083), indxname (ISO 12083), indxsubj (ISO 12083), isbn (ISO 12083), item (ISO 12083), keyphras (ISO 12083), keyword (ISO 12083), lccardno (ISO 12083), list (ISO 12083), lit (ISO 12083), location (ISO 12083), note (ISO 12083), noteref (ISO 12083), orgaddr (ISO 12083), othinfo (ISO 12083), p (ISO 12083), package (ISO 12083), pages (ISO 12083), phone (ISO 12083), price (ISO 12083), pubid (ISO 12083), pubname (ISO 12083), reportid (ISO 12083), reprint (ISO 12083), row

(ISO 12083), san (ISO 12083), secref (ISO 12083), sertitle (ISO 12083), sponsor (ISO 12083), subject (ISO 12083), subtitle (ISO 12083), supmatl (ISO 12083), table (ISO 12083), tableref (ISO 12083), tbody (ISO 12083), term (ISO 12083), title (ISO 12083), toc (ISO 12083), tstub (ISO 12083), tsubhead (ISO 12083), volid (ISO 12083)

sdapart   (ATTRIBUTE: ISO 12083)
elements: chapter (ISO 12083), section (ISO 12083), subsect1 (ISO 12083), subsect2 (ISO 12083), subsect3 (ISO 12083), subsect4 (ISO 12083), subsect5 (ISO 12083), subsect6 (ISO 12083)

sdapref   (ATTRIBUTE: ISO 12083)
elements: abstract (ISO 12083), acidfree (ISO 12083), ack (ISO 12083), acqno (ISO 12083), afterwrd (ISO 12083), appendix (ISO 12083), avail (ISO 12083), biblist (ISO 12083), catalog (ISO 12083), coden (ISO 12083), confgrp (ISO 12083), confname (ISO 12083), contract (ISO 12083), cpyrt (ISO 12083), cpyrtclr (ISO 12083), date (ISO 12083), ded (ISO 12083), deflist (ISO 12083), dformgrp (ISO 12083), dformula (ISO 12083), edition (ISO 12083), email (ISO 12083), extent (ISO 12083), fax (ISO 12083), fig (ISO 12083), foreword (ISO 12083), formula (ISO 12083), glossary (ISO 12083), indaddr (ISO 12083), index (ISO 12083), intro (ISO 12083), isbn (ISO 12083), lccardno (ISO 12083), list (ISO 12083), location (ISO 12083), nameloc (ISO 12083), nmlist (ISO 12083), notes (ISO 12083), orgaddr (ISO 12083), package (ISO 12083), phone (ISO 12083), preface (ISO 12083), price (ISO 12083), pubid (ISO 12083), pubname (ISO 12083), q (ISO 12083), reportid (ISO 12083), reprint (ISO 12083), san (ISO 12083), sponsor (ISO 12083), supmatl (ISO 12083), table (ISO 12083), toc (ISO 12083), volid (ISO 12083)

sdarule   (ATTRIBUTE: ISO 12083)
elements: body (ISO 12083), citation (ISO 12083), emph (ISO 12083), figgrp (ISO 12083), part (ISO 12083), table (ISO 12083)

sdasuff   (ATTRIBUTE: ISO 12083)
elements: q (ISO 12083)

sdasusp   (ATTRIBUTE: ISO 12083)
elements: dformula (ISO 12083), formula (ISO 12083)

seal   (ELEMENT: MIL-STD-38784)
secondary   (ELEMENT: DocBook)
secondaryie   (ELEMENT: DocBook)
secref   (ELEMENT: ISO 12083)
sect1   (ELEMENT: DocBook)
sect1info   (ELEMENT: DocBook)
sect2   (ELEMENT: DocBook)
sect2info   (ELEMENT: DocBook)
sect3   (ELEMENT: DocBook)
sect3info   (ELEMENT: DocBook)
sect4   (ELEMENT: DocBook)
sect4info   (ELEMENT: DocBook)
sect5   (ELEMENT: DocBook)
sect5info   (ELEMENT: DocBook)
section   (ELEMENT: ISO 12083, MIL-STD-38784)
security   (ATTRIBUTE: MIL-STD-38784)

elements: abbrtitle (MIL-STD-38784), applicabil (MIL-STD-38784), appltitle (MIL-STD-38784), callout (MIL-STD-38784), change (MIL-STD-38784), contractno (MIL-STD-38784), dataiden (MIL-STD-38784), def (MIL-STD-38784), deflist (MIL-STD-38784), doc (MIL-STD-38784), docpart (MIL-STD-38784), entry (MIL-STD-38784), entrytbl (MIL-STD-38784), figtable (MIL-STD-38784), figure (MIL-STD-38784), foldout (MIL-STD-38784), ftnote (MIL-STD-38784), graphic (MIL-STD-38784), hazmat (MIL-STD-38784), index (MIL-STD-38784), item (MIL-STD-38784), modelno (MIL-STD-38784), nomen (MIL-STD-38784), para (MIL-STD-38784), partno (MIL-STD-38784), precaut (MIL-STD-38784), pretmidno (MIL-STD-38784), randlist (MIL-STD-38784), remarks (MIL-STD-38784), row (MIL-STD-38784), seqlist (MIL-STD-38784), serno (MIL-STD-38784), subfig (MIL-STD-38784), subject (MIL-STD-38784), subtitle (MIL-STD-38784), table (MIL-STD-38784), tabmat (MIL-STD-38784), tctono (MIL-STD-38784), tctotbl (MIL-STD-38784), term (MIL-STD-38784), title (MIL-STD-38784), tmidno (MIL-STD-38784), tpdrno (MIL-STD-38784), typedes (MIL-STD-38784), typeno (MIL-STD-38784), verbatim (MIL-STD-38784), volume (MIL-STD-38784)

see   (ELEMENT: DocBook)
seealso   (ELEMENT: DocBook)
seealsoie   (ELEMENT: DocBook)
seeie   (ELEMENT: DocBook)
seg   (ELEMENT: DocBook, TEI-Lite)
seglistitem   (ELEMENT: DocBook)
segmentedlist   (ELEMENT: DocBook)
segtitle   (ELEMENT: DocBook)
select   (ELEMENT: HTML)
selected   (ATTRIBUTE: HTML)
      elements: option (HTML)
sepchar   (ATTRIBUTE: DocBook)
      elements: cmdsynopsis (DocBook)
seqlist   (ELEMENT: MIL-STD-38784)
seqno   (ELEMENT: MIL-STD-38784)
seriesinfo   (ELEMENT: DocBook)
seriesstmt   (ELEMENT: TEI-Lite)
seriesvolnums   (ELEMENT: DocBook)
serno   (ELEMENT: MIL-STD-38784)
sertitle   (ELEMENT: ISO 12083)
service   (ATTRIBUTE: MIL-STD-38784)
      elements: doc (MIL-STD-38784), pretmidno (MIL-STD-38784), tmidno (MIL-STD-38784)
set   (ATTRIBUTE: ISO 12083)
      elements: nameloc (ISO 12083)
set   (ELEMENT: DocBook)
setindex   (ELEMENT: DocBook)
setinfo   (ELEMENT: DocBook)
sgmltag   (ELEMENT: DocBook)
shape   (ATTRIBUTE: HTML, ISO 12083)
      elements: a (HTML), area (HTML), fraction (ISO 12083)

shortaffil   (ELEMENT: DocBook)

shortcut   (ELEMENT: DocBook)

shortentry   (ATTRIBUTE: DocBook)
    elements: informaltable (DocBook), table (DocBook)

shrink   (ATTRIBUTE: MIL-STD-38784)
    elements: pgbrk (MIL-STD-38784)

sic   (ATTRIBUTE: TEI-Lite)
    elements: corr (TEI-Lite)

sic   (ELEMENT: TEI-Lite)

sidebar   (ELEMENT: DocBook)

sigblock   (ELEMENT: MIL-STD-38784)

signed   (ELEMENT: TEI-Lite)

significance   (ATTRIBUTE: DocBook)
    elements: indexterm (DocBook)

simpara   (ELEMENT: DocBook)

simplelist   (ELEMENT: DocBook)

simplesect   (ELEMENT: DocBook)

size   (ATTRIBUTE: HTML)
    elements: input (HTML), select (HTML)

sizeid   (ATTRIBUTE: ISO 12083)
    elements: bottom (ISO 12083), fence (ISO 12083), middle (ISO 12083), post (ISO 12083), subform (ISO 12083), top (ISO 12083)

sizeref   (ATTRIBUTE: ISO 12083)
    elements: fence (ISO 12083), post (ISO 12083), subform (ISO 12083)

sizex   (ATTRIBUTE: ISO 12083)
    elements: artwork (ISO 12083), fig (ISO 12083)

sizey   (ATTRIBUTE: ISO 12083)
    elements: artwork (ISO 12083), fig (ISO 12083)

skilltrk   (ATTRIBUTE: MIL-STD-38784)
    elements: abbrsect (MIL-STD-38784), appendix (MIL-STD-38784), applicdef (MIL-STD-38784), chapter (MIL-STD-38784), ddchapter (MIL-STD-38784), dddesc (MIL-STD-38784), ddindex (MIL-STD-38784), docpart (MIL-STD-38784), figure (MIL-STD-38784), foldout (MIL-STD-38784), lrp (MIL-STD-38784), para0 (MIL-STD-38784), ratd (MIL-STD-38784), safesum (MIL-STD-38784), section (MIL-STD-38784), step1 (MIL-STD-38784), step2 (MIL-STD-38784), step3 (MIL-STD-38784), step4 (MIL-STD-38784), subpara1 (MIL-STD-38784), subpara2 (MIL-STD-38784), subpara3 (MIL-STD-38784), symsect (MIL-STD-38784), table (MIL-STD-38784), tabmat (MIL-STD-38784), tctolist (MIL-STD-38784), tctotbl (MIL-STD-38784), tmimprep (MIL-STD-38784), volume (MIL-STD-38784)

small   (ELEMENT: HTML)

smallcap   (ELEMENT: ISO 12083)

socalled   (ELEMENT: TEI-Lite)

sortas   (ATTRIBUTE: DocBook)
    elements: glossentry (DocBook), primary (DocBook), secondary (DocBook), tertiary (DocBook)

sourcedesc   (ELEMENT: TEI-Lite)

sp   (ELEMENT: TEI-Lite)

space   (ATTRIBUTE: ISO 12083)
   elements: hspace (ISO 12083), vspace (ISO 12083)
spacing   (ATTRIBUTE: DocBook)
   elements: itemizedlist (DocBook), orderedlist (DocBook)
span   (ATTRIBUTE: HTML)
   elements: col (HTML), colgroup (HTML)
span   (ELEMENT: HTML)
spanname   (ATTRIBUTE: DocBook, MIL-STD-38784)
   elements: entry (DocBook), entry (MIL-STD-38784), entrytbl (DocBook), entrytbl (MIL-STD-38784), spanspec (DocBook), spanspec (MIL-STD-38784)
spanspec   (ELEMENT: DocBook, MIL-STD-38784)
speaker   (ELEMENT: TEI-Lite)
sponsor   (ELEMENT: ISO 12083, TEI-Lite)
src   (ATTRIBUTE: HTML)
   elements: img (HTML), input (HTML), script (HTML)
srccredit   (ATTRIBUTE: DocBook)
   elements: graphic (DocBook), inlinegraphic (DocBook), lotentry (DocBook)
sssn   (ATTRIBUTE: MIL-STD-38784)
   elements: abbrsect (MIL-STD-38784), appendix (MIL-STD-38784), applicdef (MIL-STD-38784), chapter (MIL-STD-38784), ddchapter (MIL-STD-38784), dddesc (MIL-STD-38784), ddindex (MIL-STD-38784), docpart (MIL-STD-38784), figure (MIL-STD-38784), foldout (MIL-STD-38784), lrp (MIL-STD-38784), para0 (MIL-STD-38784), ratd (MIL-STD-38784), safesum (MIL-STD-38784), section (MIL-STD-38784), step1 (MIL-STD-38784), step2 (MIL-STD-38784), step3 (MIL-STD-38784), step4 (MIL-STD-38784), subpara1 (MIL-STD-38784), subpara2 (MIL-STD-38784), subpara3 (MIL-STD-38784), symsect (MIL-STD-38784), table (MIL-STD-38784), tabmat (MIL-STD-38784), tctolist (MIL-STD-38784), tctotbl (MIL-STD-38784), tmimprep (MIL-STD-38784), volume (MIL-STD-38784)
stage   (ELEMENT: TEI-Lite)
standby   (ATTRIBUTE: HTML)
   elements: object (HTML)
stanza   (ELEMENT: ISO 12083)
start   (ATTRIBUTE: ISO 12083)
   elements: overline (ISO 12083), undrline (ISO 12083)
startref   (ATTRIBUTE: DocBook)
   elements: indexterm (DocBook)
state   (ELEMENT: DocBook, ISO 12083)
status   (ATTRIBUTE: DocBook, MIL-STD-38784, TEI-Lite)
   elements: abbrsect (MIL-STD-38784), appendix (DocBook), appendix (MIL-STD-38784), applicdef (MIL-STD-38784), article (DocBook), availability (TEI-Lite), bibliodiv (DocBook), bibliography (DocBook), book (DocBook), caution (MIL-STD-38784), chapter (DocBook), chapter (MIL-STD-38784), ddchapter (MIL-STD-38784), dddesc (MIL-STD-38784), ddindex (MIL-STD-38784), dedication (DocBook), deflist (MIL-STD-38784), del (TEI-Lite), docpart (MIL-STD-38784), figtable (MIL-STD-38784), figure (MIL-STD-38784), foldout (MIL-STD-38784), glossary (DocBook), glossary (MIL-STD-38784), glossdiv (DocBook), internatlstd (MIL-STD-38784), line (MIL-STD-38784), lrp (MIL-STD-38784), mrrespns (MIL-

STD-38784), note (MIL-STD-38784), para (MIL-STD-38784), para0 (MIL-STD-38784), part (DocBook), pgbrk (MIL-STD-38784), preface (DocBook), randlist (MIL-STD-38784), ratd (MIL-STD-38784), refentry (DocBook), reference (DocBook), refsect1 (DocBook), refsect2 (DocBook), refsect3 (DocBook), safesum (MIL-STD-38784), sect1 (DocBook), sect2 (DocBook), sect3 (DocBook), sect4 (DocBook), sect5 (DocBook), section (MIL-STD-38784), seqlist (MIL-STD-38784), serno (MIL-STD-38784), set (DocBook), step1 (MIL-STD-38784), step2 (MIL-STD-38784), step3 (MIL-STD-38784), step4 (MIL-STD-38784), subfig (MIL-STD-38784), subpara1 (MIL-STD-38784), subpara2 (MIL-STD-38784), subpara3 (MIL-STD-38784), symsect (MIL-STD-38784), table (MIL-STD-38784), tabmat (MIL-STD-38784), tctolist (MIL-STD-38784), tctono (MIL-STD-38784), tctorow (MIL-STD-38784), tctotbl (MIL-STD-38784), teiheader (TEI-Lite), tmidno (MIL-STD-38784), tmimprep (MIL-STD-38784), volume (MIL-STD-38784), warning (MIL-STD-38784), warnpage (MIL-STD-38784), wpgentry (MIL-STD-38784)

step (ELEMENT: DocBook)
step1 (ELEMENT: MIL-STD-38784)
step2 (ELEMENT: MIL-STD-38784)
step3 (ELEMENT: MIL-STD-38784)
step4 (ELEMENT: MIL-STD-38784)
street (ELEMENT: DocBook, ISO 12083)
strong (ELEMENT: HTML)
structfield (ELEMENT: DocBook)
structname (ELEMENT: DocBook)
style (ATTRIBUTE: HTML, ISO 12083)
elements: a (HTML), abbr (HTML), acronym (HTML), address (HTML), area (HTML), b (HTML), bdo (HTML), big (HTML), blockquote (HTML), body (HTML), box (ISO 12083), br (HTML), button (HTML), caption (HTML), cite (HTML), code (HTML), col (HTML), colgroup (HTML), dd (HTML), del (HTML), dfn (HTML), div (HTML), dl (HTML), dt (HTML), em (HTML), fence (ISO 12083), fieldset (HTML), form (HTML), fraction (ISO 12083), h1 (HTML), h2 (HTML), h3 (HTML), h4 (HTML), h5 (HTML), h6 (HTML), hr (HTML), i (HTML), img (HTML), input (HTML), ins (HTML), kbd (HTML), label (HTML), legend (HTML), li (HTML), link (HTML), map (HTML), noscript (HTML), object (HTML), ol (HTML), optgroup (HTML), option (HTML), overline (ISO 12083), p (HTML), post (ISO 12083), pre (HTML), q (HTML), samp (HTML), select (HTML), small (HTML), span (HTML), strong (HTML), sub (HTML), sup (HTML), table (HTML), tbody (HTML), td (HTML), textarea (HTML), tfoot (HTML), th (HTML), thead (HTML), tr (HTML), tt (HTML), ul (HTML), undrline (ISO 12083), var (HTML)
style (ELEMENT: HTML)
sub (ELEMENT: HTML)
subfig (ELEMENT: MIL-STD-38784)
subform (ELEMENT: ISO 12083)
subject (ATTRIBUTE: DocBook)
elements: glossdef (DocBook)
subject (ELEMENT: DocBook, ISO 12083, MIL-STD-38784)
subjectset (ELEMENT: DocBook)
subjectterm (ELEMENT: DocBook)

subjinfo   (ELEMENT: MIL-STD-38784)
subjlwr   (ATTRIBUTE: MIL-STD-38784)
   elements: subjinfo (MIL-STD-38784)
subjup   (ATTRIBUTE: MIL-STD-38784)
   elements: subjinfo (MIL-STD-38784)
subpara1   (ELEMENT: MIL-STD-38784)
subpara2   (ELEMENT: MIL-STD-38784)
subpara3   (ELEMENT: MIL-STD-38784)
subscript   (ELEMENT: DocBook)
subsect1   (ELEMENT: ISO 12083)
subsect2   (ELEMENT: ISO 12083)
subsect3   (ELEMENT: ISO 12083)
subsect4   (ELEMENT: ISO 12083)
subsect5   (ELEMENT: ISO 12083)
subsect6   (ELEMENT: ISO 12083)
substeps   (ELEMENT: DocBook)
subtitle   (ELEMENT: DocBook, ISO 12083, MIL-STD-38784)
subtype   (ATTRIBUTE: TEI-Lite)
   elements: seg (TEI-Lite)
summary   (ATTRIBUTE: HTML)
   elements: table (HTML)
sup   (ELEMENT: HTML, ISO 12083)
superscript   (ELEMENT: DocBook)
supersed   (ELEMENT: MIL-STD-38784)
supmatl   (ELEMENT: ISO 12083)
suppl   (ELEMENT: MIL-STD-38784)
surname   (ELEMENT: DocBook, ISO 12083)
symbol   (ELEMENT: DocBook)
symsect   (ELEMENT: MIL-STD-38784)
symtitle   (ELEMENT: MIL-STD-38784)
synopfragment   (ELEMENT: DocBook)
synopfragmentref   (ELEMENT: DocBook)
synopsis   (ELEMENT: DocBook)
systemitem   (ELEMENT: DocBook)
t2page   (ATTRIBUTE: MIL-STD-38784)
   elements: front (MIL-STD-38784)
tabindex   (ATTRIBUTE: HTML)
   elements: a (HTML), area (HTML), button (HTML), input (HTML), object (HTML),
   select (HTML), textarea (HTML)
table   (ELEMENT: DocBook, HTML, ISO 12083, MIL-STD-38784, TEI-Lite)
tablelist   (ELEMENT: MIL-STD-38784)
tableref   (ELEMENT: ISO 12083)
tabmat   (ELEMENT: MIL-STD-38784)
tabstyle   (ATTRIBUTE: DocBook, MIL-STD-38784)
   elements: informaltable (DocBook), table (DocBook), table (MIL-STD-38784),
   tabmat (MIL-STD-38784)
tagsdecl   (ELEMENT: TEI-Lite)

tagusage   (ELEMENT: TEI-Lite)

target   (ATTRIBUTE: TEI-Lite)
elements: catref (TEI-Lite), gloss (TEI-Lite), note (TEI-Lite), ptr (TEI-Lite), ref (TEI-Lite)

targetdocent   (ATTRIBUTE: DocBook)
elements: olink (DocBook)

targetend   (ATTRIBUTE: TEI-Lite)
elements: note (TEI-Lite)

targorder   (ATTRIBUTE: TEI-Lite)
elements: ptr (TEI-Lite), ref (TEI-Lite), xptr (TEI-Lite), xref (TEI-Lite)

targtype   (ATTRIBUTE: TEI-Lite)
elements: ptr (TEI-Lite), ref (TEI-Lite), xptr (TEI-Lite), xref (TEI-Lite)

taxonomy   (ELEMENT: TEI-Lite)

tbdepth   (ATTRIBUTE: MIL-STD-38784)
elements: figtable (MIL-STD-38784)

tbody   (ELEMENT: DocBook, HTML, ISO 12083, MIL-STD-38784)

tbwidth   (ATTRIBUTE: MIL-STD-38784)
elements: figtable (MIL-STD-38784)

tctolist   (ELEMENT: MIL-STD-38784)

tctono   (ELEMENT: MIL-STD-38784)

tctorow   (ELEMENT: MIL-STD-38784)

tctotbl   (ELEMENT: MIL-STD-38784)

td   (ELEMENT: HTML)

tei   (ATTRIBUTE: TEI-Lite)
elements: gi (TEI-Lite)

tei.2   (ELEMENT: TEI-Lite)

teiform   (ATTRIBUTE: TEI-Lite)
elements: abbr (TEI-Lite), add (TEI-Lite), address (TEI-Lite), addrline (TEI-Lite), anchor (TEI-Lite), argument (TEI-Lite), author (TEI-Lite), authority (TEI-Lite), availability (TEI-Lite), back (TEI-Lite), bibl (TEI-Lite), biblfull (TEI-Lite), biblscope (TEI-Lite), body (TEI-Lite), byline (TEI-Lite), catdesc (TEI-Lite), category (TEI-Lite), catref (TEI-Lite), cell (TEI-Lite), change (TEI-Lite), cit (TEI-Lite), classcode (TEI-Lite), classdecl (TEI-Lite), closer (TEI-Lite), corr (TEI-Lite), creation (TEI-Lite), date (TEI-Lite), dateline (TEI-Lite), del (TEI-Lite), distributor (TEI-Lite), div (TEI-Lite), div0 (TEI-Lite), div1 (TEI-Lite), div2 (TEI-Lite), div3 (TEI-Lite), div4 (TEI-Lite), div5 (TEI-Lite), div6 (TEI-Lite), div7 (TEI-Lite), divgen (TEI-Lite), docauthor (TEI-Lite), docdate (TEI-Lite), docedition (TEI-Lite), docimprint (TEI-Lite), doctitle (TEI-Lite), edition (TEI-Lite), editionstmt (TEI-Lite), editor (TEI-Lite), editorialdecl (TEI-Lite), eg (TEI-Lite), emph (TEI-Lite), encodingdesc (TEI-Lite), epigraph (TEI-Lite), extent (TEI-Lite), figdesc (TEI-Lite), figure (TEI-Lite), filedesc (TEI-Lite), foreign (TEI-Lite), formula (TEI-Lite), front (TEI-Lite), funder (TEI-Lite), gap (TEI-Lite), gi (TEI-Lite), gloss (TEI-Lite), group (TEI-Lite), head (TEI-Lite), hi (TEI-Lite), idno (TEI-Lite), imprint (TEI-Lite), index (TEI-Lite), interp (TEI-Lite), interpgrp (TEI-Lite), item (TEI-Lite), keywords (TEI-Lite), l (TEI-Lite), label (TEI-Lite), language (TEI-Lite), langusage (TEI-Lite), lb (TEI-Lite), lg (TEI-Lite), list (TEI-Lite), listbibl (TEI-Lite), mentioned (TEI-Lite), milestone (TEI-Lite), name (TEI-Lite), note (TEI-Lite), notesstmt (TEI-Lite), num (TEI-Lite), opener (TEI-Lite), orig (TEI-Lite), p (TEI-Lite),

    pb (TEI-Lite), principal (TEI-Lite), profiledesc (TEI-Lite), projectdesc (TEI-Lite), ptr (TEI-Lite), publicationstmt (TEI-Lite), publisher (TEI-Lite), pubplace (TEI-Lite), q (TEI-Lite), ref (TEI-Lite), refsdecl (TEI-Lite), reg (TEI-Lite), rendition (TEI-Lite), resp (TEI-Lite), respstmt (TEI-Lite), revisiondesc (TEI-Lite), row (TEI-Lite), rs (TEI-Lite), s (TEI-Lite), salute (TEI-Lite), samplingdecl (TEI-Lite), seg (TEI-Lite), seriesstmt (TEI-Lite), sic (TEI-Lite), signed (TEI-Lite), socalled (TEI-Lite), sourcedesc (TEI-Lite), sp (TEI-Lite), speaker (TEI-Lite), sponsor (TEI-Lite), stage (TEI-Lite), table (TEI-Lite), tagsdecl (TEI-Lite), tagusage (TEI-Lite), taxonomy (TEI-Lite), tei.2 (TEI-Lite), teiheader (TEI-Lite), term (TEI-Lite), text (TEI-Lite), textclass (TEI-Lite), time (TEI-Lite), title (TEI-Lite), titlepage (TEI-Lite), titlepart (TEI-Lite), titlestmt (TEI-Lite), trailer (TEI-Lite), unclear (TEI-Lite), xptr (TEI-Lite), xref (TEI-Lite)

teiheader   (ELEMENT: TEI-Lite)

term   (ELEMENT: DocBook, ISO 12083, MIL-STD-38784, TEI-Lite)

termlength   (ATTRIBUTE: DocBook)
    elements: variablelist (DocBook)

tertiary   (ELEMENT: DocBook)

tertiaryie   (ELEMENT: DocBook)

text   (ELEMENT: TEI-Lite)

textarea   (ELEMENT: HTML)

textclass   (ELEMENT: TEI-Lite)

tfndisplay   (ELEMENT: MIL-STD-38784)

tfnid   (ELEMENT: MIL-STD-38784)

tfnref   (ELEMENT: MIL-STD-38784)

tfntype   (ATTRIBUTE: MIL-STD-38784)
    elements: tfnid (MIL-STD-38784)

tfnval   (ATTRIBUTE: MIL-STD-38784)
    elements: tfnid (MIL-STD-38784)

tfoot   (ELEMENT: DocBook, HTML)

tgroup   (ELEMENT: DocBook, MIL-STD-38784)

tgroupstyle   (ATTRIBUTE: DocBook, MIL-STD-38784)
    elements: entrytbl (DocBook), entrytbl (MIL-STD-38784), tgroup (DocBook), tgroup (MIL-STD-38784)

th   (ELEMENT: HTML)

thead   (ELEMENT: DocBook, HTML, MIL-STD-38784)

time   (ELEMENT: TEI-Lite)

tip   (ELEMENT: DocBook)

title   (ATTRIBUTE: HTML)
    elements: a (HTML), abbr (HTML), acronym (HTML), address (HTML), area (HTML), b (HTML), bdo (HTML), big (HTML), blockquote (HTML), body (HTML), br (HTML), button (HTML), caption (HTML), cite (HTML), code (HTML), col (HTML), colgroup (HTML), dd (HTML), del (HTML), dfn (HTML), div (HTML), dl (HTML), dt (HTML), em (HTML), fieldset (HTML), form (HTML), h1 (HTML), h2 (HTML), h3 (HTML), h4 (HTML), h5 (HTML), h6 (HTML), hr (HTML), i (HTML), img (HTML), input (HTML), ins (HTML), kbd (HTML), label (HTML), legend (HTML), li (HTML), link (HTML), map (HTML), noscript (HTML), object (HTML), ol (HTML), optgroup (HTML), option (HTML), p (HTML), pre (HTML), q (HTML), samp (HTML), select (HTML), small (HTML), span (HTML), strong (HTML), style (HTML), sub (HTML),

sup (HTML), table (HTML), tbody (HTML), td (HTML), textarea (HTML), tfoot (HTML), th (HTML), thead (HTML), tr (HTML), tt (HTML), ul (HTML), var (HTML)

title   (ELEMENT: DocBook, HTML, ISO 12083, MIL-STD-38784, TEI-Lite)

titleabbrev   (ELEMENT: DocBook)

titlefont   (ATTRIBUTE: MIL-STD-38784)
     elements: wpgentry (MIL-STD-38784)

titlegrp   (ELEMENT: ISO 12083)

titlepage   (ELEMENT: TEI-Lite)

titlepart   (ELEMENT: TEI-Lite)

titlestmt   (ELEMENT: TEI-Lite)

tmidno   (ELEMENT: MIL-STD-38784)

tmidnolen   (ATTRIBUTE: MIL-STD-38784)
     elements: idinfo (MIL-STD-38784)

tmimprep   (ELEMENT: MIL-STD-38784)

to   (ATTRIBUTE: TEI-Lite)
     elements: xptr (TEI-Lite), xref (TEI-Lite)

toc   (ELEMENT: DocBook, ISO 12083)

tocback   (ELEMENT: DocBook)

tocchap   (ELEMENT: DocBook)

tocentry   (ATTRIBUTE: DocBook)
     elements: informaltable (DocBook), table (DocBook)

tocentry   (ELEMENT: DocBook)

tocfront   (ELEMENT: DocBook)

toclevel1   (ELEMENT: DocBook)

toclevel2   (ELEMENT: DocBook)

toclevel3   (ELEMENT: DocBook)

toclevel4   (ELEMENT: DocBook)

toclevel5   (ELEMENT: DocBook)

tocpart   (ELEMENT: DocBook)

token   (ELEMENT: DocBook)

top   (ELEMENT: ISO 12083)

topic   (ATTRIBUTE: MIL-STD-38784)
     elements: modreq (MIL-STD-38784)

topmar   (ATTRIBUTE: MIL-STD-38784)
     elements: colspec (MIL-STD-38784), table (MIL-STD-38784), tabmat (MIL-STD-38784), tgroup (MIL-STD-38784)

tpdr   (ELEMENT: MIL-STD-38784)

tpdrlocation   (ELEMENT: MIL-STD-38784)

tpdrno   (ELEMENT: MIL-STD-38784)

tr   (ELEMENT: HTML)

trademark   (ELEMENT: DocBook)

trailer   (ELEMENT: TEI-Lite)

tstub   (ELEMENT: ISO 12083)

tsubhead   (ELEMENT: ISO 12083)

tt   (ELEMENT: HTML)

type   (ATTRIBUTE: DocBook, HTML, ISO 12083, MIL-STD-38784, TEI-Lite)
     elements: a (HTML), abbr (TEI-Lite), anchor (TEI-Lite), biblscope (TEI-Lite), brk

(MIL-STD-38784), button (HTML), dataiden (MIL-STD-38784), date (ISO 12083), del (TEI-Lite), distrib (MIL-STD-38784), div (TEI-Lite), div0 (TEI-Lite), div1 (TEI-Lite), div2 (TEI-Lite), div3 (TEI-Lite), div4 (TEI-Lite), div5 (TEI-Lite), div6 (TEI-Lite), div7 (TEI-Lite), divgen (TEI-Lite), emph (ISO 12083), emphasis (MIL-STD-38784), head (TEI-Lite), idno (TEI-Lite), input (HTML), interp (TEI-Lite), interpgrp (TEI-Lite), lg (TEI-Lite), link (DocBook), link (HTML), list (ISO 12083), list (TEI-Lite), name (TEI-Lite), note (TEI-Lite), num (TEI-Lite), object (HTML), olink (DocBook), overline (ISO 12083), param (HTML), ptr (TEI-Lite), q (TEI-Lite), ref (TEI-Lite), rs (TEI-Lite), s (TEI-Lite), script (HTML), seg (TEI-Lite), simplelist (DocBook), stage (TEI-Lite), style (HTML), teiheader (TEI-Lite), term (TEI-Lite), time (TEI-Lite), title (TEI-Lite), titlepage (TEI-Lite), titlepart (TEI-Lite), ulink (DocBook), undrline (ISO 12083), xptr (TEI-Lite), xref (TEI-Lite)

type   (ELEMENT: DocBook)

typedes   (ELEMENT: MIL-STD-38784)

typeno   (ELEMENT: MIL-STD-38784)

typewrit   (ELEMENT: ISO 12083)

ul   (ELEMENT: HTML)

ulink   (ELEMENT: DocBook)

unclear   (ELEMENT: TEI-Lite)

undrline   (ELEMENT: ISO 12083)

unit   (ATTRIBUTE: ISO 12083, MIL-STD-38784, TEI-Lite)

elements: abbrsect (MIL-STD-38784), appendix (MIL-STD-38784), applicdef (MIL-STD-38784), artwork (ISO 12083), chapter (MIL-STD-38784), ddchapter (MIL-STD-38784), dddesc (MIL-STD-38784), ddindex (MIL-STD-38784), docpart (MIL-STD-38784), fig (ISO 12083), figure (MIL-STD-38784), foldout (MIL-STD-38784), lrp (MIL-STD-38784), milestone (TEI-Lite), para0 (MIL-STD-38784), raid (MIL-STD-38784), safesum (MIL-STD-38784), section (MIL-STD-38784), step1 (MIL-STD-38784), step2 (MIL-STD-38784), step3 (MIL-STD-38784), step4 (MIL-STD-38784), subpara1 (MIL-STD-38784), subpara2 (MIL-STD-38784), subpara3 (MIL-STD-38784), symsect (MIL-STD-38784), table (MIL-STD-38784), tabmat (MIL-STD-38784), tctolist (MIL-STD-38784), tctotbl (MIL-STD-38784), tmimprep (MIL-STD-38784), volume (MIL-STD-38784)

units   (ATTRIBUTE: DocBook)

elements: area (DocBook), areaset (DocBook), areaspec (DocBook)

url   (ATTRIBUTE: DocBook)

elements: ulink (DocBook)

usage   (ATTRIBUTE: TEI-Lite)

elements: language (TEI-Lite)

usemap   (ATTRIBUTE: HTML)

elements: img (HTML), input (HTML), object (HTML)

userinput   (ELEMENT: DocBook)

userlevel   (ATTRIBUTE: DocBook)

elements: abbrev (DocBook), abstract (DocBook), accel (DocBook), ackno (DocBook), acronym (DocBook), action (DocBook), address (DocBook), affiliation (DocBook), alt (DocBook), anchor (DocBook), appendix (DocBook), application (DocBook), area (DocBook), areaset (DocBook), areaspec (DocBook), arg (DocBook), artheader (DocBook), article (DocBook), artpagenums (DocBook), attribution (DocBook), author (DocBook), authorblurb (DocBook), authorgroup (DocBook), authorinitials (DocBook), beginpage (DocBook), bibliodiv (DocBook), biblioentry (DocBook), bibliography (DocBook), bibliomisc (DocBook), bibliomixed (DocBook), bibliomset (DocBook), biblioset (DocBook), blockquote (DocBook), book (DocBook), bookbiblio (DocBook), bookinfo (DocBook), bridgehead (DocBook), callout (DocBook), calloutlist (DocBook), caution (DocBook), chapter (DocBook), citation (DocBook), citerefentry (DocBook), citetitle (DocBook), city (DocBook), classname (DocBook), cmdsynopsis (DocBook), co (DocBook), collab (DocBook), collabname (DocBook), command (DocBook), comment (DocBook), computeroutput (DocBook), confdates (DocBook), confgroup (DocBook), confnum (DocBook), confsponsor (DocBook), conftitle (DocBook), contractnum (DocBook), contractsponsor (DocBook), contrib (DocBook), copyright (DocBook), corpauthor (DocBook), corpname (DocBook), country (DocBook), database (DocBook), date (DocBook), dedication (DocBook), docinfo (DocBook), edition (DocBook), editor (DocBook), email (DocBook), emphasis (DocBook), entry (DocBook), entrytbl (DocBook), envar (DocBook), epigraph (DocBook), equation (DocBook), errorcode (DocBook), errorname (DocBook), errortype (DocBook), example (DocBook), fax (DocBook), figure (DocBook), filename (DocBook), firstname (DocBook), firstterm (DocBook), footnote (DocBook), footnoteref (DocBook), foreignphrase (DocBook), formalpara (DocBook), funcdef (DocBook), funcparams (DocBook), funcprototype (DocBook), funcsynopsis (DocBook), funcsynopsisinfo (DocBook), function (DocBook), glossary (DocBook), glossdef (DocBook), glossdiv (DocBook), glossentry (DocBook), glosslist (DocBook), glosssee (DocBook), glossseealso (DocBook), glossterm (DocBook), graphic (DocBook), graphicco (DocBook), group (DocBook), guibutton (DocBook), guiicon (DocBook), guilabel (DocBook), guimenu (DocBook), guimenuitem (DocBook), guisubmenu (DocBook), hardware (DocBook), highlights (DocBook), holder (DocBook), honorific (DocBook), important (DocBook), index (DocBook), indexdiv (DocBook), indexentry (DocBook), indexterm (DocBook), informalequation (DocBook), informalexample (DocBook), informaltable (DocBook), inlineequation (DocBook), inlinegraphic (DocBook), interface (DocBook), interfacedefinition (DocBook), invpartnumber (DocBook), isbn (DocBook), issn (DocBook), issuenum (DocBook), itemizedlist (DocBook), itermset (DocBook), jobtitle (DocBook), keycap (DocBook), keycode (DocBook), keycombo (DocBook), keysym (DocBook), keyword (DocBook), keywordset (DocBook), legalnotice (DocBook), lineage (DocBook), lineannotation (DocBook), link (DocBook), listitem (DocBook), literal (DocBook), literallayout (DocBook), lot (DocBook), lotentry (DocBook), manvolnum (DocBook), markup (DocBook), medialabel (DocBook), member (DocBook), menuchoice (DocBook), modespec (DocBook), mousebutton (DocBook), msg (DocBook), msgaud (DocBook), msgentry (DocBook), msgexplan (DocBook), msginfo (DocBook), msglevel (DocBook), msgmain (DocBook), msgorig (DocBook), msgrel (DocBook), msgset (DocBook), msgsub (DocBook), msgtext (DocBook), note (DocBook), olink (DocBook), option (DocBook), optional (DocBook), orderedlist (DocBook), orgdiv (DocBook), orgname (DocBook), otheraddr (DocBook), othercredit (DocBook), othername (DocBook), pagenums (DocBook), para (DocBook), paramdef (DocBook), parameter (DocBook), part (DocBook), partintro (DocBook), phone (DocBook), phrase (DocBook), pob (DocBook), postcode (DocBook), preface

(DocBook), primary (DocBook), primaryie (DocBook), printhistory (DocBook), procedure (DocBook), productname (DocBook), productnumber (DocBook), programlisting (DocBook), programlistingco (DocBook), prompt (DocBook), property (DocBook), pubdate (DocBook), publisher (DocBook), publishername (DocBook), pubsnumber (DocBook), quote (DocBook), refclass (DocBook), refdescriptor (DocBook), refentry (DocBook), refentrytitle (DocBook), reference (DocBook), refmeta (DocBook), refmiscinfo (DocBook), refname (DocBook), refnamediv (DocBook), refpurpose (DocBook), refsect1 (DocBook), refsect1info (DocBook), refsect2 (DocBook), refsect2info (DocBook), refsect3 (DocBook), refsect3info (DocBook), refsynopsisdiv (DocBook), refsynopsisdivinfo (DocBook), releaseinfo (DocBook), replaceable (DocBook), returnvalue (DocBook), revhistory (DocBook), revision (DocBook), revnumber (DocBook), revremark (DocBook), row (DocBook), sbr (DocBook), screen (DocBook), screenco (DocBook), screeninfo (DocBook), screenshot (DocBook), secondary (DocBook), secondaryie (DocBook), sect1 (DocBook), sect1info (DocBook), sect2 (DocBook), sect2info (DocBook), sect3 (DocBook), sect3info (DocBook), sect4 (DocBook), sect4info (DocBook), sect5 (DocBook), sect5info (DocBook), see (DocBook), seealso (DocBook), seealsoie (DocBook), seeie (DocBook), seg (DocBook), seglistitem (DocBook), segmentedlist (DocBook), segtitle (DocBook), seriesinfo (DocBook), seriesvolnums (DocBook), set (DocBook), setindex (DocBook), setinfo (DocBook), sgmltag (DocBook), shortaffil (DocBook), shortcut (DocBook), sidebar (DocBook), simpara (DocBook), simplelist (DocBook), simplesect (DocBook), state (DocBook), step (DocBook), street (DocBook), structfield (DocBook), structname (DocBook), subject (DocBook), subjectset (DocBook), subjectterm (DocBook), subscript (DocBook), substeps (DocBook), subtitle (DocBook), superscript (DocBook), surname (DocBook), symbol (DocBook), synopfragment (DocBook), synopfragmentref (DocBook), synopsis (DocBook), systemitem (DocBook), table (DocBook), tbody (DocBook), term (DocBook), tertiary (DocBook), tertiaryie (DocBook), tfoot (DocBook), tgroup (DocBook), thead (DocBook), tip (DocBook), title (DocBook), titleabbrev (DocBook), toc (DocBook), tocback (DocBook), tocchap (DocBook), tocentry (DocBook), tocfront (DocBook), toclevel1 (DocBook), toclevel2 (DocBook), toclevel3 (DocBook), toclevel4 (DocBook), toclevel5 (DocBook), tocpart (DocBook), token (DocBook), trademark (DocBook), type (DocBook), ulink (DocBook), userinput (DocBook), varargs (DocBook), variablelist (DocBook), varlistentry (DocBook), void (DocBook), volumenum (DocBook), warning (DocBook), wordasword (DocBook), xref (DocBook), year (DocBook)

valign   (ATTRIBUTE: DocBook, HTML, MIL-STD-38784)
elements: col (HTML), colgroup (HTML), entry (DocBook), entry (MIL-STD-38784), row (DocBook), row (MIL-STD-38784), tbody (DocBook), tbody (HTML), tbody (MIL-STD-38784), td (HTML), tfoot (DocBook), tfoot (HTML), th (HTML), thead (DocBook), thead (HTML), thead (MIL-STD-38784), tr (HTML)

value   (ATTRIBUTE: HTML, TEI-Lite)
elements: button (HTML), date (TEI-Lite), docdate (TEI-Lite), input (HTML), interp (TEI-Lite), num (TEI-Lite), option (HTML), param (HTML), time (TEI-Lite)

valuetype   (ATTRIBUTE: HTML)
elements: param (HTML)

var   (ELEMENT: HTML)

varargs   (ELEMENT: DocBook)
variablelist   (ELEMENT: DocBook)
varlistentry   (ELEMENT: DocBook)
vendor   (ATTRIBUTE: DocBook)
elements: abbrev (DocBook), abstract (DocBook), accel (DocBook), ackno (DocBook), acronym (DocBook), action (DocBook), address (DocBook), affiliation (DocBook), alt (DocBook), anchor (DocBook), appendix (DocBook), application (DocBook), area (DocBook), areaset (DocBook), areaspec (DocBook), arg (DocBook), artheader (DocBook), article (DocBook), artpagenums (DocBook), attribution (DocBook), author (DocBook), authorblurb (DocBook), authorgroup (DocBook), authorinitials (DocBook), beginpage (DocBook), bibliodiv (DocBook), biblioentry (DocBook), bibliography (DocBook), bibliomisc (DocBook), bibliomixed (DocBook), bibliomset (DocBook), biblioset (DocBook), blockquote (DocBook), book (DocBook), bookbiblio (DocBook), bookinfo (DocBook), bridgehead (DocBook), callout (DocBook), calloutlist (DocBook), caution (DocBook), chapter (DocBook), citation (DocBook), citerefentry (DocBook), citetitle (DocBook), city (DocBook), classname (DocBook), cmdsynopsis (DocBook), co (DocBook), collab (DocBook), collabname (DocBook), command (DocBook), comment (DocBook), computeroutput (DocBook), confdates (DocBook), confgroup (DocBook), confnum (DocBook), confsponsor (DocBook), conftitle (DocBook), contractnum (DocBook), contractsponsor (DocBook), contrib (DocBook), copyright (DocBook), corpauthor (DocBook), corpname (DocBook), country (DocBook), database (DocBook), date (DocBook), dedication (DocBook), docinfo (DocBook), edition (DocBook), editor (DocBook), email (DocBook), emphasis (DocBook), entry (DocBook), entrytbl (DocBook), envar (DocBook), epigraph (DocBook), equation (DocBook), errorcode (DocBook), errorname (DocBook), errortype (DocBook), example (DocBook), fax (DocBook), figure (DocBook), filename (DocBook), firstname (DocBook), firstterm (DocBook), footnote (DocBook), footnoteref (DocBook), foreignphrase (DocBook), formalpara (DocBook), funcdef (DocBook), funcparams (DocBook), funcprototype (DocBook), funcsynopsis (DocBook), funcsynopsisinfo (DocBook), function (DocBook), glossary (DocBook), glossdef (DocBook), glossdiv (DocBook), glossentry (DocBook), glosslist (DocBook), glosssee (DocBook), glossseealso (DocBook), glossterm (DocBook), graphic (DocBook), graphicco (DocBook), group (DocBook), guibutton (DocBook), guiicon (DocBook), guilabel (DocBook), guimenu (DocBook), guimenuitem (DocBook), guisubmenu (DocBook), hardware (DocBook), highlights (DocBook), holder (DocBook), honorific (DocBook), important (DocBook), index (DocBook), indexdiv (DocBook), indexentry (DocBook), indexterm (DocBook), informalequation (DocBook), informalexample (DocBook), informaltable (DocBook), inlineequation (DocBook), inlinegraphic (DocBook), interface (DocBook), interfacedefinition (DocBook), invpartnumber (DocBook), isbn (DocBook), issn (DocBook), issuenum (DocBook), itemizedlist (DocBook), itermset (DocBook), jobtitle (DocBook), keycap (DocBook), keycode (DocBook), keycombo (DocBook), keysym (DocBook), keyword (DocBook), keywordset (DocBook), legalnotice (DocBook), lineage (DocBook), lineannotation (DocBook), link (DocBook), listitem (DocBook), literal (DocBook), literallayout (DocBook), lot (DocBook), lotentry (DocBook), manvolnum (DocBook), markup (DocBook), medialabel (DocBook), member (DocBook), menuchoice (DocBook),

modespec (DocBook), mousebutton (DocBook), msg (DocBook), msgaud (DocBook), msgentry (DocBook), msgexplan (DocBook), msginfo (DocBook), msglevel (DocBook), msgmain (DocBook), msgorig (DocBook), msgrel (DocBook), msgset (DocBook), msgsub (DocBook), msgtext (DocBook), note (DocBook), olink (DocBook), option (DocBook), optional (DocBook), orderedlist (DocBook), orgdiv (DocBook), orgname (DocBook), otheraddr (DocBook), othercredit (DocBook), othername (DocBook), pagenums (DocBook), para (DocBook), paramdef (DocBook), parameter (DocBook), part (DocBook), partintro (DocBook), phone (DocBook), phrase (DocBook), pob (DocBook), postcode (DocBook), preface (DocBook), primary (DocBook), primaryie (DocBook), printhistory (DocBook), procedure (DocBook), productname (DocBook), productnumber (DocBook), programlisting (DocBook), programlistingco (DocBook), prompt (DocBook), property (DocBook), pubdate (DocBook), publisher (DocBook), publishername (DocBook), pubsnumber (DocBook), quote (DocBook), refclass (DocBook), refdescriptor (DocBook), refentry (DocBook), refentrytitle (DocBook), reference (DocBook), refmeta (DocBook), refmiscinfo (DocBook), refname (DocBook), refnamediv (DocBook), refpurpose (DocBook), refsect1 (DocBook), refsect1info (DocBook), refsect2 (DocBook), refsect2info (DocBook), refsect3 (DocBook), refsect3info (DocBook), refsynopsisdiv (DocBook), refsynopsisdivinfo (DocBook), releaseinfo (DocBook), replaceable (DocBook), returnvalue (DocBook), revhistory (DocBook), revision (DocBook), revnumber (DocBook), revremark (DocBook), row (DocBook), sbr (DocBook), screen (DocBook), screenco (DocBook), screeninfo (DocBook), screenshot (DocBook), secondary (DocBook), secondaryie (DocBook), sect1 (DocBook), sect1info (DocBook), sect2 (DocBook), sect2info (DocBook), sect3 (DocBook), sect3info (DocBook), sect4 (DocBook), sect4info (DocBook), sect5 (DocBook), sect5info (DocBook), see (DocBook), seealso (DocBook), seealsoie (DocBook), seeie (DocBook), seg (DocBook), seglistitem (DocBook), segmentedlist (DocBook), segtitle (DocBook), seriesinfo (DocBook), seriesvolnums (DocBook), set (DocBook), setindex (DocBook), setinfo (DocBook), sgmltag (DocBook), shortaffil (DocBook), shortcut (DocBook), sidebar (DocBook), simpara (DocBook), simplelist (DocBook), simplesect (DocBook), state (DocBook), step (DocBook), street (DocBook), structfield (DocBook), structname (DocBook), subject (DocBook), subjectset (DocBook), subjectterm (DocBook), subscript (DocBook), substeps (DocBook), subtitle (DocBook), superscript (DocBook), surname (DocBook), symbol (DocBook), synopfragment (DocBook), synopfragmentref (DocBook), synopsis (DocBook), systemitem (DocBook), table (DocBook), tbody (DocBook), term (DocBook), tertiary (DocBook), tertiaryie (DocBook), tfoot (DocBook), tgroup (DocBook), thead (DocBook), tip (DocBook), title (DocBook), titleabbrev (DocBook), toc (DocBook), tocback (DocBook), tocchap (DocBook), tocentry (DocBook), tocfront (DocBook), toclevel1 (DocBook), toclevel2 (DocBook), toclevel3 (DocBook), toclevel4 (DocBook), toclevel5 (DocBook), tocpart (DocBook), token (DocBook), trademark (DocBook), type (DocBook), ulink (DocBook), userinput (DocBook), varargs (DocBook), variablelist (DocBook), varlistentry (DocBook), void (DocBook), volumenum (DocBook), warning (DocBook), wordasword (DocBook), xref (DocBook), year (DocBook)

verbatim   (ELEMENT: MIL-STD-38784)
verdate   (ATTRIBUTE: MIL-STD-38784)

elements: abbrsect (MIL-STD-38784), applicdef (MIL-STD-38784), contents (MIL-STD-38784), dddesc (MIL-STD-38784), ddindex (MIL-STD-38784), doc (MIL-STD-38784), figure (MIL-STD-38784), foldout (MIL-STD-38784), foreword (MIL-STD-38784), glossary (MIL-STD-38784), idinfo (MIL-STD-38784), illuslist (MIL-STD-38784), internatlstd (MIL-STD-38784), intro (MIL-STD-38784), lep (MIL-STD-38784), lrp (MIL-STD-38784), para0 (MIL-STD-38784), preface (MIL-STD-38784), ratd (MIL-STD-38784), safesum (MIL-STD-38784), subpara1 (MIL-STD-38784), subpara2 (MIL-STD-38784), subpara3 (MIL-STD-38784), symsect (MIL-STD-38784), table (MIL-STD-38784), tablelist (MIL-STD-38784), tabmat (MIL-STD-38784), tctolist (MIL-STD-38784), tctotbl (MIL-STD-38784), tmimprep (MIL-STD-38784), warnpage (MIL-STD-38784)
verrefpt   (ATTRIBUTE: MIL-STD-38784)
elements: figtable (MIL-STD-38784), legend (MIL-STD-38784)
verrem   (ATTRIBUTE: MIL-STD-38784)
elements: abbrsect (MIL-STD-38784), applicdef (MIL-STD-38784), contents (MIL-STD-38784), dddesc (MIL-STD-38784), ddindex (MIL-STD-38784), doc (MIL-STD-38784), figure (MIL-STD-38784), foldout (MIL-STD-38784), foreword (MIL-STD-38784), glossary (MIL-STD-38784), idinfo (MIL-STD-38784), illuslist (MIL-STD-38784), internatlstd (MIL-STD-38784), intro (MIL-STD-38784), lep (MIL-STD-38784), lrp (MIL-STD-38784), para0 (MIL-STD-38784), preface (MIL-STD-38784), ratd (MIL-STD-38784), safesum (MIL-STD-38784), subpara1 (MIL-STD-38784), subpara2 (MIL-STD-38784), subpara3 (MIL-STD-38784), symsect (MIL-STD-38784), table (MIL-STD-38784), tablelist (MIL-STD-38784), tabmat (MIL-STD-38784), tctolist (MIL-STD-38784), tctotbl (MIL-STD-38784), tmimprep (MIL-STD-38784), warnpage (MIL-STD-38784)
verstat   (ELEMENT: MIL-STD-38784)
verstatpg   (ATTRIBUTE: MIL-STD-38784)
elements: doc (MIL-STD-38784)
vita   (ELEMENT: ISO 12083)
void   (ELEMENT: DocBook)
volid   (ELEMENT: ISO 12083)
volnot   (ELEMENT: MIL-STD-38784)
volnum   (ELEMENT: MIL-STD-38784)
volume   (ELEMENT: MIL-STD-38784)
volumenum   (ELEMENT: DocBook)
vplace   (ATTRIBUTE: MIL-STD-38784)
elements: graphic (MIL-STD-38784)
vscale   (ATTRIBUTE: MIL-STD-38784)
elements: graphic (MIL-STD-38784)
vspace   (ELEMENT: ISO 12083)
warnbox   (ATTRIBUTE: MIL-STD-38784)
elements: wpgentry (MIL-STD-38784)
warning   (ELEMENT: DocBook, MIL-STD-38784)
warnpage   (ELEMENT: MIL-STD-38784)
weight   (ATTRIBUTE: DocBook)
elements: subject (DocBook)
who   (ATTRIBUTE: TEI-Lite)

elements: q (TEI-Lite), sp (TEI-Lite)

width   (ATTRIBUTE: DocBook, HTML)
elements: col (HTML), colgroup (HTML), example (DocBook), graphic (DocBook), img (HTML), informalexample (DocBook), inlinegraphic (DocBook), literallayout (DocBook), object (HTML), programlisting (DocBook), screen (DocBook), table (HTML)

wordasword   (ELEMENT: DocBook)

wpgentry   (ELEMENT: MIL-STD-38784)

wsd   (ATTRIBUTE: TEI-Lite)
elements: language (TEI-Lite)

xptr   (ELEMENT: TEI-Lite)

xref   (ATTRIBUTE: MIL-STD-38784)
elements: modreq (MIL-STD-38784)

xref   (ELEMENT: DocBook, MIL-STD-38784, TEI-Lite)

xrefid   (ATTRIBUTE: MIL-STD-38784)
elements: extref (MIL-STD-38784), ftnref (MIL-STD-38784), location (MIL-STD-38784), para (MIL-STD-38784), tfnref (MIL-STD-38784), xref (MIL-STD-38784)

xreflabel   (ATTRIBUTE: DocBook)
elements: abbrev (DocBook), abstract (DocBook), accel (DocBook), ackno (DocBook), acronym (DocBook), action (DocBook), address (DocBook), affiliation (DocBook), alt (DocBook), anchor (DocBook), appendix (DocBook), application (DocBook), area (DocBook), areaset (DocBook), areaspec (DocBook), arg (DocBook), artheader (DocBook), article (DocBook), artpagenums (DocBook), attribution (DocBook), author (DocBook), authorblurb (DocBook), authorgroup (DocBook), authorinitials (DocBook), beginpage (DocBook), bibliodiv (DocBook), biblioentry (DocBook), bibliography (DocBook), bibliomisc (DocBook), bibliomixed (DocBook), bibliomset (DocBook), biblioset (DocBook), blockquote (DocBook), book (DocBook), bookbiblio (DocBook), bookinfo (DocBook), bridgehead (DocBook), callout (DocBook), calloutlist (DocBook), caution (DocBook), chapter (DocBook), citation (DocBook), citerefentry (DocBook), citetitle (DocBook), city (DocBook), classname (DocBook), cmdsynopsis (DocBook), co (DocBook), collab (DocBook), collabname (DocBook), command (DocBook), comment (DocBook), computeroutput (DocBook), confdates (DocBook), confgroup (DocBook), confnum (DocBook), confsponsor (DocBook), conftitle (DocBook), contractnum (DocBook), contractsponsor (DocBook), contrib (DocBook), copyright (DocBook), corpauthor (DocBook), corpname (DocBook), country (DocBook), database (DocBook), date (DocBook), dedication (DocBook), docinfo (DocBook), edition (DocBook), editor (DocBook), email (DocBook), emphasis (DocBook), entry (DocBook), entrytbl (DocBook), envar (DocBook), epigraph (DocBook), equation (DocBook), errorcode (DocBook), errorname (DocBook), errortype (DocBook), example (DocBook), fax (DocBook), figure (DocBook), filename (DocBook), firstname (DocBook), firstterm (DocBook), footnote (DocBook), footnoteref (DocBook), foreignphrase (DocBook), formalpara (DocBook), funcdef (DocBook), funcparams (DocBook), funcprototype (DocBook), funcsynopsis (DocBook), funcsynopsisinfo (DocBook), function (DocBook), glossary (DocBook), glossdef (DocBook), glossdiv (DocBook), glossentry (DocBook), glosslist (DocBook), glosssee (DocBook), glossseealso (DocBook), glossterm (DocBook), graphic (DocBook), graphicco (DocBook), group

(DocBook), guibutton (DocBook), guiicon (DocBook), guilabel (DocBook), guimenu (DocBook), guimenuitem (DocBook), guisubmenu (DocBook), hardware (DocBook), highlights (DocBook), holder (DocBook), honorific (DocBook), important (DocBook), index (DocBook), indexdiv (DocBook), indexentry (DocBook), indexterm (DocBook), informalequation (DocBook), informalexample (DocBook), informaltable (DocBook), inlineequation (DocBook), inlinegraphic (DocBook), interface (DocBook), interfacedefinition (DocBook), invpartnumber (DocBook), isbn (DocBook), issn (DocBook), issuenum (DocBook), itemizedlist (DocBook), itermset (DocBook), jobtitle (DocBook), keycap (DocBook), keycode (DocBook), keycombo (DocBook), keysym (DocBook), keyword (DocBook), keywordset (DocBook), legalnotice (DocBook), lineage (DocBook), lineannotation (DocBook), link (DocBook), listitem (DocBook), literal (DocBook), literallayout (DocBook), lot (DocBook), lotentry (DocBook), manvolnum (DocBook), markup (DocBook), medialabel (DocBook), member (DocBook), menuchoice (DocBook), modespec (DocBook), mousebutton (DocBook), msg (DocBook), msgaud (DocBook), msgentry (DocBook), msgexplan (DocBook), msginfo (DocBook), msglevel (DocBook), msgmain (DocBook), msgorig (DocBook), msgrel (DocBook), msgset (DocBook), msgsub (DocBook), msgtext (DocBook), note (DocBook), olink (DocBook), option (DocBook), optional (DocBook), orderedlist (DocBook), orgdiv (DocBook), orgname (DocBook), otheraddr (DocBook), othercredit (DocBook), othername (DocBook), pagenums (DocBook), para (DocBook), paramdef (DocBook), parameter (DocBook), part (DocBook), partintro (DocBook), phone (DocBook), phrase (DocBook), pob (DocBook), postcode (DocBook), preface (DocBook), primary (DocBook), primaryie (DocBook), printhistory (DocBook), procedure (DocBook), productname (DocBook), productnumber (DocBook), programlisting (DocBook), programlistingco (DocBook), prompt (DocBook), property (DocBook), pubdate (DocBook), publisher (DocBook), publishername (DocBook), pubsnumber (DocBook), quote (DocBook), refclass (DocBook), refdescriptor (DocBook), refentry (DocBook), refentrytitle (DocBook), reference (DocBook), refmeta (DocBook), refmiscinfo (DocBook), refname (DocBook), refnamediv (DocBook), refpurpose (DocBook), refsect1 (DocBook), refsect1info (DocBook), refsect2 (DocBook), refsect2info (DocBook), refsect3 (DocBook), refsect3info (DocBook), refsynopsisdiv (DocBook), refsynopsisdivinfo (DocBook), releaseinfo (DocBook), replaceable (DocBook), returnvalue (DocBook), revhistory (DocBook), revision (DocBook), revnumber (DocBook), revremark (DocBook), row (DocBook), sbr (DocBook), screen (DocBook), screenco (DocBook), screeninfo (DocBook), screenshot (DocBook), secondary (DocBook), secondaryie (DocBook), sect1 (DocBook), sect1info (DocBook), sect2 (DocBook), sect2info (DocBook), sect3 (DocBook), sect3info (DocBook), sect4 (DocBook), sect4info (DocBook), sect5 (DocBook), sect5info (DocBook), see (DocBook), seealso (DocBook), seealsoie (DocBook), seeie (DocBook), seg (DocBook), seglistitem (DocBook), segmentedlist (DocBook), segtitle (DocBook), seriesinfo (DocBook), seriesvolnums (DocBook), set (DocBook), setindex (DocBook), setinfo (DocBook), sgmltag (DocBook), shortaffil (DocBook), shortcut (DocBook), sidebar (DocBook), simpara (DocBook), simplelist (DocBook), simplesect (DocBook), state (DocBook), step (DocBook), street (DocBook), structfield (DocBook), structname (DocBook), subject (DocBook), subjectset (DocBook), subjectterm (DocBook), subscript

(DocBook), substeps (DocBook), subtitle (DocBook), superscript (DocBook), surname (DocBook), symbol (DocBook), synopfragment (DocBook), synopfragmentref (DocBook), synopsis (DocBook), systemitem (DocBook), table (DocBook), tbody (DocBook), term (DocBook), tertiary (DocBook), tertiaryie (DocBook), tfoot (DocBook), tgroup (DocBook), thead (DocBook), tip (DocBook), title (DocBook), titleabbrev (DocBook), toc (DocBook), tocback (DocBook), tocchap (DocBook), tocentry (DocBook), tocfront (DocBook), toclevel1 (DocBook), toclevel2 (DocBook), toclevel3 (DocBook), toclevel4 (DocBook), toclevel5 (DocBook), tocpart (DocBook), token (DocBook), trademark (DocBook), type (DocBook), ulink (DocBook), userinput (DocBook), varargs (DocBook), variablelist (DocBook), varlistentry (DocBook), void (DocBook), volumenum (DocBook), warning (DocBook), wordasword (DocBook), xref (DocBook), year (DocBook)

year   (ELEMENT: DocBook)

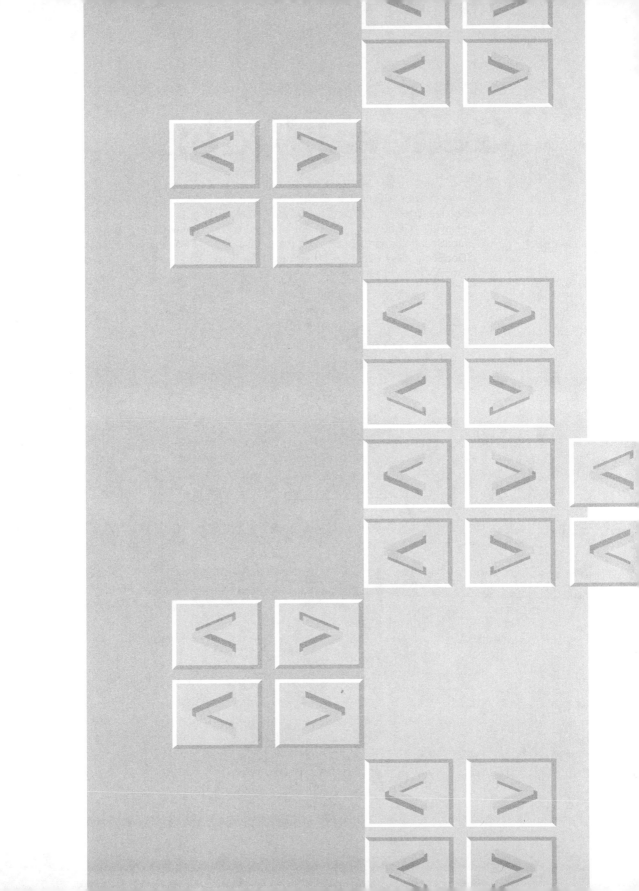

General Index

Index

Symbols

#FIXED keyword 22, 288
#IMPLIED keyword 23
#REQUIRED keyword 23

A

AAP
    See Association of American Publishers (AAP)
additional tag sets (TEI) 64
AFDR 271
    See Architectural Form Definition
      Requirements (AFDR)
age
    as influence on author's expectations 109
Air Transport Association (ATA) 70
alternation 187, 189, 198
American National Standards Institute (ANSI)
  48
anchor 81

ANSI
    See American National Standards Institute
      (ANSI)
ANY keyword 12, 192
architectural attribute renamer 307
architectural attribute renamer attribute 306,
  319
architectural document 275, 276, 302
architectural engine 288
architectural form 288
architectural form attribute 300, 308
Architectural Form Definition Requirements
  (AFDR) 271
architectural forms xxxiv, 46, 271, 274
    architectural document 275
    architectural similarities in model DTDs 278
    architecture use declaration attributes 290
    attribute form 274
    attribute forms 306
    attributes 318
    automatic derivation 292, 312
    basic forms 299
    concepts 268
    configuration 289

default notation 324
deriving attribute values from content 322
deriving content from attribute values 320
document exchange 269
element form 274
element forms 299, 303
ignoring data 291
meta-DTDs 272, 327
muliple DTDs for one document 272
notation form 274
notation forms 307
original SGML syntax 292
practical uses 276
renaming attributes 291
resolving IDREF 325
role of client document 273
setup 289
SGML 308
suppressing processing 291, 313
syntax 286, 310
terminology 282
types of forms 274
used for DTD extension 276
used for extended validation 282
used for multi-use documents 280
used for software reusability 278
architectural processing
    See architectural forms
architecture base declaration 294
architecture bridge form name 326
architecture notation declaration 295
architecture suppressor attribute 314
architecture use declaration 290, 312
architecture use declaration attributes 290
Association of American Publishers (AAP) 48
ATA
    See Air Transport Association (ATA)
ATA 2100 DTDs 70
attribute definitions 18
attribute form 240, 274
    term 274
attribute list declaration 18
    syntax 17
        attribute type 18
        default value 21
        multiple declarations 23

SGML facilities 24
attribute list declarations
    precedence 5
attribute name 18
attribute type 18
attributes
    global attributes 107
    object-oriented approach 105
authoring tools
    automatic insertion of attributes 126
    automatic insertion of elements 122
authors xxxii, 87
authors' DTD modifications 158

▌B

backwards compatibility
    changes to attribute default value 195
    repetition 194
backwards-compatibility 181, 203
    alternation 186, 196
    ANY and EMPTY 192
    attribute types 196
    attributes 193
    changes in combination 188
    entity declarations 203
    omissibility 183, 195
    repetition 181
    whitespace handling 205
base architecture 272, 273
base tag set (TEI) 64
block content 139, 140
book-oriented DTDs xxxii, 44
bracketed text 34
business rules 148

▌C

CALS DTD
    See also MIL-STD-38784 DTD
CALS Initiative 70
CALS table model 70

CDATA keyword 18
choice 9
client document 273
client DTD 272, 288
conditional section
    syntax 38
conditional sections 38
containers 166
content model 6, 7, 12
    SGML 7
content particle 9, 10, 16
content particles 9
content specification 6, 7, 12
context 146, 165
customization 246
    adding new element types 249
    authoring DTDs 247
    avoiding authoring errors 248
    reasons 246
    restructuring a DTD 250
customized DTDs
    advantages 46

D

dangerous mixed content 16
data attribute form 274
    See SGML
data attributes 36
    See SGML
    uses 37
data text 34
database-oriented DTDs xxxii, 44
Davenport Group 55
    home page 62
    mailing list 62
declared content 7, 15
declared values 24
default general entity 33
default value 18
default values 21
derived DTD 272
    See client DTD
descriptive 148

descriptive DTD 136
Digital Equipment Corporation 55
DocBook DTD
    customization 254
    introduction 54
    stability 55
document exchange
    resolving conflicting expecations 113
document processing
    advantages of a DTD 145
    advantages of containers 165
    authors' intentions 147
    authors' modifications 158
    constraint 147
    editorial policy 148
    generic element types 155
    handling recursion 150
    IMPLIED attributes 170
    non-XML constraints 149
    recursion
        hidden 152
    role attributes 155
    role of the parser 147
    structural context 165
document type declaration 4, 218
    freezing a DTD version 179
    syntax 4
    treatment in HTML browsers 78
DTD consistency 88
DTD design
    authors' requirements 87
    backwards compatibility 178
    backwards-incompatible changes 181
    choice 247
    criteria for easy learning 174
    criteria for easy use 174
    customization 246
    descriptive and prescriptive DTDs 136
    document processing considerations 144
    ease of use 118
    element type classes 104
    engineers' requirements 87
    flexibility 135
    generic element types 142
    global attributes 107
    inline element types 138

internal and external consistency 97
learning requirements 94
limiting choice 131
naming 98, 110
parallel design 100
physical effort 120, 130
role attributes 140
structural expectations 112
writers' requirements 87
DTD intuitiveness 88
DTD size 88, 89
DTD users xxxii

E

editorial policy 148
education
as influence on author's expectations 109
Electronic Publishing Special Interest Group
(EPSIG) 48, 54
home page 54
Electronic Text Center 70
element content 8
element form 274
term 274
element forms 300
element type 6
element type declaration 6
syntax 5
content specification 7
element type 6
SGML facilities 13
employer
as influence on author's expectations 109
EMPTY keyword 12, 192
enabling 148
enabling architecture(s) 273
enabling DTD 136
encompassing architecture 273
ENTITIES keyword 19
entity
as attribute value 19, 32
entity boundaries 32
entity declaration 29, 37

boundaries 32
syntax 28
entity definition 31
entity location 30
external entity 30
general entities 29
internal entity 30
parameter entities 29
SGML facilities 32
unparsed entities 31
entity declarations 203
precedence 5
ENTITY keyword 19
entity references
treatment in HTML browsers 78
entity structure 214
enumerated type 18, 20
EPSIG
See Electronic Publishing Special Interest
Group (EPSIG)
exceptions 14
limiting recursion 151
exchange 216
exchange DTDs 43
exclusion exceptions xxxiii, 14
Exeter SGML Archive 54
extensible DTD 158
external definition 30
external DTD subset 4, 5, 7
external entities 215

F

forbidden 183, 184, 191, 192, 202
fragments 214
advantages 217
context 220, 231, 237
cross-references 220, 232, 238
local entity declarations 224, 234, 241
reparenting 230
replacing with subdocuments 235
stand-alone documents 218
Fujitsu 55

G

GCARI
 See Graphic Communications Association
  Research Institute (GCARI)
gender
 as influence on author's expectations 109
General Document DTD 78
general entities 28
general entity 29, 31
generic element 140
generic element type 142, 156
generic element types 155, 156
Graphic Communications Assocation Research
 Institute (GCARI) 54
Graphic Communications Association Research
 Institute (GCARI) 48

H

HaL Computer Systems 55
Hewlett-Packard 55
Hitachi 55
HTML DTD
 applets 81
 cross-references 81
 customization 260
 familiarity 111
 frameset version 77
 introduction 77
 lack of sectioning element types 79
 popularity 77
 relationship to General Document DTD 78
 relationship to LaTeX 78
 strict version 77
 transitional version 77
HyTime 146
 cross-references 239
 home page 146
 value reference 240

I

ID keyword 19, 222
IDREF keyword 20, 222
IDREFS keyword 20, 222
inclusion exceptions xxxiii, 14
industry-standard DTDs 43
 advantages 47
information-content-oriented DTDs 44
information-processing specialists xxxii
inheritance
 in XML and SGML 245
internal DTD subset 4, 5
 XML restrictions on parameter entities 4
internal entity 30
International Organization for Standardization
 (ISO) 48, 54
intuitiveness 109
ISO
 See International Organization for
  Standardization (ISO)
ISO 12083 DTD
 customization 262
 introduction 47
 stability 49
ISO 8879:1986: General Document DTD 78

L

language
 as influence on author's expectations 109
LaTeX 78
learning requirements 89
logical structure 28
logical unit xxxvi, 90, 140
logical units 89, 131, 135, 174

M

marked sections
 treatment in HTML browsers 78

meta-DTD 272, 273, 300
meta-DTD(s) 272
meta-DTDs 272
Microsoft 55
MIL-STD-38784 DTD
    customization 261
    introduction 70
    table model 70
mixed content xxxiii, xxxv, 8, 12, 29, 146
model DTDs 44
    authors' modifications 160
    common architecture 278
    constraint in placement of elements 149
    containers 168
    customization 252
    descriptive and prescriptive structures 137
    element-type classes 103, 106
    exchange 115
    generic element types 157
    global attributes 108
    IMPLIED attributes 172
    inline element types 139
    lack of generic element types 143
    learning requirements 96
    naming 99, 110
    placement of data and subdocument entities
        164
    predictability of attributes 127
    predictability of elements 124
    predictability of sectioning elements 124
    recursion 153
    revision cycles 179
    role attributes 142, 157
    selection criteria 44
    success at limiting choice 134
    use of role attributes 92
model group 7

N

name length
    short element and attribute names 99
nationality
    as influence on author's expectations 109

NDATA entities
    See unparsed entities
NDATA keyword 31
NMTOKEN keyword 20, 222
NMTOKENS keyword 20, 222
non-recursive element types 50
non-repeatable 11, 133, 181, 182
notation
    as attribute value 21
notation declaration 36
    syntax 36
        SGML facilities 36
notation form 274
    term 274
notation forms 308
NOTATION keyword 21
notations
    uses 36
Novell 55

O

O'Reilly & Associates 55
object-oriented programming 245
occurrence indicators 9, 10
Official Navy Baseline Tagset Library 77
omissibility 101, 183, 189, 198
omitted tag minimization 14
optional 11, 122, 123, 127, 183, 184, 192,
    202, 208
ordered 122, 198, 199
ordering 198
overhead of adding markup 120

P

parallel design 100
parameter entities 29
    for general configuration 159
    XML restrictions in internal DTD subset 4
parameter entity 31
parsed entity 31

physical structure 28
predictability 146
processing instruction 39
    syntax 39
    uses 39
processing instructions
    SGML facilities 40
processing software 145
profession
    as influence on author's expectations 109
professional specialization
    as influence on author's expectations 109
properly nested 32
public identifier 30
PUBLIC keyword 30
publication-oriented DTDs 44

R

recursion 150
    hidden 152
    in model DTDs 153
    limiting with SGML exclusion exceptions 151
relational databases
    mixed content 146
repeatable 11, 182
repetition 101, 181, 188, 189, 198
required 11, 122, 123, 126, 133, 183, 184, 191, 208
reserved names 4
restrictive 181, 184
reuse of information 216
revision management 216
role attribute 90, 95, 140, 142
    abuse 92
    creating additional logical units
        See also logical unit
    used in model DTDs 92
role attributes 155

S

sample term xxxvi
sequence 9
SGML
    #CURRENT keyword 227
    additional attribute default values 25
    additional attribute types 24, 202
    additional external entity types 35
    architectural forms 292, 326
        architecture base declaration 294
        architecture entity declaration 296
        architecture notation declaration 295
        architecture support attributes 297
        attributes 323
        automatic derivation 313
        data attribute form 274
        notation forms 308
        suppressing processing 317
    backwards compatibility 198
    CDATA external entities 35
    CONREF attributes 25
    content model 7
    CURRENT attributes 25
    dangerous mixed content 16
    data attributes 37
    declared content 15, 201
    default entity 33
    entities
        data text 34
    exceptions 14, 202, 228, 235, 243
    external identifiers 33
    global attributes 28
    limiting recursion 151
    markup minimization 207
    mixed content 16
    multiple attribute definition lists 26
    multiple element types 13
    NAME keyword 222
    NAMES keyword 222
    omitted tag minimization 13
    ordering 198
    placement of data and subdocument entities 163
    record ends 210

SDATA external entities 35
SUBDOC entities 35
SUBDOC keyword 242
unordered content 17
WebSGML 26, 28
SGML University
DTD list 77
SGML/XML Web Page xxxii
socio-economic status
as influence on author's expectations 109
specific character data 34
string type 18
subdocuments 235
Sunsoft 55
system identifier 30
SYSTEM keyword 30

T

TEI
See Text Encoding Initiative (TEI)
TEI DTD
additional tag sets 64
base tag set 64
customization 257
introduction 63
online documentation 70
TEI-Lite DTD
home page 69
introduction 62
online documentation 70
Text Encoding Initiative (TEI) 62
home page 69
The Santa Cruz Operation 55
tokenized type 18, 19
true inline content 139
typing 196

U

U.S. Navy 77
unconstrained role attributes

See also role attribute
Unisys 55
University of Virginia
Electronic Text Center 70
unordered 123, 198, 199
unordered content xxxiii, 17
unparsed entities 31, 308
unparsed entity 163

V

value reference 240
value reference (HyTime) 240
valueref 240
See value reference (HyTime)

W

W3C
See World Wide Web Consortium
WebSGML
global attributes 28
multiple attribute definition lists 26
World Wide Web Consortium 78
home page 82

X

XML
reserved names 4
restrictions on parameter entities in internal
DTD subset 4
XML and SGML
major structural differences xxxiii
XML Linking Language (XLL)
cross-references 240

LICENSE AGREEMENT AND LIMITED WARRANTY

READ THE FOLLOWING TERMS AND CONDITIONS CAREFULLY BEFORE OPENING THIS CD PACKAGE. THIS LEGAL DOCUMENT IS AN AGREEMENT BETWEEN YOU AND PRENTICE-HALL, INC. (THE "COMPANY"). BY OPENING THIS SEALED CD PACKAGE, YOU ARE AGREEING TO BE BOUND BY THESE TERMS AND CONDITIONS. IF YOU DO NOT AGREE WITH THESE TERMS AND CONDITIONS, DO NOT OPEN THE CD PACKAGE. PROMPTLY RETURN THE UNOPENED CD PACKAGE AND ALL ACCOMPANYING ITEMS TO THE PLACE YOU OBTAINED THEM FOR A FULL REFUND OF ANY SUMS YOU HAVE PAID.

1.   **GRANT OF LICENSE:** In consideration of your purchase of this book, and your agreement to abide by the terms and conditions of this Agreement, the Company grants to you a nonexclusive right to use and display the copy of the enclosed software program (hereinafter the "SOFTWARE") on a single computer (i.e., with a single CPU) at a single location so long as you comply with the terms of this Agreement. The Company reserves all rights not expressly granted to you under this Agreement.

2.   **OWNERSHIP OF SOFTWARE:** You own only the magnetic or physical media (the enclosed CD) on which the SOFTWARE is recorded or fixed, but the Company and the software developers retain all the rights, title, and ownership to the SOFTWARE recorded on the original CD copy(ies) and all subsequent copies of the SOFTWARE, regardless of the form or media on which the original or other copies may exist. This license is not a sale of the original SOFTWARE or any copy to you.

3.   **COPY RESTRICTIONS:** This SOFTWARE and the accompanying printed materials and user manual (the "Documentation") are the subject of copyright. The individual programs on the CD are copyrighted by the authors of each program. Some of the programs on the CD include separate licensing agreements. If you intend to use one of these programs, you must read and follow its accompanying license agreement. If you intend to use the trial version of Internet Chameleon, you must read and agree to the terms of the notice regarding fees on the back cover of this book. You may not copy the Documentation or the SOFTWARE, except that you may make a single copy of the SOFTWARE for backup or archival purposes only. You may be held legally responsible for any copying or copyright infringement which is caused or encouraged by your failure to abide by the terms of this restriction.

4.   **USE RESTRICTIONS:** You may not network the SOFTWARE or otherwise use it on more than one computer or computer terminal at the same time. You may physically transfer the SOFTWARE from one computer to another provided that the SOFTWARE is used on only one computer at a time. You may not distribute copies of the SOFTWARE or Documentation to others. You may not reverse engineer, disassemble, decompile, modify, adapt, translate, or create derivative works based on the SOFTWARE or the Documentation without the prior written consent of the Company.

5.   **TRANSFER RESTRICTIONS:** The enclosed SOFTWARE is licensed only to you and may not be transferred to any one else without the prior written consent of the Company. Any unauthorized transfer of the SOFTWARE shall result in the immediate termination of this Agreement.

6.   **TERMINATION:** This license is effective until terminated. This license will terminate automatically without notice from the Company and become null and void if you

fail to comply with any provisions or limitations of this license. Upon termination, you shall destroy the Documentation and all copies of the SOFTWARE. All provisions of this Agreement as to warranties, limitation of liability, remedies or damages, and our ownership rights shall survive termination.

7. **MISCELLANEOUS:** This Agreement shall be construed in accordance with the laws of the United States of America and the State of New York and shall benefit the Company, its affiliates, and assignees.

8. **LIMITED WARRANTY AND DISCLAIMER OF WARRANTY:** The Company warrants that the SOFTWARE, when properly used in accordance with the Documentation, will operate in substantial conformity with the description of the SOFTWARE set forth in the Documentation. The Company does not warrant that the SOFTWARE will meet your requirements or that the operation of the SOFTWARE will be uninterrupted or error-free. The Company warrants that the media on which the SOFTWARE is delivered shall be free from defects in materials and workmanship under normal use for a period of thirty (30) days from the date of your purchase. Your only remedy and the Company's only obligation under these limited warranties is, at the Company's option, return of the warranted item for a refund of any amounts paid by you or replacement of the item. Any replacement of SOFTWARE or media under the warranties shall not extend the original warranty period. The limited warranty set forth above shall not apply to any SOFTWARE which the Company determines in good faith has been subject to misuse, neglect, improper installation, repair, alteration, or damage by you. EXCEPT FOR THE EXPRESSED WARRANTIES SET FORTH ABOVE, THE COMPANY DISCLAIMS ALL WARRANTIES, EXPRESS OR IMPLIED, INCLUDING WITHOUT LIMITATION, THE IMPLIED WARRANTIES OF MERCHANTABILITY AND FITNESS FOR A PARTICULAR PURPOSE. EXCEPT FOR THE EXPRESS WARRANTY SET FORTH ABOVE, THE COMPANY DOES NOT WARRANT, GUARANTEE, OR MAKE ANY REPRESENTATION REGARDING THE USE OR THE RESULTS OF THE USE OF THE SOFTWARE IN TERMS OF ITS CORRECTNESS, ACCURACY, RELIABILITY, CURRENTNESS, OR OTHERWISE.

IN NO EVENT, SHALL THE COMPANY OR ITS EMPLOYEES, AGENTS, SUPPLIERS, OR CONTRACTORS BE LIABLE FOR ANY INCIDENTAL, INDIRECT, SPECIAL, OR CONSEQUENTIAL DAMAGES ARISING OUT OF OR IN CONNECTION WITH THE LICENSE GRANTED UNDER THIS AGREEMENT, OR FOR LOSS OF USE, LOSS OF DATA, LOSS OF INCOME OR PROFIT, OR OTHER LOSSES, SUSTAINED AS A RESULT OF INJURY TO ANY PERSON, OR LOSS OF OR DAMAGE TO PROPERTY, OR CLAIMS OF THIRD PARTIES, EVEN IF THE COMPANY OR AN AUTHORIZED REPRESENTATIVE OF THE COMPANY HAS BEEN ADVISED OF THE POSSIBILITY OF SUCH DAMAGES. IN NO EVENT SHALL LIABILITY OF THE COMPANY FOR DAMAGES WITH RESPECT TO THE SOFTWARE EXCEED THE AMOUNTS ACTUALLY PAID BY YOU, IF ANY, FOR THE SOFTWARE.

SOME JURISDICTIONS DO NOT ALLOW THE LIMITATION OF IMPLIED WARRANTIES OR LIABILITY FOR INCIDENTAL, INDIRECT, SPECIAL, OR CONSEQUENTIAL DAMAGES, SO THE ABOVE LIMITATIONS MAY NOT ALWAYS APPLY. THE WARRANTIES IN THIS AGREEMENT GIVE YOU SPECIFIC LEGAL RIGHTS AND YOU MAY ALSO HAVE OTHER RIGHTS WHICH VARY IN ACCORDANCE WITH LOCAL LAW.

ACKNOWLEDGMENT

YOU ACKNOWLEDGE THAT YOU HAVE READ THIS AGREEMENT, UNDERSTAND IT, AND AGREE TO BE BOUND BY ITS TERMS AND CONDITIONS. YOU ALSO AGREE THAT THIS AGREEMENT IS THE COMPLETE AND EXCLUSIVE STATEMENT OF THE AGREEMENT BETWEEN YOU AND THE COMPANY AND SUPERSEDES ALL PROPOSALS OR PRIOR AGREEMENTS, ORAL, OR WRITTEN, AND ANY OTHER COMMUNICATIONS BETWEEN YOU AND THE COMPANY OR ANY REPRESENTATIVE OF THE COMPANY RELATING TO THE SUBJECT MATTER OF THIS AGREEMENT.

Should you have any questions concerning this Agreement or if you wish to contact the Company for any reason, please contact in writing at the address below.

Robin Short
Prentice Hall PTR
One Lake Street
Upper Saddle River, New Jersey 07458

About the CD-ROM

Platform

All operating systems (web browser required).

Contents

Item	Format	Platform
General information	HTML	any
XML/SGML links	HTML	any
DTDs and catalog	SGML	any
SP parser	source	any (32-bit OS required)
SP parser	binaries	Windows 95/NT, Linux
AElfred XML parser	source/binaries	any (Java support required)

Getting Started

Load the page "index.htm" from the root directory of the CD-ROM and follow instructions.

Plug-and-Play Support

There is a web of XML and SGML pages available on the CD-ROM for offline browsing, starting with "index.htm" in the root directory. There are also four ways that you can use the CD-ROM for plug-and-play parsing:

1. you can try a live demonstration of XML parsing in any Java-enabled web browser
2. you can use Microstar's free AElfred XML parser directly from the CD-ROM, either on its own or as part of your own Java applications
3. you can use all of the SGML DTDs and entity sets on the CD-ROM directly in any SGML tool that supports standard SGML Open entity catalogs, since all SGML support files are fully catalogued
4. (Windows 95/NT or Linux only) You can run the binaries for the SP XML/SGML parser directly from the CD-ROM

Prentice Hall does not offer technical support for this software. However, if there is a problem with the media, you may obtain a replacement copy by emailing us with your problem at discexchange@phptr.com